★★★★★★★★★

DARK AND BLOODY GROUND

★★★★★★★★★

ALSO BY THOMAS AYRES

That's Not in My American History Book

★★★★★★★★★★★★★★

DARK AND BLOODY GROUND

★★★★★★★★★★★★★★

The Battle of Mansfield and the
Forgotten Civil War in
Louisiana

THOMAS AYRES

TAYLOR TRADE PUBLISHING

Dallas, Texas

Published by Taylor Publishing Company
1550 West Mockingbird Lane
Dallas, Texas 75235

Library of Congress Cataloging-in-Publication Data
Ayres, Thomas, 1936–
    Dark and bloody ground : the battle of Mansfield and the forgotten Civil
War in Louisiana / Thomas Ayres.
        p.   cm.
    Includes bibliographical references (p.) and index.
    ISBN 0-87833-180-8 (cloth)
        1. Louisiana—History—Civil War, 1861–1865—Campaigns. 2. United
States—History—Civil War, 1861–1865—Campaigns. 3. Mansfield
(La.), Battle of, 1864. 4. Louisiana—History—Civil War, 1861–1865—
Social aspects. 5. United States—History—Civil war, 1961–1865—Social
aspects. I. Title.

E470.7 .A97 2001
973.7'3—dc21   00-067669

10 9 8 7 6 5 4 3 2 1

Printed in the United States of America

☆☆☆☆☆☆☆☆☆☆☆☆☆☆☆☆☆

To Bea,
whose smile lit my path

✮✮✮✮✮✮✮✮✮✮✮✮✮✮

Contents

1863
Mud and Blood

1864
Dark and Bloody Ground

✩ ✩ ✩ ✩ ✩ ✩ ✩ ✩ ✩ ✩ ✩ ✩ ✩

Acknowledgments

AS A SMALL BOY, Raymond Sullivan sat in front of a fireplace and listened to my great-grandfather and his old Confederate buddies spin war stories. Years later, I sat in Raymond Sullivan's living room and listened to him retell those stories. Raymond, an elderly cousin, provided a direct link to my Confederate ancestors and ignited an interest in the Civil War that has not waned. He is gone now, but in the stories he told me lies the genesis of this book.

Many contributed to the research on which this work is based. Most helpful was Steve Bounds, curator at the Mansfield Battlefield Museum. Deeply involved in writing a dissertation on the Battle of Mansfield, he is probably the foremost expert on the Texas regiments that fought there. Park Ranger Scott Dearman walked the battlefield with me, revealing details one can never find in libraries.

Likewise, I have stood on the redoubts of the old Star Fort at Morgan City with historian Roger Busbice while he explained how the Confederate "Mosquito Fleet" came out of the swamps to surprise Union occupiers. I am grateful to Patrick Hotard, former curator at the Brown-Sanders Museum in Morgan City for providing insight into the bayou battles that raged along Bayou Teche. I was dismayed to learn of the recent closing of this facility. For those interested in this phase of the Civil War in Louisiana, the museum's material can now be found at the Morgan City Library.

Greg Davies, Winn Parish historian, was helpful in compiling information on the life and service of Colonel William Walker, about whom very little has been written until now.

No one is more knowledgeable than historian Andrew Capone of Donaldsonville on the battles fought in South Louisiana. Walking with him along the banks of Bayou Lafourche, one can almost feel the crash of cannons, hear the yells of desperate men, and smell the smoke that covered the adjacent fields more than a century ago.

In telling this story, I have relied heavily on the writings of others, including Arthur W. Bergeron, Jr., Ronald A. Mosocco, and many others. Especially helpful was John D. Winters's *The Civil War in Louisiana*. Also, Richard Taylor's *Destruction and Reconstruction*, originally published in 1879, is essential reading for those interested in the Civil War west of the Mississippi River. Exchanges of dialogue were created based on details taken from the principal figures' diaries, memoirs, and documents.

Finally, I am grateful to the editors at Taylor Publishing Company—especially to Fred Francis, who sometimes makes me appear to be a better writer than might be the case.

★ ★ ★ ★ ★ ★ ★ ★ ★ ★ ★ ★ ★ ★

Introduction

AS SURELY AS smoke rises from the ashes of war, so rise war's legends and myths. The history of warfare is never objective. It is written by victors. Napoleon Bonaparte understood the process when he said, "What is history but a fable agreed upon?" Indeed the closets of our past hide many a skeletal chapter, and many a hero or villain has been shrouded in obscurity. But when fable distorts history and myth veils truth for no good reason but to sanitize the past, our historians do us a disservice.

No historical event has been more thoroughly reported than the American Civil War. More has been written about it than any other single event in our history—memoirs, biographies, diaries, collections of letters by the great and obscure; analytical accounts of battles great and small; reference works that might best be weighed by the ton; countless millions of words poured into the covers of an Everest of books. Volumes detailing Civil War muster rolls, dog-eared by use, line our library shelves. The Civil War occupies hundreds of Web sites. With each new issue, several current magazines reanalyze Civil War battles and the movements and motives of the men who fought them.

No magazines specialize in reporting the events of World War I. One will not find World War II muster rolls prominently displayed on the shelves of the local library. Reenactors do not gather on weekends to recreate the landing at Inchon. Why then are we so obsessed with a conflict decided well over a century ago? Why do Civil War buffs create miniature battlefields, accurate to the last detail, and spend hours maneuvering imaginary regiments about them? Why do white Southerners ride around with bumper stickers displaying the Confederate flag above a caption that says, "Forget, Hell!" We even have video games that allow us to fight the battles all over again—and again, as if the outcomes were not decided by our ancestors, long in their graves.

In spite of all that has been written about the Civil War, no event in our history is more misunderstood. In many ways this war has grown beyond history to embrace mythology. One has only to examine the titles of best-selling novels like *The Killer Angels* and *Gods and Generals* to realize this fact. Angels? Gods? One imagines that the battles of Gettysburg and Shiloh might have been fought beyond the clouds above Pennsylvania and Tennessee. But when the clouds of myth are parted on the war that will not end, a simple truth emerges. Although a war was won, the dispute was never fully settled. In fact, the U.S. Civil War may never be settled because its roots are embedded in pre–medieval Europe and nourished by the blood of a thousand wars.

Many issues contributed to the atmosphere that divided our nation and led us to war in 1861—slavery, tariffs, regional pride, and a struggle for political and commercial superiority among them. But the war had only one cause. Finally, the American Civil War was a cultural conflict fought for economic, political, and social power. We brought it with us from beyond the Atlantic—from the bloody plains of Normandy, Saxony, England, Scotland, and Ireland where Celt, Anglo, Norman, Saxon, and Gaul had fought with lance and sword for countless generations.

There was never anything grand, glorious, or remotely civil about the Civil War. It was a brutal extension of those old clan wars—one final, great bloodletting between the obstinate, and stubbornly independent, agrarian Celtic culture of the nineteenth-century South and the puritanical, pragmatic, industrious, and impatient Anglo-Saxon culture of the Northeast. The rebel yell heard at Shiloh was the same as the one that chilled the spines of English soldiers and Roman legions before them on the moors of Scotland. And that is why Great Britain's civil war and our own continue to this day.

The two sides clearly had to go to war. By 1860 the rhetoric of the statesmen had created a chasm of hatred so wide it could only be bridged by the bodies of the masses. Well before a Confederacy existed, Southern governors had committed acts of war by seizing Federal installations and expelling Federal troops. Well before the shells screamed above Fort Sumter or Abraham Lincoln gave his first inaugural address, or a single Southern state seceded, Union strategists were planning a military conquest of the South.

The war was divided into three theaters of operation—the East, the West, and the Gulf. It would require four years for the North to squeeze the final breath from Robert E. Lee's army at Appomattox and conclude the war in the East. William T. Sherman's March to the Sea and conquest of the Carolinas brought the Western Campaign to a successful conclusion. This book is about the third theater of that war—the one history forgot. The Gulf Campaign to conquer the southernmost states west of the Mississippi River was the only unsuccessful phase of the war for the Union. It came to an abrupt halt in a blood-soaked Louisiana wheat field on the outskirts of a small woodland town named Mansfield.

One will not find Mansfield listed among the great battles of the Civil War. In fact, one seldom finds it mentioned at all. Kenneth C. Davis's popular book, *Don't Know Much about the Civil War*, has a subtitle that promises: *Everything You Need to Know About America's Greatest Conflict but Never Learned.* Yet, in 486 pages, he never mentions the Battle of Mansfield. He devotes only one sentence to General Nathaniel Banks's Red River Campaign and perhaps a page of text to the Battle for New Orleans—the turning point on which hinged the very outcome of the war. Davis cannot be faulted for his oversight, which is typical among historians.

There is no good reason that Mansfield should not take its place among the classic battles of the Civil War. It certainly deserves more from history than relegation to footnote, if for no other reason than because it delayed the conquest of Atlanta and extended the war for several months. It was not a great battle when compared to the collisions of massive armies at places like Gettysburg, Antietam, Chancellorsville, Shiloh, and Bull Run. Still, more than forty thousand men were in the field at Mansfield, and the following day at Pleasant Hill, and the fighting was as fierce as any of the war.

The war in Louisiana never equaled the legendary grandeur of the conflicts in Virginia, Maryland, and Pennsylvania, or the struggles between colossal armies east of the Mississippi River. The Gulf Campaign (called the Trans-Mississippi Department on the rebel side) was an isolated, dirty little war fought along the winding bayous and in the swamps, cane brakes, and pine hills of the state. Badly outnumbered, the Confederate Army fought a cat-and-mouse war, constantly in retreat with only an occasional opportunity to turn and bloody its pursuer. Still, it managed to avoid destruction for two years before falling upon a much larger Federal army at Mansfield with a fury not taught in military academies. During those two years, some six hundred clashes took place between rebel and Union armies in Louisiana, ranging from minor skirmishes to major battles. Remarkably, when the war ended, the Confederates still controlled 90 percent of the state, as well as the southern half of Arkansas and all of Texas.

The Battle of Mansfield was the last major Confederate victory of the Civil War, as well as the culmination of an unsavory episode in our nation's past. From the beginning, President Lincoln and Union General in Chief Henry Halleck mistakenly viewed Louisiana as a pacification problem rather than a serious military challenge. In fact, they could not have picked a more difficult locale to conquer or a more difficult people to pacify. Louisiana was not like any other state. Its people were not like those of any other state. A humid, semitropic climate that spawned clouds of disease-bearing mosquitoes spread sickness among Union troops. A topography ranging from dense swamp and marshland to heavily forested hills with narrow, muddy roads made it difficult to maneuver large armies. Its treacherous streams, with their shifting sandbars and unpredictable water levels, frustrated the Union's gunboat captains. Louisiana's diverse amalgamation of cultures—ranging from Creole to Cajun French, English, Spanish, Redbone, Creoles of Color, German, Italian, Scots-Irish, a large population of free blacks, including many who owned slaves, and some slaves who refused to be freed—confounded and frustrated occupying troops. Northern soldiers had never seen such people—or even dreamed they existed. And out of their frustration in dealing with cultures they could not understand evolved a tragic and little-known chapter in our history.

The atrocities committed by Federal troops against the civilian population of Louisiana—black and white, rich and poor—is a stain upon our past that in some ways exceeded the brutality of Sherman's march through Georgia and the Carolinas. Long before Sherman's troops arrived in Georgia, they had pillaged and burned their way through central Louisiana. Sherman justified his actions in Georgia and the Carolinas as acts committed during an active military campaign. But in Louisiana, atrocities were committed against civilians by troops of occupation, leaving little room for justification. No military rationale existed for the senseless burning of Alexandria. The ruthless destruction of Donaldsonville and shelling of civilians at Baton Rouge by Union gunboats had no purpose other than wanton destruction.

Union forces were not alone in the commission of acts of brutality. In the final, lawless months of the war, marauding bands of outlaws ravaged the countryside. Some gangs were made up of Confederate Army deserters. Others included Union sympathizers who used the war as an excuse to raid, burn, and murder the innocent. In the waning days of the conflict, roving bands of outlaws fought each other as well as Union and Confederate cavalry over the meager spoils that remained.

It was a period of rampant greed, corruption, and government-sanctioned trade with the enemy. The U.S. government, in collusion with turncoat planters and New England cotton brokers, sent freed slaves back to the fields to feed the textile mills of the North even as men were dying to end slavery. Men made great fortunes overnight, even as women and children starved in the hinterlands. The freemen of New Orleans were befriended, then betrayed, by Union officials, and Lincoln emancipated the slaves of the South but not those in South Louisiana.

Some of our ancestors, as well as our historians, chose to bury this chapter of our history in the ashes of that war. This book tells the story of that tumultuous time, the men and women who lived it, and the events that led them to a climactic day at a place called Mansfield.

✮ ✮ ✮ ✮ ✮ ✮ ✮ ✮ ✮ ✮ ✮ ✮ ✮

Prologue

APRIL 8, 1864— It was late afternoon when the two armies finally faced each other across a large open field on the Moss Plantation three miles south of a small woodland town named Mansfield. Shells screamed above as artillerymen gauged distance. Without orders, several Cajuns from the 18th Louisiana Regiment had advanced from the protection of a pine forest, crouching and crawling on hands and knees to lie prone atop a slight rise in the open field and snipe at Union officers. The Yankees responded, and a spirited firefight was building. Down a narrow dirt road, among a cluster of mounted officers, General Alfred Mouton watched the action unfold, the glint in his eyes indicating that he might be more proud than concerned by his troops' breach of discipline. The 18th was his old regiment. He had helped form it back in Vermillionville and led it into the mouth of Yankee cannons at Shiloh. If he had a musket at this moment, instead of the responsibility of divisional command, he might even be joining them.

Turning toward the sound of hoofbeats in the soft sand along the shoulder of the road, he saw General Richard Taylor approaching, greatcoat flapping, face flushed with excitement, teeth clamped on his ever present cigar. He reined his horse before Mouton's group even as a string of artillery rounds splintered limbs in the trees behind them. Taylor lifted his field glasses and studied the movement of enemy troops behind a rail fence a half mile away. For days he had been retreating before General Nathaniel Banks's Union Army. Only the previous morning, Taylor received long-awaited reinforcements, bringing the strength of his army to eighty-eight hundred.

Taylor's was a patchwork army, pieced together from the remnants of previously decimated units. It included old men and young boys better suited to home guard than to battlefield combat. Dismounted Texas cavalry had been converted to infantry because he had only a few light regiments of infantry at his disposal. One could not send horses charging into canister—only men. Across an unplanted wheat field, Taylor faced artillery far superior to his own and a rapidly deploying Union Army of thirty thousand that included ten thousand battle-tested veterans on loan to Banks from General William T. Sherman at Vicksburg.

Among the rebel officers beside the road was General Camille Armand Jules Marie, Prince de Polignac, commander of a brigade of Texas cavalry. Having served as a lieutenant in the French Army in the Crimea, Polignac had no illusions about the reality of warfare. For some time he had been studying the steady arrival and deployment of Federal troops, his concern increasing with the appearance of each new regiment. To the west the sun was nearing the tree line. No more than three hours of daylight remained, hardly time for either side to mount a full-scale attack. But if they waited until morning, Polignac knew Banks would have his full force in position. He lowered his field glasses and turned to Taylor.

"What shall we do, sir?" he asked.

"Little Frenchman," Taylor calmly replied, "I am going to fight Banks here if he has a million men."

He watched as another group of skirmishers from the 18th emerged from the forest and made its way into the open field.

"It appears your Louisianans are anxious for a fight, Mr. Mouton," he said.

The Cajun rose in his stirrups and drew his sword. "They are, sir!"

"Then they may advance and engage the enemy," he said.

☆ ☆ ☆ ☆ ☆ ☆ ☆ ☆ ☆ ☆ ☆ ☆ ☆ ☆

1860

Babylon of the South

For out of the north there cometh up a nation against
her, which shall make her land desolate.

JEREMIAH 50:3
THE JUDGMENT OF BABYLON

1

A Good Year

NEW ORLEANS, DECEMBER 1—In the good years, December in New Orleans was a time of festivity, and 1860 was a good year. Although cotton yields were average, the sugar crop was abundant, and both fetched good prices, which meant plentiful money. Nothing made New Orleans more festive than an ample supply of funds. Glad-handing bankers, merchants, factors, and planters filled the tables at Moreau's and Victor's restaurants, their conversations' steady drone about commerce and politics mingling with occasional laughter and the clatter of glassware. In a back room at the Boston Club, the third oldest private club in the country, members with more means than rationale played a card game called whist for stakes that could run to several hundred dollars a hand. In the evenings the elite of the city congregated at the St. Louis and St. Charles hotels, filling the ornate drawing rooms and salons of those great caravansaries. They arrived with elegant ladies on their arms and with daughters whose dark, Creole eyes flicked dangerous glances at the sons of planters from upriver plantations. The opera season was underway, and the brilliance of the audience far exceeded the talent of the tenor. Beautiful women filled the city—bedecked in diamonds and brocaded dresses from the best shops of Paris. Not even the election of a Republican president and talk of secession and war could dampen the gaiety of the season.

Louisiana was a world unto itself in 1860, and New Orleans a city unlike any other. It was 1833 when Captain James E. Alexander warned the uninitiated: "Let no one judge of America from New Orleans, for it is altogether sui generis." By 1860 it was even more so. Having existed for a century and a half under five flags, its 150,000 inhabitants consisted of a polyglot mixture of French, Spanish, Creole, Cajun, Negro slave and freedman, late-arriving Anglo-Saxon and Jewish businessmen and migrants from every part of Europe—Germans, Italians, native Frenchmen, Britons, Scotsmen, and especially Irishmen.

Twelve thousand free blacks inhabited New Orleans. Most prominent was a large and relatively prosperous community of Creoles of Color—a result of many generations of intimate liaison between colonial Frenchmen and their African slaves. Trapped in a classless void between black and white, these proud, elegant people of light brown skin and gentle manner had created their own social island. Some Creoles of Color had been educated in Paris. Many were successful businessmen, professionals, landlords, planters, plantation owners, and owners of slaves themselves. They owned much of the real estate of the city, including many of its boarding houses and restaurants. They held their own gala balls, and attended the opera—sitting in their own segregated section of the theater even as their enslaved brethren were auctioned in the lobby of the St. Charles, just down the street.

In New Orleans, the institution of slavery itself had become a confusing mixture of tolerance and suppression. Unlike the slaves who toiled in the sugarcane and cotton fields of the hinterlands, many of the city slaves were tradesmen and craftsmen whose owners hired them out and received a portion of their earnings while allowing the bondsmen freedom to go and come as they pleased. Some even owned homes and property, in direct violation of Louisiana law. In fact, the weekend loitering of slaves on the streets of New Orleans had become such an issue, letters to the editor were appearing in the *Daily Picayune* admonishing owners for not exerting more control.

Among the visitors in awe of the city was a young New Yorker named Henry B. Whipple. In a letter to home, he provided an incisive description of the city he would label "That Great Southern Babylon":

> The truth is New Orleans appears to me to be at the extreme of everything . . . the busiest and the most dull, the most wicked and the most orderly. They have, in truth, the most business, the best land, the prettiest of women, the fastest of horses and the most delightful climate. It rains harder, it is more dusty. Changes take place here with almost the rapidity of thought. Today rich, tomorrow poor, today well, tomorrow dead, today hot, tomorrow cold, today dry, tomorrow wet, suffocating for air one day and the next suffering from extreme winds which almost vie with a hurricane in their fierceness. . . . An observing man can see as much of the world and of diversified character here as in any city in the Union. It is the grand reservoir of the great West.

Indeed, it *was* a reservoir.

Although Louisiana's agrarian economy relied on two staples—sugar and cotton—New Orleans's commerce was fueled by a plethoric, three-thousand-mile-long horn of plenty: the mid-nineteenth-century Mississippi River Valley. Products of every description flowed south along the waterway to be factored, bought, sold, and swapped on the docks and levees lining the Port of New Orleans, before finally being shipped to the ports of the world. Manufactured products, dry goods, and the tools of agriculture flowed back up the river aboard paddlewheel steamers. The banking houses of New Orleans, among the most respected in the world—their vaults bloated with deposits, their transactions backed by the great banks of New York and Europe—fueled this beehive of prosperity at the base of the nation's great waterway.

New Orleans was the largest, most cosmopolitan, and richest city in the South in 1860, and the third largest in the nation. More than half of the nation's millionaires resided in the elegant plantation homes and ornate dwellings that lined the river from New Orleans to Natchez, Mississippi. All of these factors, in combination with a bizarre political atmosphere, made the Babylon of the South a world unto itself. Rooted in tradition, yet progressive in business and banking; it presented a paradoxical potpourri of commercial frenzy and genteel leisure, wealth and poverty, open arms and closed societies, notorious brothels and great cathedrals. New Orleans caused outsiders to despair at trying to understand it.

Likewise, even the most informed Easterner failed to visualize the vastness of the Mississippi River Watershed. The valley that once spawned the great mound-building empires of pre-Columbian America covered 1.2 million square miles. It was two thousand miles from New Orleans to the highest point of navigation on the Ohio River, three thousand to the farthest navigable reaches of the Missouri. Hundreds of streams fed the Mississippi, creating twenty thousand miles of navigable waterways, all flowing toward New Orleans. Ten million people inhabited the valley, almost all of them living within a few miles of a waterway. The area developed so rapidly that analysts of the day predicted the population would swell to 25 million by 1870. And while 1860 was a good year, prospects for the next decade exceeded calculation.

Between October and May the products of people who labored beside the Mississippi and its tributaries flowed through New Orleans aboard every conceivable type of waterborne conveyance—keelboats, barges, flatboats, square riggers, and steamers painted in gaudy colors. Some riverboats arrived with cotton stacked so high on deck that only their pilot houses and stacks peeked over the top. Waiting for their cargo was an armada of oceangoing steamers, brigs, schooners, and sloops, and a fleet of puffing tugboats to maintain order. More than sixty varieties of produce descended on New Orleans each winter. Bales of cotton and hogsheads of sugar towered as high as houses and covered acre upon acre along the levee. Along the water's edge sat piled bags of feathers, barrels of corn, bundles of leather, carrots of tobacco, firkins of butter, hogsheads of molasses, kegs of lard, puncheons of rum, reels of yarn, sacks of wheat, and tierces of flaxseed. A curious mix of merchants, factors, planters, traders, brokers, and riverboat and sea captains strolled the waterfront, buying, selling, and tabulating while an army of dockside laborers, predominantly black and Irish, worked shoulder to shoulder, loading, unloading, shifting, and sorting.

Solon Robinson, a Northern journalist who toured the cities of the South in the 1850s, observed this scene of organized confusion and wrote: "One would just as well undertake to show the magnitude of the ocean and the fearful raging of the storm at sea . . . as to try to give an idea of the business upon the levee here by a string of words and figures."

If Robinson had been around in 1860, he would have reported that the rich river deltas of the relatively small state of Louisiana, much of it still undeveloped, produced 96 percent of the nation's sugar and 17 percent of its cotton. But Louisiana's production represented only a small portion of the goods that came down the river and through the Port of New Orleans. In fact, New Orleans handled half of all the cotton produced in the United States, and its total exports rivaled those of any other port in the world. Although restrictive tariffs limited New Orleans's imports, its cotton exports alone exceeded the total exports of all Northern ports.

At the center of Robinson's "raging storm" of commerce, bringing a degree of order to it, were the most colorful characters on the waterfront. They were the factors—the deal makers, the link between seller and buyer, banker and broker, planter and merchant. Dressed in jackets of gaudy colors and broad stripes, cocked hats tilted in defiance of fashion, they strutted the levees, advancing money on crops yet to be planted, trading, arranging, and pocketing profits.

The factor was equally at ease dealing with a backwoods ruffian with a few bundles of hides to sell or a bejeweled banker sporting lace cuffs and pinkie rings. He might frequent the lowest waterfront dives by day before emerging in tie, tails, and top hat at the evening opera. He advertised his services in agricultural and business journals like *De-Bows Review*, *Price-Current,* and the *Commercial Bulletin*, all faithfully subscribed to by upriver planters. His manner and dress often belied the fact that he might be a millionaire, on paper if not in hard currency.

Although the Eastern business establishment stood in awe of New Orleans's rapid growth and economic might in 1860, some parties were concerned. For two decades, Eastern industrialists, with the help of federal subsidies, had extended railroads in a desperate attempt to divert the growing raw wealth of the upper Mississippi and Ohio River valleys to East Coast factories and ports. Detroit and Chicago likewise had built railroads in an effort to siphon trade northward to the Great Lakes. The Crescent City's southern neighbors also grew increasingly jealous of New Orleans. Alabama had spent vast sums building a state-supported railway system to direct produce to the Port of Mobile. But manmade conveyances could not compete with nature's great North American highway. Despite the efforts of others, the currents of the Mississippi continued to funnel goods downriver. New Orleans continued to prosper, and 1860 emerged as yet another good year. Ledgers showed profits, from the shops on Conti Street to the largest of the surrounding sugar plantations, and the city celebrated its continuing prosperity.

At Victor's Restaurant, the factors and their associates were questioning the wisdom of investing in a new canal extension while speculation in upstate farmland promised far greater profits. Soaring prices for prime delta land, brought on by the steady migration of planters from the burned-out hill farms of eastern Mississippi and northern Alabama, had created an unprecedented demand for open farmland. Even poor-dirt farms in the North Louisiana sand hills, once selling for a few cents an acre, now brought ten dollars, and river bottomland was going for forty dollars an acre. An astute businessman could make a fortune overnight in the land business.

In the posh environs of the Boston Club, shielded from the masses, Louisiana's movers and shakers congregated to discuss the great issues in candid conversation. Governor Thomas Overton Moore spent as much time there as he did at the state Capitol in Baton Rouge. Fueled by brandy and juleps, the talk revolved around race horses, sugar prices, deals, and politics. United States Senators John Slidell and Judah Benjamin were frequent visitors. Momentous decisions were made here, without a vote cast or a constituent consulted. The club also consumed many of its members' idle hours, to the dismay of their homebound wives. Dick Taylor, son of the late President Zachary Taylor and owner of a large plantation just north of the city, spent so much time at the club his wife, Mimi, likened it to a rival mistress.

By December 1860, all conversations at the Boston Club eventually came around to the new Republican president. Almost everyone agreed that separation from the Union was inevitable. Still, a few held onto a thread of hope that Louisiana, somehow, might avoid secession. They based that hope on the premise that, regardless of the rhetoric of those who had elected Lincoln, the president would not bite the hand that fed the federal treasury. The inescapable truth was that Southern agriculture filled the treasury's coffers, and slavery fueled Southern agriculture. The South provided 75 percent of federal revenues. To abolish slavery would not only bankrupt Southern planters, it would also devastate Eastern shipping, cripple Northern industry, and close some of New York's most prestigious banking houses.

Some hoped that England, with four hundred thousand textile workers depending on Southern cotton for a livelihood, would pressure Lincoln to maintain the status quo until some kind of compromise could be arranged. In fact, many rational-thinking businessmen and plantation owners were convinced the slavery issue would resolve itself if the North did not press the matter. Few expected the institution to last beyond another ten years anyway. Many large plantation owners had begun to question the profitability of the system. During the sugar cane grinding season, free blacks, as well as white workers, routinely were hired to supplement slave labor on the plantations. Owners gladly paid a freedman thirty-five dollars per month to fill a seasonal labor demand while avoiding the expense of having to house and feed him for the remainder of the year.

When all arguments for maintaining or abolishing slavery were stripped bare, one inescapable reality remained. The slaves of the South represented far more than a source of labor. Adult male slaves, valued at eight hundred to three thousand dollars each, represented the bulk of the assets of most planters—collectively worth more than lands, homes, livestock, buildings, and machinery. Simply to release the slaves, as advocated by the abolitionists, would not only create social chaos, it would collapse the economy. If the slaves were to be set free, such an action must occur gradually and with some form of government compensation.

At the forefront of the avowed separatists was the governor. Thomas Moore owned a large plantation on Bayou Beouf near Alexandria and held slaves of his own. For years, Louisiana's rabble-rousers had been clamoring for separation from the Union. Few took them seriously until Moore openly advocated secession. With the posting of the results of the presidential election in November, the movement attracted alarming support. Joining the radicals were an increasing number of state and local politicians more inclined to drift with the shifting winds of opinion than vote their convictions. The first signs of war fever surfaced in New Orleans, when radical businessmen began sponsoring newly formed citizen militias. These units were a far cry from the proud old, socially elite militias that were a tradition in the city. Included in the ranks of these upstart militias were waterfront rabble more inclined to drink than drill. Lacking weapons or discipline, they marched about for a few minutes each week before retiring to the taverns for a night of drinking.

On the issue of secession, most New Orleans citizens adopted a wait-and-see attitude. Theirs was an old city, jaded by political upheaval. Pestilence, plagues, floods, hurricanes, armies, and governments had come and gone, and the city had survived them all. Change always came slowly to New Orleans because those who tried to change it too quickly simply found themselves absorbed by it.

The slavery issue aside, some in the New Orleans business community supported secession for pragmatic reasons. The prospect of an independent Louisiana being able to lower burdensome tariffs on imports flowing through the port provided a mighty incentive for separation. A tariff reduction would entice European imports away from the East Coast, allowing New Orleans to replace New York as supplier of goods for the growing Mississippi River Valley. But if secession was to come, it had to be a careful, step-by-step process. The South needed Northern markets as surely as the North needed the produce and raw materials of the South. Cool heads must prevail. Compromises must be made to avoid inciting the North to war. A war would benefit no one. The first rule of business was that when business was good, one did not tamper with its means, and business in 1860 was very good.

* * *

FASHION PLANTATION, DECEMBER 15—Twenty-five miles north of New Orleans, Dick Taylor sat in his office at the rear of the house, working on his long-neglected account books, when the dogs began barking, announcing the arrival of company. Earlier he had visited the site where workers were extending a levee in an ongoing effort to reclaim one of his fields from floodwaters in time for planting. He had returned with mud on his boots and left them with William Hawkins, his house servant, to be cleaned. By the time he retrieved the boots and made his way to the front of the house, an impatient and clearly excited Braxton Bragg was waiting for him in the foyer.

"South Carolina will secede within the week," he announced without waiting for a salutation. "Their assembly is meeting in Columbia on Monday, and there is no doubt about the outcome. The governor has summoned me to Baton Rouge, and he wants you there as well."

At age forty-three, Braxton Bragg had a full beard already streaked with gray. His most prominent feature, a set of unruly brows, produced a permanent scowl above sunken eyes that reflected a slight hint of wildness. He was the owner of a large sugar plantation on Bayou Lafourche near Thibodaux, some forty miles to the west. Three days earlier Governor Moore had appointed him to the State Militia Board. The appointment had surprised Taylor since Bragg was an open, and frequently vocal, opponent of secession. However, Taylor suspected Bragg's first loyalty was to opportunity rather than a cause. He long since had concluded that Bragg's opposition to secession owed more to a concern that it would interfere with sugar prices, rather than any deep-felt sympathy for preserving the Union.

Before marrying into money and becoming a planter, Bragg spent almost twenty years in the United States Army. He had served under Taylor's father, Zachary Taylor, in Mexico, during which time he established a reputation for combativeness with fellow officers, as well as the enemy. In spite of that reputation, Bragg had a reverence that bordered on childlike devotion to Zack Taylor, and it seemed to Dick that, though unsolicited, he had inherited that loyalty. Although no one else could get along with Braxton Bragg, Dick Taylor had never experienced anything but the utmost courtesy in his dealings with him.

"You can tell the governor I will leave for Baton Rouge on Monday," Taylor informed him. Bragg seemed disappointed that he was not prepared to depart sooner. Declining an invitation to stay for refreshments, he said he intended to proceed at once to Baton Rouge. He had stepped out on the porch when he paused and looked around as if to be certain they were alone.

"I believe the governor has it in mind to seize the river forts," he said. "If he does that, there might be bloodshed before this is over."

Taylor could not suppress a fleeting, sardonic smile. He reacted not to the grim prospect of Bragg's prophecy, but to the fact that at least one other person in the state government had recognized that bloodshed might be a consequence of secession. Taylor had been preaching that message to his legislative colleagues for months. He had repeated the warning so often that most of his friends considered him a fanatic on the subject. Even the governor, who had a great deal of respect for Taylor's opinions on other matters, had grown weary of his calamitous predictions. Governor Moore was stubbornly determined to separate Louisiana from the Union by any means, and he remained convinced that the North did not have the stomach for a fight.

As he watched Bragg's carriage disappear around a bend in the road toward St. Charles Station, Taylor wondered if his account books and finances might be doomed to permanent disorder. Since Moore became governor, he felt he had devoted far too much time to his official duties in Baton Rouge, and far too little to Mimi, the children, and the plantation, especially since he became chairman of the Louisiana Senate Committee on Federal Relations. His role as a senate leader arose as a result of circumstance more than choice; he cared little for the gritty business of politics, although he did enjoy the company of its practitioners. By nature Taylor was not a mover and shaker but rather a social animal at home in the halls of power. He had an affinity for good brandy, good cigars, and clever after-dinner repartee. In such settings he was content to let others engage in serious discourse while he provided commentary, usually laced with philosophical witticism rather than deep insight.

This latest break from official duty had allowed Taylor to remain at home for only three days before being called back to Baton Rouge. There seemed little likelihood that things would improve. During a just-completed special session, the Louisiana Senate had set January 7 as the date for statewide elections to select delegates to a Secession Convention. But as far as Taylor was concerned, elections, conventions, and grand speeches had become a waste of time—little more than the trumpet's blare before the joust. That Louisiana would secede, he had no doubt. That secession would bring on a war, he was certain.

* * *

If the United States had been a monarchy instead of a troubled democracy in 1860, Dick Taylor might have been an aristocrat instead of a farmer. He was a handsome man of thirty-four with dark, intelligent eyes and a broad forehead made to appear even broader by a slightly receding hairline. He sported a beard, neatly trimmed in the latest European style. Proud of his athletic build as a youth, he had become concerned by the recent hint of a paunch, the appearance of which he might have denied had it not begun to test the buttons on his vest.

Taylor represented the sixth generation of one of America's most respected families. Zachary Taylor, his father, had been the twelfth president of the United States. He was a cousin to James Madison, and third cousin to Robert E. Lee. Their great-grandfather, James Taylor, had acquired ten thousand acres in Orange County, Virginia, back in the 1720s and established a successful farm operation that became the foundation for, to some extent, the Taylor, Madison, and Lee family fortunes.

Dick bore the name of his grandfather and inherited his adventurous spirit. The first Richard Taylor celebrated his graduation from college by exploring the Kentucky wilderness and traveling down the Mississippi River to New Orleans. A hero in the American Revolution, he had risen to the rank of lieutenant colonel in the 2nd Virginia Regiment. Following the war he married Sarah Dabney Strother, also from a respected Virginia family. To this union, Zachary Taylor was born in Orange County in 1784. Zachary was still a toddler when Richard and Sarah moved to Kentucky and established a large plantation near Louisville, where Zachary grew to manhood, the beneficiary of a privileged childhood and a tutored education.

At age twenty-four, following a tradition established by many of his ancestors, he chose the military as a career. Commissioned a first lieutenant, he fought in the War of 1812 and rose in rank. In 1819, he traveled to Louisiana to command troops stationed along the Sabine River border with Mexico. In 1823 he purchased a four-hundred-acre Louisiana cotton plantation in West Feliciana Parish, twenty miles north of Baton Rouge. Assigned to duty in Kentucky, he hired a manager to run the plantation and, in 1824, moved his family to Louisville. On January 27, 1826, Peggy Taylor gave birth to a son. After five daughters, the arrival of a boy was cause for celebration in the Taylor household. They named him Richard after his eighty-one-year-old grandfather. To distinguish him from his grandfather, they called him Dick.

Dick Taylor was two years old when his father was assigned to command Fort Crawford, a wilderness outpost on the banks of the Mississippi River in southwestern Wisconsin. There he grew into precocious youth, playing with the Indian children and dealing out a great deal of misery to a succession of teachers at the post school. At age nine, he demonstrated his inherent leadership qualities by organizing a mass exodus from the confines of the classroom. Trailed by Indian playmates and a group of white children from the post school, Dick led his band of truants on an excursion into the wilderness. For two days they eluded their adult pursuers while having a grand time of it before finally being captured and returned to their classroom prison. The episode convinced Zachary it was time to send his son to Louisville to live with relatives in a more structured society. Dick would not see his father again for five years.

He was a bright, headstrong youngster, prone to occasional temper tantrums and, according to his father, stubborn enough to argue with a fence post. He constantly challenged his tutors who, nevertheless, managed to educate him well enough so that, at age seventeen, he entered the junior class at Yale University. Outgoing and well liked by his classmates, he was among the first to close a textbook and lift a tankard. One classmate described him as "always finely dressed, popular, generous, talented, and rather easygoing." A good student if not an outstanding one, he could be obsessive in his pursuit of knowledge, if a subject captured his interest. A voracious reader, he enjoyed European history, or, more precisely, its wars and the military leaders who fought them.

In 1845, at age nineteen, Dick received his diploma from Yale. That same spring an event took place four thousand miles away that would have a lasting impact on his life. Mexico broke off diplomatic relations with the United States over the U.S. annexation of Texas, and his father went to Corpus Christi with fifteen hundred troops to counter the threat of a Mexican incursion into disputed territory between the Nueces and Rio Grande rivers.

With the outbreak of the Mexican War, Zachary Taylor won a series of brilliant victories in Northern Mexico. Commanding an army of twenty-three hundred at Palo Alto, he scattered a Mexican army of more than six thousand. At Resaca de la Palma, he routed an army of seventy-five hundred. After a hard-fought, five-day battle to capture Monterrey, he marched his troops toward Buena Vista. There, outnumbered three to one, he defeated a Mexican force of fifteen thousand under Santa Anna, effectively ending the war in Northern Mexico. Two young officers were responsible for holding Taylor's left flank against a massive attack at Buena Vista—Jefferson Davis and Braxton Bragg. Among the witnesses to the strategies that produced this string of victories was young Dick Taylor, who spent his summer vacation in the field with his father.

The Mexican War was the first to be reported by telegraph. Daily reports from the front appeared in newspapers back home, and in a matter of weeks Zachary Taylor vaulted from relative obscurity to national hero. Meanwhile, his son returned home to earn his own dubious notoriety—as a ladies' man, high-stakes card player, and horse player—at the better clubs, race tracks, and grand ballrooms of New Orleans and Natchez. He was especially well known at the exclusive resorts lining the beach at Pascagoula, Mississippi, where the social elite of the Gulf South congregated.

At seventeen, Dick had begun experiencing occasional headaches, accompanied by pain in his back and legs. When he finally sought medical attention, he learned that he had the beginnings of rheumatoid arthritis. He used the diagnosis as an excuse to spend a great deal of time visiting hot springs resorts from Virginia to the Gulf Coast, ostensibly to receive therapy and medical treatment. The resorts were hubs for social activity, and young Taylor seemed to devote more time to socializing than he did to engaging in physical rehabilitation. Zack Taylor never fully believed the arthritis story, his suspicions reinforced by rumors that his son's physical condition did not prevent his dancing the most lively reels as he endeared himself to a succession of Southern belles from some of the Old South's most prominent families. To pry him away from such corruptive influences, Zachary had Dick enrolled at Harvard and the University at Edinburgh, Scotland. However, an advanced education little interested young Taylor at that stage of his life, and his stays at those institutions were brief.

Upon Zachary's return home, "Old Rough and Ready," as his men called him, was overwhelmed by the adulation heaped upon him. Impressed by his popularity, leaders of the Whig Party came calling, urging him to become their nominee for the presidency. However, Zack Taylor abhorred politics and had never bothered to vote in an election, much less go to the trouble to join a political party. The Whigs finally convinced him to become their standard-bearer, but the campaign almost ended before it began. While visiting New Orleans in January 1848, Zachary was felled by a seizure that partially paralyzed him.

The illness stunned Dick, who regarded his father as a distant, larger-than-life figure who, surely, would live forever. Zachary Taylor spent more than a month recuperating at the family home near Baton Rouge. There, at his bedside, Dick began to know his father without the uniform, and the father came to realize that his wayward son might benefit from some assigned responsibility. Zachary had purchased a nineteen-hundred-acre cotton plantation named Cypress Grove, located thirty miles above Natchez on the east bank of the river. Cypress Grove had never been fully developed, and Zachary urged twenty-two-year-old Dick to go there and take over its management.

Arriving at Cypress Grove in February 1848, Dick found a primitive main house, along with outbuildings and slave quarters in need of repair. He supervised spring planting and had begun making improvements to the buildings when he became aware of a demand for cypress lumber in the region. Since the plantation contained several hundred acres of giant cypress trees, he constructed a sawmill, which proved to be a far more lucrative operation than cotton farming. His father was elected president that November, running on a one-plank platform that promised preservation of the Union while maintaining a balance of power between the slave and free states. He carried seven of the fifteen free states, in spite of the fact that he owned more than one hundred slaves back in Louisiana.

In the spring of 1849, even as President Taylor struggled with the manmade disaster of slavery, a natural disaster descended on his son at Cypress Grove. Mississippi floodwaters rose to record levels, breaking the levees and destroying the cotton crop. If not for the sawmill, the Taylors might have been financially ruined. In the spring of 1850, the waters rose even higher and again covered the plantation. At that point, Dick urged his father to purchase a less vulnerable plantation. With Zachary's permission, he bought Fashion Plantation, twenty-five miles north of New Orleans. It was an old estate with manicured grounds, a beautiful, two-story home, and twelve hundred acres, most of which were cleared for the cultivation of sugar cane. A few weeks after the purchase, Dick learned that his father had fallen ill. Four days later, he was stunned by news that his father had died.

Old Rough and Ready died from an intestinal inflammation on July 9, 1850, after standing for hours during a Fourth of July ceremony. Almost immediately, rumors circulated that he had been poisoned by his enemies who, by then, were legion on both sides of the slavery issue. Dick dismissed the rumors, assuming his father had died of natural causes.

From his father, he inherited two plantations totaling 3,100 acres, $21,000 in cash, and 147 slaves. At age twenty-four, overnight, he had become one of Louisiana's most prominent planters. He also had become a substantial debtor, having inherited a $100,000 liability with the properties.

In February 1851, Dick surprised his friends and family when he married a beautiful and vivacious French Creole teenager named Myrtle Bringier, from one of the wealthiest families in Louisiana. The twenty-five-year-old groom was a socially polished man of the world, his bride an impulsive and fun-loving seventeen-year-old. Taylor had met "Mimi," as she was called, two years earlier while his father was campaigning for president. Dick accompanied him to a dinner party hosted by Duncan Kenner, a state legislator who had wed Mimi's older sister, Nadine. Although young Taylor was accustomed to flirtatious glances from beautiful women, the dark-eyed, fifteen-year-old who boldly returned his gaze across the dinner table that evening strangely mesmerized him.

During their courtship, Mimi endured teasing by her French friends and younger siblings, who considered Taylor an English "dandy." They giggled behind his back and made jest of his stylish long hair and fashionable, European-style dress. It was a courtship that might not have taken place a generation earlier. For many years, wealthy Catholic Creole families refused to allow their daughters to marry Anglo Americans. However, by the 1850s, many planters of English descent could match the wealth and social status of the richest Creole families, and intermarriage had become common.

The contrasting personalities of the newlyweds seemed to make them compatible. Taylor was cultured and reserved, while Mimi was spontaneous in word and deed, often to the amusement of her husband. Frederick Law Olmsted, a writer for the *New York Times*, described Mimi as "a devil of a Creole wife—young, childish, whimsical, comical." They had four children—Louise Margaret, named for Taylor's mother; Elizabeth, called Betty after Dick's sister; Zachary, called Zack; and Richard, who Mimi nicknamed "Dixie." Taylor was openly affectionate with his children and devoted to Mimi. He seemed to draw energy from her youthful spontaneity. Their only domestic difficulty resulted from his addiction to the card tables at the Boston Club and the time he spent at the Metairie race track.

In the summer of 1853 Taylor was visited by Olmsted, on assignment to produce a series of articles on the South for the *New York Times*. Put in touch with Taylor through a mutual Yale friend, Olmsted was duly impressed by Fashion Plantation and its owner. Although he later savaged the South in his writings, Olmsted had only high praise for Taylor. Upon assuming ownership of Fashion, the first thing Taylor did was tear down the old slave cabins and build new ones, complete with board floors and verandahs. Olmsted viewed these quarters favorably, comparing them to New England cottages. The writer reported that Taylor's slaves were well clothed and had warm coats for winter. His bondsmen ate from the same stores and gardens as the Taylor family. They received health care from a physician on retainer. Taylor allowed older, retired slaves to grow separate gardens and paid them for their produce. The slaves were given Sundays off, and he often granted Saturdays, as well as holidays and special occasions like weddings and funerals. At Christmas, Taylor distributed to his slave families one dollar for each hogshead of sugar produced on the plantation. He divided the money—usually amounting to about five hundred dollars—and gave it to the head of each family household to be spent as they wished. He also gave them a week off for Christmas celebration before breaking ground for a new planting season. Although Olmsted expressed the opinion that any slave in the South would prefer freedom, he noted a genuine affection existed between Taylor and his bondsmen that went beyond the bounds of master and slave.

The proslavery ranting of Southern fire-eaters like William Yancey of Alabama incensed Taylor because they fed the flames of abolitionist rhetoric, and he ranked such men alongside Northern radicals. In Taylor's analysis, the debate did not concern slavery, but rather tyranny. Although cast in the role of aristocratic planter, he long ago had detached himself both philosophically and emotionally from any personal responsibility for the institution of slavery. In fact, he considered himself a slave to the system. "The South would have been better off if the institution never existed," he told Olmsted during his visit. "I could have prospered without slavery—but I am trapped by it."

Like his father, Dick Taylor had little interest in politics but, due to his prominence, he could not avoid being shoved into Louisiana's always perking pot of political gumbo. He served as a delegate to the Whigs' nominating convention at Donaldsonville in 1851. In 1854 the Whig Party disintegrated over the issue of slavery, leaving him little choice but to join the Democratic Party. In 1855 he was elected to the state senate without conducting a campaign, which he considered beneath his dignity. In fact, during his entire political career, he never made a campaign speech. By the spring of 1860 Taylor had become disillusioned with the democratic process, at least as it was practiced in Washington. He believed the system had been perverted to benefit individuals at the expense of the public good.

The election of Lincoln in November left no doubt in his mind as to the inevitability of secession. As chairman of the Senate Committee on Federal Relations, he had tried without success to convince his peers that war loomed on the horizon. He read the Northern newspapers and followed events in Washington. He occasionally communicated with old New England classmates. He knew the Yankee mind-set and was convinced the radical abolitionists of New England were not the problem. They only wanted to free the slaves of the South. Far more dangerous, Taylor believed, were Northern industrialists, financiers, and political power brokers who wanted to control the South's wealth.

* * *

After Bragg departed for Baton Rouge, Taylor went out to look for Tom Strother. Tom was his childhood playmate, slave, and friend, who now did more to run Fashion Plantation than did Taylor. He found him at the barn saddling the children's new pony, the acquisition of which had caused a great deal of excitement in the household and now inspired an argument between the Taylor daughters. Louise, age nine, and Betty, age seven, were engaged in a spirited debate over who would be the first to ride the pony. Apparently the brown and white spots decorating the animal made it a more desirable mode of transportation than the old pony, with its ordinary reddish-brown coat.

Their father settled the dispute by awarding the first ride to three-year-old "Little Zack." With his son clinging to the saddle horn, Taylor took the reins and carefully led the pony around the barnyard. He did not return to his office that afternoon, and the account books would remain in their usual state of disarray atop his desk for weeks before he returned to them.

★ ★ ★

SOCIETY HILL, DECEMBER 17—A year after the senate campaign, Eleanora Gray remained bitter over its outcome. She had no doubt that a vote of the people would have put her husband in the United States Senate instead of Judah Benjamin. But the Louisiana General Assembly, not the people, decided the election. And, when the brandy bottles were empty in the back rooms of the Boston Club and the smoke-filled hotel rooms of Baton Rouge—when the deals were struck, and the payoffs consummated—Henry Gray lost the election.

Henry was far more philosophical about the loss than was his wife. Having dabbled in politics for years, he knew that Benjamin and the New Orleans crowd would fight like hell to avoid relinquishing the power of a U.S. Senate seat to an outsider from North Louisiana. Now that the issue was decided, Henry desired only to return to the simple life of gentleman farmer and country lawyer. Drained of energy and emotion, he had vowed not to seek public office again.

With Eleanora, it was different. Left up to her, she would have stormed the hallowed chambers of the Capital Building and chased the political manipulators from their sanctuary, just as Jesus had driven the money changers from the temple. Eleanora had always been more ambitious than her husband, in business as well as politics. The product of a wealthy old South Carolina family on her mother's side, she was described by a friend as "a young lady of rare attainment who contributed greatly in furthering the intellectual pursuits and political aspirations of her husband."

By December 1860 Henry had exhausted himself trying to fulfill Eleanora's ambitions for him. He was forty-four years old and content to remain in the scenic hill country beyond the east bank of the winding Red River in northwest Louisiana. Although the sandy loam soil lacked the richness of the reddish earth of the flat deltas on the other side of the river, it produced profitable yields of cotton and enough grain per acre to provide winter forage for the livestock and food for family and slaves. Finally, those conditions were all that was required for a successful farm operation, and Henry Gray ran a successful plantation.

The region was known as Brush Valley when he purchased 332 acres and moved there in 1851. The families of several well-educated and wealthy planters from South Carolina came to settle around him, creating something of a cultural island in the North Louisiana wilderness. The dress and manner of the newcomers prompted residents of the nearby river town of Coushatta to rename the area Society Hill.

Society Hill actually consisted of many hills. They rose steeply above lush valleys where networks of spring-fed creeks and branches flowed. Negotiating the narrow roads that wound through the region, travelers unexpectedly found grand, often ornate homes along the way. Over the years, Gray had purchased several hundred additional acres in various locations. By 1860, his fifty-two slaves had cleared a large portion of his scattered holdings for cultivation, and he was running a substantial farm operation. He supplemented his income by practicing law in Coushatta and at the Bienville Parish courthouse at Sparta, some twenty-five miles away. Quiet and reserved outside the courtroom, he was a dynamic orator before the bar, and spectators often overflowed the benches when Henry Gray argued a case.

Unimposing, Gray stood only five-four, with wide shoulders and stubby legs. A full beard, somewhat out of fashion for the time, contributed to a top-heavy appearance. Still, he had a commanding presence with piercing blue eyes behind which, one had the impression, resided boundless wisdom.

Henry Gray was of German descent, his ancestors having arrived in the Americas via a circuitous route. Before being Americanized, the family name was DeGraw. Henry's great-great-grandfather had been a member of the King's Guards at Potsdam and later an officer in the Royal Prussian Army before falling out of favor with the Royal Court. In the mid-1700s, he and several other military families fled to England to avoid political persecution. Welcomed there as heroes, they received land grants in South Carolina. During the American Revolution, the Grays remained loyal to the king of England, with the exception of Henry's grandfather. He joined the Colonial Army and fought against his brother, an officer in the British Army. Henry's father (also named Henry) served as an officer in the United States Army in the War of 1812.

Henry Gray Jr. was born January 19, 1816. He grew up in a cultured household in Lauren's District, South Carolina; graduated from South Carolina College in 1834; studied law and was admitted to the bar. In 1838, he moved to Winston County in eastern Mississippi where he served as district attorney for six years. Eleanora Howard, the daughter of a wealthy local planter, became smitten by the young attorney and they married in 1841. In 1846 she talked him into running for the state legislature, to which he was elected. However, he served only one session before resigning. He later ran for the U.S. Congress on the Whig ticket but was narrowly defeated, prompting the first of many pledges to give up politics.

Moving to Louisiana, Gray established a law practice and managed to stay out of politics until the 1856 presidential election, when he was an elector on the Democratic ticket. In 1859 he canvassed the state in an aggressive campaign for the U.S. Senate seat of Judah Benjamin. On the eve of the General Assembly vote, Gray was confident he would win. However, last-minute vote switching produced fifty-seven ballots for Benjamin to Gray's fifty. The Know-Nothing Party candidate, Randall Hunt, received five votes, leaving Benjamin with a majority.

Because of his sporadic plunges into political waters, Gray was well known in Southern politics and acquainted with many of its practitioners, including two who would have a profound influence on his future. One was a Mississippi politician named Jefferson Davis. The other was a Louisiana state senator named Dick Taylor.

* * *

SHREVEPORT, DECEMBER 20—James Hamilton Beard had been pacing the levee for some time when the stacks of the steamboat finally appeared above the tree line down the river. He watched as the steamer came into full view and slowly made its way through the rust-colored waters of the Red River. James could not suppress a temptation to critique the pilot's performance as the craft slid to the far side of the channel in preparation for its approach to the levee.

Lining the levee were factors and merchants, along with dockworkers, black and white. They clustered around fires, unmindful of color or social standing in their efforts to stay the cold. James waited on an order of goods for his store, but that was only an excuse for his presence. He loved the waterfront and visited it at every opportunity. He liked the people there, the frenetic pace, the very smell of it. He had been a riverboat captain before settling down to the somber life of retail merchant. Now his wife, Kate, provided the adventure in his life, and a daughter named Corinne inspired him to sell dry goods.

From his youth, James was one of those rare, adventurous souls inclined to act while others discussed. Orphaned at eleven, by age twenty-seven he had willed himself to a position of influence and relative wealth in the raw, rapidly growing river town of Shreveport—some three hundred miles from New Orleans geographically, but a world away in appearance and attitude. He was a partner in Childers & Beard, a large mercantile store located on Shreveport's busy Texas Avenue, just two blocks from the town's bustling waterfront. At the popular establishment, men gathered around a cast-iron heater on frosty mornings to talk of horses, crops, women, and politics. Although Lincoln's inauguration remained two months away, at Childers & Beard the issue of secession was not even a matter for debate. Everyone favored it. The only question was whether the Yankees would fight and, if they did, how long it would take to whip them. The prevailing joke reasoned that since most of the boys from DeSoto Parish could shoot a running squirrel through the eye at fifty yards, it would require only about a hundred of them to overrun New York City.

Just across the Red River, Bossier Parish already had seceded from the Union. Reacting to Lincoln's election, a large crowd gathered at Rocky Mount on November 26 to cheer parish officials as they passed an ordinance of secession and voted to organize the Minute Men of Bossier Parish. Not to be outdone, Beard began taking names and recruiting volunteers for a Shreveport militia. Although domestic responsibility prevented him from piloting a riverboat, he saw nothing wrong with organizing a militia company. He could do that without leaving the store. He even intended to tell Kate about it when the time was right.

* * *

In 1860 Shreveport appeared a rough-hewn, miniature replica of New Orleans in terms of commerce, if not ornate architecture, sophistication, progressive thought, and population diversity. It was a boisterous, rapidly growing town of three thousand, its citizenry dominated by Scots-Irish migrants from the Carolinas by way of Georgia, Alabama, and Mississippi, and new arrivals from the docks of New Orleans who had made their way upriver looking for opportunity.

Unlike New Orleans, Shreveport had few freedmen, only twenty-one in town. Shreveport's slaves existed in a restrictive environment different than the relaxed atmosphere in New Orleans. A curfew required all bondsmen to be in their homes by nightfall, with one notable exception. The City Council had passed a resolution allowing members of the locally popular Shreveport Ethiopian Band "to assemble together to practice on their instruments: Provided they always notify one of the town constables of the time and place of their meetings . . . and always close their practicing and return home by eleven o'clock P.M."

Norman Davis, a freedman who also happened to be one of the city's wealthiest businessmen, led the band. He ran a Texas Avenue barber shop next door to the Powell Hotel, a few doors down from Beard's store. As Shreveport had grown, Davis parlayed ten acres of downtown real estate into a fortune. Some of the town's finest homes and most successful business establishments sat on lots he developed. The Ethiopian Band performed at all of the city's galas during the holiday season, and the citizens of Shreveport considered themselves lucky to have someone of Davis's musical ability in their culture-starved town. As for Davis, he started the band for the simple reason that he loved to play the violin. He continued with the band because it generated enough income to allow several of his musicians to purchase their freedom.

Rounding out the city's population mix was a sprinkling of Anglo Americans who had come west to work on a river-clearing project; Irishmen employed on a railroad extension between Shreveport and Marshal, Texas; Jewish businessmen from the Caribbean and East Coast; Germans from a failed communal settlement in nearby Claiborne Parish; and a few inhabitants of Spanish descent from the Sabine River bottomlands. The German influence appeared most noticeably in a notorious area of town called Mugginsville—so named for the ceramic beer steins on the tables of the beer gardens clustered there. Thanks to Irish patronage, some of those establishments turned a tidy profit, enabling several German saloonkeepers to join the ranks of Shreveport's more successful businessmen.

In a little over a decade, Shreveport had grown from trading post to trade center, its rough face belying its status as the commercial hub for a large, tristate area. Cotton arrived at its waterfront via trains of cargo wagons all the way from Fannin County, Texas; Southern Arkansas; and North Central Louisiana. Poor-dirt farmers and open range herders from the pine hills, who farmed in summer and trapped the creeks and bayous in winter, arrived daily, their wagons piled high with cotton and bundles of furs and cowhide leather to be shipped downriver to New Orleans.

For years, a massive 150-mile-long log jam that clogged the Red River stunted the region's growth. In 1835, Captain Henry Shreve finally removed the tangle of trees and vegetation, washed from the banks of the river over many years, allowing a small trading post to grow into a thriving commercial hub appropriately named Shreve's Port. With the opening of the river to navigation, planters and merchants poured into the area much like the floodwaters that visited the valley each spring.

In ten short years, Shreveport evolved from log-and-plank frontier town to booming inland port city with multistory brick buildings and a cluster of fairly elegant homes protected by a network of levees. South and west of the city, rust-colored Delta farmlands, among the most fertile in North America, stretched for miles before merging with rolling pine hills. Along narrow roads traversing the area, small farm communities clustered around rough-board churches—creating little towns with colorful names like Red Bluff, Keatchie, Grand Cane, and Kingston. Into this area came James Beard in his twentieth year to seek his fortune. He was a handsome young man of obvious education if not means, personable in manner, and fueled by youthful ambition. He had piercing eyes, a sincere smile, and a dimple in his prominent chin that the ladies no doubt found charming.

He came from sturdy Carolina stock. In 1831 Edward Derrell Beard and his bride,

Caroline Rembert, left Orangeburg, South Carolina, on a journey of three hundred miles, lured by a promise of available farmlands in Alabama where the U.S. government was in the process of removing Native Americans from their ancestral homes. The Beards settled in Lowndes County, Alabama, and there James was born, the first of seven stairstep Beard children. In August 1844 Caroline Beard was eight months pregnant when her husband fell victim to a cholera epidemic. Less than a year later, Caroline also died, leaving eleven-year-old James orphaned with two brothers and four sisters.

The children were separated and parceled out, to be raised by friends and neighbors. No records indicate with whom James lived, although he may have lived with the family of E. C. Norris, since it appears he assumed the role of protector for his infant brother Ned, who was taken in by the Norrises. Few details survive of James's adolescent years but the fact that he was articulate in speech, accomplished in letters, and had a head for numbers attests to more than a passing brush with formal education.

In the early 1850s James Beard showed up in the town of Red Bluff, some twenty-five miles south of Shreveport. The fact that the Norris family had moved from Alabama and lived nearby in DeSoto Parish further indicates a connection to that family. James found employment as manager of a dry goods store owned by Charles Edwards. By 1856, he was captain of a river steamboat, also owned by Edwards. He must have been a skilled captain just to negotiate the Red River with its narrow channel, shifting sandbars, and rapidly rising and falling water levels. For almost two years he plied the waters between Shreveport and New Orleans without any recorded disaster befalling him or his craft.

On September 30, 1857, the dashing steamboat captain married Catherine Tomkies, the daughter of a prominent family at Kingston. Kate, as she was called, was petite, pretty and, like the groom, well-educated. She possessed a keen wit, evidenced by the letters she wrote to James during his absences from home.

The following year James gave up the river life to become a partner in Childers & Beard Mercantile, located in what the local newspaper described as "a spacious brick building" at the corner of Texas Avenue and Spring Street in the heart of Shreveport's business district. His rapid accumulation of wealth attests to the success of the venture. The 1860 Census reveals that he owned a home valued at sixty-five hundred dollars and held personal property worth twenty-seven thousand dollars.

Although James lived and worked in Shreveport, he and Kate maintained a home in Kingston, some twenty miles downriver. A large showplace of a house, it had two stories and a wide front porch with eight columns. James called it "Auburnia" in obvious tribute to his Alabama roots. He quickly earned the respect of his business peers in Shreveport as well as that of his neighbors in Kingston as evidenced by the fact that, at age twenty-five, he was "Raised to the sublime degree of Master Mason" in Jefferson Lodge No. 138 at Kingston.

In February 1860 James and Kate had a daughter they christened Corinne Gayle. Her arrival subdued the restless spirit of her father for a time as he and Kate wrapped their world around the child. On December 20, 1860, as Kate Beard made plans for her ten-month-old daughter's first Christmas, she had no way of knowing that future holidays would become a time of sad reflection rather than joy. As Kate played with her daughter, the South Carolina Assembly voted to secede from the Union and James Beard recruited the final enlistees for a militia company he would call the "Shreveport Greys"—120 men, without guns, uniforms, or any knowledge of warfare, but bound to fight for Louisiana.

* * *

NEW ORLEANS, ÐECEMBER 20—The news from Columbia fell on New Orleans like a bombshell. Telegraph keys across the city clattered confirmation that South Carolina had seceded from the Union. Even as some citizens took to the streets to celebrate, others berated the South Carolina Assembly for acting irresponsibly. Many believed it was far too early for such drastic action, and that if the Southern states were to separate, they should go out together. The South Carolina secession had changed everything. It forced a decision few were ready to make.

In 1860 Louisianans were divided into four camps on the politics of secession: the "secessionists," who advocated immediate separation; the "co-operationists," most of whom adopted a wait-and-see attitude; the "doubtfuls," who could not make up their minds; and "Unionists," who left no doubt about their loyalty to the Union. In the rural parishes of North Louisiana, where Scots-Irish settlers dominated, the sentiment was largely secessionist. However, Unionist pockets existed even there. The isolated and clannish Cajun French to the southwest, most of whom did not speak English, were among the "doubtfuls," being more loyal to their own culture than to any government. The upriver planters and plantation owners were rabid secessionists, as were most of the politicians they influenced. The sugar cane planters of South Louisiana, having just experienced a bountiful year, were split in their sentiments. If a statewide referendum had taken place on December 19, the co-operationists would have prevailed. That changed overnight. The secession of South Carolina, and subsequent actions by Governor Moore, quickly altered the mood of the people.

Even as the wisdom of South Carolina's decision was being debated in the drawing rooms of the St. Louis Hotel, over the linen-draped tables at Victor's, and across the whist tables at the Boston Club, church bells began to toll across the city. They signaled the first rustling of the winds of a coming storm, not unlike one of the hurricanes that occasionally crossed the Mississippi River Rigolets to visit the city. Moderates and Unionists looked on in dismay as increasing numbers of celebrants appeared on the streets. New Orleans was a city where revelry was a way of life—where even a funeral provided cause for celebration. By nightfall, an infectious joy swept the city. Caught up in the excitement of the moment, city officials called a special meeting that evening. They voted to hold an official ceremony the following day to celebrate South Carolina's brave action.

* * *

NEW ORLEANS, ÐECEMBER 21—By eleven o'clock Friday morning, a large crowd had gathered on Camp Street, many drawn by the spectacle rather than conviction to a cause. Miniature flags bearing the pelican symbol—the sovereign banner of Louisiana—waved defiantly above a boisterous crowd. The "blue cockade," a pelican button with two streamers attached to it, the secessionist badge once worn by only the most militant, now appeared on almost every lapel.

A cheer rose from the crowd with the appearance of a large Louisiana flag being unfurled from the third-floor window of the building at 72 Camp Street, headquarters for the Southern Rights Association. Following speeches in French and English in support of South Carolina and Southern rights, a band struck up *le Marseillaise,* and as a roar of approval from the crowd drowned the final notes, a militia cannon of the Washington Artillery boomed in the distance. It was answered by another cannon. Promptly at noon, on cue, heavy guns began to fire all about the city—hundreds of cannons, creating a din as reassuring as it was deafening to the crowd. If war should come, New Orleans was prepared to defend herself. Surely, no army could stand against such mighty armament.

★ ★ ★ ★ ★ ★ ★ ★ ★ ★ ★ ★ ★ ★

1861

The Marching Street

War
I do abhor,
And yet how sweet
The sound along the marching street.

RICHARD LE GALLIENNE
THE ILLUSIONS OF WAR

★ ★ ★ ★

2

★ ★ ★ ★

Old Zack's Flag

BATON ROUGE, JANUARY 10—It came as no surprise to Major Joseph Haskin of the United States Army when the rebels came to take the Federal arsenal. He just did not expect to see them so soon. They began collecting at the end of Third Street at mid-morning, a motley congregation of perhaps a hundred men clutching old muskets and shotguns and shivering in the cold wind that gusted up from the river. A smartly dressed officer approached under a flag of truce, and Haskin recognized Braxton Bragg, an ac-quaintance from his service in Mexico. Beside him walked Dick Taylor, with whom Haskin had established a cordial relationship during his dealings with the governor's of-fice. They saluted and exchanged greetings. Bragg, sporting the twin stars of a colonel on his collar, announced that he was there in his capacity as head of the Louisiana State Militia. He presented Haskin a letter bearing the seal and signature of the governor of Louisiana:

> The safety of the State of Louisiana demands that I take possession of all govern-ment property within its limits. You are, therefore, summoned hereby to deliver up the barracks, arsenal and public property now under your command. With the large force at my disposal, this demand will be enforced. Any attempt at defense on your part will be a rash sacrifice of life.

Haskin responded by arguing that, unlike South Carolina and Mississippi, Loui-siana had not seceded from the Union. It was still a part of the United States and bound by its laws. Under those conditions, the major said, he could not comply with the gover-nor's demand.

"I am not concerned with law or legality," Bragg told him. "I have orders to take this facility and I will do it. Any resistance on your part will result in bloodshed, and it will be on your hands, not mine."

Bragg had assembled three militia companies from Baton Rouge and three from sur-rounding parishes—a battalion-size force of about five hundred men. Because there were hotheads in the ranks capable of provoking hostilities, Bragg was reluctant to place them in a confrontational situation. He had ordered most of the men to remain bivouacked on the grounds in front of the State Capital Building, selecting only one hundred men to accompany him to the arsenal.

Bragg informed Haskin that he had a larger force at his disposal and expected reinforcements from New Orleans to arrive at any moment. Haskin had only sixty artillerymen ensconced in the white, Doric-columned pentagon barracks beside Third Street. Across the street, overlooking the Mississippi River, sat the arsenal he was bound by orders to defend. There, Lieutenant J. W. Todd and another twenty men of the ordnance corps waited with their weapons at the ready. Haskin requested that he be allowed to confer with his men before making a decision.

Upon the departure of Bragg and Taylor, Haskin ordered a cannon wheeled forward and pointed down the street in the direction of the rebels. But even as his cannoneers took their stations, reinforcements from New Orleans began arriving from the direction of the waterfront. These troops were unlike the others. They came up from the river in close ranks, dressed in crisp uniforms, marching in cadence with banners flying. A look of concern clouded the major's face. Instead of rabble, a well-disciplined army was deploying before him.

Governor Moore's plan to take the arsenal had been cloaked in such secrecy, even the officers assigned to carry it out lacked full information. Taylor was almost as startled as Haskin by the appearance of so many troops from New Orleans. Unlike Bragg's ragtag militiamen, Colonel James Walton had assembled an elite force—the very best from long-established militias around New Orleans. The men had been ordered to report to the New Orleans waterfront on Sunday night. There they were hustled on board the steamboat *National* without being told their destination until well on their way to Baton Rouge.

Walton was commander of the Washington Artillery, a battalion composed of members from the finest families of New Orleans and the surrounding area. Membership was by invitation only, and its enlistees were carefully screened according to social standing and military background.

Word that New Orleans troops had arrived in Baton Rouge angered Bragg's militiamen at the Capital Building. They had come to fight, not stand by while New Orleans reaped accolades for capturing the arsenal. Incensed, most of Bragg's militiamen picked up their gear and went home.

That afternoon, Bragg, Taylor, and Colonel Walton tried to convince Haskin to surrender the arsenal peacefully. By late afternoon, the major had exhausted their patience. They gave him until 5 P.M. to capitulate or face attack. Just before the deadline, Haskin led his men from the buildings to stack their arms. He asked Taylor for a receipt for all government property seized in order to satisfy his superiors. Taylor assured him a receipt would be forthcoming from the governor and prepared an agreement of surrender:

> Upon the demand of Governor Moore, supported by six hundred men, Major Haskin, from necessity, surrenders the barracks, arsenal and all public property therein, receipt to be given by Governor Moore for the same. The officers and enlisted men of the United States are to leave by river transport for some point above

and beyond the State of Louisiana, taking their personal effects, infantry armament, camp and garrison equipage and twenty days ration and to move within thirty-six hours.

As Taylor watched Colonel Walton's men take possession of the buildings and lower the Stars and Stripes in front of the barracks, he wondered what his father would think of the day's events. When Zack Taylor was president he threatened to hang any member of Congress who dared advocate from the floors of the U.S. House or Senate a state's secession. Now, a decade later, his son was committing armed aggression against the Union his father had sworn to preserve, and presiding over the lowering of a flag for which his father spent a lifetime fighting wars. Although Zack Taylor was long in his grave, his son had never fully escaped his shadow. Seldom did he make a decision without wondering if it would meet with his father's approval. He had resolved this latest inner conflict by rationalizing that the Union his father fought to preserve in 1850 was not the same Union of 1860.

The Whig Party that put Zachary Taylor in the White House had ceased to exist. It had been usurped by radicals and reformed as the Republican Party. Dick Taylor believed that party had fallen into the hands of men who would destroy the South to advance their personal ambitions. He had read the writings of radicals like Edward Atkinson and Amos Lawrence, both of whom advocated a conquest of the South and its resettlement with immigrants from the North. Lawrence, a Massachusetts textile baron, had written that "because of the obstinacy of the rebels it will be necessary to ruin them completely and settle their lands with Yankees." Some of the same old power brokers with whom his father once grappled when he was in the White House now embraced resettlement by "right thinking" Yankees. The flood of New England abolitionists into Kansas in 1855 and its bloody aftermath had convinced Taylor that the scheme was more than idle talk.

If not a participant in Washington intrigue, Dick Taylor was at least schooled in its surreptitious workings. With each new wave of immigrants into the Mississippi River Valley, the nation's balance of power shifted slowly westward. The question had become whether the industrial Eastern Seaboard or the rapidly expanding West would be the center of political power in the United States. Long before there was a Republican Party, there had been a theory, if not a plan, grinding its way through the gears of Washington's rumor mill. If a political party could free the four million slaves of the South and permit eligible males to vote, the shift in electoral power would allow that party to dominate the White House and Congress for generations. Taylor believed that such cocktail-party conversation had become the behind-the-scenes Republican agenda, and he concluded that the only way Northern radicals could achieve their agenda was by military conquest. Even if Lincoln was an honorable man, it would not matter, Taylor believed, as the people who had orchestrated his election were not honorable men.

He watched with mixed emotions as the Pelican Flag of Louisiana fluttered in the Gulf breeze above the Third Street barracks even as Colonel Walton's men folded the banner of his father at the base of the flagpole. What would Old Zack Taylor have done?

He concluded that Old Zack would have taken the damn arsenal.

✳ ✳ ✳

The inventory was impressive: Fifty thousand stands of small arms, four howitzers, twenty pieces of heavy ordinance, one battery of six-pound cannons, one battery of twelve-pounders, three hundred barrels of powder, and a large quantity of ammunition. The muskets were old smooth-bores, some of which had been converted for percussion firing. Some were left over from the War of 1812. Although outdated, enough armament and ammunition was available to supply a sizable army.

Taylor approved of taking the arsenal, but questioned the wisdom of doing so before Louisiana seceded. Governor Moore defended his timing, pointing out that he intended to seize all military facilities in the state before President Buchanan had a chance to reinforce them or to remove or destroy their weapons.

"Within two weeks, Louisiana will become an independent republic," the governor predicted. "I will not allow those weapons to be turned on Louisiana citizens now or in the future."

✳ ✳ ✳

FORT JACKSON, JANUARY 11—Even as the arsenal was being inventoried, a detachment of the Louisiana State Militia, under Adjutant General Maurice Grivot and Major Paul E. Thread, steamed downriver toward the twin forts guarding the Mississippi River, some seventy miles below New Orleans. By the time the sun broke over the tree line along the east bank of the river, Grivot had a sufficient number of troops deployed to demand the surrender of Fort Jackson. The old fort was heavily fortified with cannon and munitions but only lightly manned. Orderly Sergeant Henry Smith, in charge of the small Federal garrison, knew immediately that he had little choice but to capitulate. Once the Louisiana Militia was in control of Fort Jackson, Federal soldiers at Fort St. Philip, just across the river, also surrendered. General Grivot then sent a force on down the river to take Fort Pike, a less important fortification guarding the downriver Rigolets.

Within days, Fort McComb, near New Orleans, would be placed under siege. Sergeant D. Wilbur surrendered the facility and awarded himself a vacation, writing to his superiors, "I turned over all of the property under protest, closed my public accounts, transmitted them to the departments to which they belong and, as there is no use at present for an ordnance sergeant at this post, I will request leave of absence for three months to visit my family in Portland, Maine." With that, the sergeant departed for home.

True to his word, in a matter of days Governor Moore took control of all key military facilities in the state and expelled most of the Federal troops stationed in Louisiana. Since the citizenry could not make up its mind on the issue of secession, by a vote of one, the governor had decided for them. In the process, he effectively declared war on the United States of America.

✳ ✳ ✳

PINEVILLE, JANUARY 11—At a quiet campus nestled beneath towering pine trees that gave the town its name, the superintendent of the Louisiana State Seminary and Military Academy was visibly shaken by news of the takeover of the arsenal and river forts. William Tecumseh Sherman immediately grasped the significance of the governor's action even if the governor did not. It amounted to nothing less than armed insurrection by a state against the federal government.

At age forty, William Sherman, West Point graduate and Mexican War hero, had failed at every civilian career endeavor, save this one. He had failed as a banker, real estate agent, architect, and lawyer before finding his niche as an educator. He had taken on the task of converting the seminary at Pineville into a state-supported military school that, eventually, would become Louisiana State University. He liked his new job and was good at it. He was a good administrator, firm but fair. Although some of his students considered him too stern, their parents were delighted at his insistence on discipline. He moved comfortably among the social elite of Pineville and Alexandria. He had earned respect and grew increasingly comfortable in his adopted state among old friends who had risen to power in the state government. Dick Taylor, with whom he had become acquainted eight years earlier when he commanded the army's commissary depot at New Orleans, was one of his strongest supporters. Braxton Bragg, with whom he had served in Mexico and who had recommended him for the job, was one of the governor's top aides. His students came from the wealthiest and most influential families in the state. Two sons of P. G. T. Beauregard were in his classes, and Beauregard stood next in line to become the superintendent at West Point.

By his nature Sherman was a man of unyielding conviction. He had informed Bragg when he took the job that if Louisiana ever seceded he would resign. He had reached the decision not out of sympathy for the abolitionist movement—he had no strong opinion one way or the other on the issue of slavery—but because he held an uncompromising loyalty to the United States Army.

Only that week it had become clear to him that Louisiana probably would secede. In a January 7 election called by Governor Moore, a majority of the delegates selected were prosecession. But the convention to vote on secession remained two weeks away, and Sherman, a man devoted to protocol, had decided to wait on the outcome.

Sherman frequently pointed out to his Northern friends and relatives that Louisiana was not like other Southern states. "Louisiana is not ultra," he wrote to his wife, noting that "its people have always treated me with the greatest kindness and courtesy." He recalled an incident almost a year earlier when the newly inaugurated governor attempted to test him on the issue of slavery. The occasion was a dinner party hosted by the governor at his New Orleans residence. In attendance were some of the most important citizens of the state as well as the socially prominent of New Orleans. After dinner, when the ladies had departed the dining room, brandy glasses were filled, cigars were lit, and the men settled into serious conversation. Governor Moore immediately challenged Sherman by noting that his brother, John Sherman, a Republican congressman, seemed to be an avowed abolitionist.

"Some of our people wonder that you should be here at the head of an important state institution," Moore said. "Just what are your views on slavery, Mr. Sherman?"

state institution," Moore said. "Just what are your views on slavery, Mr. Sherman?"

Sherman calmly responded that his brother was far from being a radical abolitionist. "He would not of himself take from you by law or force any property whatever, even slaves," he said.

"What about your views, Mr. Sherman?" the governor had prodded him. "What would you do in our place?"

The superintendent had chosen his words carefully.

"I believe Southerners would be better served if they raised the status of their slaves," he said. "If I were in your place, I would begin by prohibiting the separation of slave families. I would educate them to read and write and raise them nearer the status of human beings. Not only would it produce more productive work, it would appease many in the North who view the current treatment of slaves as inhuman."

At that point Lieutenant Governor Henry Hyams pounded the table and said, "By God, he is right!" Others had nodded agreement. Memory of their reaction had sustained Sherman's hope that Louisiana might avoid the pitfall of secession. But that was before Lincoln's election, South Carolina's secession, and the governor's foolhardy seizure of Federal facilities. His decision made for him, Sherman sat at his desk and wrote his resignation.

A few days later, during a farewell ceremony, Sherman walked down the line of cadets, shaking hands and saying a few words of encouragement to each student. But when he stood to give his farewell speech, his voice choked and tears filled his eyes. He excused himself and left the ceremony with the realization that the next time he saw some of the young men looking up at him, it would be on a battlefield.

★ ★ ★

ON THE RED RIVER, JANUARY 23—In spite of the humid chill in the air, Captain James Beard stood on the deck of the riverboat plowing its way northward through the swift currents of the Red River. By day's end, he would be home. He was anxious to see Kate and Corinne. His daughter was almost a year old now, filled with curiosity, and no item left within reach was safe from her grasp. Already she could stand by clinging to his thumbs, her chubby legs wobbling beneath her. At each absence he seemed to miss some remarkable new feat of Corinne's, and he wondered what it would be this time. He hoped it would not be her first steps. That was his ongoing project, and he wanted to be there when his daughter passed that noteworthy milestone.

Though he hated to be away from home, James Beard had felt compelled to make this particular journey. On January 11 he received word of the takeover of the arsenal at Baton Rouge. On the morning of January 12 he was on a steamer bound for Baton Rouge, determined to secure rifles for his Shreveport Greys. He anticipated his mission would require no more than a week when he set out, but that was before he ran into bureaucratic snarls in Baton Rouge. The mission had consumed eleven days, and he looked forward to getting home—and to witnessing the expressions on the faces of his men when they saw the stack of crates on the deck. So persistent was he in Baton Rouge they had entrusted him with 350 muskets—enough to outfit three full companies. He was unperturbed that he did not have a single round of ammunition.

It had been an eventful three weeks for the young merchant-turned-soldier. On New Year's Day, his Greys were accepted as a company in the Louisiana State Militia and Beard was elected captain. A newspaper article described the unit as "unarmed and un-equipped . . . but ready to fight for Louisiana."

Even as nimble feminine fingers stitched uniforms, Captain Beard relentlessly drilled the men who would wear them. In his journal, Private William Moore of the Greys noted with pride that on January 4 "I drilled in uniform for the first time." By January 8 the Greys had honed their marching skills and increased their confidence sufficiently to march in a parade celebrating the anniversary of the Battle of New Orleans, and Private Moore proudly wrote: "By drilling in public [it was] the first time that I made my appearance in daylight with a uniform on."

Grateful to be on his way home, Beard remained nonetheless dazed by the events that swirled around him during his trip. The state capital was a whirlwind of excitement and rumor. In one three-day period, Mississippi, Florida, and Alabama had seceded, and Georgia joined them a week later. He had learned that, in addition to seizing the river forts, the governor ordered the seizure of a United States ship undergoing repairs at Algiers, an act sure to steam some collars in Washington. Even as Beard left Baton Rouge, delegates to the Louisiana Secession Convention were arriving for the opening assembly on January 23. He had come across George Williamson, an acquaintance from Shreveport who was there as a delegate from Caddo Parish. Through Williamson, Beard met several delegates from other regions. All seemed confident that there would be no war. The abolitionists were a small minority, he was assured, and the majority of Yankees did not want to fight.

* * *

BATON ROUGE, JANUARY 26—A blanket of gray, created by fog mixed with chimney smoke, lay upon the city that fateful Saturday. In spite of a damp chill in the air, by noon citizens overflowed the drafty, Gothic old State House overlooking the river. Others gathered in clusters out on the lawn. Inside, the low drone of assembled men drifted from the legislative chamber where delegates to the Secession Convention were taking their places. The gallery was packed to standing room and, down the hallway, people stood shoulder-to-shoulder in the lobby. For three days the high-ceilinged hallways had echoed speeches of reason and absurdity, sprinkled with angry outbursts and pleadings for calm. But there would be no speeches today. The time for talk had passed. The day of decision had arrived.

As people outside awaited word of the proceedings and Governor Moore waited in the wings of the House Chamber, Chairman Alexandre Mouton, president of the Senate and himself a former governor, pounded his gavel until the room fell silent. In stentorian tones, Mouton opened the session. He warned those in the gallery to conduct themselves with more decorum than they had exhibited in the past and asked for a word of prayer before the delegates cast their votes.

* * *

Never in its troubled history had Louisiana experienced a political upheaval like the one that culminated in the old building that drab winter day. And the man who stoked Louisiana's political furnace from ember to inferno was Governor Thomas Moore. A year earlier, in his inaugural address on January 23, 1860, he had stunned the state's moderates by suggesting outright separation from the United States. In a speech, in which he labeled 1860 as "Louisiana's Year of Decision," he concluded by stating: "In the North, a widespread sympathy with felons has deepened a distrust in the permanent federal government and awakened sentiments now favorable to a separation of the states."

It was a radical pronouncement for its time. The presidential election was almost a year away, and John C. Fremont was expected to be the nominee of the hated Republican Party. The Democrats had beaten Fremont in 1856 and had no reason to believe they would not do it again. In January 1860, when Governor Moore made his "Year of Decision" speech, Abraham Lincoln had not appeared on the political horizon. An Illinois lawyer and former U.S. Representative who had lost a Senate election to Stephen Douglas, Lincoln's political career until that time was more often a subject for jest rather than serious consideration. Over the years he had lost no less than nine elections. No one, not even the affable Lincoln, who often made jokes about his political ineptitude, could have predicted that he might become the Republican standard-bearer in the most important presidential election in the history of the nation.

Governor Moore's controversial speech sparked an interest in national politics unparalleled in Louisiana until that time. The upheaval began on March 5, 1860, when Louisiana's Democratic power brokers quietly gathered in Baton Rouge to select delegates to the national presidential nominating convention. Under the guiding influence of Governor Moore and former Governor Mouton, twelve hand-picked delegates were chosen to attend the Democratic National Convention at Charleston, South Carolina. All were involved in some way with Louisiana's sugar or cotton industries and, to a man, they favored secession. Dick Taylor was among those chosen.

News of the makeup of the delegation, and the secrecy surrounding its selection, outraged South Louisiana's moderates. However, they could do little except voice their displeasure and write letters to the newspapers. There was no Republican caucus in Louisiana that year because there was no Republican Party in the state.

From the moment the gavel fell on the Democratic Convention in Charleston, the meeting was doomed to disorder. Northern and Southern Democrats could not agree on plank, platform, or candidate, splitting the once solid old party apart at its partisan seams. As the convention dissolved into riotous shouting, the Louisiana contingent walked out. Alabama, Texas, Arkansas, and Florida quickly followed. Even South Carolina's delegation finally walked out of its own convention.

Taylor had gone to Charleston convinced that the South's only hope of salvation was a Democratic victory in the fall presidential election. Disturbed by the walkout, he assumed the role of mediator. With delicate diplomacy, he brought together leaders of the opposing sides for a late-night meeting at a hotel. Although the scene was less contentious than the one on the convention floor, it soon became apparent that no agreement would be struck between the fire-eaters of the South and co-operationists of the North. When the convention broke up, Taylor returned home convinced the Democratic Party was doomed and that the South would be best served if its leaders forgot politics and prepared for war.

Even as the Charleston debacle came to a merciful end, a group of Democrats bolted the party and met in Richmond. There they formed the National Constitutional Union Party and selected John Bell of Tennessee, a moderate who opposed secession, as its nominee. Bell and the new party attracted immediate support among moderates in New Orleans and South Louisiana.

Meanwhile, the regular Democrats met in Baltimore, where they proceeded to dismantle what was left of the party. Once more they split over the issues of slavery and states' rights and finally held not one, but two, nominating conventions. The main body of delegates selected Stephen Douglas as its candidate while a splinter group of Southerners, including the Louisiana delegation, nominated John C. Breckinridge of Kentucky, the nation's vice president and a strong advocate for states' rights.

The ensuing presidential campaign in Louisiana was almost as tumultuous as the Democrats' nominating process. Great rallies were held, complete with barbecues and blaring bands. New newspapers sprang up overnight in support of one candidate or the other. Night parades, lighted by hundreds of torches wound through city streets. In the North Louisiana pine hills, farmers traveled for miles and gathered beneath brush arbors to hear orations by famous politicians of the day. Supporters planned grand balls in the cities and fiddle dances in the hinterlands to rally support for their candidates.

On November 6, 1860, Louisiana voters flocked to the polls in unprecedented numbers. With solid support from the rural parishes, Breckinridge received 22,681 votes—winning 36 of the state's 48 parishes. Bell, the moderate, ran a close second with 20,204 popular votes but carried only nine parishes. Within those parishes were the population centers of Monroe, Alexandria, Baton Rouge, and New Orleans. Of the state's larger cities, only Shreveport supported Breckinridge. Douglas received only 7,625 votes and won just three South Louisiana parishes—all predominantly Cajun French.

Louisiana's electorate might as well have stayed at home. Lincoln and the Republicans had won the election before the first vote was cast. Although he did not appear on the ballot in most Southern states, Lincoln carried seventeen of the nation's thirty-three states and won the electoral vote by a wide margin.

As the results were tabulated and word filtered south that Lincoln had become president with less than 40 percent of the popular vote, Louisiana's enthusiasm for the electoral process turned from disbelief to anger. Newspapers ran blistering editorials, lamenting the unfairness of the process. Reverend Benjamin Palmer, a leading spokesman for secession, who had a Bible verse to counter every argument against slavery, stirred the pot of discontent by holding rally after rally, and railing against the "Black Republican devils of the North who have sold their souls to Satan." Governor Moore, an incurable opportunist, promptly took advantage of citizen outrage and called the State Legislature into a special session "to consider Louisiana's future."

The legislature approved the governor's request for a convention to begin on January 23 to decide the question of Louisiana's possible secession, and a statewide election of convention delegates was set for January 7. The election was still three weeks away when South Carolina seceded from the Union, an event that had a marked effect on the Louisiana vote. By election day, states rights rallies throughout the state had clearly altered public opinion. Louisianans went to the polls and elected eighty secessionist delegates, many of them from the rural parishes of North Louisiana. The co-operationists claimed forty-four delegates. Even New Orleans, always the calm eye of every storm, had sent a narrow secessionist majority to the convention. Six doubtfuls were chosen, all from South Louisiana. Accepting the result as a mandate, Governor Moore issued his secret orders for the militias to seize the river forts and the arsenal at Baton Rouge.

* * *

If 1860 was the "Year of Decision," the day of decision for Louisiana was January 26, 1861. For three days the House Chamber in the State Capital Building had echoed passionate oratory. Governor Moore had opened the convention by explaining his decision to use the State Militia to seize U.S. military facilities without consulting the legislature:

> Near this capital, where the delegates of the sovereign people were about to assemble was a military depot, capable, in unscrupulous hands, of being overawing and restraining the deliberations of a free people. I decided to take possession of the military posts and munitions of war . . . to prevent a collision between Federal troops and the people of the state.

Missing from the governor's remarks was an explanation of how eighty troops might have intimidated an entire state or why he chose to seize nonmilitary federal facilities.

To the displeasure of the governor, co-operationist delegates tried to delay a vote on secession by offering a string of resolutions. Charles Bienvenu, the delegate from Plaquemines, offered a resolution to submit the question of secession to a vote of the people. It was narrowly defeated.

At the height of the debate, Governor Moore, one of the Boston Club's better card players, played his trump. It came in the form of a letter from Washington, D.C., signed by U.S. Senators John Slidell and Judah Benjamin and Louisiana Representatives T. G. Davison and John Landrum. In it the lawmakers revealed that General Winfield Scott, commander-in-chief of the United States Army, already had drawn up a secret plan for a military conquest and subjugation of the Southern states. The revelation brought cries of outrage from the gallery. "Louisiana must never submit to such coercion by force of arms," the governor railed from the podium. When the pandemonium finally subsided a large number of co-operationists had joined the ranks of the secessionists.

By the time Delegate James G. Taliaferro of Catahoula Parish rose to speak, he realized that little tolerance remained for a message of moderation. Still he remained determined to give his speech.

"The delegate from the parish of Catahoula opposes, unqualifiedly, the separate secession of Louisiana from the Federal Union," he said, and a murmur went through the chamber before a rare silence fell upon the assembly. Speaking in a calm voice, Taliaferro systematically dismantled the argument for secession. Secession, he insisted, would not bring about the salvation of Louisiana, only its destruction. He concluded his speech with a foreboding prophecy:

"Secession will bring anarchy and war, as it will assuredly bring ruinous exactions upon property. . . . [It will bring] a withering blight upon the prosperity of the state and a fatal prostration of all its great interests."

Taliaferro left the podium to hoots and catcalls.

By the afternoon of January 26, when Chairman Mouton finally called for a vote and the secretary called the roll, only an occasional "nay" came from the respondents. The final vote was 113 to 17 for secession. *Harper's Weekly* reported in its February 9, 1861, issue that some delegates were in tears as they cast their votes. Mouton affirmed the result, declared Louisiana "a free, sovereign, and independent republic," and brought down his gavel.

Harper's Weekly described the resulting scene:

Capt. [Henry] Watkins then entered the Convention with a pelican flag with Governor Moore and his staff and put the flag in the hands of the President [Mouton] amidst tremendous excitement. A solemn prayer was offered. . . .

With the final amen, a cheer went up from the gallery. As word reached those in the rotunda a wild celebration began. The excitement spread to the crowd outside. The governor, flanked by Bragg and Watkins, shouldered his way through the celebrants to a flagpole in front of the Capital Building and raised the banner of the new republic. Unionists and moderates, who had gathered in small groups to await the inevitable, stood by, solemnly watching the ceremony. As word of the vote spread, the throaty thunder of cannons echoed from their riverside emplacements and church bells joined in, creating a symphony of celebration, salvation, and impending doom.

Amidst the tumult, a solitary figure in a black greatcoat made his way through the crowd. Dick Taylor, his dark eyes fixed in distant thought, seemed hardly to notice those who offered congratulations. Consumed by his own thoughts he shouldered his way outside. He was deeply troubled by the joyous nature of the celebration taking place and wanted no part of it. Although he had voted for secession, the assembly's scornful reaction to Taliaferro's prophecy concerned him for Taylor knew it was accurate. In his memoirs, he later recalled his thoughts as he left the State House that day:

At the time . . . I marveled at the joyous and careless temper in which men, much my superiors in sagacity and experience consummated these acts [of secession]. There appeared the same general *gaite de coeur* that M. Olliver [sic] claimed for the Imperial Ministry when war was declared against Prussia. The attachment of the northern and western people in the Union, their superiority in numbers, in wealth and especially in mechanical resources; the command of the sea; the lust of rule and territory . . . and nowhere in greater degree than in the South; all of these facts were laughed to scorn, or their mention was ascribed to timidity and treachery. As soon as the convention adjourned, finding myself out of harmony with prevailing opinion as to the certainty of war and necessity for preparation, I retired to my estate, determined to accept such responsibility only as it came to me unsought.

Dick Taylor was physically and emotionally drained. He only wanted to go home and sit undisturbed in his library with a good book, a cigar, and a slow fire in the fireplace. He wanted to sit with Mimi on the back verandah overlooking his fields and listen to the laughter of his children playing games as the sun settled behind the moss-draped oaks lining the bayou. A sharp pain in his back extended down his thighs. He could not be certain if the damp cold, exhaustion, or the tension had triggered it. But he knew from experience that relief came only with rest, and that there would be precious little rest in the days to come.

★ ★ ★

Taylor had barely arrived home when he received word that Chairman Mouton had called for the Secession Convention to reconvene in New Orleans on the twenty-ninth. New Orleans had been chosen over Baton Rouge because the capital did not have enough luxury hotel rooms to accommodate the discerning demands of the delegates. Foremost on the agenda was the selection of delegates to represent Louisiana at Montgomery, Alabama, where representatives from the seceding states were to meet on February 4 to form a Confederacy of Southern states. Taylor learned that he would not be going to Montgomery. Mouton had chosen him to chair a Committee on Louisiana Military and Naval Affairs. He was instructed to provide an assessment of the state's readiness in the event of hostilities. Taylor felt some gratification that Mouton at least acknowledged the possibility of hostilities.

★ ★ ★

NEW ORLEANS, FEBRUARY 2—Taylor presented a compelling report to the committee, although no one seemed especially interested in it. He emphasized that the North would never give up New Orleans and the mouth of the Mississippi River without a fight because the river was vital to the economy of the midwestern states.

Taylor recommended an immediate appropriation to arm and professionally train two full regiments and asked for funding for extensive repairs to the old river forts. He urged the committee to approve funds for the purchase of new, English Enfield rifles, pointing out that the smooth-bore muskets from the Baton Rouge arsenal were outdated. Taylor also wanted to build forts along the Mississippi River at Louisiana's northern border to prevent an invasion from that direction. His only ally was Pierre Beauregard, who had just arrived in the city after resigning as superintendent of West Point.

As the United States Army's top engineer, Beauregard was more familiar than anyone with the river forts, having completed an assessment of their worthiness several years earlier. He warned committee members that, in their current condition, the forts were incapable of stopping a modern invasion fleet. The forts, equipped with outdated, smooth-bore Columbiad cannons, were built to stop slow-moving sailing ships, not modern, steam-driven men-of-war. Beauregard also thought that the forts might be vulnerable to infantry assault when the river was low and recommended fortifications to repel such an attack. He noted that dense forest along the banks of the river would shield enemy vessels, allowing them to move within easy range of Fort Jackson and suggested removing those trees to provide the fort's gunners a clear field of fire. He urged the installation of an elaborate series of floating booms connected with heavy chains and cable to span the river just below the forts. He envisioned an obstruction that would allow ships to pass up and down the river but that could be hauled quickly into place to halt invading warships under the guns of Fort Jackson and Fort St. Philip. Governor Moore agreed that it was a good concept but far too expensive. The committee members listened politely, then recommended a transfer from the state's Swamp Lands Fund to the Defense Fund of six hundred thousand dollars, a fraction of the money needed to accomplish Taylor's goals and Beauregard's grand designs for the river forts.

Unable to convince the committee to purchase Enfield rifles, Taylor met with Horace Fulkerson, the purchasing agent offering to secure the weapons for Louisiana. He suggested that Fulkerson approach Braxton Bragg, who headed the State Militia Board, but Fulkerson reported back to Taylor that he was rudely received by Bragg: "In his sententious, brusque manner he informed me, with the wave of his hand, that Louisiana had all the arms she needed." In fact, Bragg had become something of an arms supplier. With the approval of the governor, he sent thousands of muskets and large quantities of ammunition from the Baton Rouge arsenal to the governor of Mississippi for its state militia.

Bragg's reaction to Fulkerson's visit disturbed Taylor. He assumed it was Bragg's petty way of responding to his recent alliance with Beauregard at the committee hearings. Bragg's and Beauregard's egos were of such proportion there was hardly space for both of them in the same room. Beauregard felt slighted when Governor Moore failed to appoint him to head the State Militia Board. Having secured that appointment, Bragg compounded the alienation by offering Beauregard the number-two spot in the militia, more as an instrument of humiliation than a sign of respect. Beauregard did not even respond to the offer. In one of the most regressive career moves in military history, he enlisted as a private in the Orleans Guards Militia rather than serve under Bragg. Taylor had been more amused than concerned by the almost childlike jealousy of the two men, until it manifested in Bragg's refusal to consider the purchase of Enfield rifles.

Taylor found more cause for concern when told of the reaction of one of the committee members to his warnings of war: "If Taylor is right and it becomes necessary, a hundred thousand men are ready to take Washington and overrun the northern states in less than a month," the delegate boasted to colleagues. When informed of the statement, Taylor bristled, "Ask the gentleman if it is his intention for that mighty force to stone the North into submission."

★ ★ ★ ★

3

★ ★ ★ ★

The Man and the Hour

NEW ORLEANS, FEBRUARY 12—Secession and the threat of impending war did not slow New Orleans's annual orgy of self-indulgence. The two-month festival of joy and debauchery always began in mid-December and did not end until Ash Wednesday, when repentant revelers with soot-marked faces filled the cathedrals to confess their sins. The winter of 1860–61 proved no exception, except for the appearance of decorative, often garish military uniforms at the grand balls. With the approach of Mardi Gras, the wealthy donned bright costumes and bejeweled masks, dancing the latest waltzes at the city's great hotel ballrooms while the working class filled the bars and taverns of the Vieux Carre. The madness climaxed on Shrove Tuesday when all elements of the city came together for one great, spasmodic celebration, and the Mistick Krewe of Comus staged the parade that signaled the end of Mardi Gras and the beginning of confession and repentance.

The parade of 1861 was especially spectacular. With a theme of "Scenes from Life," it began with a procession of colorfully attired Negroes carrying torches. They were trailed by scores of musicians playing the liveliest tunes of the day. Then came members of the Mistick Krewe of Comus in their masks and marvelous costumes, depicting, in order, childhood, youth, adulthood, and old age. Finally, as the distant music faded, the last depiction of the evening made its appearance: A large, shadowy figure moved along Canal Street, trailing the parade. The image was that of a giant, shrouded skeleton. Many in the crowd, by then too drunk to grasp the foreboding symbolism, cheered him.

★ ★ ★

Adding to the beehive atmosphere of the city during the season of frivolity was the formation of numerous militia companies in New Orleans and throughout Louisiana. Citizens gathered to applaud as these would-be soldiers drilled on designated marching streets, showing off their fancy steps. Nothing was uniform about these hurriedly assembled units, not even their uniforms. Each company tried to outdo the next in decorative garb. As a result, the uniforms of the proud defenders of Louisiana progressed from outlandish to absurd.

No two companies dressed alike. No two marched alike or adhered to anything resembling a code of military standards. Some companies quickstepped through their drills while others stomped. There was a company made up of Greek immigrants bedecked in native uniforms, another composed of German gymnasts, and yet another of professional gamblers. Firemen formed a company and policemen another. The military frenzy extended beyond New Orleans. At Keatchie in DeSoto Parish, Scotsmen formed a militia company called The Highlanders. Their uniforms featured plaid kilts. A wealthy cotton farmer in Catahoula Parish outfitted an entire company with modern rifles, sabers, ammunition, uniforms, tents, and all of the latest military equipment from Europe.

The "Zouave craze" influenced the dress of several of the early New Orleans volunteer companies. It began when a group of touring actors from Europe performed a play at the Orleans Theater depicting what one newspaper described as "a bloody drama of the Crimean War." Dressed in colorful costumes of Turkish military design, these soldier-thespians strutted about the stage and acted out mock battles that left the audience in awe. The show proved so popular the troupe remained in New Orleans for several weeks before touring other Louisiana cities. By the time the ensemble returned to New Orleans for a series of encore performances, some of the individual actors had become so popular that militia company commanders invited them to lecture on military tactics.

Whether any of these theatrical tactics were ever put to military use is unknown, but the actors left a legacy: a proliferation of the most impractical military garment ever devised—the Zouave uniform. It consisted of colorful kepi caps; decorative, waist-length, close-fitting jackets; billowing flannel pantaloons; and white, buttoned leggings. But even these uniforms varied widely. Caps ran the length of the color scale and no two jackets were of the same hue or design. Some pantaloons were red while others were blue, and for those who could not make up their minds, there were stripes.

Among the first companies formed in New Orleans was an outfit that adopted the name Tiger Rifles, perhaps the most dysfunctional military company ever assembled. Its early recruits were hard-drinking Irishmen from the brawl-infested dives and gambling dens of the New Orleans waterfront. Later, when it became necessary to fill out the company ranks, they recruited men directly from the city jail. The company commander, Captain Alex White, was a con man who recently had spent time in prison for pistol whipping a passenger on a riverboat, and rumors spread that he was wanted up north for killing a man over a card game. White claimed to be a veteran of the Mexican War but no one could be certain of his background because White was not his name. He had so many aliases no one knew who he was. For White and his Tigers, military service seemed little more than an excuse to engage in the greatest drunken adventure of their lives.

At first the company gained attention for its bright Zouave uniforms and unique marching style. Then it became notorious for a succession of brawls with other companies and tavern patrons. When an antagonist could not be found, the Tigers fought among themselves. The fancy uniforms, often slept in and rarely washed, soon were soiled, and an unkempt appearance became a Tiger Rifles trademark. They would be among the first units sent to Virginia and the first into the fire because everyone with whom they came into contact wanted to get rid of them. But the Tiger Rifles were destined to become one of the most storied outfits in military history.

In the midst of this chaotic frenzy of military disorganization arrived a man whose name would be linked forever to the Tiger Rifles. He was Roberdeau Wheat, a bear of a man whose exploits as a soldier were legend in New Orleans. Wheat stood six-four and weighed 275 pounds. A soldier of fortune, he had been fighting wars with little pause since he was a teenager. He had fought in the War with Mexico. He later led filibuster expeditions in Mexico, Nicaragua, and Cuba. Wheat was in Italy serving with Garibaldi when he received word that Louisiana had seceded, and he immediately boarded a ship for the United States. So highly regarded was Wheat as a soldier that General Winfield Scott personally met him in New York and urged him to join the Union Army. Wheat declined and proceeded to New Orleans where he was commissioned a major and given command of the Louisiana 1st Special Battalion, consisting of five companies numbering some five hundred men. One of those companies was the rowdy Tiger Rifles. Another was made up entirely of gamblers. The tamest of its companies was the Catahoula Guerrillas—described by an officer from their hometown as "a bunch of free booters and robbers."

These were the men Major Rob Wheat led to Virginia. The battalion eventually assumed the name Louisiana Tigers, taken from the Tiger Rifles. Before they were through, many a Union officer would wish that he had never heard of them.

★ ★ ★

MONTGOMERY, ALABAMA, FEBRUARY 16—The frail-appearing man who emerged from the train into a misting morning rain hardly fit the image portrayed in the local newspapers. Jefferson Davis looked gaunt and pale as he paused to address the crowd that had braved a wind-driven rainstorm to greet him. He had been ill for weeks, unable to shake a recurring fever and respiratory condition. He had waited in the shelter of the railcar until the worst of the storm passed, and when he finally stepped onto the platform, an ovation from the crowd seemed to ignite the political fire in the man. His back stiffened and his voice rose above the applause. The message was brief. All the new Confederacy wanted, he said, was to be left alone. "The time for compromise has now passed," Davis declared. "The South is determined to maintain her position, and make all who oppose her smell Southern powder and feel Southern steel if coercion is persisted in. We ask nothing. We want nothing; we have no complications."

The selection of Jefferson Davis as president of the new Confederacy had surprised him as well as most of those people who considered themselves politically aware. When the delegates of the seven seceding states met in Montgomery, William Yancey of Alabama or Robert Toombs of Georgia seemed the likely candidates to lead the new confederation. Davis, having recently resigned from the United States Senate, was not even involved in the formation of the Confederacy. He did not seek political appointment and, in fact, did not want one. He was a soldier. The governor of Mississippi had promised him command of the Mississippi Militia. That was the job he wanted. If there was going to be a war, he could not imagine that he would not be in the middle of it.

The delegates settled on Davis as a last-minute compromise candidate. Georgia had withdrawn Toombs's name from consideration, and the delegates were reluctant to place a proslavery fire-eater like Yancey or Georgia's Alexander Stephens, considered by many to be a co-operationist, at the head of the new Confederacy. Davis was considered a man of even temper and reason and was well respected in Washington. If hostilities should come, the delegates believed he would be an able military leader. After all, he was a Mexican War hero and former U.S. secretary of war in the Pierce administration.

That evening, in the grand ballroom of the Exchange Hotel, it became clear the fire-eaters had accepted Davis when Yancey stood to introduce the new president to a packed house. He praised Davis as the greatest of statesmen, the bravest of soldiers, and a patriot of the South. "The man and the hour have met," he said. The words brought the crowd to its feet and a thunderous ovation filled the room.

* * *

The Confederacy's man of the hour was fifty-four years old. He was born, the last of ten children, in a log cabin in Kentucky, only 110 miles from the birthplace of Abraham Lincoln. His father was a horse trader who had received just enough education to appreciate the benefits of a good one. Sam Davis resolved that his sons would have the best education he could afford. By the time Jeff was born his older brother, Joseph, had established himself as a lawyer in Natchez and made enough money to acquire vast land holdings. When Jeff was four, his father sold his horses and moved to Mississippi to live near Joseph and become a cotton farmer. He sent his younger son off to Saint Thomas School in Kentucky—one of the best prep schools in the South at the time. At twelve, Jeff demonstrated a natural inclination for rebellion when he announced he was quitting school. His father responded by sending him to the fields to pick cotton with the slaves. After two weeks of dragging a cotton sack, young Jeff was ready to resume his education. He was only thirteen when he entered Transylvania University at Lexington, Kentucky. He was away at school when his father died.

Joseph Davis took his little brother under a protective wing. His law practice, farm operations, and business dealings had made him wealthy but prevented him from fulfilling an ambition to enter the political arena. Through sibling proxy, Joseph proposed to catapult Jeff to the political heights he himself was denied. Joseph believed if one aspired to high public office, the first requirement was attendance at West Point. He used his influence to secure for his little brother an appointment there.

The most remarkable thing about Cadet Davis's West Point experience was that he was not drummed out of the corps. A frequent patron of Benny Havens's off-limits tavern, Davis narrowly escaped court-martial when caught there on several occasions. On one visit to the watering hole, he evaded detection by running through the night and tumbling down a forty-foot cliff. Although cut and bruised, he miraculously escaped serious injury.

Cadet Davis was a practical joker. One day, during ordnance class, he "accidentally" lit the fuse to a grenade and calmly turned to the instructor. "What shall I do, sir?" he said. "This fireball is ignited." The astonished teacher responded by making a dash for the door even as Davis defused the grenade and tossed it out the window. He also organized a notorious Christmas party that turned into a drunken celebration. Informed that his old nemesis, Captain Ethan Hitchcock, was on the way to break up the party, Davis turned to the revelers and shouted: "Hide the grog, boys! Old Hitch is coming." As it turned out, Old Hitch was standing directly behind him.

Davis was arrested and confined to his room, which set off the most violent riot in the history of the academy. Davis's drunken companions and Hitchcock's friends squared off in a bloody battle in which the sides bombarded each other with firewood. The fight turned ugly when a cadet with a saber chased an officer across the grounds and a pistol shot of undetermined origin narrowly missed Hitchcock. Davis, having consumed more than his share of the aforementioned grog, was confined to his room, and he slept through the whole affair. His friends were court-martialed while Davis was reprimanded, and he somehow managed to stay in school long enough to graduate near the bottom of his class.

He was commissioned a second lieutenant and assigned the ignoble task of going into the wilderness to establish a sawmill and supply lumber for the Army. That winter, he contracted pneumonia and almost died. The illness damaged his lungs and left him vulnerable to respiratory ailments for the remainder of his life.

Davis's bravery in the Black Hawk War against the Sac and Fox tribes in northern Illinois impressed Colonel Zachary Taylor sufficiently for the commander to have the young lieutenant transferred to Fort Crawford as his aide. Davis's unorthodox style of command was hardly reflective of his West Point training. When a private refused to obey an order, instead of putting him on report, Davis lit into him with his fists. Having subdued the soldier, Davis informed him he would not report the incident since it was a man-to-man fight.

Taylor and Davis had a good relationship until the young lieutenant became smitten by the colonel's eighteen-year-old daughter, Sarah. Zachary Taylor loved the army, but did not trust its young officers around his daughters. Taylor and his wife, Peggy, had parented five daughters but only three survived, the two oldest girls having died in childhood during a yellow fever epidemic in Louisiana. Against his wishes, their third daughter, Ann, married an army surgeon and was struggling in near poverty while trying to raise two daughters at Fort Snelling. When Taylor learned that Davis was courting Sarah behind his back, the colonel threatened to shoot his aide. Fortunately for Davis, Peggy Taylor calmed her husband, and Lieutenant Davis was promptly transferred to Fort Smith, Arkansas—but not before he asked Sarah to marry him, and she accepted.

They were apart for two years but in the summer of 1835, Davis resigned from the army and went to Louisville, Kentucky, where Sarah was staying with relatives. They married in a small ceremony attended by several members of the Taylor family, including nine-year-old Dick. Sarah did not invite her father to the wedding.

The couple moved into Joseph Davis's palatial Hurricane Plantation home near Natchez while Jeff Davis prepared nearby Briarfield Plantation for his bride. Two months after the wedding, Sarah became bedridden with a fever. She died that September of malaria, just three months after the wedding.

As far as Jeff Davis was concerned, his life had ended as well. He became a brooding recluse and fell into a disturbing depression. Joseph finally talked his brother into taking a trip. He sailed to Havana, New York, and Washington, but the trip did not help. Returning to Mississippi, Davis entered a seven-year hermitage. During that time, his only friends were Joseph and a slave named James Pemberton. To occupy his time, Davis read—volume after volume on history, government, war, and politics—absorbing the book knowledge that had been of little interest to him at West Point. He studied the lives of the Founding Fathers and developed a fascination for the wording of the Constitution. For years, he studied and analyzed its every line. Finally, in 1843, his brother dragged him out of the shadows and shoved him into politics.

A week before election day that year, the Democratic candidate for the state legislature dropped out of the race. Joseph talked Davis into letting him enter his name on the ballot. Although the district was a Whig stronghold, Davis ran a strong race and barely lost. His near win caught the attention of the state's Democratic leaders and also provided a second benefit. While campaigning, he met Varina Howell, the cultured daughter of a Natchez lawyer and granddaughter of an eight-term governor of New Jersey. She and Davis were married the following year.

In 1845, Davis was elected to the U.S. House of Representatives. He gained attention by strongly opposing legislation that would limit immigration: "Do you gentlemen forget," he said from the well of the House, "that among the signers of the Declaration of Independence [there were] eight actual foreigners and nine who were the immediate descendants of foreign parents?"

His oratory inspired John Quincy Adams to remark, "That young man is no ordinary man. Mind me, he will make his mark."

Davis lived to regret another of his speeches. During a debate on whether the nation should maintain a strong professional army or depend on citizen volunteers, Representative Andrew Johnson stated that an ordinary citizen could perform just as well as any professional soldier. Being a West Pointer, Davis rose to challenge the statement. He cited the record of Zachary Taylor and asked, "Could a blacksmith or tailor have procured those results?" Johnson immediately charged that Davis had insulted him because he once was a tailor. Johnson, a man of shallow intellect, was sensitive to the fact that he had no formal education. His wife had taught him to read and write. Nothing about Johnson suggested that he might become president of the United States. But, four years later, destiny rather than ability thrust him into that role following Lincoln's assassination and he would exact his revenge on Davis.

With the outbreak of the Mexican War in 1846, Davis resigned from the House to serve under General Taylor and led a Mississippi infantry regiment into Northern Mexico. Before leaving Washington he argued with General Winfield Scott, who had insisted that flintlock muskets were sufficient to subdue the Mexicans. Davis went over Scott's head and ordered percussion rifles for his men but, in doing so, he created a lifelong enemy in Scott.

Zachary Taylor's string of victories in Mexico made "Old Rough and Ready" so popular that President James K. Polk became alarmed. Polk had handpicked Scott to succeed him in the White House. But it was Taylor, a man with no political ambition or aptitude, who had emerged as the popular choice for the office. Left alone, Taylor might have ended the Mexican War in a matter of weeks, if not days. He was stopped, not by the Mexican Army, but by Polk, who ordered him to hold his position and send half of his force to General Scott for an ill-conceived, and unnecessary, coastal invasion at Vera Cruz. This strictly political decision left Taylor sitting at Buena Vista with less than five thousand troops, short on ammunition and supplies, and facing Santa Anna's force of fifteen thousand men and superior artillery.

Santa Anna promptly attacked him, the bulk of his force, including his cavalry, striking Taylor's lightly manned left flank. Davis and his Mississippi Rifles Regiment had the misfortune to be holding the position. Outnumbered nine to one on that side of the field, low on ammunition, and almost certain to be overrun, Davis formed his men into a V with the opening facing the enemy. As Santa Anna's troops charged, a young artillery officer named Braxton Bragg wheeled cannons into position to support the Mississippians. The Mexican cavalry charged into the jaws of the V and was destroyed by a withering crossfire. Crushed, Santa Anna withdrew the remnants of his army and fled south. Zachary Taylor became the hero of Buena Vista but Jeff Davis had won the battle. Taylor acknowledged as much in his report. He also personally thanked Davis. "My daughter was a better judge of men than I," he admitted, finally ending their estrangement.

Jeff Davis went on to serve in the U.S. Senate. As secretary of war in the administration of weak-willed Franklin Pierce, he became the most powerful man in Washington for a time. Pierce relied on him for advice on all matters, foreign and domestic. Later, as talk of secession stirred the political pot in Washington, Davis worked for a compromise solution. He was willing to compromise on many issues, including slavery, but refused to yield when it came to the rights of states. He insisted that one of those rights guaranteed by the Constitution was for a state to secede from the Union if it so desired. When Mississippi seceded, he stood before his Senate colleagues, bid them a tearful farewell, and returned home. He was at Briarfield, helping Varina set out rose cuttings, when the telegram from Montgomery arrived, informing him that he had become president of the new Confederate States of America.

* * *

JACKSON, MISSISSIPPI, FEBRUARY 16—Leaving the plantation in Louisiana in the capable hands of his wife Eleanora, Henry Gray left for Mississippi in early February. He arrived at Jackson prepared to offer his services to the new commander of the Mississippi Militia, only to learn that his old friend, Jeff Davis, was the new president of the Confederate States of America. Henry considered returning home and volunteering his services in Louisiana. However, Mississippi officials urged him to remain as a civilian volunteer until a suitable appointment could be arranged for him. Their arguments convinced him to cast his lot with the Mississippi Militia.

Most Federal facilities in Mississippi and Alabama had been seized by local militias or abandoned by the United States Army. However, the forts around Pensacola and those along the Florida coast remained in Union hands. Gray assumed that Mississippi troops would be called on to help liberate those forts, and he would see some quick action. Instead, he ended up cooling his heels in Jackson, assisting with organizing and outfitting regiments for the Confederate Army.

The "suitable position" promised him did not materialize, and Gray continued to serve as a volunteer for several months before he tired of the duty and accompanied a regiment of Mississippi troops to Montgomery, and from there to Virginia, as a civilian advisor. However, his stay in Virginia would be brief. President Davis soon urged him to return to Louisiana to raise additional regiments for the Confederate Army.

* * *

NEW YORK CITY, MARCH 30—As one Southern state after another seceded in the early weeks of 1861, many in the North seemed content to let them go. That attitude was reflected in editorials appearing in Northern newspapers, but by mid-March, a parade of powerful businessmen, bankers, and politicians had enlightened editors on the economic consequences of letting the South go. The result was a series of editorials like the one that appeared in the *Manchester Union Democrat*: "If the Southern Confederacy will not employ our ships or buy our goods . . . what is our shipping without it? The transportation of cotton and its fabrics employ more ships than all other trade. It is very clear that the South gains by this process and we lose. No—we must not let the South go."

The *New York Evening News* called for an immediate blockade of all Southern ports: "Either revenue from duties must be collected in the ports of the rebel states or the ports must be closed. . . . If neither of these things be done, our revenue laws are substantially repealed. The sources which supply our treasury will be dried up. . . . The nation will become bankrupt before the next crop of corn is ripe."

The *New York Times* predicted that, if nothing was done, New Orleans would flourish while grass grew in the streets of New York City. In a March 30, 1861, editorial, the *Times* made a prediction:

> If the manufacturer at Manchester [England] can send his goods into the Western states through New Orleans at less cost than through New York, he is a fool for not availing himself of his advantage. . . . With the loss of our foreign trade, what is to become of our public works, conducted at the cost of many millions of dollars to turn into our harbor the products of the interior? Once at New Orleans, goods may be distributed over the whole country, duty free. With us it no longer is an abstract question—one of Constitutional construction or of the reserved or delegated power of the state or federal government, but of material existence. . . . We were divided and confused till our pockets were touched.

The first distant rumblings of war from the North were coming, not from drums on parade grounds, but from the newspaper presses of the port cities along the Eastern seaboard.

* * *

MONTGOMERY, APRIL 10—By early April, two men knew a great war was about to commence and both knew where and how it would start. Like schoolboys facing off on a playground, Lincoln and Davis each waited for the other to blink. The chip in that deadly standoff, delicately balanced on the shoulder of destiny, was a concrete enclave rising out of the harbor at Charleston, South Carolina.

From the day of South Carolina's secession, President-elect Lincoln knew there would be a fight. During the campaign, he expressed a willingness to compromise on any number of issues that divided North and South, including slavery. But under no circumstance would he allow the nation to be split in two. His Southern counterpart, President Davis, had realized that war was inevitable well before he gave his emotional farewell speech in the Senate. He had been a part of the hopeless compromise process in Washington, and he knew too many men of influence on both sides were unwilling to yield.

Following his election, Lincoln remained in Illinois, uncharacteristically silent, leaving the lame-duck Buchanan to stew in the White House. Lincoln might have soothed Southern passions with a few well-chosen words of reassurance. He might have warned in advance that secession would be answered by armed intervention. He did neither, leaving Southern fence-straddlers with the mistaken impression that the North might not be willing to go to war over Southern secession. Through the upheaval of the winter of 1860–61, Lincoln remained ensconced with his Republican advisors in Illinois, forming a new government and planning for the conflict.

In late February 1861 Virginia made one final attempt to bring the states of the South back into the Union. Trapped between North and South, Virginia's leaders arranged a "peace conference" in Washington. Representatives from twelve Northern and eight Southern states assembled to seek a common ground for reconciliation. They managed to agree on a compromise based on an earlier plan put forth by Senator John J. Crittenden. Finally, the fate of the compromise hinged on what President-elect Lincoln thought of it. Lincoln refused to endorse, condemn, or comment on it. The plan was presented to the Senate for approval and defeated by one vote.

Southern moderates were at last jarred awake to the likelihood of war on March 4. In his inaugural address, Lincoln finally spelled out his position. "No state, upon its own mere action, can lawfully get out of the Union," he said. He indicated that he would use force to preserve the Union, noting, "In your hands, my dissatisfied fellow countrymen, and not in mine, is the momentous issue of *civil war.*"

A long-abandoned old fort in Charleston Harbor was the tinderbox, waiting for a spark. Forts Sumter and Moultrie had been subjects of contention between Washington and South Carolina well before Lincoln and Davis took their respective offices. South Carolina wanted the small Federal force occupying the forts to leave. President Buchanan had refused to abandon the facilities but agreed not to reinforce them. When the Army abandoned Moultrie because of its vulnerability and moved into Sumter, the fort became more of a symbol than a threat. An outdated facility, Sumter was worth little to the North, and it was of no real value to South Carolina. Yet, both were ready to go to war over it.

Both Davis and Lincoln viewed Sumter as a means to an end. Davis saw a confrontation over the fort as a lever to bring the balking border states into the Confederacy. Virginia, Maryland, Tennessee, Kentucky, and Missouri wavered between secession and Union loyalty. Lincoln saw Sumter as a means to rally support for a war he knew was inevitable. Most Northerners were not ready to go to war over the issues of slavery or secession in the spring of 1861, especially those in New York and the border states. But Lincoln was convinced that, if the Confederacy fired on the flag of the United States, an outraged North would unify behind him. He prodded Davis into doing just that when he announced his intention to reinforce Sumter. The following day, Davis responded by requesting that Southern governors send him whatever troops they could spare.

Governor Moore received a telegram asking for three thousand men from Louisiana plus whatever arms, ammunition, and equipment he could supply. On April 9, as the Federal steamer *Baltic* left New York harbor with provisions and reinforcements for Sumter, Davis called a cabinet meeting at Montgomery to discuss the crisis. One by one the cabinet members sided with Davis's decision to expel Federal troops from the fort. The lone dissenter was Secretary of State Robert Toombs, whose protest was prophetic:

> The firing on that fort will inaugurate a civil war greater than any the world has ever seen," he told Davis. "It is suicide. It is murder, and will lose us every friend in the North. You will wantonly strike a hornets' nest, which extends from mountains to ocean; and legions, now quiet, will swarm out and sting us to death. It is unnecessary. It puts us in the wrong. It is fatal.

Davis was unswayed by Toombs's argument. Having placed newly appointed Brigadier General Pierre Beauregard in command at Charleston, Davis sent word on April 10 for him to expel Federal troops from Fort Sumter. Davis made it clear to Beauregard that it must be the Confederate Army, not the South Carolina Militia, that initiated hostilities.

★ ★ ★ ★

4

★ ★ ★ ★

The Hornets' Nest

CHARLESTON, SOUTH CAROLINA, APRIL 14—Pierre Beauregard struck the "hornets' nest" at 4:30 A.M. on April 14, 1861, when Captain George James sent a mortar shell arching high into the night sky above Charleston Harbor. It was a signal for shore batteries rimming the harbor to open up on the island fortress sitting in the bay.

Major Robert Anderson, commander at Fort Sumter, sent his men to the parapets to respond. Ironically, in 1780 his father, Major Richard Anderson, had defended Charleston harbor against a fleet of British warships from the parapets of Fort Moultrie. Now Anderson found himself under attack from the very fort his father once commanded.

In its January 5, 1861, issue, *Harper's Weekly* reported to its Northern readers that the "gallant Major Anderson" had abandoned Fort Moultrie and moved his troops into Fort Sumter, described as "a work of great strength, and, with the force now in it, commanded as it is, can be held securely against any army South Carolina can bring against it." In fact, Anderson had only seventy-six troops inside Sumter's fifty-foot-thick walls, and eight of those were musicians who comprised a brass band.

The residents of Charleston were jarred from their sleep in the predawn darkness when thirty cannons and seventeen mortars opened fire. Thousands of men, women, and children, some still in nightclothes, climbed onto fences, into trees, and atop roofs to witness the spectacle. With the coming of dawn, they saw to their disappointment that most of the Confederate fire was landing beyond the fort. But with daylight, the mortar operators found their range and shells began exploding inside Sumter's walls. The shelling continued throughout the day. Gun crews inside the fort occasionally fired back with no apparent effect, except for a pair of stray forty-two-pound balls that crashed through the roof of a Charleston resort hotel, resulting in what a newspaper reporter described as "a miscellaneous scattering" of the guests.

By noon, flames leapt above the walls of Fort Sumter and reached its powder magazine. Captain Abner Doubleday (destined to become famous as the "inventor" of baseball rather than for his military accomplishments) described the scene inside the fort: "The roaring and crackling of the flames, the dense masses of whirling smoke, the bursting of the enemy's shells and our own which were exploding in the burning rooms . . .

and the sound of masonry falling in every direction made the fort a pandemonium."

Remarkably, the rain of fire and metal from the shores of Charleston harbor inflicted not a single casualty upon the defenders. But after thirty-four hours of bombardment, with the interior of the fort reduced to rubble, Major Anderson had little choice but to surrender. Before lowering the United States flag, he ordered nothing less than a one-hundred-gun salute in its honor. Halfway through the ceremony one of the fort's cannons exploded. Five soldiers were wounded and a young cannoneer named Daniel Hough was killed. He was the first to die in a conflagration that eventually would consume more than 683,000 lives.

* * *

The capture of Sumter vaulted Pierre Gustave Toutant Beauregard from hero to legend. Before the war, the little French Creole soldier was about as close to Southern nobility as one could achieve without wearing a crown. His family was among the wealthiest and most respected in Louisiana. His father could trace his French lineage back to the thirteenth century along a royal ancestral chain that had been alternately in and out of favor with the French crown. His mother was a DeReggio, a family that claimed descent from Italian nobility.

Pierre was born in 1818, the third of seven children. The Toutant Beauregards lived on a vast estate twenty miles below New Orleans. A family with its roots clinging to Old World ways and values, they were both rich and arrogant. Above all, they were French, and contemptuous of everything and anyone Anglo-Saxon. Pierre was twelve years old before being exposed to the English language, and that exposure took place in New York rather than Louisiana. After receiving an elementary education at a French school in New Orleans, his father sent him to a French school in New York run by two brothers who had been high-ranking officers under Napoleon Bonaparte. Young Pierre found their war stories fascinating and decided to be a soldier. Although not pleased by the decision, his father arranged an appointment to West Point and Pierre entered the academy at sixteen. He graduated in 1838, ranking second in a class of thirty-four.

By age twenty-three, he already was recognized as one of the army's top young engineers. In 1841, he married Marie-Laure Villere, from another old and wealthy Creole family. They lived on her family's estate in Plaquemines Parish for several years before moving to New Orleans. Marie-Laure bore him two sons before Pierre was called to duty in the war with Mexico, where he served under Winfield Scott and with another young army engineer named Robert E. Lee. Following the war Beauregard was assigned to evaluate the nation's coastal forts, including those in Louisiana, and to make repairs where needed. Limited funds prevented him from accomplishing anything beyond a few superficial repairs, but nobody had more knowledge of the strengths and weaknesses of U.S. coastal fortifications than Beauregard.

In 1850, tragedy struck when Marie-Laure died while giving birth to a daughter. A few years later, Beauregard married Caroline Deslonde—a union that quickly accelerated his career as she was the sister of U.S. Senator John Slidell, the most powerful politician in Louisiana and one of the most influential in Washington. By 1861, Beauregard stood next in line to become the superintendent at West Point. Ironically, he received the appointment the day before the Louisiana Secession Convention met in Baton Rouge. When word of Louisiana's secession reached him, Beauregard resigned from the U.S. Army. His tenure as head of West Point had lasted only four days.

The resignation made him an instant hero in the South. The newspapers nicknamed him "Little Napoleon." Jefferson Davis commissioned him the first brigadier general in the Confederate Army. With the bombardment of Fort Sumter, Beauregard's popularity soared to such heights it inspired songs about him, and a great deal of bad poetry, one notable example being: "With cannon and musket, with shell and petard / We salute the North with our Beauregard." Mercifully, the author remains unknown.

* * *

NEW ORLEANS, APRIL 18—The morning after the surrender of Fort Sumter, President Lincoln announced that an "insurrection" existed in the South and called for seventy-five thousand volunteers to suppress the rebellion. That afternoon, Governor Thomas Moore received a telegram from Jefferson Davis asking for another five thousand volunteers from Louisiana in addition to the forty-seven hundred he already had promised. Within minutes, Captain James Beard in Shreveport received a telegram informing him the Shreveport Greys were activated. He was to report to the Shreveport docks the following morning, fully equipped and prepared for departure.

For weeks, the Greys had attended gala balls and received the praise of adoring wives and sweethearts, politicians and businessmen. They had marched to the cheers of the crowd and seen their names in print in the local newspaper. Young boys looked up to them as heroes of the highest order.

Early on the afternoon of April 16, a large crowd gathered on the levee to watch the Greys board the steamer *Louis d'Or*. The atmosphere was festive. Beard embraced Kate and promised that he would write often. Several members of her family were there to see him off, and waiting nearby was Alonzo Tomkies, a family household slave who was a favorite of Kate's. Since James and Kate did not own slaves, Kate had "borrowed" Alonzo to accompany James as his manservant. James had resisted the idea, whereupon Kate's suggestion became a demand. Also present was sixteen-year-old Ned Beard, who had been pestering his brother for weeks to join the Greys. James had refused to enlist him but finally agreed to allow Ned to accompany the unit as far as New Orleans on the condition that he then would return home. Having said his good-byes, James, escorted by Alonzo and Ned, boarded the steamer and lifted his hat to the cheers of the crowd. A reporter for the *Shreveport Daily News* described the scene as the *Louis d'Or* left the dock:

> The levee was crowded with ladies, gentlemen and children, anxious to have another look at the brave defenders of our rights. As the boat left the shore, the band of the Caddo Rifles struck up a very appropriate tune, 'The Girl I Left Behind Me,' and the cannon was made to belch forth its thundering sound. . . . The best citizens, the very best men of Shreveport—its gentlemen—make up the file of this company. Captain

James H. Beard is worthy of his command and will make his mark or nature made a mistake when she marked the man. If the war lasts, we shall hear from James H. Beard.

The departure had been so hurriedly organized, several wives and mothers had to accompany the boys in order to finish sewing some of the uniforms before they reached New Orleans. As the boat made its way down the winding river, people lined the levee at each town, hamlet, and plantation dock to cheer them. The following morning, as they approached the levee at Alexandria, a cheering crowd and a seven-gun salute greeted them. There was a great deal of excitement when Governor Moore and his wife made an appearance and announced they would accompany the Greys as far as Baton Rouge. The governor gave a brief inspirational talk and afterward conversed with James in private for a time before retiring. Meanwhile, the governor's wife volunteered to assist the ladies of Shreveport in sewing the last of the uniforms as the boat continued down the river.

Upon their arrival at New Orleans on the eighteenth, the boys from Shreveport were in awe of the activity along the waterfront—a teeming tangle of humanity beneath a forest of ships' masts. Men seemed to be loading and unloading cargoes everywhere. Soldiers in uniforms of the most gaudy colors and outlandish fashion moved about in ragged ranks, disembarking and boarding transport steamers as their officers barked orders—some in languages the men of Shreveport had not heard before.

Marching through the outskirts of the city, the Greys were surprised when girls of unusual beauty gathered in clusters on street corners to wave and call to them. A young lady boldly ran forward to present Private Stephen Hackett with a silk handkerchief. Surprised by the act, his face flushed crimson.

"We love you, brave soldiers," the girls called to them.

"We love you, Hackett," his comrades hooted and catcalled as they marched. The private placed the perfume-scented trophy inside his jacket and tried to ignore them.

When at last Captain Beard's men reached their assigned campsite on the outskirts of the city, they finally faced the harsh reality of soldiering. Having walked just four miles, they were exhausted, more from a loss of sleep than the trek. Many of the men, like Hackett, had never traveled more than a day's ride from Shreveport and the journey down the river had been so filled with adventure they dared not sleep for fear of missing something. Many were footsore from newly purchased, ill-fitting civilian footwear. In this state of discomfort and fatigue they came upon crudely constructed barracks in a muddy field near an abandoned cotton gin. Private Moore wrote of the accommodations: "It is such a place as decent men never had to submit to before."

Two days after arriving in New Orleans, the Greys departed their muddy campsite and boarded the steamer *Florida* for a trip to Mobile. From there, they walked forty-five miles to Pollard, Florida, and boarded a train for the final few miles to Fort Barrancas at Pensacola. Accompanying them was Ned Beard. James had become concerned that, in his absence, Ned might join another company and concluded the safest thing to do was take him along. At least he would be able to keep an eye on his impulsive little brother.

★ ★ ★

WASHINGTON, D.C., APRIL 19—On Wednesday, April 17, just two days after the surrender of Fort Sumter, President Lincoln was informed that Virginia not only had refused to provide troops to the government, but its lawmakers were meeting in assembly to consider secession. Any hope that Virginia might remain neutral was dashed on Thursday, when the militias seized the U.S. Customs House and Post Office in Richmond. Lincoln was further distressed by news that a secessionist flag had been raised over Federal Hill in Baltimore. That same day, F. P. Blair reported back to Lincoln that he had met with Robert E. Lee and offered him command of the Union Army, and Lee had declined it.

Things did not improve on Friday, when word arrived that riots had broken out in Baltimore. A Massachusetts regiment was changing trains on its way to Washington when a mob began throwing stones and shots were fired. When the mayhem ended, four soldiers and nine civilians were dead.

Meeting with his cabinet, Lincoln emphasized that Maryland would be kept in the Union under force of arms. Should Maryland secede, the nation's capital would be geographically cut off from the rest of the Union. Lincoln ended a busy day by issuing a proclamation calling for a blockade of all ports of the seceding Southern states—a decision that would have a profound effect on Louisianans.

* * *

NEW ORLEANS, MAY 2—A week after the surrender of Fort Sumter, an announcement appeared in the April 21, 1861, issue of the *New Orleans Daily Picayune*.

DEFENDERS OF THE NATIVE LAND

We, the undersigned natives of Louisiana, assembled in committee, have unanimously adopted the following resolution: Resolved that the population to which we belong, as soon as a call is made to them by the governor of this state, will be ready to take up arms and form themselves into companies for the defense of their homes, together with the other inhabitants of this city, against any enemy who may come and disturb its tranquillity.

The notice concluded with an appeal for volunteers. Fifteen hundred men answered the call. They overflowed the auditorium at the Convent School. What distinguished this gathering of militia volunteers from others in New Orleans was that all were black freedmen or, as they preferred, "hommes de couleur libre"—free men of color.

The response to the notice overwhelmed Armand Lanusse and Charles Sauvenet. They had intended to form two or three companies when they placed the announcement. Now they faced the prospect of organizing a full regiment, and even then hundreds of volunteers would be turned away.

Lanusse and Sauvenet were among the city's intellectual elite. Lanusse was the principal at Convent School, established in 1833 as the first free school for black children in the United States. He also was a poet, whose works had been published in a book of poetry titled *Les Cenelles*. Sauvenet was a teacher fluent in German, Spanish, French, and

English and frequently served as a translator in court cases, as well as business matters.

The formation of a black militia regiment anywhere in the Confederacy except New Orleans would have been bizarre. But black men had been fighting in wars to protect the city for one hundred and fifty years. Armed slaves and freedmen joined the French Colonial Army in 1727 to fight in the Choctaw Indian wars. In 1735, forty-five blacks were listed in the ranks of French troops stationed in New Orleans. When Louisiana was ceded to Spain in 1762, the tradition of blacks serving in the military continued. During the American Revolution, black soldiers fought with the Spanish to help capture British forts at Baton Rouge and Natchez. Six months later they participated in the conquest of Mobile and Pensacola. When the United States purchased Louisiana in 1803, blacks continued to serve in the local militias. In 1811 blacks in the New Orleans Home Guard were called out by the governor to help put down a slave insurrection, and they were with Andrew Jackson in 1815 when he defeated a British invasion force on the plains of Chalmette, saving New Orleans from enemy occupation.

Unlike other Southern states, Louisiana was heavily influenced by French and Spanish occupation in its attitudes toward slavery. French army officers and government officials, upon returning to their homeland, often freed their slave mistresses and children, sometimes leaving them their holdings. During Spanish rule, free blacks routinely obtained land grants. From these practices evolved a unique culture of well-educated and often wealthy free men of color.

Within days of the gathering at Convent School, a regiment was formed and officers selected. They called themselves the Native Guards. The officers' corps, in addition to Lanusse and Sauvenet, included Arnold Bertonneau, a wealthy wine merchant; Louis Gollis, a cigar manufacturer with vast real estate holdings; Florville Gonzales, who ran a popular coffeehouse; and Joseph Lavigne, who owned a grocery store.

In its April 27 issue, the *New Orleans Daily Crescent* published a glowing article on the Native Guards, noting, "They will fight the Black Republicans with as much determination and gallantry as any body of white men in the service of the Confederate States."

The reason they were willing to fight was as simple as the fact that, in 1860, New Orleans's free men of color paid city taxes on $15 million worth of property. Although some of them owned slaves, few condoned the institution and most could have cared less about the new Confederacy. Their loyalty was to New Orleans. They were willing to fight for their property and hard-earned status. Many of those who made up the community of "hommes de couleur libre" had earned the respect of the whites of the city. The professionals, many of them trained in Paris, included doctors, dentists, architects, engineers, teachers, and ministers. Among the artisans were musicians, silversmiths, portrait painters, and at least one sculptor whose works would receive acclaim in France. The businessmen were prosperous, and the tradesmen among the most skilled in the world. Within the ranks of the freedmen were several successful money brokers and, according to the 1860 census, two citizens who listed their occupations as "capitalists."

On May 2, Governor Moore sat at his desk in Baton Rouge and signed documents accepting the New Orleans Native Guards into the Louisiana State Militia. He issued commissions to the regiment's line officers, all of whom were black. He then appointed

Colonel Henry D. Ogden to command the regiment. The colonel was white.

* * *

PENSACOLA, FLORIDA, MAY 7—Upon his arrival at Fort Barrancas, overlooking Pensacola Bay, Dick Taylor found his old friend Braxton Bragg in a state of agitation. As the newly appointed commander at Pensacola, Bragg had a problem and, as he often did on such occasions, he wrote to Taylor, requesting his counsel. Actually, Bragg had written Taylor several letters, the final one containing a thinly veiled cry of desperation. Its tone prompted Taylor to visit. Thanks to Bragg's friendship with Davis, he had been promoted to brigadier general in the newly created, and extremely dysfunctional, Confederate States Army. From the window of his barracks office, he looked out on Confederate camps springing up around the bay. He also had a clear view of Fort Pickens, rising like a low, natural outcrop above a small spit of sand a mile and a half offshore in Pensacola Bay. Above Pickens, waving its defiance, a United States flag floated on the Gulf breeze.

"There are no more than a hundred men out there and most of them are seamen," Bragg said. "I should have taken the island when I arrived here but the secretary would not give me permission to do so, much less an order. And now that Mr. Beauregard has taken Sumter, they want to know why I haven't taken Pickens."

Taylor surmised that, more than counsel, Bragg needed someone upon whom he could unburden his frustrations. With Bragg's field glasses, Taylor scanned the island.

Santa Rosa was barely an island and Pickens seemed hardly a fort when viewed on its landward side. The fort had been built to repel an attack from the open waters of the Gulf, leaving its landward back door vulnerable to assault. That situation had been partly remedied by the energy of the fort's occupants, who had managed to turn some of the guns inland and fortify the back of the facility with a substantial wall of sand. Bragg was capable of subduing Pickens with superior artillery, but he and the Federal commander had reached a gentlemen's agreement. In the absence of orders from their superiors, they would maintain a standoff if the Federals did not attempt to resupply the island. Although circumstances had changed, Bragg still felt bound by the agreement. Besides, he pointed out to Taylor, he had problems that were even more pressing.

"They are sending me more troops than I can accommodate, and I am supposed to train them for Richmond," he said. "Everything goes to Richmond. I have more than four thousand men here with more arriving every day, and not a disciplined company among them. The men elect their own officers, and the officers refuse to discipline the men. I tell you it is an unholy system. When I arrived the regimental commander could not get his men out of the taverns long enough for a review. I closed the taverns and confiscated the whiskey. Now there is more whiskey than there was before. The officers are worse to drink than the men. Yet, I am supposed to train them and take Pickens at the same time."

Although unspoken, Taylor perceived that Bragg's discontent stemmed from rumors that Beauregard would be placed in command of the main Confederate Army in Virginia. The prospect of training troops for Beauregard apparently was more than the

Bragg ego could absorb.

The general finally came around to his purpose for writing to Taylor.

"In all of these camps, there is not a single subordinate upon whom I can rely," he said. "I need you to help me organize the training, supply, and transportation of these men. Troops are leaving here without ammunition, food, or equipment, much less training."

Taylor thought about it. Things were critical back at Fashion Plantation. Upon inheriting Fashion, he had whittled down a one-hundred-thousand-dollar debt over the years in spite of maintaining a lavish lifestyle that included some substantial losses at the Boston Club and the Metairie Racetrack. But back-to-back crop failures in 1856 and 1857 had plunged him into debt, more deeply than before. He had swallowed his pride and secured loans totaling more than two hundred thousand dollars—some secured by his wife's family, others by his brother-in-law, Martin Gordon Jr., who also served as his factor. The cane crop of 1860 had been Taylor's best ever—930 hogsheads of sugar. One more such crop and he would be able to retire much of that debt. It was not a time to be in Pensacola when so much depended on him back at Fashion. Reluctantly, he agreed to stay for a couple of weeks to lend what assistance he could, making it clear to Bragg he then must return home and attend to business.

* * *

YORKTOWN, VIRGINIA, JULY 4—From the day James Beard arrived at Yorktown with his company, it was obvious that his battalion commander, Colonel Charles Dreux, was itching to get at the Yankees. Upon arriving in Virginia, the Greys had been assigned to the defense of Yorktown on the lower Virginia peninsula. For weeks they had remained behind breastworks, with the enemy encamped within a half-day's march at Hampton Roads. Knowledge that Yankees were no more than ten miles away fed Dreux's impatience. By the Fourth of July, he could be restrained no longer—not even by a direct order to remain in a defensive position at Yorktown.

Rumors that a band of Union soldiers had left their camp to loot homes in the area finally provided the excuse Dreux needed to act. Applying his own theorem, he reasoned that an attack on the raiders could be considered a defensive action and made plans to seek out the Yankee raiders and ambush them.

Beard thought the colonel's plan ill-advised from its conception and wanted no part of it. He concluded early on that Dreux was a politician first and soldier second. A New Orleans lawyer and state legislator, Dreux had campaigned for battalion commander as if running for public office. What concerned Beard more than Dreux's plan of action was his method of selecting men for the mission. Instead of an organized company, the colonel chose twenty volunteers from each company of the battalion, assembling a force of one hundred. He prevailed upon a cavalry officer to loan him a half dozen horsemen to act as scouts and requisitioned a small howitzer. There was a festive atmosphere, and an obvious absence of discipline, when the men marched out of camp and headed south along the Newport News Road to look for Yankees. Watching them depart, an officer remarked to Beard that the exercise appeared more typical of country boys embarking on a Saturday night coon hunt than soldiers on a military mission.

* * *

YORKTOWN, JULY 5—It was near noon when the column returned, walking slowly up the road. Lying in a wagon was the corpse of Colonel Dreux, pierced in the chest by a single minié ball. Instead of surprising the Yankees, he had led his men into an ambush. Having spent a lifetime seeking notoriety in a continuing quest for public approval, he finally had earned the distinction of becoming the first Louisiana soldier killed in the war.

Dreux was not the only casualty. Young Stephen Hackett lay in the wagon beside him. Upon lifting the blanket and seeing the youthful face drained of life, Beard was overcome by nausea. Among the personal items he found was a ladies handkerchief with a hint of perfume still clinging to it. He buried it with the boy. That night, he sat at the table in his tent and struggled with the words as he penned a letter to the boy's family. It was the hardest thing he had ever done. With time and practice, he would become more proficient at the task.

* * *

MANASSAS JUNCTION, VIRGINIA, JULY 7—General Beauregard looked up at the officer standing at attention before his desk and did not know what to make of him.

"Lieutenant Colonel Polignac, reporting for assignment, sir!"

The voice was heavily accented. Beauregard immediately recognized it as the kind of stilted but precise English one learns in a French classroom.

The uniform was far more impressive than the man wearing it, and the name was more impressive than the uniform. Camille Armand Jules Marie, Prince de Polignac, a soldier of fortune, did not look like a soldier at all. However, the rows of gold braid adorning his uniform certainly qualified him as the most grandly attired lieutenant colonel Beauregard had ever seen.

Camille Polignac was of average height, but his slender build and erect bearing made him appear taller. He had delicate features that bordered on effeminate, making him look younger than his twenty-nine years. He was meticulously groomed and, to offset his youthful appearance, sported a substantial mustache, heavily waxed in an attempt to make him appear more ferocious. His most notable feature was a set of dark, intelligent eyes that swept the room even as he stood at attention.

Although not technically a prince, Camille Polignac came from a wealthy and respected French family descended from royalty. Inspired by patriotism and a yearning for adventure, he had joined the French Army at twenty-one. He fought with the Franco-British expeditionary force against the Russians at Sevastopol and was nearby when Lord Cardigan led the legendary charge of the British Light Brigade at Balaclava. In 1855 Polignac distinguished himself sufficiently to receive a battlefield promotion to lieutenant. With the end of the Crimean War, he returned to France and continued to serve in the military until early in 1859, when his restless nature prompted him to resign and embark on a bold business venture.

He traveled to Central America, intending to establish a shipping line between Europe and the potential raw wealth of Central and South America. He lived in Costa Rica for a time and traveled extensively before settling in Nicaragua, arriving there at a time when the government was in the turmoil of civil insurrection. In Nicaragua, he was distracted from business matters when the president employed him as a military advisor to help organize and train the national army. In that capacity Polignac came to know Alexander Dimitri, a Louisianan serving as United States ambassador to Nicaragua.

Dimitri was impressed by Polignac's character, as well as his military background. As rumors of a civil war in the United States approached reality, they discussed the possibility of Polignac returning to Europe to recruit experienced French officers for the Confederate Army. Meanwhile, Dimitri had written to his friends, Slidell and Benjamin, about Polignac's availability for such a mission. The recruiting trip never materialized but, with the firing on Fort Sumter, Polignac sent a letter to Beauregard, volunteering his services to the Confederate Army. Beauregard promptly accepted the offer.

Polignac sailed to New York, arriving there on July 2, 1861. With some difficulty, he made his way to Richmond and reported to the War Department. He was commissioned a lieutenant colonel in the Confederate Army and told to report to Beauregard in the field at Manassas, where a defense was being readied in anticipation of an assault by Union forces.

From the beginning, the prospect of meeting Polignac intrigued Beauregard. Like any military professional, he had closely followed the events of the Crimean War and studied its great battles. The chance to discuss the war with one of its participants presented a rare opportunity. But even as he welcomed the Frenchman, he was uncertain as to how he might best employ Polignac's expertise. Because of the youthful appearance, grand uniform, and heavy accent, Beauregard thought it unwise to place Polignac in direct command of the rough-hewn, rank-and-file sons of the South who comprised his army. He decided to assign Polignac to his personal staff.

Beauregard need not have worried. Before the war was ended, Camille Armand Jules Marie, Prince de Polignac, would lead Southern soldiers into many a bloody battle.

★ ★ ★

NEW ORLEANS, JULY 14—The visit to Fashion was a fleeting one for newly commissioned Colonel Dick Taylor, consisting of a day spent with Mimi and the children before he and Tom Strother departed for the railway station in New Orleans. They arrived just in time to shoulder their way through the crowd and board an express that was bound for the Confederate capital at Richmond. As he settled into the comfort of the leather seat and the train lurched forward, Taylor realized that this was the first time in days he actually had time to reflect on the frenetic events of the past week.

Overnight he had become an officer in the Confederate Army, responsible for 10 companies totaling 942 men and comprising the newly formed 9th Louisiana Infantry Regiment. His men had preceded him to Richmond, departing on a troop train three days earlier. Taylor was reassured, knowing they were under the watchful eye of his second in command. He had complete confidence in Lieutenant Colonel Edward Randolph, a no-nonsense, Mexican War veteran and strict disciplinarian. Taylor now concerned himself with traveling to Richmond as quickly as possible. Rumors circulated that a great battle was about to take place at a little town just across the Potomac from Washington, and he intended to be there when the shooting started.

The two weeks Taylor promised Braxton Bragg at Pensacola had turned into two months. He had become so entangled in his duties as a civilian advisor that he could not gracefully detach himself. Although he was reluctant to admit it, the entanglement, finally, was a willing one. After two weeks, there remained too much work to be done, and the same was true the following week and the one after that. Without realizing it, Dick Taylor had stumbled into his destiny at Pensacola. As spring turned to summer and a blazing sun beat down on the sandy beaches, it occurred to him that he had a natural aptitude for soldiering, or more precisely, for military organization. He discovered that if one exudes authority, other men will do his bidding. As the days slid by, he organized a workable training schedule for the troops at Fort Barrancas. He also made arrangements for the transportation of troops, munitions, and supplies to Virginia.

Before Taylor arrived in Pensacola, a member of the Shreveport Greys had rearranged a citizen's hairstyle with a rifle butt at a local tavern. The incident set off a bloody brawl between soldiers and patrons that caused a great deal of embarrassment for Bragg. To discourage such after-hours encounters, Taylor instructed officers to drill the men in the soft sand along the shoreline. It was an especially unpleasant summer, of which a visiting English journalist wrote: "The temperature here is as high as that of Calcutta." The blistering sand quickly sapped strength from the legs of the marchers, rendering them too weary to engage in mischief at the end of the day. In a letter home, a Louisiana soldier complained: "They have us living like crabs in the sand down here." Throughout the camps, a recurring, plaintive cry arose from the ranks: "When are we going to Richmond?" Meanwhile, in Richmond, Davis's advisors informed him that soldiers arriving from Pensacola seemed to be the best trained in the entire Confederate Army.

From the beginning, Bragg was persistent in his efforts to convince Taylor to accept an officer's commission. Taylor repeatedly declined, assuring Bragg that he was perfectly content in the role of civilian advisor. At one point Bragg even wrote to the War Department recommending that Taylor be commissioned a brigadier general, noting, "He has become a necessity to me."

On July 3, Bragg called Taylor to his office and shoved a telegram across his desk. It was from Governor Moore, granting Taylor the rank of full colonel and assigning him command of the newly formed 9th Louisiana Infantry Regiment. He was to report to his unit and accompany it at once to Richmond for assignment. Taylor considered turning down the commission. He was still smarting from the governor's casual dismissal of his report to the Committee on Military and Naval Affairs. However, in light of the fact that the war he predicted was now upon them, and his critics had been proven wrong, Taylor rationalized that the appointment might be considered a validation of his position. He accepted the command.

Arriving in New Orleans, he found a city infected with war fever. Some time was required to arrange transportation to Camp Moore, eighty miles to the north in a dense pine forest. There he sought out his regiment for review and was pleasantly surprised. Compared to the motley-appearing units around it, the 9th epitomized efficiency, thanks to a heavy dose of drilling under the guidance of Lieutenant Colonel Randolph. Taylor learned that most of his troops came from the small farms of the North Louisiana hill country—many of them the sons of successful planters, and most having benefited from at least minimal exposure to education. Also in the ranks were rural merchants, clerks, teamsters, and German and Irish laborers. Included in the mix was an officers' corps that included several small-town lawyers, doctors, and preachers. Although impressed by the quality of his men, Taylor was disappointed to learn that his elevation to regimental command was not the result of a commission from a repentant governor, but an election by the rank and file. He was further humbled by the revelation that he was chosen for no better reason than he happened to be the former brother-in-law of Jeff Davis. The greatest fear among the men at Camp Moore was not the prospect of dying in battle, but the possibility that the war might end before they could fight in it. The men of the 9th had concluded that if anyone could expedite their transfer from the humid drilling grounds of Camp Moore to the real war in Virginia, it was Jeff Davis's brother-in-law. Taylor did not have the heart to tell them that, although he had known Davis most of his life, their relationship was something less than intimate.

Dick Taylor had been only six years old when he first saw Lieutenant Davis at Fort Crawford, Wisconsin. Slender, handsome, and self-confident, Davis stood out among the young officers at the post. Dick could remember the strange way his sister Sarah acted when Jeff was around. He also could recall his father bellowing in a fit of rage, "I'll be damned if another daughter of mine will marry into the army!"

Dick had been delighted when Sarah volunteered to take him and Betty on long walks in the forest. It mystified him how they always seemed to meet Lieutenant Davis during those walks. While Dick and Betty played nearby, Sarah and Jeff would sit, talking quietly and gazing dreamily into each other's eyes. Only later did Dick realize that he and Betty had been pawns, used by Sarah to avert suspicion that she was meeting a forbidden boyfriend.

Dick knew of his father's outrage over those clandestine meetings, but was unaware that the colonel considered shooting Sarah's boyfriend or that Davis had responded by threatening to challenge his father to a duel. The wedding took place when he was only nine. He personally liked Davis and could not understand why his father disliked him. Later, when news arrived of his big sister's death, Taylor never fully accepted it. He found it easier to imagine that Sarah was simply away, living on a plantation in Mississippi.

As an adult, Dick had seen Davis on occasion in Natchez, Vicksburg, and New Orleans. Although their relationship was cordial, it never progressed to true friendship—perhaps because each reminded the other of their mutual loss. Taylor's men knew nothing of all of this. They only knew that three days after their newly elected colonel's arrival at Camp Moore, they were on a train bound for Richmond.

Taylor delayed his departure for two reasons—one professional, the other personal. While at Pensacola, he had watched regiment after regiment depart for the front without a single blanket or round of ammunition, only to find none available in Richmond.

He was determined that would not happen to his men. From Camp Moore, he went to New Orleans and there, by force of will and several outbursts of invective that effectively cowed a succession of bureaucrats, he obtained one hundred thousand rounds of ammunition and enough field equipment to accommodate his regiment. After arranging for its shipment north, he rented a carriage and traveled to Fashion Plantation to say good-bye to his family.

At Fashion Taylor faced a dilemma he had not anticipated. He intended to take William with him to Virginia as his valet, but the choice did not sit well with Tom Strother. In his teen years, Tom had assisted his uncle, Charles Strother, as body servant to Zachary Taylor during his campaigns in Florida and Mexico. Tom figured if he was good enough to go to war with Mister Zack, he should be able to accompany Mister Dick. Taylor was hesitant to take Tom because he had the responsibility of a large family, while William was single. William also could read and write, which would be an asset in the field. But when it became apparent that Tom's feelings were hurt, Taylor made a last-minute decision.

"If you're going with me, you should pack your bags and bring the buggy around," he gruffly instructed Tom.

"They is already packed," Tom informed him.

Taylor said good-bye to each of his slave families gathered in the front yard. He embraced his daughters, Margaret and Louise, admonishing them to mind their mother and study their lessons for the tutor. He hugged the boys—Zack, who had just turned four, and Dixie, who had learned to walk during his father's absence. He attempted to cheer Mimi, assuring her that he would not take chances. The dancing Creole eyes that had captured his heart at the dinner party those many years before were glazed with moisture when he gave her a farewell embrace. He tethered his favorite horse, a black stallion, to the back of the carriage. Mimi watched in tight-lipped silence as the carriage disappeared in the direction of St. Charles Station. She waited until it was well out of sight before she released her tears.

★ ★ ★ ★

5

★ ★ ★ ★

Itching for a Fight

SUDLEY SPRINGS, VIRGINIA, JULY 21—As the first rays of dawn filtered through the foliage, Major Rob Wheat scanned the woods beyond Bull Run Creek. For three hours he had listened to the movement of men and artillery positioning for battle on the other side of the stream. In the half-light of morning he rode his horse across the creek to see if he could take a look at the enemy. He went some distance along the bank, but did not encounter pickets. Wheat and his Louisiana Tigers Battalion were positioned near the Carter House at Sudley Springs on the extreme left of the rebel line. His responsibility was to hold the Confederate left for there was not a man beyond him and his troops.

As he impatiently waited, the distant boom of a cannon interrupted the morning stillness. He heard the shell explode a mile to his right near the Stone Bridge where Colonel "Shanks" Evans and his South Carolina boys were camped. Even as the rumble of cannon fire slowly built to a roar, Wheat whirled his horse about and dashed down the line, to the cheers of his men.

* * *

There was a great deal of confusion, but few military secrets when the armies of North and South collided that Sunday morning at Bull Run Creek. Union General Irvin Mc-Dowell knew the strength and approximate deployment of twenty thousand Confederate troops dug in along an eight-mile-long line behind the creek. Pierre Beauregard knew that McDowell was bringing thirty-four thousand troops out of Washington with the intention of crushing him in a frontal assault. The respective generals did not rely on intelligence for such information. All they had to do was read the Washington and Richmond newspapers, which faithfully reported the strength and movements on both sides. No two armies ever faced each other with more familiarity and uncertainty.

Prodded by Lincoln to engage the rebels and quickly end the war, a reluctant Mc-Dowell had formed up his army on July 16 and paraded it through Washington. Wildly cheering crowds lined the streets to witness the pageantry of a mighty army marching off to war. Regimental flags snapped in the breeze. Bands played stirring anthems in time to the rhythmic sound of marching men. As the last columns passed, spectators were greeted by yet another army—one of politicians, bureaucrats, and businessmen in fancy carriages, triumphantly waving to the crowd.

Two days after leaving Washington, McDowell's army had straggled only twenty miles to camp near Centerville, Virginia, still some eight miles from the rebel line. McDowell required two more days to bring up artillery and supplies, and yet another day to position his forces for battle. The delay would be disastrous for McDowell. It allowed Confederate General Joe Johnston time to bring another eight thousand troops to the front, increasing rebel strength to twenty-eight thousand men.

The disorganization apparent in McDowell's movements did not escape the attention of Beauregard. By Saturday afternoon, the impatient Creole had decided to launch a surprise attack the following morning. At two o'clock on Sunday morning, however, Union line officers began rousing their troops and forming battle lines, and at daylight, the Union artillery barrage opened hostilities, and sporadic fighting erupted along the length of the rebel defense. In the beginning, there was more noise than substance to the battle as inexperienced soldiers on both sides discharged artillery and rifle fire over the heads of the enemy. After feinting an assault on the Confederate center, McDowell sent two divisions in a sweep around the rebel's left flank. That is how Roberdeau Wheat and his 450 Louisiana Tigers ended up facing more than 10,000 Yankees at Sudley Springs. If Wheat had known the odds, he might not have attacked them.

At 9:45 A.M., as Union General Ambrose Burnside sent his brigade across the creek, Wheat led his wildly screaming Tigers in a charge that sent the startled Federals into retreat. Three times Wheat's men charged, prompting a desperate Burnside to call for reinforcements. In his report, General Beauregard described the action: "The enemy soon galled and staggered by the fire and, pressed by the determination with which Wheat handled his battalion, hastened up three other regiments."

Overwhelmed by numbers and under intense fire, Wheat withdrew to a field where several haystacks offered cover. From there, his small force put down a steady fire that checked the Union advance. While positioning his troops, Wheat was struck by a minié ball and fell heavily to the ground. In his report, he described the incident in the simplest of terms: "While in the act of bringing up the rest of my men I was put hors de combat by a minié ball passing through my body." It was a literal description. The ball went through him from side to side, piercing a lung.

When Captain Buhoup saw Wheat fall, he rallied his company around the bleeding commander. Wheat ordered the men to leave him but they refused. While some formed ranks and furiously fired and reloaded to keep the enemy at bay, others made a litter of rifles. Under heavy fire they carried the major to safety. "Lay me down, boys!" he admonished them time after time. "You must save yourselves." But they refused to lay him down.

Recognizing that Wheat's battalion was under a major attack, Colonel Evans left four of his companies to defend Stone's Bridge and sent six to reinforce the besieged Louisianans.

Hard-pressed by the enemy, Wheat's men, joined by Evans's South Carolinians, retreated to Matthews Hill where they attempted to make a stand. Outnumbered twenty to one, the little band of Louisianans had held back two divisions for more than an hour, buying precious time for Beauregard to bring up reinforcements on that side of the field.

Among the reinforcements were General Thomas J. Jackson's Virginia regiments. Just before noon, at Henry Hill, they met a Union attack and drove the Federals into retreat. Inspired by Jackson's disregard for danger in the face of heavy fire, General Bernard Bee raised his sword and yelled to his disorganized Texans: "Look! There is Jackson, standing like a stone wall! Rally behind the Virginians!" Within minutes the man who immortalized Jackson as "Stonewall" lay dead on the battlefield.

The Federal attack stalled all along the line. At 12:30 P.M., there was a lull in the fighting as McDowell reorganized his army for another assault. It came shortly after 1:30 P.M. when he sent sixteen thousand infantry against sixty-five hundred rebels defending Henry Hill—the Louisiana Tigers among them. A charge by Jackson's 2nd, 4th, and 5th Virginia regiments broke the Union center even as Wheat's battalion struggled to hold the rebel left. As Captain Alex White dashed down the line to rally his Tiger Rifles, his horse was shot from beneath him. He immediately leaped to his feet, retrieved his sword, waved it defiantly, and urged his men to hold their ground.

At that critical moment, a shout came from the rear: "Hurrah for the Tiger Rifles!" The shout came from Colonel Harry Hayes, commander of the Louisiana 7th Regiment. Immediately behind him were the Louisiana 6th and 8th. "Charge for the Tigers and for Louisiana!" Hayes shouted as his men surged forward. Although they had marched eight miles on the double to reach the front, they charged as if they were fresh. Joining their Louisiana brethren, the Tigers advanced to drive the Federals from the field. Among the Yankee regiments driven back were those under the command of General William T. Sherman. Among the line officers in the Louisiana regiments that pursued him were some of his former students.

Seeing his army in disarray, McDowell ordered a general withdrawal. He intended to fall back to Centerville and reorganize his ranks, but as his soldiers crossed Bull Run Creek, they came upon a scene no one could have anticipated. There on the opposite bank were hundreds of civilians who had ridden out from Washington to witness the battle as if it were a spectator sport. Dressed in Sunday finery, they had brought picnic baskets and erected awnings to protect the ladies from the sun. Hundreds of buggies and fancy carriages lined the road. The sight of Union soldiers fleeing back across the stream set off a panic among the spectators.

In the weeks before the battle, Northern newspapers had published articles about a Confederate "black horse cavalry." According to rumor, it was composed of the most vicious cutthroats imaginable—men who had vowed never to take a prisoner alive. Word that these merciless, mythical horsemen were advancing and cutting down all in their path, turned retreat into a hysterical stampede by soldiers and civilians. As overturned carriages and abandoned supply wagons clogged roadways, soldiers threw down their weapons and fled in all directions.

General McDowell and his staff looked on in horror as the largest army ever assembled in America up to that time disintegrated before their eyes.

* * *

While the legend of "Stonewall" Jackson was born at Bull Run Creek, another legend also emerged from the chaos at Manassas—the ferocious fighting ability of Wheat's Louisiana Tigers Battalion. A British journalist who witnessed the battle wrote of them, "These heroic soldiers sustained every shock with unwavering courage and on more than one occasion dropped their rifles and rushed among the enemy with long Bowie knives. As the majority of Wheat's command were Louisiana Irish, they robbed the dead of their whiskey and were in high spirits when ordered to expel Sherman and Keyes."

* * *

Dusk was settling on the battlefield when the train carrying Colonel Taylor's 9th Louisiana Regiment finally reached the rail yard at Manassas Junction. It had required more than eighteen hours for it to chug the ninety miles from Richmond to Manassas, and the battle had ended well before Dick Taylor got there. As he stepped from the train and caught the scent of smoke in the evening air, evidence of the day's battle surrounded him. Wounded men were everywhere, sitting on the station platform, in the street, and resting beneath a nearby grove of trees. Meanwhile, another train, apparently loaded with the more seriously wounded, was just pulling out of the station. Asked how the battle had gone, a corporal assured Taylor, "They say we whupped 'em, sir." As his troops disembarked, Taylor told Randolph to bivouac the men and be ready for combat on short notice. He then set out through a confusing maze of humanity, horses, mules, and rumbling wagons to look for General Beauregard.

It had been a frustrating two days for Taylor. He arrived in Richmond the previous afternoon, amid rumors that the long-awaited big battle was about to take place at Manassas. He found his regiment camped on the outskirts of Richmond and then proceeded to the office of Leroy Walker, the new secretary of war. Walker, a gentleman from Alabama who owed his appointment to his friendship with Taylor's old fire-eater adversary, William Yancey, was obviously devoid of even a hint of managerial ability. Once Taylor cornered him, the secretary moaned that the colonel would have to wait his turn because thousands of men were camped outside the city waiting for ammunition. Informed that the 9th possessed its own ammunition and equipment, and desired nothing more than transportation to the front, Walker's face lit with delight. He summoned an aide and told him to arrange for a train to immediately transport the regiment to Manassas. An hour later, Taylor was informed a train would be available at nine o'clock that night. It did not show up until after midnight.

The journey from Richmond to Manassas was one of the most frustrating experiences of Taylor's life. In his writings, he described the locomotive as "a machine of the most wheezy and helpless character." At the approach of each grade the soldiers had to leap off the train and trot beside it to lighten the load. The more impatient sometimes reached the crests of the hills ahead of the train. The less energetic straggled along, requiring the engineer to wait for them at the top of each hill.

If cursing won wars, the conflict would have been decided that day. During those snaillike climbs, the men of the 9th acquired an appreciation for fine invective as practiced by their colonel. They had never heard such cursing. It was a prosaic blend of the most foul words imaginable, mixed with French and occasionally flavored by Latin. In the ranks they opined that the blasphemous outbursts of their commander, not the coal bin, powered the reluctant locomotive up the steeper grades.

As they approached Manassas that Sunday afternoon, they could hear the thunder of cannons over the distant hills. Leg weary, they struggled up the grades toward the sound. The rumble grew louder until the pop of individual field pieces could be distinguished above the roar. The great battle was raging within earshot and they were missing it.

"At every halt of the wretched engine, the noise of battle grew more and more intense, as did our impatience," Taylor later wrote. As for the legendary display of colorful language that so impressed his men, he noted: "I hope the attention of the recording angel was engrossed that day in other directions."

Having missed the fight, Taylor sought out line officers from a nearby regiment who had been in the battle. He learned the Yankee army had been routed, leaving arms, equipment, and wounded on the field. There was speculation they would move on Washington the following day, capture the Capitol, and end the war.

As Taylor made his way through the night, seeking the location of General Beauregard's headquarters, he was surrounded by confusion. Officers stopped him to inquire if he had seen a particular regiment. Men milled about as if lost while others gathered in clusters to recount the events of the day. Occasional nervous laughter erupted from clusters of soldiers. Others sat alone in silence. Now and then a soldier fired a weapon into the air for no good reason. He was informed that Beauregard's headquarters was in the McHenry house, but no one seemed to know the location of the McHenry house. Taylor finally stumbled upon it more by accident than design. A staff officer informed him the general was unavailable and instructed Taylor to return to his men and wait for orders in the morning.

Back at camp, Tom Strother had Taylor's tent prepared and a meal waiting for him. Having been up for more than thirty hours, the colonel had no difficulty falling asleep. As instructed, Tom awakened him at daybreak. Impatiently, Taylor waited for his orders, pacing in front of his tent as the hours slid by. Late in the morning a messenger from headquarters finally arrived. The orders were to wait for further orders.

* * *

BULL RUN CREEK, JULY 24—The morning after the Confederate victory at Bull Run, General Thomas J. Jackson, while in his tent having his wounded hand stitched by a surgeon, commented to fellow officers, "Give me ten thousand fresh troops and I would be in Washington by tomorrow."

Unlike Johnston and Beauregard, Jackson had grasped the reality of the moment. He had watched McDowell's army melt before his eyes, had stepped over their discarded weapons and haversacks, and seen the resignation of defeat in the eyes of the captured. All of the subconscious knowledge he had absorbed from the late-night study of his West Point textbooks, all of his experience in Mexico, every fiber in his soldier's heart cried out for him to pursue the enemy.

Jackson's estimate of the number of troops needed to capture Washington was grossly inflated. A cavalry force of a thousand might have ridden, unopposed, through the streets of the capital that Monday morning. A regiment could have taken Arlington Heights and planted cannons overlooking the city. So complete was the rout of Mc-Dowell's army, it required weeks for Union officers to round up enough men to assemble anything resembling an organized military defense of Washington. Not only had thousands of the Union rank and file thrown away their weapons and gone home, many an officer had joined them.

For three days, Jackson kept his men on twenty-four-hour alert, prepared to advance on Washington at a moment's notice. Impatiently, he awaited orders to do so. He reissued ammunition to his troops and had them keep three days of cooked rations in their haversacks. From the heights near Centerville, he could see the spires of the churches of Washington and knew the Potomac bridges lay, unguarded, before him. He paced and waited for orders that never came.

Encamped near the Manassas rail yard, Dick Taylor was equally mystified by the absence of orders. He sensed that a great opportunity had been missed. In his memoirs, he wrote that "a strong brigade could have stormed into the streets of Washington and taken Baltimore." He cited Napoleon's axiom that a victorious army should always pursue and destroy a defeated foe to avoid having to fight that enemy again.

Union officials confirmed Jackson and Taylor's assessment of Washington's vulnerability in the days following Bull Run. Secretary of War Edwin Stanton wrote, "The capture of Washington seems now to be inevitable; during the whole of Monday and Tuesday, it might have been taken without resistance. The rout, overthrow, and demoralization of the whole army is complete."

General George McClellan, who would replace McDowell as commander of the Union Army, was asked to assess the situation and issue a report. Arriving in Washington five days after the battle, he rode through the streets observing the chaos and confusion:

> I found no preparations whatever for defense [sic], not even to the extent of putting the troops in military position. Not a regiment was properly encamped, not a single avenue of approach guarded. All was chaos, and the streets, hotels and barrooms were filled with drunken officers and men, absent from their regiments without leave. . . . Many had gone to their homes, their flight from Bull Run terminating in New York, or even in New Hampshire and Maine. There was really nothing to prevent a small cavalry force from riding into the city. . . . If the Secessionists attached any value to the possession of Washington, they committed their greatest error in not following up the victory of Bull Run.

In the wake of Bull Run, many were willing to take credit for victory, but none for "the greatest error" that would extend the war for four years, rain death and destruction upon the states of the South, and eventually consume more than 600,000 lives.

General Beauregard blamed Davis. In his official report on the battle, Beauregard stated that his intention from the beginning was to cross the Potomac, relieve Maryland,

and capture Washington, but Davis rejected the plan. The president responded by insisting he had never seen such a plan, much less rejected it, and he accused Beauregard of "an attempt to exalt yourself at my expense." In all likelihood, Beauregard's plan never progressed beyond Joe Johnston.

Beauregard also criticized the confusing command structure imposed by Davis. Under the arrangement, Johnston commanded all forces in Virginia, including Beauregard's troops. This structure created a situation in which Beauregard was responsible for battlefield strategy without actually being in command of the men under him. In the wake of Manassas, Beauregard insisted that his troops be separated from Johnston's and placed under his independent control.

Meanwhile, Johnston had a gripe of his own. In the overall Confederate chain of command, he ranked behind Robert E. Lee, Albert Sidney Johnston, and Samuel Cooper. Before the war, Johnston had been quartermaster general in the United States Army while the others held the rank of colonel. Johnston thought he should outrank the three men above him and accused Davis of favoritism. Against that backdrop of political intrigue the overly bold Beauregard and ever cautious Johnston fought and won the Battle of Manassas.

Following Manassas, Johnston excused his inaction by claiming that Confederate forces were too confused to pursue the retreating Federals. In truth, the army was not nearly so confused as the general. Of the twenty-eight thousand rebel troops at Manassas that day, only eighteen thousand were actually engaged. Within two days after the battle, another ten thousand men had arrived from Richmond, giving Johnston twenty thousand troops in ranks, fully armed, supplied, and anxious to fight. Within a week Johnston had more than forty thousand troops at his disposal but no plans to march on Baltimore or Washington. Finally, the confusion that cost the Confederacy a complete victory was not in the ranks of the army but in the timid soul of Joe Johnston and in the hallways of the Capitol in Richmond, where Walker, Benjamin, Lee, and Davis were so mired in the logistics of putting an army in the field that they failed to develop a strategy in the event they were victorious.

During his brief passage through Richmond, Dick Taylor had seen the campfires of scores of volunteer regiments in the fields and on the hillsides around the city. Over one hundred thousand volunteers had flocked to Richmond that spring and summer. Most waited in vain for arms, ammunition, and equipment while the pathetically disorganized Walker paced his office, expending his energy on insignificant bureaucratic matters. Even as needed supplies sat in railcars and warehouses throughout the South, thousands of volunteers had gone home. In the weeks following the victory at Bull Run, thousands more would leave, convinced the war was over.

Forgotten in all of the post-battle chaos, Dick Taylor's 9th Louisiana waited near the rail yard. But the sharply analytical mind of their colonel was not idle. Taylor knew the war was far from over. And he had observed enough to realize that an army in the field could not depend on Richmond to sustain it. He made a promise to himself that no regiment he commanded would ever break ranks following a battle. And he vowed that, given the opportunity, he would pursue a retreating enemy to the doorstep of its home.

* * *

KINGSTON, LOUISIANA, AUGUST 17—Even as James Beard supervised the construction of fortifications around Yorktown, Kate Beard and eighteen-month-old Corinne sat on the floor at Auburnia, writing a letter to Papa.

"Don't spill the ink," Kate cautioned as she held her daughter's hand and carefully dipped the pen in the inkwell. Slowly, she guided it toward a scrap of paper. At that point Corinne's genetically inspired independence took charge. Her hand became the guiding force and the "O" that Kate was helping her craft became something resembling a squiggly "Z."

Kate laughed and managed to catch the small hand before it could ram the pen back into the inkwell.

"Oh well," she laughed. "I think Papa will get the message."

When it came to writing to Papa, Corinne's attention span rarely lasted beyond the first few letters, at which time the missive became a series of meandering lines that only a father could appreciate. Capturing the pen from the clutches of tiny fingers, Kate resumed her own letter to James:

> Mary [Kate's sister-in-law] went to the kitchen just awhile ago and she [Corinne] came running to me and said "Mama, Mary gone." She makes gestures equal to a Frenchman, draws her face up and wags her head about. You would hurt yourself laughing at her. I know well enough who she will love the best when you come home, for she takes a fancy to any man she meets. The poor little thing is downstairs now, calling me. I did not answer her and she said "Mama gone." I am sitting on the floor and now she is sitting by me trying to pick off a watermelon seed that has stuck to the bottom of her foot. I'll just send the seed for you to look at.

Carefully, Kate tied a small ribbon around a lock of Corinne's hair. She folded the paper containing her daughter's scribbling and placed it in the envelope along with her own letter, the lock of hair, and a tiny watermelon seed.

* * *

NEW ORLEANS, SEPTEMBER 29—Following the Confederate victory at Manassas, Governor Thomas Moore felt more confident than ever that the war would not reach Louisiana. Like others in the Deep South, he embraced the possibility that a truce might be forthcoming once Lincoln realized that he could not subdue the Confederate Army. Under the worst scenario, the governor assumed the shooting war would be confined to Virginia and the border states. But by autumn, he was in a state of near panic. Federal troops had occupied Ship Island and warships had sealed off the mouth of the Mississippi River. From Pensacola, Bragg reported that he was under attack from Fort Pickens and newly arrived Union warships. Federal forces controlled western Virginia, opening the doorway for an invasion of Kentucky and Eastern Tennessee. The Union Army had invaded Missouri in force, and a bitter struggle for control of the upper Mississippi River was under way. The river forts, once thought impregnable, now appeared vulnerable to enemy infantry. Most disturbing of all was talk of an attack on New Orleans by warships in the Gulf of Mexico.

By September 1861, Governor Moore realized that he had precious few resources to resist an assault on New Orleans. He had armed and supplied more than twenty thousand Louisianans to serve in other theaters and now had fewer than four thousand poorly armed and untrained militia troops to protect his own state. Arms and ammunition seized from the Baton Rouge arsenal had been sent to militias in Mississippi and Alabama and to the Confederate Army at Montgomery. The Washington Artillery, made up of the best-trained cannoneers in the South, had departed with their heavy guns. In fact, only 158 heavy guns remained to protect all of Louisiana—with precious little shot and powder to prime them. Even if he had the necessary troops, there were no qualified officers to train them. The state's best men were in distant camps—including the young cadets from the Louisiana State Seminary, who were in great demand as line officers in Virginia.

Some of New Orleans's leading citizens had expressed their concerns to the governor for months. But only after a firsthand inspection of the city's defenses did Moore realize the extent of New Orleans's vulnerability. There seemed to be no single strategy to defend the city. Planning was piecemeal and actual preparation almost nonexistent. Virtually nothing had been done to fortify the plains below New Orleans. Although trenches were dug, there were no gun emplacements or troops to man them. The river forts, vital to the city's defense, remained unimproved. On September 29, Governor Moore sent an urgent letter to Judah Benjamin, the new secretary of war, pleading for men, competent officers to train them, and for weapons, munitions, and saltpeter to make gunpowder. Reluctantly, he also asked Benjamin to replace General David Twiggs, the man responsible for the sorry state of New Orleans's defenses: "I have about 3,500 men in camp and have not arms for them all. I am now sorry that I ever sent off so many as they . . . are so occupied I fear I shall not get them back when needed."

In a letter dated September 15, a New Orleans businessman named A. B. Roman expressed even greater alarm in a letter to Jefferson Davis:

> It is generally admitted that we are not now prepared to offer . . . an efficient resistance. Our militia . . . can hardly be considered as organized. As we have no muskets to give them they will have to use such shotguns as they can procure, and could scarcely get at the present time powder enough to fire a few rounds. If you except the two forts above the entrance of the Mississippi, there is not a single fortification on our coast which can stand a coup de main. Preparations for their defense are now undertaken which ought to have been completed long ago.

At seventy-one years of age and in failing health, Major General David Twiggs was the wrong man in the wrong place at the wrong time. Before the war, he had been the second highest ranking officer in the United States Army. A brevet major general with almost a half century of service behind him, only Winfield Scott outranked him. Twiggs was commander of the Department of Texas, headquartered at San Antonio when, on

February 18, 1861, he issued General Order No. 5. The order, posted on the same day that Lincoln was inaugurated, turned over all United States military facilities in Twiggs's department to the Texas State Militia. The action, taken two weeks *before* Texas seceded from the Union, stunned Washington's hierarchy. Lincoln was livid when informed of the action. Twiggs was charged with treason and immediately dismissed from the U.S. Army.

Davis promptly commissioned Twiggs a major general and gave him command of coastal defenses from Pascagoula, Mississippi, to Brownsville, Texas. The decision would cost the Confederate cause dearly.

Twiggs was welcomed as a hero upon his arrival in New Orleans to assume his duties. The people of New Orleans and Davis did not realize that Twiggs was in ill health and had been suffering bouts of dementia. Upon arriving in the Crescent City, he spent most of his time in his living quarters. When he did go to work, Twiggs remained in his office, rarely venturing out to inspect troops or fortifications, or the war plants where production of weapons, ammunition, and military supplies had become disorganized and plagued by corruption.

Six months after his arrival, Twiggs departed New Orleans under a cloud of controversy, having done nothing to protect the only city in the South with a manufacturing base capable of sustaining the Confederate war effort.

* * *

WASHINGTON, D.C., OCTOBER 7—By the autumn of 1861, there was no more hectic location on earth than the corridor outside Abraham Lincoln's office as he tried to rebuild his shattered army while dealing with a level of political intrigue unprecedented even in Washington, D.C. From the day of his election, he was besieged by favor seekers, and smoke had hardly cleared above Bull Run Creek when a new wave of lobbyists descended on him. Industrialists, contractors, businessmen, power brokers, politicians, con men, and crooks clogged the hallways, creating incredible chaos. They came seeking contracts for everything from buttons to bullets to beef. Elderly, retired officers showed up clutching battle plans. Senators sought officers' commissions for ne'er-do-well sons-in-law. Governors arrived with pet industrialists in tow seeking contracts on warships and cannons to destroy warships. Some came to peddle influence and others to sell their souls—if there was a profit in it.

Adding to Lincoln's dilemma, the ceaseless clamor of abolitionists demanded that he immediately send a great army to smite the rebels. But at that critical juncture, Lincoln was more concerned with fortifying than smiting. In those early days of his presidency, the affable Midwestern lawyer had a difficult time saying no. He had yielded to political pressure rather than logic and sent a green army to Manassas with disastrous results. And now he agreed to the "Texas Plan."

A version of the "Texas Plan" had been around since 1846 when, after a bitter fight in Washington, Texas entered the Union as a slave state—a status the textile barons and abolitionists of New England refused to accept. The plan was the brainchild of Edward Everett Hale of Worcester, Massachusetts, who first outlined it in a pamphlet titled

How to Conquer Texas Before Texas Conquers Us. He advocated the organization of a great army of free-soil settlers to migrate to Texas and wrest that state from the clutches of slave holders by sheer weight of numbers. Utilizing Texas's open, fertile lands, these Northern farmers would demonstrate to the world how cotton could be produced without slave labor. According to Hale, Texas could produce all of the cotton needed to run the textile mills of New England.

In 1854 Hale's plan was put into action—not in Texas, but in Kansas. Eli Thayer, who lived just down the street from Hale, used his friend's concept to flood Kansas with free-soil immigrants. He formed the Massachusetts Emigrant Aid Society to recruit and finance New Englanders willing to go to Kansas. Other emigrant aid societies soon sprang up throughout the East, sending thousands of immigrants to Kansas. The result was a bloody war between Missouri pro-slavers and Kansas free-soilers, a conflict that consumed almost four hundred lives and left hundreds of farms and small towns in smoking ruins. But from the ashes, Kansas emerged a free state.

The events in Kansas were not lost on Frederick Olmsted, Dick Taylor's old friend from the *New York Times* who once wrote a glowing article about Fashion Plantation. In the mid-1850s, as Olmsted's reportorial journey through the South had progressed, so had the bias in his writings. His readers back East did not want to read about planters who treated their slaves well. They wanted their beliefs reinforced by plantation horror stories. Olmsted did not disappoint them. At the urging of his editors, his role changed from reporter to propagandist. In his dispatches, all Southern villages became squalid hamlets and their inhabitants, lazy dolts. Only two classes of whites existed in Olmsted's South—greedy plantation owners, who squeezed their wealth from the blood and sweat of their slaves, and poor whites, all of whom were uneducated, slothful louts. In Northern minds, Olmsted established a contemptible Southern stereotype that was easy to despise—an image that would be perpetuated for generations beyond the Civil War.

In 1857, Olmsted published a book entitled *A Journey Through Texas.* In it he praised the richness of the land while savaging those who lived there. Like Hale, he concluded that if practical New Englanders occupied the rich fields of Texas, they would be able to grow all of the cotton needed up North—effectively putting the slave states of the South out of business. Olmsted's book received rave reviews in New York and New England newspapers. It also attracted the attention of Massachusetts textile barons like Amos Lawrence and Edward Atkinson.

In the spring of 1861 as North and South prepared for war, Atkinson published a booklet titled "Cheap Cotton by Free Labor." In it he advocated the formation of a great Northern army capable of invading, subduing, and colonizing a conquered Texas. Soldiers who volunteered for this noble mission would receive grants to the lands of former slave holders. Atkinson's solution to the fate of the freed slaves was rather callous: "Labor or starvation would be his [the freed slave's] only choice and . . . labor upon the cotton field would be the easiest and most profitable in which he could engage. [If he will not work] let him starve and exterminate himself, if he will, and so remove the negro question—still, we must raise cotton."

By the fall of 1861, the war had created a cotton shortage that was being felt throughout the Northern economy. A third of New England's 4,745,750 spindles sat idle. Backed by Governor John A. Andrew of Massachusetts and other powerful politicians, the textile barons demanded an immediate invasion of Texas. Lincoln attempted to calm them by promising such an expedition at the earliest practical moment. However, George McClellan, his top-ranking general, opposed a Texas invasion. McClellan preferred Winfield Scott's Anaconda Plan, which called for splitting the Confederacy in two by securing the Mississippi River, and squeezing the economic life from the Southern states east of the river. Scott had dismissed a coastal invasion of Texas, pointing out that conquest of the interior would require a large army. Since there were few railroads and the state's inland streams were too shallow to support gunboats, supplying such an army would be a major problem.

Although McClellan and Scott rarely agreed on anything, both were convinced that control of the Mississippi was vital to Union success. And McClellan convinced Lincoln that the capture of New Orleans must take precedence over an invasion of Texas. McClellan believed the most practical route to Texas was not by coastal invasion, but via the Red River, which flowed through the heart of Louisiana to the Texas border. New Orleans, he insisted, was the keystone that supported the Gulf Coast states and the entire Mississippi River Valley. Capture New Orleans, McClellan assured Lincoln, and the entire valley would crumble.

* * *

GALVESTON, TEXAS, OCTOBER 7—Brigadier General Paul O. Hebert stood at the window of his hotel room and watched rivulets of water trail one another down the panes. His mood was no less gloomy than the weather outside. His mission was not going well. Sent to Texas to organize a defense of the state, he had discovered that Texas did not want to be organized. He could not decide if the problem was the independent nature of Texans or their inherent mistrust of Louisiana Frenchmen. Whatever the cause, his inability to alarm the state's leaders to the possibility of an invasion or to rally them to prepare a defense of their coastal cities frustrated him.

Upon his arrival in Galveston, the general found Texas's most important port city virtually defenseless. Although Texas regiments were active from Virginia to New Mexico, those who remained at home seemed convinced they were too far removed from the fighting for it to ever reach them. Hebert knew the war was far from over. The War Department had informed him that three coastal cities were targeted for Northern invasion—New Orleans, Mobile, and Galveston.

Texas was vital to the Confederacy. Not only was it a source of beef, grain, and manufactured goods for the rebel armies, it was the back door to the Confederacy. Its border with Mexico provided a conduit for foreign trade around Union warships in the Gulf of Mexico. Even more important, if Texas should fall, Louisiana, Arkansas, and Missouri would be trapped between Union armies, dooming the Confederacy west of the Mississippi River.

Hebert had pleaded with the governor, his superiors in the Confederate high command, and his old friend Judah Benjamin to send him men and artillery. Instead of arms and troops, he received letters of encouragement. In fact, Benjamin even suggested that

Hebert raise more regiments in Texas for service in the East. Finally, as a last resort, Hebert sat at the small desk in his hotel room and penned an open letter he would print on broadsides and send to the state's newspapers:

TO THE MEN OF TEXAS:

Texans: It is more than probable that your state will soon be invaded by the sea coast. The enemy's resources for such an attack would seem to be formidable. Yours to meet and defeat it lie almost entirely in your own strong arms, brave hearts and trusty rifles.

Our infant government has achieved wonders, but yet it must largely rely upon the states that created it. . . . Look not to Richmond, then, for all your military inspiration and guidance. Remember the days of yore, when your own red right hands achieved your independence, and while some of your hardy sons are prepared to share the glory to be won in Virginia, Kentucky, and Missouri and others to guard the highway to the Pacific, which they have won against superior arms and numbers, be it your portion of the duty which you owe them and yourselves to keep your soil free from the enemy's touch and to preserve, unsullied, the fame of the Texas ranger. Let every man then clean his old musket, shot-gun or rifle, run his bullets, fill his powder horn, sharpen his knife and see that his revolver is ready to hand, as in the trying but glorious days when Mexico was your foe.

Organize at once into companies, if possible into battalions, and report to me promptly at Galveston. . . . Be ready to march at a moment's notice and wait for orders. Rely upon it that I shall not fail to call you when needed and, when I call, I know that you will come. I am too near San Jacinto's field to doubt for a moment that even against overwhelming numbers you will gladly rally to the defense of your homes, your families, and your liberties.

Our enemy may succeed from his superior armaments, in ravaging your sea coast, but, God willing, and you aiding, he will never hold a foot of your soil—never!

BRIGADIER GENERAL PAUL O. HEBERT

Those lines inspired the appearance of some of the most colorful and daring warriors of the Civil War—the Texas cavalrymen who would defend Louisiana. To prevent the invasion of their state, they would fight in the hills, cane brakes, and bayou country of their neighbor. Their weapons were varied. Most did not have standard uniforms. Their mounts ranged from thoroughbreds to motley nags. They were cocky, headstrong, impossible to discipline, and unwilling to walk, but they would prove to be among the fiercest fighters ever assembled.

★ ★ ★

CENTERVILLE, VIRGINIA, NOVEMBER 29—It was an unusually mild day for late November, and newly commissioned Brigadier General Dick Taylor took advantage of a break in the weather to drill the men relentlessly. He had wheeled the regiments right flank, to the front, then left, until their legs became so heavy they were shuffling instead of marching. When the order to dismiss finally came, it was answered by a collective groan instead of the usual cheer. Uniforms dark with sweat, shoulders hunched under the weight of backpacks and rifles, the men straggled back into camp to collapse beside their tents.

"I wish the Lord would send a miracle to cure Ole Dick Taylor's damned arthurritis, afore it kills us all," was a common lament among the troops.

Although he was one of the youngest brigadier generals in the Confederate Army, Taylor's recurring bouts with arthritis had become legend. The troops knew that their general's personality changed in direct correlation to the limp in his stride. When it became pronounced, even the regimental colonels avoided him.

Handing the reins of his horse to Tom Strother, Taylor slowly dismounted and slapped his gloves against his thighs, sending out a cloud of dust. He entered his tent, dropped the flap, and collapsed on the cot. He had not sought the promotion to brigadier, the responsibility of brigade command or the headaches that came with managing thirty-eight hundred men. But, cast in the role, he was determined that the 1st Louisiana Brigade would be the best in the Confederate Army. Only one thing prevented him from accomplishing that goal—Major Wheat's Tigers. Wheat's battalion should have been the best unit in the brigade. They had proven their bravery at Manassas, and on the drill field, their columns were the sharpest in the brigade, in spite of those garish Zouave uniforms Taylor so detested. But off the field, Wheat's outfit was the most lawless collection of con men, gamblers, thieves, drunkards, and brawlers Taylor had ever encountered. The Tiger Rifles Company in Wheat's battalion was the worst of all, and Taylor blamed Captain Alex White, who he considered more of a ring leader than a company commander.

Taylor had become weary of punishing the entire brigade for violations committed by Wheat's battalion. He considered dispersing them into other units but rejected the idea for fear they would contaminate the entire brigade. He pleaded with Joe Johnston to transfer the whole battalion to another brigade but the general refused, assuring Taylor he had every confidence in his ability to whip them into shape. Besides, Johnston finally confessed, no one else would have them.

✴ ✴ ✴

Taylor's leap in rank, from regimental colonel to brigadier general, had been unexpected. Some high-ranking officers openly expressed their resentment, pointing out that he was not a West Pointer and had no formal military training. What many did not realize was that he might have been the best prepared of all the young Confederate generals. He had read the biographies of Europe's great military leaders and locked their strategies in an unfailing memory. He had stood at his father's shoulder in Mexico and watched him mark his maps and maneuver his ranks.

However, Taylor recognized that his promotion had little to do with merit and a lot to do with his old friend Judah Benjamin, his former brother-in-law Jeff Davis, and the political intrigue that permeated Richmond. There a war was being waged not on a battlefield but in the corridors of the Capitol, where the forces of Joe Johnston and Pierre

Beauregard vied for control of the army of Virginia. As the troops sat idle in their camps that fall, Johnston emerged victorious and Beauregard paid dearly for his criticism of Davis. Johnston assumed overall command of the army in Virginia and Beauregard was demoted to corps commander.

Meanwhile, north of the Potomac, General George McClellan was assembling a second great Union army and preparing it for a spring offensive against Richmond. To meet the challenge, Johnston began reorganizing his army. Beauregard's corps ended up with eight brigades. Taylor's 9th Louisiana Regiment, along with the 6th, 7th and 8th regiments and Wheat's battalion comprised the 1st Louisiana Brigade. At first this new brigade came under the command of Brigadier General William H. T. Walker, a fifty-four-year-old veteran of the Seminole and Mexican wars.

From the beginning, Taylor had driven his North Louisiana country boys in the 9th harder than other regimental colonels had driven their units. He took them on long marches, under full packs. He tolerated no stragglers, alternately bawling out and cajoling those who fell behind. The men grumbled but ultimately responded to Taylor's discipline until it became a badge of shame to lag. "Colonel Taylor aspires to have the most orderly regiment in the service," a soldier wrote home. "True he is quite rigid in his discipline, as all military commanders should be, but he is a gentleman in every sense."

In mid-September, as Yankee and rebel troops warily watched each other across the Potomac, a succession of camp diseases swept the Confederate ranks. The 9th Louisiana was hit especially hard. Soldiers from the rural South, having never been exposed to some childhood diseases, were particularly vulnerable. One epidemic after another swept the winter camps, felling the troops with measles, mumps, typhoid, and whooping cough. Pneumonia often followed, and death. "I passed days in the hospital, nursing the sick and trying to comfort the last moments of many poor lads, dying so far from home and friends," Taylor noted in his memoirs.

By the end of September, the 9th Louisiana had lost more than a hundred men to death and medical discharge. Hundreds more lay ill. At one time, Taylor had no more than three hundred troops in his regiment available for duty. As death visited the camps with increasing frequency, the men became jaded to it. A private in the 9th wrote home, "One of the Bossier boys died day before yesterday and one of ours today and it seemed to me that it was not noticed no more than if a dog had died."

By the first week in October, Taylor himself lay bedridden, burning with fever, his body virtually paralyzed by the rheumatoid arthritis that always plagued him with the coming of cold weather. Upon learning of his condition, his sister, Betty Dandridge, who lived at Winchester, Virginia, insisted on personally nursing him back to health. She moved in with friends at Fauquier Springs, just twenty miles from the Confederate camp and had her brother transported there. She stayed with him, day and night, patiently mopping his brow and administering his medicines. At Fauquier Springs, while bedridden, Taylor learned that he had been promoted to brigadier general and given command of Walker's brigade.

The news disturbed him. He had worked hard to overcome the perception that he was given regimental command for no reason other than his relationship to Jeff Davis. Taylor also had a great deal of respect for General Walker, who was far superior to many of his peers in military expertise. When word reached Taylor that Walker had resigned from the army over the incident, he rose from of his sick bed and went to Richmond to seek an audience with Davis.

The president greeted him warmly, as if relieved to see a friendly face. They conversed casually about mutual acquaintances for a time before Taylor came to the purpose for his visit. He asked Davis to cancel the promotion, pointing out the unfairness to Walker. He also informed the president that the promotion vaulted him over three regimental colonels who had seniority, including Colonel Isaac Seymour, an old friend from New Orleans who owned the *Commercial Bulletin* newspaper. "Were I in his place, I would resent such a promotion," Taylor said.

Davis listened patiently to his concerns and promised to consider them. He explained that the promotion was part of an overall plan to achieve cohesiveness in the army by brigading all regiments by states. Since the 1st Brigade was a Louisiana unit, he wanted a Louisianan in command.

"I am besieged by governors and legislators trying to push political generals upon me," Davis complained. "If I do not fill these positions now with those I can trust, they will end up in the hands of men in whom I have no confidence at all."

As for Walker, Davis confided that he had offered Walker command of a Georgia brigade and the general decided not to accept it. The president assured Taylor he would consider all aspects of the question and inform him of his decision by mail.

Taylor departed Richmond feeling confident the promotion would be rescinded. Upon his return to camp on November 3, he was surprised to be cordially greeted and congratulated by Colonel Seymour and the other regimental commanders. Taylor learned that Davis had written letters to each of them explaining the rationale for his decision.

"They [the letters] went on to soothe the feelings of these officers so effectually as to secure me their hearty support," Taylor wrote.

General Walker also helped solidify Taylor's acceptance by the brigade's officers and men. Walker let it be known that he had complete confidence in Taylor. As a symbol to the men, upon his departure, Walker left Taylor his tent and equipment. As a benefit of Walker's hard work, Taylor inherited one of the best-trained brigades in the army—and it might have been the best disciplined except for Wheat's troops.

Although not a strong disciplinarian, Rob Wheat managed to maintain a degree of control over the Tigers until his wound at Manassas incapacitated him for several months. During his convalescence, the Tigers resumed their wayward ways. When Taylor assumed brigade command, he attempted to bring them under control, without a great deal of success. In fact, his entire command was becoming known as the Louisiana Tigers, an embarrassment to Taylor.

When General Johnston refused to transfer the battalion, Taylor asked for his support in matters of discipline.

"You do what is necessary to tame the Tigers and I will back you," Johnston assured him.

* * *

It was near midnight when Taylor was awakened by the orderly.

"They are drunk again and fighting, sir," he said.

"Who is drunk and fighting?"

"The Tigers."

Taylor loosed a blast of profanity in the darkened tent. Slowly, he swung his legs over the edge of the cot. Grimacing with pain, he pulled on his boots, draped the great-coat over his shoulders, and followed the orderly into the chill of the night. Near the commissary, a group of grim-faced officers stood guard over several sullen men sitting on the ground. As he approached, one of the officers started to speak but Taylor lifted his hand.

"Put them in the guardhouse," he bluntly instructed. "I will deal with them in the morning. I do not even want to hear their story tonight."

As the offenders were herded away, Taylor turned on the officers.

"Who is responsible for those men?" he said.

"Captain White," said an officer.

"Where is Captain White?"

"He's on leave, sir."

Taylor breathed a deep sigh. Captain White was on leave more often than on duty.

"Then I suggest the next in command exercise control over these men," Taylor said. "And you can begin by informing Captain White's men that the next soldier who creates a disturbance this night will face a firing squad."

Even as he turned away, the officers scattered, thankful to escape the full wrath of their commander. Back in his tent, Taylor finally managed to doze off. He awakened from a restless slumber with Tom Strother standing over him with a lantern. An apologetic orderly stood in the doorway.

"There's been another disturbance, sir," the orderly reported with obvious reluctance.

Taylor sat up in bed. "What have they done now?"

"Some of the men attacked the guard and tried to break the others out of the guardhouse," he said. "We have two of them in custody."

"Is the guard hurt?"

"He's been in better health, sir."

"Secure them and post armed guards," Taylor instructed. "By God, I will have them shot. This nonsense will end now."

★ ★ ★

CENTERVILLE, VIRGINIA, DECEMBER 9—Sobriety came to the Louisiana Tigers on a frosty morning in early December. Minutes before the execution was to take place, Taylor still debated whether he should pardon privates Dennis Corkeran and Michael O'Brien. To do so would make him popular with the troops. It also would make him appear weak. Rob Wheat had pleaded with him to spare the lives of the men, promising to keep a tighter rein on the battalion. Taylor refused, stating that if he did not establish discipline now, it would cost far more than two lives when fighting resumed in the spring.

He watched as the priest prayed with Corkeran and O'Brien. They knelt, heads bowed, hands bound to stakes, their billowing red, white, and blue stripped Zouave pantaloons covering the ground around them. Before being bound and blindfolded, the condemned men had calmly opened their jackets to expose their naked chests for the firing squad. The previous night, they had written a joint statement to their fellow soldiers: "We acknowledge the justice of our sentence," it read. "May the rendering up of our lives prove a benefit . . . and a lesson to all to guard against the vice of drunkenness." To the firing squad they requested, "Please do not mangle us. Aim for our hearts." They concluded the message with, "Tigers, a last farewell!"

The entire division stood at attention as the firing squad, composed of twenty-four members of the Tiger Rifles, took its position fifteen yards in front of the condemned men. Conspicuously absent from the ceremony was Major Wheat. He remained in his tent, refusing to witness the event.

The men in the firing squad stood with faces grim, their eyes looking beyond their kneeling comrades. Half of their muskets contained blanks. None knew whose musket had the live round. Unknown to members of the firing squad, Taylor had ordered a company from the 8th Regiment, with weapons loaded, to line up directly behind the firing squad as a precaution. Captain White, his face approximating the color of his assumed name, looked to Taylor, as if hopeful the general might yet call off the affair. Instead, Taylor nodded for him to proceed. White reluctantly raised his sword.

The orders came—raise muskets . . . aim . . . fire! The thunder of twenty-four muskets shattered a dead silence. Corkeran and O'Brien slumped forward. A lone, anguished cry, more animal-like than human, rose from the ranks. A young soldier broke from the lines of the Tiger Rifles and ran forward to cradle the head of Dennis Corkeran in his arms. He wept uncontrollably. The soldier was Danny Corkeran, the slain man's brother.

As orders dismissing the regiments echoed down the line, Taylor walked slowly back to his tent. The sight of a weeping Danny Corkeran holding his dead brother had brought tears to the eyes of many a soldier. For a fleeting moment Taylor wondered what he was doing in this place of mud, misery, and death, so far from Fashion Plantation, participating in so bizarre an event. He missed his beautiful, fun-loving wife and the laughter of his children. He steeled his jaw sufficiently to restrain the moisture building in his own eyes. And he wondered if somewhere within himself he possessed the character to face death with the quiet bravery shown by privates Corkeran and O'Brien that morning.

They were the first executions in the Confederate Army. Although the newspapers criticized Taylor, the event earned him the respect of his fellow officers. It also earned him, at long last, the respect of the Louisiana Tigers.

★ ★ ★

NEW ORLEANS, DECEMBER 30—William J. Seymour was easily distracted from his duties that day. From the window of his office at the *Commercial Bulletin*, he watched the movement of troops near the waterfront. They were on their way to Tennessee to bolster General Albert Sidney Johnston's western defense forces. The Union Army had already moved into Kentucky, and bitter fighting raged in Missouri. Given a choice, William would have locked the doors of the office and joined their ranks. Instead, he returned to his desk where a half-written editorial awaited him.

He had never shared his father's passion for journalism. Isaac Seymour had founded the *Commercial Bulletin* and in twelve years built it into one of the most respected financial journals in the South. But for William, editing the *Bulletin* represented a job more than a passion, far more confining than rewarding. Because of the demands of the job, he considered himself no less a slave than Henry, who swept out the pressroom. Unlike Henry, he was bound by unyielding deadlines, temperamental typesetters, compositors, pressmen, lazy reporters, and advertisers with impossible demands. Having occupied the editor's chair since June, his reportorial fire had burned itself out. William Seymour did not want to be an editor. He wanted to be a soldier.

A letter from his father lay on his desk beside the unfinished editorial. Several days earlier, Richard Taylor, commander of the 1st Louisiana Brigade in Virginia, had offered William an appointment as aide-de-camp on his staff. The letter from his father urged William to turn down the commission and stay at the newspaper.

Colonel Isaac Seymour commanded the 6th Louisiana Infantry Regiment under Taylor. He made it clear that, if William accepted the appointment, he would have to give up his own command and return to New Orleans to run the newspaper. In the letter, Isaac never addressed William's suggestion that someone else be hired to manage the newspaper in his absence.

Isaac Seymour loved journalism only slightly less than he loved the military, and William had grown up listening to his father's war stories. Isaac had fought in the Seminole Wars in 1836 and the Mexican War a decade later. With the end of the Mexican War, Winfield Scott appointed him governor of Santa Anna's home province with his headquarters in the Castle of Perote. In fact, it was Isaac who escorted the exiled Santa Anna to the coast and put him on a boat to Jamaica. But that was long ago when his father was a young man. Isaac Seymour was fifty-seven now and not in the best health. William had been relieved when his father survived Manassas, but he worried that the old man might not survive a winter in Virginia under the harsh conditions described in his letters.

The Seymours descended from one of Connecticut's most distinguished families. Among their relatives was Horatio Seymour, a leading politician in that state and a one-time presidential candidate. Isaac was born in Savannah, Georgia, in 1804. He graduated with honors from Yale in 1827 and moved to Macon where he opened a law office. He married Caroline Whitlock in 1829 and William was born in 1832, the only one of five Seymour children to survive. Three of his siblings died in infancy. A sister, Catherine, died at nineteen. Isaac quit his law practice the year William was born to become a journalist. As editor of the *Georgia Messenger* he developed an interest in politics and became an active member of the Whig Party and a leading figure in Georgia politics. He served six years as the mayor of Macon before resigning the office to fight in the Mexican War.

Following the war, Isaac moved to New Orleans and established the *Commercial Bulletin*. It began as a financial publication, but its editorial scope expanded over the years to include politics and stories of general interest.

In 1852 William disappointed his father by dropping out of Hobart College in New York state. Isaac promptly put him to work as assistant editor of the newspaper. By 1860 the Seymours had become a political force in Louisiana and stood among the social elite of New Orleans.

When Louisiana seceded, Isaac had joined a local militia, and when the Confederate 6th Louisiana Infantry was formed in June 1861, he was elected its commander. The regiment, composed largely of Irish immigrants, was among the first units sent to Virginia. With his departure, Isaac had turned the newspaper over to William. He did so with a degree of concern, since William had never exhibited the energy, intensity, or ambition of a born newspaperman. Upon his departure for the front, Isaac wrote to a friend, "William has arrived at that age that he must depend upon himself. He has the whole business given to him and he must depend upon his own wit . . . to carry it through."

William Seymour sat at his desk and pondered the predicament his father's proposition posed. With the coming of spring, great armies would be on the move. Historic events would unfold across the continent . . . but he would not be there to witness them. He reached for his pen and composed an apologetic letter to Taylor, declining the appointment, then wrote a quick note to his father and finally retrieved the half-written editorial. At any moment, the typesetter would poke his head inside the door to remind him they were past deadline. As he finished his piece, William could not know that destiny would soon thrust him into one of the most spectacular, and critical, battles of the war.

★ ★ ★

Through the spring and early summer of 1861, the Union Navy's Gulf Coast blockade amounted to little more than a cat-and-mouse game between Admiral David Porter's small fleet of U.S. warships and the blockade runners out of New Orleans, Mobile, Galveston, and Indianola. By autumn the game turned serious. The arrival of additional U.S. warships in the Gulf of Mexico, along with coal to power them and men to service them, had tipped the scales of advantage to the Federal fleet. Coal stations, repair yards, and supply depots had been established on a string of coastal islands from Virginia to Texas, including a critical outpost at Ship Island off the coast near the Louisiana-Mississippi border. In a reversal of fortune, Pensacola had come under bombardment by Fort Pickens, supported by U.S. warships patrolling the bay. Porter's fleet had effectively sealed the passes through the Rigolets at the base of the Mississippi River. Only the occasional blockade runner slipped past the Federal ships guarding them, and by year's end, New Orleans felt the effects of the blockade.

Coffee had become so scarce it was selling for $1.50 a pound, when it could be found at all, a devastating deprivation for a population addicted to the stimulant. One enterprising citizen came up with a coffee substitute made from ground-up sweet potatoes and a potpourri of other, unidentified ingredients. However, the concoction did little to satisfy the cravings for caffeine. Soap, another item in short supply, was selling for a dollar a bar. During the harvest season, North Louisiana's farms provided an adequate, if not abundant, food supply for their Crescent City brethren. Produce and meats from East Texas still arrived in New Orleans via riverboats from Shreveport. But, by the end of the year, food shortages were becoming common. Fish and shrimp had disappeared from market stalls. Flour sold for astronomical prices. The only meat available in quantity was bacon, and there was an abundant supply of molasses and corn meal. Cornbread flapjacks, molasses, and fried bacon became a staple meal for rich and poor alike.

When Louisiana seceded from the Union in January 1861, thirty-three shipping lines operated out of New Orleans. Total commerce for the 1860–61 harvest season was almost $500 million. By the end of 1861, there were no oceangoing shippers at New Orleans and the port was effectively closed. Unsold cotton bales and hogsheads of sugar piled up along the levees at New Orleans and factors refused to accept shipments from upriver planters. As a result, all along the Mississippi, Red, and Ouachita rivers, mountains of cotton bales remained stacked beside the docks at cities and small river towns alike.

In October, at the urging of Governor Moore, Jefferson Davis appointed Major General Mansfield Lovell to replace the doting General Twiggs. Lovell took command of the newly created Department Number One. Headquartered at New Orleans, Lovell had responsibility for coastal defenses from Pensacola to Texas. The promotion enraged Braxton Bragg, who had been sitting at Pensacola, pleading in vain for heavy guns to contend with the batteries of Fort Pickens. Bragg immediately dispatched a letter to Governor Moore: "The command at New Orleans was rightly mine. I feel myself degraded by the action of the government and shall take care they know my sentiments."

In a subsequent letter, Bragg attacked the character of Lovell and expressed an opinion that his selection was tainted by politics if not by an outright payoff: "But for his inordinate vanity, he would be a fine soldier. Still, we could do as well without him and he can't make me believe he was not bought." It was one of those rare occasions when Bragg was right. New Orleans, indeed, would have been better off without Mansfield Lovell.

★ ★ ★ ★ ★ ★ ★ ★ ★ ★ ★ ★ ★ ★

1862

The Beast at the Gate

If they do not respect the stars in our flag,
they will feel its stripes.

BENJAMIN BUTLER

★ ★ ★ ★

6

★ ★ ★ ★

Lull before the Storm

WASHINGTON, D.C., JANUARY 9—Although Admiral David G. Farragut had never set foot on Ship Island, he was familiar with it. As a boy he had sailed past the island many times and wondered what mysteries lay beyond the glistening white sand of its beaches. He had seen the shaft of light from its lighthouse reflect upon the waves as it sliced the night and he wondered what kind of man would live there, so isolated from civilization, just to keep it burning. Farragut had grown up on the family farm not far from where the Pascagoula River emptied into the Gulf of Mexico. As a boy he accompanied his father on business trips to New Orleans and never failed to be fascinated by the mysterious island, looming dark and foreboding, fifteen miles out in the Gulf. Now at sixty years old he was going to return to Ship Island and the land of his early boyhood, not to visit, but to conquer it.

The case on his desk held orders from Secretary of the Navy Gideon Welles, appointing him commander of the newly formed Western Gulf Blockading Squadron. He was to proceed immediately to Philadelphia where his flagship, the *USS Hartford*, was being outfitted. In spite of the secrecy surrounding his mission, Farragut knew for some time of a buildup for an assault on New Orleans. What surprised him was his selection to command it. Some of Washington's most influential congressmen opposed his appointment to any vital role in the war effort because of his Southern background. However, Gideon Welles knew where David Farragut's allegiance lay. He maintained total dedication to the United States Navy and, given an order, Welles knew that Farragut would kick down the gates of hell to carry it out. The orders that accompanied the appointment were simple:

> When you are completely ready, you will collect what vessels can be spared from the blockade and proceed up the Mississippi River and reduce the defenses which guard the approaches to New Orleans, when you will appear off that city and take possession of it under the guns of your squadron, and hoist the American flag thereon, until troops can be sent to you. . . . There are other operations of minor importance which will commend themselves to your judgment and skill, but which must not be allowed to interfere with the great object in view, the certain capture of New Orleans.

Most of Farragut's armada had departed Hampton Roads, Virginia, on December 22, bound for Ship Island. The fleet consisted of men of war, schooners outfitted with thirteen-inch mortars, shallow draft gunboats, transports, coal tenders, and troop ships. By the time the fleet was fully assembled on the Gulf Coast, it would be the most powerful single naval force in the history of the nation until that time.

* * *

WASHINGTON, D.C., JANUARY 19—By December 1861 Major General Benjamin F. Butler, commander of the Department of New England, was being besieged by Massachusetts politicians and businessmen to organize an invasion of the Deep South, where millions of bales of cotton were being hoarded. The New England textile industry, long insulated by pet tariffs and fed by cheap Southern cotton, was in deep trouble. The Union blockade had worked far too well, and the small amount of cotton that snuck past Union warships went to France and England. At the outbreak of the war many believed cotton imports from India might make up for the loss of Southern cotton. Instead, Indian cotton also was going to England.

Butler, ever anxious to accommodate his powerful Massachusetts supporters, wrote a letter to General George McClellan, in which he proposed to lead an invasion of the Texas Gulf Coast. McClellan did not bother to answer him, the only response being a brief acknowledgment by an aide that the general had received the letter. Butler, who never counted patience among his limited virtues, decided to bypass McClellan. Learning that his good friend Edwin Stanton had just been appointed secretary of war, Butler immediately departed for Washington. On January 19, 1862, over breakfast at Stanton's home, Butler presented his own version of the Texas Plan.

He proposed to recruit an army of fifteen thousand New England volunteers and land them at Indianola on the Texas coast. From there, he would drive inland to capture San Antonio while a second army, under "Bloody Jim" Lane of Kansas, invaded Texas from the north. Butler believed those armies could crush resistance in a matter of weeks, after which time he would march into Louisiana and Arkansas. Butler also hoped to pick up a large number of recruits in Texas. His intelligence told him there was widespread Union sympathy in North Texas, where settlers from the Midwest were concentrated, and in the hill country beyond San Antonio, home to a large German population.

Butler assured Stanton the conquest of Texas would serve multiple purposes. In addition to cutting off the rebels' foreign trade through Mexico, Butler predicted that contraband cotton seized by an invading force would pay for the expedition and save the New England textile industry. Taking a page from Atkinson's booklet on Texas resettlement, he proposed that members of his volunteer army be given the lands they conquered, creating a slave-free society of New England landowners in the Lone Star State. With a new growing season about to begin, by autumn they would be able to supply the textile mills with more than enough cotton to make up for that lost because of the war. Stanton liked the plan. However, he and Butler did not realize that Lincoln had already selected New Orleans as the target for a Gulf Coast invasion.

In November 1861 Navy Commander David D. Porter had presented a secret plan for the capture of New Orleans. Upon reviewing it, Lincoln had turned to Secretary of the Navy Gideon Welles and brusquely remarked, "Why haven't we already done this?" Stanton, having been named secretary of war only three days before his meeting with Butler, had not been briefed on Porter's plan or Farragut's appointment. And, unknown to Lincoln, the reason it had not been done was because General McClellan had put the Louisiana campaign on hold for reasons that had little to do with military considerations. McClellan intended to lead the expedition himself.

McClellan had political ambitions far beyond even those of Butler. He envisioned himself not only the savior of the Union, but as its next president. He planned to crush Joe Johnston's rebel army in Virginia that spring, then lead his forces south for a full-scale attack on New Orleans that summer. McClellan figured the South would not survive such a one-two punch. The war would be over by the end of the year, at which time he would emerge a national hero. If anyone in Washington had bothered to read the New York newspapers, they would have known McClellan's plans. He revealed them in October during a boastful interview when he stated with absolute confidence, "I will knock them to pieces at New Orleans."

When Stanton approached Lincoln with Butler's Texas Plan, he learned from the president that New Orleans, not Texas, was targeted for invasion. An angry Stanton demanded to know why he had not been consulted. If New Orleans was the objective, Stanton insisted that Butler, not McClellan, command the campaign. To Stanton's surprise, Lincoln agreed. He had been trying to figure out what to do with the volatile Butler. From the beginning of the war he had held no less than three commands. In each case, Lincoln was forced to transfer him because he could not get along with his fellow generals. Although well connected politically in New England, Butler was not popular in Washington. Winfield Scott and McClellan could hardly stand him. On one occasion when Lincoln asked McClellan where he should assign Butler next, McClellan replied, "As far away as possible." Thus Ben Butler ended up on a ship bound for Louisiana instead of Indianola, Texas.

* * *

As the calendar leaf turned on 1862, Lincoln accepted the fact that there would not be a quick conclusion to the war. The armies of North and South watched each other across the Potomac that winter as the president juggled problems from Missouri to Pennsylvania Avenue. A War Department corruption scandal forced him to fire Secretary of War Simon Cameron. In Missouri, General John Fremont, in defiance of Lincoln's orders, announced the emancipation of the slaves of Missouri. When Lincoln tried to fire him, Fremont had his troops detain the president's messengers so that papers dismissing him could not be delivered. Meanwhile, McClellan's army sat idle in winter quarters draining the defense budget, even as the general demanded more men and equipment before moving on Richmond.

Lincoln's problems extended all the way to London and Paris. The British Parliament debated a declaration of war against the United States over the Trent Affair, in which a British ship was stopped on the high seas by a U.S. man-of-war and Confederate diplomats James Mason and John Slidell were taken prisoner. Meanwhile, the French had exerted their influence in Mexico. Although officially neutral, France openly traded with the Confederacy through Mexico, and there was nervous speculation that the French might enter the conflict on the side of the rebels in Texas. Compounding Lincoln's problems, New England's abolitionists exerted intense political pressure to prosecute the war even as New York's bankers urged him to end it.

★ ★ ★

NEW ORLEANS, JANUARY 26—With the dawning of the new year, it seemed the people of New Orleans awakened from the warmth of a delusional dream and stepped onto the cold floor of reality. As word spread that a fleet of Federal warships was anchored at Ship Island, there were rumors that an attack on the city was imminent. The war that Louisianans thought would never reach them had arrived at their threshold.

Along the waterfront, the ring of hammers on metal could be heard as workers labored to convert a motley assortment of river steamers and tugboats into ships of war. The fires of the city's foundries glowed in the night, and molten metal flowed into casts from which emerged Confederate cannons. The engines that drove the textile plants rumbled, and the clack-clack of looms chattered day and night. In the late afternoons, a new sound joined the industrial symphony. From the backyards of the city and along the banks of its canals came the pop of pistol fire. Afternoon target practice had become the latest social recreation for the ladies of New Orleans. Under the watchful eyes of husbands and fathers, the women of the city clutched pistols in delicate, gloved hands, pointed them at swatches of cloth nailed to trees, closed their eyes, and winced when the weapons fired. If the Yankees came, the women of New Orleans were prepared to protect their honor.

No citizen felt the shock of impending crisis more deeply than Governor Moore, who spent far more time in New Orleans now than he did in Baton Rouge. To the governor, it seemed the Confederate government had become an all-consuming monster, devouring arms, goods, and equipment as quickly as they could be produced. Each time a gunboat was outfitted and armed for the protection of New Orleans, it had to be sent upstream to meet another threat from the north. With the arming of each new regiment came desperate pleas from Beauregard and Johnston for its transfer to Tennessee or Richmond. Now faced with the threat of invasion, the governor had neither guns, manpower, nor fortifications to defend his state. He had armed and sent fifteen thousand Louisianans to Virginia and another ten thousand to defend the upper Mississippi River Valley. The Baton Rouge arsenal had been depleted.

Moore had only 158 heavy guns to defend all of Louisiana, including three hundred miles of coastline and four hundred miles of a river navigable by the enemy's heavily armed, oceangoing men-of-war. Only eight thousand Confederate troops remained in Louisiana from the latest draft. Less than half of those were armed and none had received proper training. For many, their only training consisted of digging trenches around New Orleans. On paper the governor could count almost fifteen thousand men in state and local militias, but of those, only about three thousand were armed with personal weapons ranging from rusty shotguns to ancient muskets and pistols. However, even that did not matter because there was no ammunition for them. The problem was never a lack of volunteers. The population had responded, but anyone with military experience had left the state, and no qualified officers remained to train new volunteers.

The governor blamed Twiggs and Manfield Lovell for the sorry state of preparedness. Instead of concerning himself with the defense of New Orleans, Lovell tried to endear himself to Richmond by responding to every request for men and arms. Only recently, without consulting the governor, Lovell had committed two new Louisiana regiments to General Beauregard at Corinth, Mississippi, and promised to deliver three more as soon as they could be organized.

Frustrated and filled with the fear of impending disaster, Governor Moore finally did what any self-respecting politician would do. He ordered a grand military parade to reassure the citizens of New Orleans that they had nothing to fear.

The parade took place on January 26. More than twenty thousand men formed ranks and marched down Canal Street. The city turned out to cheer the troops, but even the most patriotic had to notice the absence of weapons in the ranks and the advanced ages of some of the marchers. Aside from the three thousand rifles or shotguns, there appeared only the occasional saber or pistol. Most of the men were in civilian dress. The best armed and best dressed unit in the procession was the Louisiana Native Guards Regiment, whose members had armed and outfitted themselves. Marching crisply in step with backs stiff and shoulders squared, they drew the loudest applause of all the regiments.

That night the city's ballrooms were alive with music and laughter, as were its waterfront taverns. Even as Farragut's fleet stood poised to strike from the south and Grant's gunboats from the north, New Orleans celebrated—at least for a day.

★ ★ ★

BATON ROUGE, FEBRUARY 18—At first Governor Moore did not believe the reports about Fort Donaldson. But as details of the disaster trickled in by telegraph, disbelief turned to anger. A brigadier general named Gideon Pillow had surrendered an important fort on the Cumberland River, virtually without a fight. With it, he surrendered fourteen thousand Confederate soldiers, twenty thousand small arms, forty-eight field pieces, seventeen heavy guns, three thousand horses and mules, and vast stores of food, clothing, and ammunition. With the stroke of a pen, Gideon Pillow had inflicted more damage to the Confederacy than had all Union generals and their legions combined.

The governor paced his office far into the night. Many of those soldiers, so casually sacrificed by Pillow, were Louisiana boys—trained and armed at great expense to Louisianans. They wore uniforms made from the cloth of Louisiana looms and sewn by mothers, wives, and sweethearts. Many of the small arms and field pieces and much of the ammunition, food, and equipment, now lost, had been sent up the river from New Orleans and Baton Rouge at great cost and sacrifice. Jeff Davis had promised the governor he could bring those troops home if Louisiana was threatened. Now they were gone.

Moore swore that never again would he blindly send men and arms to such distant venues to be wasted by fools.

✴ ✴ ✴

Abraham Lincoln frequently complained of the ineptitude of his Union generals, but none of them approached the incompetence of one of Jeff Davis's appointments. On Sunday, February 16, 1862, with a single order, Gideon Pillow surrendered the Confederacy's keystone fort in the upper Mississippi River Valley. In doing so, he gave up Missouri and Kentucky, most of Tennessee and northern Arkansas, and left the door open for a Northern invasion of the lower Mississippi and Cumberland rivers. The blow staggered the South and forced Confederate generals Albert Sidney Johnston and Pierre Beauregard to hurriedly reorganize their plans for a defense of the southernmost states.

The greatest mystery surrounding the debacle at Fort Donaldson was why President Davis approved Pillow's appointment as a general—much less allowed him to command a vital fortification. Pillow was a notorious incompetent. As an officer in the Mexican War, he once ordered his men to dig trenches on the wrong side of a breastworks, resulting in heavy casualties during an attack.

Fort Donaldson was located on high ground overlooking the Cumberland River near its juncture with the Mississippi. Well-situated and sufficiently armed to defend against gunboats, its only vulnerability was an attack by land forces. To defend against an assault by Union infantry, Albert Johnston pulled fifteen thousand rebel troops out of Bowling Green, Kentucky, and sent them on a forced march to Donaldson. When Pillow assumed command of the fort on February 9, he had some seventeen thousand troops to defend the fortification. General Grant's gunboats attacked the fort on February 14 and were quickly repulsed. Several of Grant's boats were damaged, two of them badly enough to be put out of commission. However, with the appearance of Federal ground troops, Pillow panicked and fled the fort, leaving orders for his second in command to surrender it. General Simon Bolivar Buckner dutifully followed orders and sent a letter of surrender to a surprised General Grant, who was making plans for a long siege. Several thousand rebel troops refused to surrender and left the fort before they could be captured, including fifteen hundred under Nathan Bedford Forrest. The remainder were taken prisoner without having a chance to defend the fort or to fight their way out.

With the fall of Fort Donaldson, Louisianans suddenly found themselves not only threatened from the south, but vulnerable from the north as well.

✴ ✴ ✴

NEW ORLEANS, APRIL 9—Shortly after daylight, citizens began gathering in clusters at the windows of the city's newspaper offices. By mid-morning the clusters grew to crowds that spilled into the streets. Word spread that the first casualty figures were being posted from a great battle in Tennessee at a place called Shiloh. The early reports of the battle were encouraging. But as the day wore on, columns containing the names of the battle's casualties grew longer, and a picture of unimagined human destruction emerged. Heartrending wails were heard, followed by weeping, as wives and mothers found the names of loved ones in the seemingly endless columns. In just one battle the Confederate Army had lost 10,000 men—killed, wounded, and missing. There was little consolation that Union losses were placed at 13,000. Among the 1,723 Confederates listed as dead was General Albert Sidney Johnston, commander of the western forces.

No one could imagine a battle that would claim so many lives. And for what? When it was over, the armies were back where they started. Hardly a family in Louisiana escaped the effects of the Shiloh casualty reports. Everyone knew someone on the list. If not a husband, son, or sweetheart, it was a neighbor down the street or the boy on the next farm. As Louisiana grieved, its citizenry paid little heed to another report in the newspapers. On April 7, near New Madrid on the Mississippi River, the Confederate fort at Island Number Ten fell to the Yankees. The river was now open to Memphis, only 170 miles upstream from the Louisiana border.

＊　＊　＊

THE RAPPAHANNOCK RIVER, APRIL 17—The rains of early March had turned the snows of February to slush along the roads of Northern Virginia when Joe Johnston received intelligence that McClellan was planning to flank him by moving up the peninsula with more than one hundred thousand men. By then, Johnston's Confederate Army had dwindled to only forty thousand troops scattered across the Virginia countryside. Under pressure from the politicians back in Richmond, he had adopted a lenient furlough policy that winter, allowing thousands of troops to return home. What he failed to consider was the twelve-month enlistment problem. Even as he planned a defense of Richmond against a major Union offensive, it dawned on him that the enlistments of many of his men would be up that spring and summer, and a large number of those on furlough might not return. He decided, therefore, to withdraw his army forty miles to the south and concentrate it near the Orange Court House, well below the Rappahannock and Rapidan rivers. From there he could better defend Richmond.

As the men shivered in their tents and makeshift winter cabins, Johnston shuffled his commander structure. Among the changes, he placed Major General Richard S. Ewell in command of a division that included Dick Taylor's Brigade. Having known Ewell in Mexico, Taylor was more amused by his commander's nervous behavior than impressed by his military expertise. Indeed, Ewell was an unusual character in appearance as well as manner, with wide eyes that seemed locked in perpetual surprise, a large, hawklike nose, and a bald head that rose like a mountain peak out of an unruly hairline. In his writings, Taylor described him as "having a striking resemblance to a woodcock." Hyperactive by nature, Ewell possessed almost as many eccentricities as did Taylor, most of them related to his belief that he was the victim of an indefinable inner illness. For relief he lay on the floor in his tent, his body curled around a camp stool in a position Taylor described as unusual enough "to dislocate an ordinary person's joints."

Taylor could hardly justify criticism of eccentric contortions considering his own.

The men often made jest of the precarious way he sat his horse. To relieve the pain in his arthritic limbs, he would hook his right leg around the front of the saddle, balancing himself with his left hand resting on the rump of his horse while holding a cigar in his right. The men believed that the cigar was the key to maintaining this position, the theory being that if he ever dropped it, he would topple right out of the saddle. In fact, Taylor's unusual behavior and talent for profane expression had endeared him to his men—especially the Irish in Wheat's battalion, who agreed that he was even more skilled at vile invective than Cussin' Emmett, the battalion champion.

The pullback from Manassas began on March 9 in a driving rain laced by sleet. Taylor's brigade, by now numbering only about twenty-six hundred men, was assigned the rear guard. Taylor assigned the crucial role of skirmish unit to Wheat's Tigers. Slogging through deep mud, crossing swollen streams, and burning bridges as they went, the Tigers repeatedly ambushed the Yankees, slowing pursuit to a crawl.

Upon reaching the bridge at the Rappahannock River, Ewell received orders to secure it and hold the Union Army at bay until Johnston could extract the last of his troops beyond the Rapidan. Once that was accomplished, Ewell was to burn the bridge and move south to join forces with Johnston. Ewell's division remained at the bridge for a month, during which time he and Taylor became close friends. With little else to do, Ewell spent a great deal of time in Taylor's tent, spellbound by his stories. Dick Taylor was an encyclopedia of anecdotal stories about history's great battles and the little-known events that decided their outcomes, and Ewell never tired of listening to them.

On the morning of April 17, the boom of cannons beyond the river caused Taylor to exit his tent quickly. He ordered his men to prepare for combat even as he mounted his horse and galloped toward the sound of battle well ahead of his troops. As he approached the south end of the bridge, he spotted the bald head of General Ewell bobbing among a band of Confederates engaged in an artillery duel with a Federal battery across the river. Ewell dashed about, personally directing the fire. Seeing Taylor, he came to greet him.

"I think we surprised them," he said, even as a nearby explosion shook the ground. It appeared to Taylor that his commander was enjoying this opportunity to play soldier. As the advance elements of Taylor's troops began arriving, the outmanned Federals quickly withdrew. Taylor then saw flames leaping from the bridge.

"You set the bridge on fire!" he said.

"Why? You don't like it?" said Ewell.

Taylor knew of the orders to destroy the bridge. However, he had been pondering an alternative strategy he intended to discuss with Ewell, but never got around to it.

"One of Napoleon's officers used a similar situation to his advantage," Taylor said. "Instead of burning the bridge, he withdrew only a small part of his command and left the majority of his troops in hiding. When the enemy got half of its men across the bridge, he ambushed and defeated them. Then he burned the bridge."

Ewell gave him a look of disgust.

"Why didn't you tell me *that* story *before* I burnt the damn bridge?" he asked.

7

River of Fire

FORT JACKSON, LOUISIANA, APRIL 18—William Seymour stood at the parapet, watching Union gunboats maneuver into position along the east bank of the river just out of reach of the fort's guns, when he heard a distant boom from behind the trees on the west bank. He followed the flight of a large mortar shell as it arced high above and finally came down with a dull thud in the soft earth of the parade plain. A moment later, the shell exploded, sending dirt and debris skyward. Although William was some distance from the blast, he felt its concussion. As the smoke cleared and debris sprinkled the parapet, he saw men running across the grounds. Where the shell had landed, a gaping hole some six feet across had opened in the earth. Before he could fully grasp what was happening, another explosion ripped the parade ground, and another. There was pandemonium in the fort as men fled to the shelter of the walls while others wheeled the Columbiads on the ramparts toward the source of the fire. In an instant, the newspaperman who was afraid he would miss the war was swept up in one of the most violent battles of the conflict.

The struggle for the river forts that guarded New Orleans' threshold, began at 8:30 that morning. Under cover of darkness, Admiral David Porter anchored 14 mortar boats behind the trees lining the west bank in the bend of the river below the fort. The nearest boat was only 950 yards away and all were hidden from view from the fort. Each boat had a massive, thirteen-inch mortar that hurled 225-pound shells high into the air. The missiles rained inside the fort with uncanny accuracy. Only occasionally did a short fuse explode a shell prematurely overhead, or a stray fall outside the walls. Choked by smoke and under a ceaseless blizzard of mud and flying fragments of brick and metal, the men on the ramparts fired their cannons at an enemy they could not see.

Writing in his memoirs, William Seymour described the scene inside the fort that morning:

> Shell succeeded shell in quick succession. When these ponderous missiles fell on the
> ramparts or parade plein [sic], they sunk into the earth to a distance of six to eight
> feet and, exploding, would tear a hole in the earth large enough to admit a barrel.
> When they struck the brickwork of the fort, the crashing noise produced was almost

stunning and the bricks and mortar would fly in all directions. I saw a young fellow who had narrowly escaped from being crushed by a falling shell running away from the place, laughing in great glee, but before he had run ten yards the shell exploded, throwing fragments of brick in all directions—one of which struck this man in the back, killing him instantly.

Explosions ripped the two rear bastions of the fort, setting the officers' quarters ablaze and sending bedding, clothes, and personal belongings up in flames. As Seymour watched, six mortar boats, escorted by gunboats, appeared far downstream at the bend in the river. They maneuvered into position some three thousand to four thousand yards away, at the outer range of the fort's guns. They soon joined in the bombardment as did the gunboats with their long-range, rifled howitzers. Shells from the howitzers exploded along the fifty-foot-thick walls of the fort, showering the men on the ramparts with brick even as mortar shells exploded behind them. The barracks building caught fire, turning the interior of the fort into an inferno. The hospital building outside the fort sustained a direct hit, forcing the evacuation of its sickbay occupants. Seymour recounted:

> We returned their fire with vigor, though most of our shots fell short owing to the miserable quality of our powder. However, enough shots did threaten the boats across the river sufficiently to send them in retreat back downstream.
>
> One of the mortar vessels and one gunboat were disabled and the others retired beyond the woods. During the subsequent bombardment, we never caught sight of a single mortar vessel [behind the trees] although we heard from them with disagreeable frequency.

As dusk settled on the river, and fires raged along the interior of the walls of the fort through the wooden structures along the fort's interior walls, the frequency of the shelling slowed. Several times during the day, the men had managed to subdue the blazes, only to have the flames break out once more. A fire in the citadel that could not be extinguished threatened to spread to a magazine. The entire garrison was called out to throw wet blankets on the walls of the magazine in an effort to save it. A fire engine that had been brought down from New Orleans was wheeled out and finally managed to confine the fire to the citadel. Mercifully, just when it seemed the men could take no more, the firing ceased. Seymour wrote, "Fortunately, when this danger threatened us, and when all the men were exposed, the fire of the enemy ceased—not, as we subsequently found out, from dictates of humanity, but for the purpose of giving some rest to their gunners."

With the coming of darkness, a silence fell on the river. In less than twelve hours, more than fourteen hundred mortar shells had fallen on Fort Jackson and its walls were battered from moat to parapet. Casualties were remarkably few, considering the intensity of the bombardment. Those men who were not manning guns had been ordered to remain in the safety of the casements when not called upon to fight fires.

Seymour observed that the interior of the fort was a shambles. The parade plain was ripped and cratered. The parapets and casements had suffered terrible damage. Fire had claimed the barracks—along with the bedding and clothing of the men. Seven of the fort's heavy guns were disabled—weapons they could ill afford to lose. The guns of the fort had damaged only two of Porter's mortar boats and one of his gunboats, killing one man and wounding some fifteen others. Fort Jackson had sustained a horrific pounding, yet sustained fewer than twenty casualties, including three dead.

That night, General Johnson K. Duncan, the commander of the river forts, sent a messenger upstream with an order for Captain Renshaw to release fire rafts in an effort to dislodge the mortar boats from the shelter of the tree line. The captain botched the assignment, releasing the flaming rafts too close to the bank and too far upstream. As Duncan and Seymour looked on in disbelief, the first of the rafts drifted ashore above the fort. A second group of rafts was caught in the river current and floated harmlessly past the Federal fleet, proceeding down the channel like torchbearers on parade. Gliding along harmlessly, they burned themselves out against the banks at the Head of the Passes. Near midnight, General Duncan received a message from Captain Renshaw, apologizing for his error.

★ ★ ★

From the day he took command of the river forts, General Duncan warned his boss, Major General Mansfield Lovell, and Secretary of War Judah Benjamin that without improvements the fortifications could not repel an attack by a modern fleet. He requested larger guns and rifled howitzers to replace the old smooth-bore Columbiads on the ramparts. He sought additional men to bolster the forts' skeleton force. Duncan also complained about the inadequacy of the makeshift chain barrier across the river. To all of his concerns, the Confederate brass turned a deaf ear.

Forts Jackson and St. Philip sat seven hundred yards apart on opposite banks of the river, seventy miles below New Orleans at a place called Plaquemines Bend. Their guns looked out over a sharp bend where river traffic slowed to negotiate the curve. Key to the river's defense was a barrier to halt enemy ships in that bend. General Beauregard had recommended that a wire cable—one that could be raised or lowered—be stretched across the river. However, Lovell constructed a stationary barrier made of logs connected by chains, and with the first heavy rain, driftwood piled up against the logs and broke the barrier loose, sweeping it downriver and out to sea. A second makeshift barrier included the anchoring of several old schooners across the river and connecting them with chains. However, a wayward barge had torn away a section of this barrier.

To support the forts, New Orleans's shipyards had converted a motley assortment of watercraft to gunboats and rams—a dozen in all. Most of these vessels were old tugs coated with sheet metal and mounting one or two small cannons each. No single commander directed this strange armada. Some boats belonged to the Confederacy, others to the state of Louisiana. Three were privately owned, commanded by individual captains. Completing the defense were fifty fire rafts loaded with pine logs, coated with tar, and soaked with turpentine.

The manpower shortage at the forts was solved by conscripting workers from the city docks. Most were foreign nationals who had chosen not to enlist in the Confederate Army. Some went voluntarily, but others had to be forced at gunpoint onto the boats that took them downriver to the forts.

Meanwhile, at the Algiers shipyard, workmen labored furiously to complete the ironclad *Louisiana*. A massive ram with three-inch steel sides and sixteen heavy guns, it represented the only vessel on the Mississippi capable of contending with Union warships. Cost overruns and continuing squabbles between contractors and state officials had delayed its completion for months.

Even without the *Louisiana*, General Lovell had supreme confidence in his river defenses. Just days before the Union attack, he wrote to Benjamin, "I have no fears about the results if the enemy tries to pass our defenses."

* * *

When the war began, the two most capable officers in the United States Navy were David Farragut and David Porter. There was a bond between the two that went beyond friendship. They were stepbrothers. Farragut arrived at Ship Island in late February, but it would be the end of March before he was ready to move against the river forts. Upon his arrival he found much of the fleet in a state of disrepair. Hulls had to be patched, riggings replaced, and engines repaired. It took several weeks to bring in sufficient amounts of coal and supplies to support the operation. When he was ready, Farragut had a fleet of seventeen men-of-war. He was soon joined by Porter who commanded twenty mortar boats and seven gunboats. Combined, their fleet had 268 guns ranging from giant mortars to the rifled howitzers on the gunboats.

On March 18, the shallow-draft gunboats began towing the mortar vessels over the bar and into a deep water basin at the Head of the Passes. They anchored at Pilot Town, a small village built on stilts above the largest of the islands at the base of the Mississippi River. Two weeks were required to tow Farragut's deep-draft warships through the shallow passes into the deeper waters of the Mississippi. Gunboats went up the river to survey and mark the banks with colored rags tied to trees so that the ships' captains would know their positions in relation to the forts. The survey crews were greeted by rebel snipers sitting in trees, hidden behind cypress knees, and sometimes standing in waist-deep water at the river's edge. Musket balls pinged against metal plates and left holes in smokestacks and pilothouses. The gunboat crews answered with blasts of canister, which did little damage except to the foliage. However, the constant whistling of minié balls from rebel muskets made it impossible for the survey crews to complete their task. Upon their departure, the snipers removed most of the markers.

Meanwhile, Farragut drilled his men and prepared his ships for battle by placing chain armor around the hulls. He overlapped these with cable. Sandbags were stacked around guns, engines, and ammunition, and rope netting was rigged above the decks to protect the crewmen from flying splinters. The most abundant commodity at Pilot Town was mud. Although the men cursed it, they took advantage of its abundance, smearing it over hulls, masts, and riggings to make their ships more difficult to see at night. Whale boats with grappling hooks moved up the channels to tow away enemy fire rafts that might threaten the fleet.

To keep an eye on Union activities, the Confederates sent scouts in small skiffs and pirogues into the bayous and backwaters of the river. They strung telegraph wire from Fort Jackson to a reporting station nine miles below the forts. An unarmed old steamer named the *Star* sat anchored there to provide reconnaissance. On April 9, Farragut sent two of his warships to chase the *Star* back up the river. In spite of her age, the *Star* churned up the river, staying just out of the range of the guns of the warships until she came under the protection of Fort Jackson's Columbiads, which drove the men-of-war back downstream.

On Thursday, April 10, a violent storm roared across the region followed by a prolonged downpour that drove the rebel scouts and snipers from their flooded positions. Farragut took advantage of the opportunity and dispatched a force to cut the telegraph wire.

The following Tuesday, with the river at an unusually high stage, the entire fleet moved north and began anchoring at the bend in the river below Fort Jackson. Although the warships could not be seen from the fort, their tall masts and yardarms showed beyond the trees. General Duncan reacted by sending word for Captain John Mitchell to release some fire rafts to drift into the fleet. Instead of bringing the rafts downstream and lighting them, as instructed, Mitchell released them far upstream. Instead of intercepting Farragut's fleet, the rafts drifted into the banks at the bend of the river and burned themselves out—with one notable exception. One of the wayward rafts nudged up against a warehouse outside the fort. The wooden structure quickly went up in flames. An angry Duncan instructed Captain Renshaw on the proper handling of the rafts and sent him to take over the task from Mitchell. Captain Mitchell, a Confederate Navy officer, refused to be replaced by an army officer, causing an awkward standoff. Mitchell finally relented, making it clear that it was his decision, not Duncan's, to relinquish command of the rafts. However, when it came time for Captain Renshaw to release fire rafts, he proved just as inept as Mitchell at following instructions.

On the morning of April 16, Union gunboats moved to within two miles of the fort to draw fire to determine the range of its guns. That afternoon, the gunboats exchanged fire with the fort to distract its gunners while Porter maneuvered his mortar boats into position. He anchored them in a line against the west bank, hidden by the tree line with the lead boats sitting no more than a half mile from the walls of the fort. The following morning, five lightly armed Confederate steamers from New Orleans came down the river to test the Union fleet. They were met by a barrage from the heavy guns of Farragut's warships and quickly retreated back up the river. That evening Porter informed Farragut he was ready to launch an all-out bombardment of the forts the following day. He confidently told Farragut to have his men-of-war ready to move against New Orleans within forty-eight hours, assuring him that was all the time needed for his mortars to level Fort Jackson.

✶ ✶ ✶

ON THE MISSISSIPPI RIVER, APRIL 24—Under normal conditions, David Farragut was a patient man. But by the time darkness settled on the river on April 23, Porter's forty-eight-hour bombardment had extended to six days. At the bend in the river, Fort Jackson still stood, looming defiantly, smoke rising from its fires. Upstream, on the opposite bank, Fort St. Philip remained hardly touched. Day after day, Farragut paced the deck of the *Hartford* and watched as mortar shells rained down on Fort Jackson—more than six thousand in six days. Still, when he sent gunboats forward to test its gunners, they encountered showers of shot and shell.

On the twentieth, in an attempt to break the chain barrier that ran across the river below the forts, Farragut sent two gunboats, the *Itasca* and the *Pinola*, racing up the east bank, within range of the guns of Fort St. Philip. Under heavy fire they managed to reach the obstruction and the crews tried to blast it away with a keg of gunpowder, but the fuse failed to detonate the charge. As it turned out, they could have saved the gunpowder. The captain of the *Itasca* discovered that a break in the barrier already existed near the east bank and went through it. The barrier had been broken more than a week earlier when several barges broke loose from their moorings and slammed into it. Although Mitchell and Lovell were apprised of the break, neither had bothered to order its repair.

Seeing a fire raft bearing down on him, the captain turned the *Itasca* hard about. In doing so, he struck the barrier, became entangled, and tore an even greater hole in it before breaking free. The gunboats fled back down the river under a storm of fire from the forts, sustaining heavy damage but completing their mission.

Farragut was elated to learn that the barrier was broken. He summoned Porter and told him that he intended to run his fleet past the forts before the Confederates had a chance to repair the barrier, but Porter objected. For two days, he succeeded in restraining Farragut from launching an attack, assuring him that Fort Jackson could not long stand under the pounding it was taking. Porter believed the forts must be taken before New Orleans was assaulted. Otherwise, he said, even if Farragut managed to get some of his ships past the forts, they would be trapped upstream, their only avenue of escape a return trip under the very same guns of the forts. Two days later, with no sign that the forts were ready to surrender, Farragut would wait no longer. He announced that he was going to New Orleans even if he lost part of his fleet.

As darkness settled on the river that Wednesday, Farragut began maneuvering his ships in preparation for a run past the forts. The fleet was separated into three divisions. Captain Theodorus Bailey, aboard the *Cayuga*, commanded the first division of eight warships. He was to proceed up the east bank, as close to Fort St. Philip as possible, and lead the other ships through the break in the barrier. Farragut, with three warships, would follow the channel. He would be trailed by six warships making up the third division. Porter was instructed to move his mortar boats as close to Fort Jackson as possible and fire without pause. One warship from the third division was assigned to protect the mortar boats. Preparations complete, at nine o'clock, the men were sent to their hammocks to rest, but few slept in those next hours.

At two o'clock on the morning of the twenty-fourth, shrill whistles echoed down the river, sending men scrambling to their battle stations. At three o'clock, engines fired and the ships moved out, two-by-two, their positions slightly angled so that broadsides could be fired without striking a sister ship. Slowly they built up steam until they ran at full speed toward the guns of the river forts and the city that held the key to control of the Mississippi River.

★ ★ ★

The activity on the river that night did not escape the attention of those inside Fort Jackson. According to Seymour, preparations were under way to meet the long-awaited assault:

> Long before daylight, all of the guns were manned. The hot shot furnaces [were] in full blast, shot and shell placed near the guns and every preparation made for the fight.

Fort Jackson was not a pretty sight, with its casements blown apart and some of the fort's better guns rendered useless. Great cracks had appeared in the walls as a result of mortar shells being lobbed into the moat at their foundation. One magazine had sustained heavy damage. At great peril to their lives, the men had managed to remove the ammunition from it. Although the bombardment had caused few fatalities, a larger number of men suffered wounds, and even more were on sick call due to exposure during a chilling rainstorm that flooded the fort two days earlier. Those not ill or wounded bore up under physical and emotional exhaustion from lack of sleep, poor diet, and stress. There had been grumbling among the men, and General Duncan found it increasingly difficult to maintain discipline.

On Monday night the men were momentarily cheered by news that the *Louisiana* was on its way from New Orleans to support them. However, upon its arrival above Fort St. Philip, the men in the forts learned to their dismay that the great ironclad had to be towed into place. Its engines remained uncompleted, and the rudder and propeller were unfinished. The great warship built to save New Orleans was nothing more than a stationary battery.

When General Duncan learned that Captain Mitchell was mooring the *Louisiana* above the chain barrier, he immediately went to see him. Duncan urged him to anchor the ironclad below the barrier near Fort St. Philip so that its firepower could supplement that of the forts. Duncan pointed out that the guns of St. Philip could not aim low enough to be effective against ships running along the east bank channel. With the *Louisiana* anchored below the barrier, Union warships moving up that side of the river would come within point-blank range of its guns. Mitchell, however, refused to move the *Louisiana*. Frustrated by the obstinate attitude of the navy officer, Duncan sent a message to General Lovell, who technically commanded both army and navy forces, but who enforced his authority only reluctantly. Duncan informed Lovell that an attack was imminent and urged him to order the *Louisiana* below the barrier.

Instead of issuing the order, Lovell decided to come down the river and survey the situation. He arrived at two o'clock in the morning and was still surveying the situation at 3:30 when Admiral Porter's mortars opened up and hell broke loose on the Mississippi.

In the first barrage, shell after shell fell in rapid succession, shaking the very foundations of Fort Jackson. At one point, Seymour counted twelve shells in the air at the same time. Through the smoke, twin flares from the *Cayuga* lit the sky, signaling the beginning of the attack by the warships. The guiding red lights atop the *Cayuga*'s mast came into view as the lead ship churned up the river under a full head of steam. Like shadowy ghosts in the night, Farragut's fleet emerged from the darkness. Seymour provided a vivid description of what happened in the next few minutes:

> As soon as they were within range, the guns of both forts opened a well-directed fire upon the leading ships which was followed by broadsides after broadsides [from the ships] . . . the roar of the artillery was deafening; the rushing sound of the descending bombs; the sharp, whizzing noise made by the jagged fragments of exploded shells; the whirring of grape shot and hissing of canister balls—all calculated to disturb the equanimity [sic] of the strongest nerved man, provided he was not too much engaged to allow his mind to dwell upon them, which was the case with most of us.
>
> Soon, a lurid glow of light rested upon the fort, produced by the almost incessant discharge of our own guns and the explosions of the enemy's shells above and around us. At one time, when the din and tumult were at the highest, as I was at my post, Father Nachon, a Catholic priest, who was volunteer chaplain at the fort, placed his mouth at my ear and called out that hell could not be more terrible.

A Confederate soldier provided an even more vivid description of the battle:

> It was so dark we could see nothing, but as the second rocket faded, in one instant the whole scene was brilliantly illuminated, as if by magic. Every gun opened in the forts. The vessels poured broadside after broadside [lighting the scene so that] we could see every yard, every sail, every rope, every man in the rigging, every man at the guns in the fort, dark against the red sulphurous [sic] light. The men working the little howitzers in the rigging of the *Hartford* looked like black imps, clinging and climbing about her ropes. It was the most superb sight I ever witnessed—so flashing, so bewildering, so magnificent, so brief.

The *Cayuga* ran so close to the east bank that the guns of Fort St. Philip, trained on the middle of the river, blew away masts, sails, and rigging without striking the hull. The other ships in Bailey's division followed, throwing their broadsides into the fort. As the *Cayuga* came through the barrier, the indecisive General Lovell finally made a decision. He climbed into his boat and fled back up the river to New Orleans.

When the attack began, the six-vessel rebel defense fleet just above the forts lay at anchor, crews asleep, engines silent. Caught by surprise, crews quickly began firing engines. As the Union warships approached, two of the boats managed to build up enough steam to escape up the river. Three others sat helplessly against the bank while the *Cayuga* blasted away, riddling them and setting them on fire. Of the three Confederate rams that were destroyed, and the two that escaped, not one had fired a shot.

A brave exception to the cowardly flight of others was Captain A. F. Warley's *Manassas*, a seagoing tug converted into a ram. It was, in appearance, the strangest of all the river defense boats: its decks removed to the water line and oak timbers installed and covered with iron rails, giving it the appearance of a giant turtle. A single thirty-two-pound cannon pointed out through a trap door at the bow. As the *Cayuga* turned its guns on the *Louisiana*, the *Manassas* bore down on Captain Bailey's warship in an attempt to ram it. At that point, the *Varuna* arrived to fire a broadside into the *Manassas*. Part of the broadside struck the *Cayuga*, causing Bailey to disengage and continue on up the river. The *Varuna* did likewise, leaving the slow-moving *Manassas* behind.

Having failed to stop the two warships, Captain Warley turned his attention to the *Brooklyn*, which had become entangled in the barrier. A single shot from the *Manassas* struck the *Brooklyn* just above the waterline before the rebel vessel rammed her. However, the *Manassas*'s steam power was so low it bounced away, unable to penetrate the chain armor. The rebel gunboat, *Warrior*, came chugging down the river and tried to come to the aid of the *Manassas* but a broadside from the *Brooklyn* set her on fire, driving her to the shore. The *Manassas* then went after the Union man-of-war *Mississippi*, ramming her. Although heavily damaged, the *Mississippi* managed to stay afloat. As the first gray light of day broke the horizon, Captain Melancton sent the *Mississippi* in pursuit of the *Manassas*. While attempting to maneuver out of harm's way, Captain Warley's little ram lodged against the bank. As the *Mississippi* fired broadsides into her, the crew set a fuse to the magazine and dived into the water. A few minutes later, she drifted away from the bank and exploded, sending debris ripping through the riggings of the *Mississippi*. When the smoke cleared, the *Manassas* had simply disappeared.

Meanwhile, Admiral Farragut and his flagship were experiencing difficulty getting past the forts. Dozens of fire rafts floated downstream, the reflection from their flaming cotton bales giving the impression that the entire river was on fire. Attempting to dodge a raft, the *Hartford* became grounded under the guns of St. Philip. As the crew tried to dislodge the ship and its gunners continued to exchange fire with the forts, a small rebel tug named the *Mosher*, pushing a blazing raft, bore down on the *Hartford*. It shoved the raft against the warship and attempted to escape when a broadside sent the *Mosher* to the bottom of the river. The *Hartford* crew frantically fought the blaze caused by the raft as flames leaped up the mainmast. The men finally managed to subdue the fire and free the heavily damaged *Hartford*, which then fought its way past St. Philip and out of range of its guns.

At the Quarantine station, six miles above the forts, Captain Bailey sighted a Confederate camp. From the *Cayuga*, he sent a messenger ashore to demand its surrender. Confederate Colonel Ignatius Szymanski complied and ordered his three hundred men to stack their weapons. He had little choice for they hardly had enough ammunition to fire a single volley. Within the hour, Farragut arrived aboard his flagship. Surveying the scene, he sent a message for General Butler to bring troops to the location along a bayou that connected the Quarantine station with the Gulf. Since he did not have the time or means to secure the prisoners, Farragut paroled Szymanski and his troops and told them to return to New Orleans. Once out of sight of the gunboats, Szymanski, assuming that

New Orleans was doomed, marched his men north toward Camp Moore at Tangipahoa.

Farragut put his men to the task of burying the dead, caring for the wounded, and repairing his ships. One by one, his warships arrived, thirteen in all. Three vessels had been disabled. Although his fleet was heavily damaged, not a single ship was sunk. Total Union casualties were 39 dead, 149 wounded. The *Mississippi* suffered the greatest loss with 15 crewmen killed in its encounter with the *Manassas*. The *Cayuga* endured extensive damage, having sustained forty-two hits.

As Farragut's warships made their way past the forts and trailed the *Cayuga* up the river. Gun crews on some of the ships began firing indiscriminately into homes on the banks of the river. At one house, a girl came to the door to watch the ships go by. She was the daughter of the former United States ordnance sergeant at the river forts before they were seized by the Louisiana Militia. As the girl stood on the porch, waving to the ships, a shell struck the house, killing her.

* * *

NEW ORLEANS, APRIL 25—The sky was overcast and a light rain fell on New Orleans Friday morning as citizens emerging from their homes saw a huge column of black smoke rising above the shipyard across the river at Algiers. Word spread that Confederate soldiers were burning the ships to prevent them from falling into the hands of the enemy. That was the first indication to the people of New Orleans that the river defenses had been breached. Within minutes, flames leapt from stacks of cotton bales lining the waterfront. Warehouses caught fire as did ships anchored in the harbor. The giant alarm bell in the Christ Church tower began to toll—slowly at first, then wildly as word spread that the Yankees were coming.

They arrived at one o'clock, their warships dropping anchor along the levee in front of the city. Because of a rapid rise in the river, the guns of the ships sat nine feet above the level of the streets. New Orleans, built on a plain four feet below sea level, found itself literally under the guns of the fleet. All around the invading Yankees raged a chaotic scene. Fires were burning everywhere. Anything that might be of value to the Federals had been put to the torch, and a pall of black smoke covered the proud old city. Torrents of rain began to fall and still the fires roared. An Englishman reported: "People were amazed and could scarcely realize the awful fact, and ran hither and thither in speechless astonishment."

General Lovell did not attempt to defend the city, choosing instead to have his soldiers remove Confederate stores, weapons, and equipment. Trains of cargo wagons moved out of the city headed for Camp Moore. As the soldiers departed, some citizens began looting—government buildings at first and then private warehouses containing food. Broken sacks of rice and corn, and kegs of sugar and molasses soon littered the streets. Roads out of town became clogged with people, horses, carts, carriages, and wagons as many fled the city.

As Admiral Farragut watched, the hull of a huge ironclad vessel, flames leaping above it, came floating down the river. It was the *Mississippi*—a gunboat that had been under construction at the shipyard. Unable to move it, General Lovell had ordered it destroyed.

At two o'clock, Captain Bailey and Lieutenant George Perkins, went ashore and made their way through an angry crowd shouting obscenities, brandishing pistols, waving rebel flags, and cursing Abe Lincoln. The Union officers were spat upon and reviled with every step and greatly feared for their lives by the time they reached City Hall. There police held the crowd at bay while the two officers met with Mayor John Monroe and General Lovell. The general told Bailey he would not surrender but was removing his troops to save the city from a destructive battle. At three o'clock, Bailey and Perkins departed through the back door to avoid the angry crowd in front of City Hall. Even as they were escorted to their ship, Confederate troops boarded freight cars bound for Camp Moore. The Queen City of the South had fallen to the enemy without a struggle. It was a blow from which the Confederacy would not recover.

✶ ✶ ✶

BATON ROUGE, APRIL 27—As the carriage made its way up the River Road and approached Baton Rouge, Mimi Taylor was stunned by the destruction she witnessed. As far as she could see, columns of smoke from burning cotton and sugar rose to form an umbrella that blocked the sun. She had the children with her, and what belongings they could quickly gather before fleeing the plantation. The militiamen had shown up at Fashion the previous morning with news that New Orleans had fallen and instructions from the governor to burn all sugar stores and proceed to Baton Rouge. Mimi had summoned William and informed him that she and the children must leave. She told him to burn the sugar and look out for the well-being of the slaves.

At Baton Rouge, she discovered that the governor intended to move the state capital to Opelousas, some fifty miles to the west, and that she should proceed to that location. Accompanied by several protective state militiamen, they set out on the road to Opelousas, only to be caught up in a mass exodus. The road was clogged with vehicles ranging from fine carriages to heavy wagons filled with cotton and carts laden with hogsheads of sugar. Beside the road, families trudged with bundles of belongings on their shoulders. It was a nightmarish journey that would remain in her memory for years.

✶ ✶ ✶

When Governor Moore learned that New Orleans had fallen, he knew Baton Rouge could not be defended. As he prepared to evacuate the capital, he issued an order that all commodities that might fall into the hands of the enemy be burned. By the night of the twenty-seventh, fires lit the sky along the levees from New Orleans to Tensas Parish as tens of thousands of bales of cotton and hogsheads of sugar went up in flames. At Baton Rouge, flatboats piled high with cotton were soaked with alcohol, set on fire, and cut loose to float down the river. Many a planter and plantation owner stood on the levee that night and watched their fortunes go up in flames.

✶ ✶ ✶

WINNFIELD, APRIL 30—They came from the bottom of the manpower barrel: backwoods farmers who nursed crops from the poor dirt of the sand hills, open-range herders whose earmarked hogs and cattle ran wild in the forests, and grizzled trappers from the lowland bayou sloughs. Most of them were of Scots-Irish descent. They had arrived too late to claim the fertile farmlands that flanked North Louisiana's network of rivers, creeks, and bayous. Their destiny was to scratch a hardscrabble living from the hill country where the soil was prone to erode when it rained and turn to dust when it did not. Here a man worked from first light until dark just to survive.

These were men who stayed at home when the sons of the planters, shopkeepers, and politicians marched off to war to the tumult and cheers of patriotic fervor. To them, corn crops and curing pelts held more significance than war in Virginia. But by the end of April 1862, there were Yankee soldiers in Arkansas and Mississippi. Union gunboats were shelling Memphis. And when word reached Winn Parish that New Orleans had fallen, these hard-bitten men poured out of the woods, ready to fight for those hardscrabble hill farms.

Winn Parish was unique among its North Louisiana neighbors. A large parish with a small population, it sat isolated by dense forests and an intricate maze of creeks and bayous that ran through flats between steep hills. Only forty-six hundred people lived in the parish. There were few large planters and, thus, few slaves. Most of its citizens lived on remote farms hewn from the wilderness. They were reclusive by nature and fiercely independent. In fact, the Winn Parish governing body had refused to pledge allegiance to either the Confederacy or Union, designating their parish "The Free State of Winn." In January 1861, when its North Louisiana neighbors sent pro-secession delegates to the State Secession Convention, Winn Parish elected a co-operationist delegate by a vote of 507 to 88. But when secession came, Winn responded to the call for volunteers, quickly raising four full companies of infantry. The parish contributed no less than seven companies to the Confederacy before the war was over.

By April 1862, when Jefferson Davis signed a new conscription law and the governor sent out yet another urgent call for volunteers, few able-bodied men remained in North Louisiana, and there was only modest compliance with the conscription law in Winn Parish until news arrived that New Orleans had fallen. At that point the issue no longer was secession or cooperation, war or peace, or who was right or wrong. There was only one issue: The Yankees might have taken New Orleans but, come hell or high water, they would never take Winnfield.

Although the new draft law called for conscription of men between the ages of eighteen and thirty-five, many of those who converged on the courthouse at Winnfield were in their forties. Boys no more than fifteen showed up to raise their hands and swear they were eighteen. Many of them had never seen the inside of a schoolhouse. They came from two-room, dog-trot cabins at the outer bounds of civilization. Their education was limited to clearing new ground, tending livestock, and nursing enough food and forage from tired soil to get their families and livestock through the winter. They would not fight for Richmond, Jeff Davis, the governor, or the rich plantation owners in their fancy Delta houses. They would fight for the land and the women and the broods of barefoot children who inhabited those wilderness cabins. They and others like them filled the ranks of a ragtag army that would stand against the legions of the North, even then preparing to invade Louisiana.

* * *

Dusk was settling on the North Louisiana pine hills when Sheriff William Walker reined his mount west on the Harrisonburg Road. The horse, sensing that he was heading home, struck a brisk trot and Walker tugged the reins to keep him from breaking into a gallop. As much as he wanted to put some miles behind him before darkness set in, he did not want his horse to run himself out. This stretch of road was dangerous for anyone to be stranded after dark walking a winded horse—even the sheriff of Winn Parish.

Walker had spent several days riding the back roads, reminding potential slackers that they must comply with the draft laws. Instead of arresting violators, he urged them to go into Winnfield and sign up. Considering the independent nature of his constituents, he found it a more effective method than threats of arrest and impressment.

Although Walker's office exempted him from serving, he had resigned his position to sign up with the latest batch of recruits. The men had elected him captain of one of the companies. They were to report to Monroe within the week for assignment to a regiment. Upon his departure, his two deputies would keep the peace until the Parish police jury appointed a replacement. His decision to enlist was motivated by a simple reality. As a volunteer himself, he found it easier to tell a backwoods wife with a baby on her hip and another under her apron that her husband must go off to war.

Walker had a dual purpose in making this final swing through the southern part of the parish. A year earlier, a family from Alabama had disappeared on this stretch of road that once was a part of the old Natchez Trace. He had devoted a great deal of time to investigating the case. From the 1820s, outlaws had been preying on innocent travelers in this remote region—infamous cutthroats like Samuel Mason, the Copeland brothers and John Murrell. One by one they had been hunted down and imprisoned or hanged. Now Walker feared that yet another gang was operating in the area. Although he had no evidence, he did have a suspect. His name was Dan Kimbrell.

Kimbrell had a place on Nantachie Creek not far from the Trace. He lived there with his wife and three sons in a large old house that also served as a tavern and lodging place. Walker suspected it also might be a place to lure unwary travelers so they could be robbed and killed. Rumors circulated that Old Man Kimbrell had ridden with the Murrell gang. When Murrell was terrorizing the countryside, he tended to kill his victims, bury them deep in the wilderness, take their valuables, and send their horses and wagons to Texas to be sold. Walker suspected that something similar had happened to the family from Alabama, but lacked proof. The odds of finding a hidden burial site in the dense woods that covered these hills was not even worthy of calculation. As much as he hated to leave a potential murder case unsolved, someone else would have to keep an eye on the Kimbrells until he returned from the army.

* * *

RICHMOND, MAY 14—Major James Beard felt deeply disturbed by news that New Orleans had fallen. His immediate reaction was that he must return to Louisiana to defend his home and family. His military experience in Virginia had been less than he expected when he left Shreveport. For almost a year, he had been encamped in and around Yorktown. Except for a couple of minor skirmishes and a two-hour artillery bombardment on April 5, he had seen no real action. A timid attack by the Yankees following the bombardment hardly qualified as a battle.

Beard and his men had spent the winter drilling and building a line of fortifications along the Warwick River. As his battalion sat idle in camp, he was promoted to major and elevated to second in command of the unit. During those months of boredom, he spent a lot of time thinking about Kate and his daughter. Corinne was two years old now, and if Kate's letters were an indication, she was spoiled beyond redemption.

In early April, large numbers of Union troops landed on the peninsula. George McClellan soon had ninety thousand men in place in front of the Confederate breastworks. To oppose them, Major General John B. Magruder had only fifteen thousand troops. To confuse the Yankees, Magruder had his regiments march around in circles day and night with bugles blaring and drums pounding. The ruse worked. McClellan reported to Washington that he faced a large Confederate army at Yorktown and requested reinforcements before marching on Richmond.

In late April, General Joe Johnston ordered Magruder to retreat to Richmond where he intended to concentrate his forces in defense of the capital. As Johnston reorganized the Confederate Army, the 1st Louisiana Battalion ceased to exist and the men became part of the 1st Louisiana Infantry Regiment. Temporarily without an assignment, Beard requested a transfer back to Louisiana. On May 14, he received orders to report to Monroe, Louisiana, where he would serve as second in command in Lieutenant Colonel Jacob Shelly's 11th Louisiana Infantry Battalion. With mixed emotions Beard departed Richmond. He bid his Shreveport Greys a tearful good-bye, then boarded a train bound for Vicksburg. Within weeks, many of those men he had left behind would lie dead on bloody battlefields outside Richmond.

* * *

VICKSBURG, MAY 18—By the middle of May, David Farragut's warships, supported by just fifteen hundred infantry under the command of General Thomas Williams, had swept unopposed up the Mississippi River all the way to Vicksburg. On May 9, a landing party took possession of Baton Rouge without a shot being fired. Four days later, Union troops occupied Natchez. Farragut's juggernaut encountered no resistance until he reached the bluffs below Vicksburg on May 18. Williams sent a messenger ashore demanding surrender of the city, but Confederate Brigadier General Martin L. Smith refused. Farragut soon learned the reason for his resistance. Having sacrificed Baton Rouge and Natchez, the rebels were ready for the invaders at Vicksburg. Almost eight thousand troops had been withdrawn from Louisiana and Mississippi to defend the city. Ten large Columbiad cannons sat mounted on the high cliffs, positioned out of the range of Farragut's warships.

With only fifteen hundred troops at his disposal, General Williams could not possibly mount a land attack. He sent a message to Ben Butler in New Orleans stating his intention to return to Baton Rouge until he received reinforcements.

★ ★ ★ ★

8

★ ★ ★ ★

Stonewall's Swift Sword

SHENANDOAH VALLEY, VIRGINIA, MAY 23—Dick Taylor was not impressed by General Thomas Jackson and not happy at being assigned to his command. The last thing he wanted was to be stuck in the Shenandoah Valley with the man Ewell called "Tom Fool" while the real fighting took place around Richmond. Taylor felt further distress when he received orders detaching his brigade from Ewell's division with instructions to join Jackson's forces near New Market.

In spite of his displeasure, Taylor's arrival at New Market appeared worthy of a theatrical production. The men's rigid training was evident as the 1st Brigade marched into the valley where Jackson's ragged and combat-weary veterans camped. The old uniforms in their various shades of gray and the Zouave outfits that Taylor so detested had been replaced by brand-new uniforms, adorned with spotless white gaiters and leggings. The men marched briskly, in tight rows, in step with the lively music of the regimental bands. The mounted officers' uniforms were trimmed with gold braid and lace, their hats topped with tassels and plumes. Colorful flags with the pelican symbol floated above a sea of three thousand polished rifles and bayonets gleaming in the sunlight. Jackson's Virginians were awestruck by the spectacle. One wrote, "It was the most picturesque and inspiring martial sight that came under my eyes during four years of service."

Asked for Jackson's whereabouts, a Virginian pointed Taylor toward a lone figure sitting on a rail fence watching the show. As Taylor approached the man the first thing he noticed were the cavalry boots. They were wrinkled, unpolished, and each large enough, in Taylor's estimation, to accommodate two ordinary feet. The man who wore them was large and gangly in appearance. He wore a badly faded, old-style kepi cap with a black visor and a frayed army coat that had begun to turn brown from exposure to the sun. There was not a man in Taylor's brigade who was not better dressed than the hero of Manassas. Taylor snapped a salute and announced his name and rank.

"How far have you marched today?" Jackson asked.

"Twenty-six miles," Taylor said.

"You don't seem to have stragglers."

"I never allow stragglers," Taylor said.

"Then you must teach my people," Jackson said, looking up at him. "They straggle badly."

What Taylor did not realize was that he was at New Market precisely because his troops did not straggle. Stonewall Jackson had plans for a fast marching, well-disciplined brigade—and Taylor's spit-and-polish troops precisely fit his needs.

* * *

Jackson's first order sent the brigade on a circuitous march that made absolutely no sense to Taylor until he emerged from a tree line on a ridge and looked down upon a Federal encampment at the little town of Front Royal. During the mystery march, Taylor had commented to his grumbling colonels that Jackson obviously wanted them to enjoy "the full scenic beauty of the entire valley." In spite of the jest, as he overlooked Front Royal, the moment seemed to him "surprisingly beautiful."

In the distance the Allegheny Mountains rose majestically above the valley. To his left, Mount Massanutten soared above him, sloping down to where the forks of the Shenandoah River met about a mile beyond the town. On a plain between the forks of the river and the town, row after row of white tents housed the enemy. From the heights beyond the river, a battery of Yankee artillery looked down on two wagon bridges crossing the twin forks of the stream. To Taylor's left, a railroad bridge spanned the river.

A Jackson courier arrived with orders for Taylor to send Wheat's Tigers and a Maryland regiment assigned to him around to the east side of the town to attack from that direction. They were to be backed by the 6th Louisiana Infantry. Taylor was to take his three remaining regiments to the left and be ready to charge the enemy from the west. With the Marylanders, Taylor's force totaled some thirty-six hundred men, giving him a three-to-one advantage over the Union force at Front Royal. Jackson's Virginians, exhausted by recent fighting and long marches, remained several miles to the rear.

Taylor moved the 7th, 8th, and 9th regiments down the hillside and formed them in attack lines facing the town. A mile down the river, he spotted the movement of Federal troops in the hills on the opposite bank and decided to ride down the slope for a better view. While he scanned the enemy position with his field glasses, his horse seized the opportunity to get a drink of water. By the time Taylor realized what was happening, the animal was standing on the edge of the river with its muzzle in the water. Taylor heard a plunking sound and felt a spray of water beside him, followed by the distant report of a rifle. Suddenly, the water came alive with rifle balls fired by unseen Yankees in the hills beyond the river. His first impulse was to flee back toward his lines and out of range. He glanced over his shoulder at his men, standing in ranks, watching him. The fact that the Yankees seemed incapable of hitting anything as large as a horse emboldened him. He steeled himself, took a puff on his cigar, and waited for the horse to drink its fill as rifle balls whined about him. "A provident camel, on the eve of a desert journey, would not have laid in a greater supply of water than did my thoughtless beast," he wrote of the incident. Once satisfied, the horse raised its head, looked around, and lumbered back up the riverbank. As Taylor rode up the hillside, casually puffing his cigar, a loud cheer went up from his men and echoed down the valley.

The only person who did not appear impressed by the dramatics was Stonewall Jackson, who had just arrived on the scene. "Shall we attack, sir?" Taylor inquired. The response was a simple nod.

Under sporadic artillery fire, Taylor led his men double-quick down the slope, through a series of fields and thickets and into Front Royal. A brief, disorganized firefight endangered the citizens of the town and their habitations more than it did the participants. However, two or three companies of Yankees scurried out the other side of town where they ran into a volley from Major Wheat's battalion as it charged the Federal encampment. Fleeing across the south fork bridge, the Federals came under the umbrella of their artillery but Taylor's men continued to pursue them. Sitting on his horse on an elevation where he could survey the action, Taylor was surprised when Jackson suddenly appeared beside him.

"Your men are looting," he said.

Taylor turned his attention to the Federal encampment where Wheat's Tigers had paused to overturn tents. Clothing and bedding flew in the air as the Tigers searched for more valuable booty—like whiskey flasks. Taylor loosed an outburst and dispatched a messenger with orders for Major Wheat to immediately resume his pursuit of the enemy.

"Oh for my artillery now," Jackson said, more to himself than to Taylor. "What an opportunity for artillery." But his artillery was far to the rear.

Through his glasses, Taylor saw Federal troops setting fire to the bridge spanning the north fork of the river. If it burned before his troops crossed it, the Federal force would escape. Jackson spotted the flames at the same instant and became visibly agitated. Front Royal was only the first part of a grand scheme to surprise and destroy the bulk of General Nathaniel Banks's Union army at Strasburg before marching on Winchester. The plan existed only in Jackson's mind, as he never divulged his intentions to subordinate or superior until it was time to act. His scheme was to capture the force at Front Royal, distract Banks with cavalry, and descend on the Union Army at Strasburg with all his infantry, cavalry, and artillery. In coordination with the attack on Front Royal, Jackson had sent Colonel Thomas Flournoy's cavalry to cut the telegraph lines to Strasburg. Now he faced the prospect that a single burning bridge might upset all of his plans.

"I will try to get the men across the bridge before it burns," Taylor offered.

Jackson nodded and Taylor spurred his horse through exploding artillery rounds and toward Wheat's battalion. "The bridge!" he shouted to Wheat. "Put the men across it and give the enemy no relief."

Wheat reined his mount about and circled his sword above his head, and a cheer went up from the Tigers. The major rode toward the bridge at a full gallop. A Maryland soldier who witnessed the charge later wrote: "I shall never forget the style in which Wheat's Battalion passed us. He [the massive Wheat] was riding full gallop, yelling at the top of his voice . . . the men following after—all running—all yelling—all looking like fight." Wheat disappeared into the billowing black smoke enveloping the bridge. His troops followed, screaming like demons. Taylor sent Colonel Henry Kelly's Cajuns from the 8th Regiment after them. Kelly paused long enough to dispatch one company into the swift currents of the river to fight the flames, then ordered the remainder of his men across the bridge. The Frenchmen assigned firefighting duties plunged into the water and began scaling the pilings with amazing agility. From the edge of the river, their companions formed brigades, handing up water in anything that would hold it, including canteens and hats. Those on the pilings dashed it into the flames. Two of Kelly's men who ventured too far from shore were swept away by the current and drowned.

Taylor urged his horse onto the bridge even as one side collapsed, sending several men plunging into the river. His troops reeled backward. However, one side of the bridge remained intact and, at his urging, the men continued their crossing in single file. Fire scorched them as they dashed through the flames. Some paused to fling burning timbers from their path into the river. As Taylor coaxed his horse along the narrow pathway, through searing heat and thick smoke, he became aware that Wheat's men had flushed the Yankees from their position and cut off part of the enemy force. However, several hundred Federals could be seen escaping along the Valley road.

"Oh for my cavalry! Where is the cavalry?" came a high-pitched voice.

Taylor was stunned by the sudden appearance of Jackson at his side and marveled at how he had maneuvered across the bridge when it was choked with men. Jackson was mounted on the awkward appearing horse he always rode—an animal that Taylor concluded would have been more comfortable in front of a plow than under a cavalry saddle. He noticed that his commander's old greatcoat showed evidence of exposure to the flames and smoke. "It decidedly freshened up his uniform," Taylor later observed.

As if in answer to Jackson's plea, or perhaps summoned forth by his will, Colonel Flournoy and his cavalry appeared. Without hesitating, Jackson sent his horse in a dead run after the fleeing Union soldiers, and Flournoy's 250 horsemen fell in behind him. Taylor marveled at the surprising speed exhibited by Jackson's graceless mount as it led the cavalry in pursuit of the enemy. He also was surprised to see Major Aaron Davis, his own quartermaster officer, riding like a madman at the heels of Stonewall's steed.

"What in the name of hell is my quartermaster doing leading a cavalry charge?" Taylor yelled to no one in particular.

Jackson and the cavalry caught up with the Federals near Cedarville where the Yankees formed ranks and put up a surprisingly spirited fight. While part of Flournoy's force feinted a charge into the muzzles of several hundred Yankee muskets, the remainder of his men circled behind the enemy, forcing the exhausted Federals to surrender.

Even the stoic Jackson was pleased. By day's end, he had taken almost a thousand prisoners, a battery of rifled artillery, a large number of rifles, ammunition, and supplies. In the process, he had lost less than a hundred men. One of the casualties was Taylor's quartermaster, shot from the saddle while charging the Union line at Cedarville. "The best damn quartermaster in the army," in Taylor's estimation, was buried near where he fell. Because of Davis's ability to find canned delicacies, dried fruit, fresh vegetables, and fat beef yearlings where none seemed to exist, Taylor's brigade had enjoyed a reputation as the best fed in the army. Jealous quartermasters from other units insisted that if they had a band of thieves like the Tiger Rifles foraging for them they might have been equally well supplied. Davis was popular with the troops, and a large crowd gathered at the gravesite to hear Taylor say a few appropriate words. The major's death visibly upset

Taylor for days. "Have you ever heard of another quartermaster being killed in battle?" he lamented to his old friend, General Ewell. The general agreed that it was most unusual.

⭑ ⭑ ⭑

MIDDLETOWN, VIRGINIA, MAY 24—Upon reaching the crest of the ridge west of Middletown that afternoon, Taylor was in awe of the scene before him. No more than a thousand yards below, strung out along the Valley Pike as far as he could see, was a disorganized parade of men and wagons. Whether by luck or genius Taylor could not be certain, but Stonewall Jackson had stumbled upon General Banks's supply train.

Banks was caught in the process of concentrating his troops by moving some six thousand men from Strasburg to Winchester that morning. Jackson planned to cut him off and defeat him at Middletown. Unknown to Jackson, Banks's army already had passed Middletown by the time the Confederates arrived. What appeared before them was the supply train trailing the Union army. Taylor could not imagine a more inviting target. Soldiers, oblivious to danger, intermingled with slow-moving military wagons, sutlers' carts, livestock, and hundreds of black refugees. The wagons, laden with spoils from the surrounding countryside, rumbled along in single file, trapped between waist-high stone fences on both sides of the road.

Jackson did not try to conceal his excitement. "Bring up your troops, sir," he instructed Taylor, then turned a courier, "and bring up the artillery."

The only troops immediately available to Taylor were some 350 members of Wheat's Tigers, who had managed to stay at the heels of Ashby's cavalry during the long march from Front Royal. The remainder of his brigade was on the Middletown Road more than a mile away. Taylor instructed Wheat to form a battle line, then rode quickly to the rear to bring up the remainder of his men. Even as he rode he heard artillery open up on the Federals. In his report, Jackson described what happened next:

"In a few moments, the turnpike, which had just before teemed with life, presented a most appalling spectacle of carnage and destruction. The road was literally obstructed with the mingled and confused mass of struggling and dying horses and men."

Even as Ashby's cavalry and Wheat's screaming Tigers swept down the hillside, Taylor led the 9th Louisiana into the village, which had become clogged with confused teamsters and Union soldiers. Major Robert Dabney remembered the scene as the Louisianans arrived: "General Taylor, throwing his advance regiment into line, advanced at a double quick to the center of the village, his men cheering and pouring a terrific volley into the confused mass which filled the street."

Abandoning wagons and weapons, the enemy fled into the countryside. Taylor sent his brigade in pursuit of the Federals and looked around for the Tigers.

"The gentle Tigers were looting right merrily, diving in and out of wagons with the activity of rabbits in a warren," he wrote, "but this occupation was abandoned on my appearance and, in a moment, they were in line, looking as solemn and virtuous as deacons at a funeral."

Taylor's troops quickly rounded up two hundred prisoners, including several Yankee cavalrymen. When Taylor ordered them to dismount he was puzzled that the horsemen did not immediately comply. He realized then that they were strapped to their saddles. "Hailing from New England where horsemanship was an unknown art . . . some of the riders [had to be] given time to unbuckle."

When word came to Taylor that a large force of the enemy had drawn up in a battle line west of Middletown, he formed his men into skirmish lines. Moving toward the enemy, the brigade came under artillery fire and a single shot landed in the ranks, felling several of his men. To determine the strength and deployment of the Federal force, Taylor rode ahead of his troops. He was studying the enemy position when a shell exploded directly beneath his horse, tearing away part of the saddle blanket and covering animal and rider with dirt. "To my amazement, neither man nor horse received a scratch," he wrote. Apparently, the trajectory of the shell forced the blast beyond the horse and rider. Confederate artillery quickly unlimbered and drove the Union soldiers from their position. Several wagons went tumbling as artillery shells fell among the fleeing Federals. Pursuing the enemy, Taylor's men found row upon row of knapsacks where whole companies had abandoned them.

With no enemy before him, Taylor marched his men back through Middletown. Rain had begun to fall when he caught up with Jackson's regiments near Newtown. He found Stonewall's Virginians locked in battle with the rear elements of Banks's main army. Darkness had fallen when Taylor spotted Jackson at the head of his drenched troops, personally directing the action in a hotly contested fight. With bullets whizzing and shells exploding around him, Jackson shouted, "Charge them! Charge them!"

"I quite remember thinking at the time that Jackson was invulnerable, and that persons near him shared that quality," Taylor later wrote. He stayed at Jackson's side through the night as the "Army of the Valley" slogged through ankle-deep mud while fighting its way, yard by yard, toward Winchester. It was dangerous work as the Yankee rear guard established a pattern of ambush and retreat, and occasionally blanketed the road with artillery barrages. It was work for cavalry, but Jackson had no cavalry. Ashby's men were far to the rear, looting the wagons left in the wake of the day's fighting. Most of them had become so drunk on Yankee whiskey they openly defied their commanders. A dismayed Ashby alternately threatened and begged them to pursue the enemy, but to no avail as they busily loaded loot onto horses to take home to their families. Undaunted, Jackson used Taylor's foot soldiers as his cavalry, pushing them mercilessly through torrents of rain and mud into fire from an enemy they often could not see. Taylor's only consolation was that the enemy, in retreat, must be even more miserable.

At 2 A.M., having pushed to within two miles of Winchester, Jackson called a halt to the action. The men were falling, not from enemy fire, but from the exhaustion of ten hours of almost continuous marching and fighting. They slept sprawled in the mud or sitting in the muck, heads resting on knees. One who did not sleep was Jackson. He desperately wanted to plant his cannon on the high ground outside Winchester before daylight. Now he hoped that the elements thwarting his plans also prevented Banks from occupying those hills.

★ ★ ★

WINCHESTER, VIRGINIA, MAY 25—As the morning sun burned fog from the flats between the ridges south of Winchester, Jackson surveyed the enemy's positions. He was surprised to discover that Banks had not occupied the high ground, choosing instead to deploy his troops on either side of the turnpike on the outskirts of Winchester, as if he intended to defend the town at the risk of exposing his army.

A sudden artillery barrage to his right told Jackson that Ewell was beginning an attack on the Union left flank. He promptly ordered Brigadier General Charles Winder and his Stonewall brigade against the enemy's right flank. Almost immediately, Winder's troops found themselves pinned down by a storm of artillery and rifle fire from a ridge on the west side of the turnpike. Winder asked for reinforcements and Jackson sent word back to him: "I will send you Taylor."

Jackson had planned to hold Taylor's exhausted troops in reserve. But Taylor already had heard that his troops were needed at the front. Riding to the rear, Jackson found the brigade moving forward in battle formation. Spotting Taylor, Jackson rode up to him and pointed toward the ridge. "You must carry it," was all he said.

Surveying the position, Taylor decided to attack up a long, sloping hillside against the enemy's extreme right flank. He was moving his men into position at the foot of the hill when the Federals directed a galling artillery fire toward the Louisianans. Most of the rounds fell short, but the intensity of the fire caused the men in the ranks to flinch and duck. Taylor was furious at the breach of discipline in front of Jackson. Forgetting his commander's religious convictions, he unleashed a verbal barrage at the men—one that included some vintage Taylor cursing. "What the hell are you men dodging for?" he shouted. "If there is any more of it, I will halt you here under this fire for an hour." Backs stiffened and the men straightened their lines even as the exploding shells showered them with dirt.

Taylor felt Jackson's hand touch his shoulder. He turned, expecting a rebuke for his careless outburst. Instead, he saw a hint of mischief in Jackson's eyes. "I am afraid you are a wicked fellow," he said. With that, Jackson reined his horse about and rode to a nearby rise to watch the action. The respectful reproach was the nearest thing to praise Taylor would ever receive from his commander.

Taylor ordered colors to the front. Regimental banners and pelican flags unfurled in the breeze as the ranks moved up the hillside, slowly at first, then at double-quick. "That charge of Taylor's was the grandest I saw during the entire war," a Virginia private wrote. Major Dabney provided a vivid account of the action.

The enemy poured grape and musketry into Taylor's line as soon as it came in sight. General Taylor rode in front of his brigade, drawn sword in hand, occasionally turning his horse, at other times merely turning in his saddle to see that his line was up. They marched up the hill in perfect order, not firing a shot. About halfway to the Yankees, in a loud and commanding voice that I am sure the Yankees heard, he gave the order to charge.

A yell went up from the rebels and the blue-clad ranks broke with the first volley. The Stonewall brigade joined the Louisianans in pursuit of thousands of Yankees fleeing down the hillside into the streets of Winchester.

"The battle is won!" Jackson shouted from his hilltop. Sweeping off his battered kepi and waving it over his head, he rode after the fleeing Federals whooping and hollering like a schoolboy. Stunned by the suddenness of the defeat, General Banks tried to rally his retreating troops. Beyond the town, he waved his arms, trying to halt a Wisconsin regiment. "Stop, men!" he yelled. "Don't you love your country?" A voice rose from the ranks: "Yes, by God, and I'm trying to get back to it as fast as I can!"

From Port Royal to Winchester, Banks lost thirty-five hundred troops, killed, wounded, and captured—one-third of his army. Taking advantage of Banks's bad judgment at Winchester, Jackson routed his army, taking almost two thousand prisoners and driving the remainder of his troops across the Potomac River into Pennsylvania. He might have cut off and captured Banks's entire command if Ashby's cavalry had been at the front instead of looting wagons in the rear.

* * *

With little but open countryside and the Potomac River between Jackson and Washington, D.C., President Lincoln diverted twenty thousand men and one hundred heavy guns under Irvin McDowell to meet the threat of a possible attack on the capital. General Fremont, with fifteen thousand men, was ordered from West Virginia to the Shenandoah Valley and General Shields, with ten thousand troops, was sent to cut off the Valley Pike behind Jackson. Reinforcements were rushed to Banks. For four days, Washington, D.C., waited in panic for the expected Confederate invasion. Lincoln sometimes visited the fortifications on the outskirts of the city and gazed toward the Potomac, half expecting to see Jackson descending on him. No one knew where Stonewall's army was, its strength, or where it might strike next. With less than seventeen thousand men, he had tied up three Union armies totaling fifty thousand troops and paralyzed another one hundred thousand under George McClellan outside Richmond.

On June 1, with his army depleted to less than sixteen thousand, Jackson departed Winchester, not to attack Washington, but to escape back down the Shenandoah Valley with the fruits of victory, including vast stores of food, blankets, equipment, arms, and ammunition. Pursued by three armies trying to cut him off, he paused to bloody the noses of Fremont and Shields at Mt. Carmel, Harrisonburg, and Cross Keys before defeating Fremont in a vicious battle at Port Republic. Finally, with three Union armies at bay in the valley, he slipped away to join Confederate forces defending Richmond.

A Georgia private who saw Taylor's brigade on the march from the Valley to Richmond inspected the cannons the Louisianans had captured in the fighting at Port Republic and wrote: "The bullet marks and blood-splattered guns showed the nature of the fighting at the hands of the Louisiana Tigers." He noted that their horses, wagons, and equipment looked used up. "But the soldiers—how lean and ragged, yet how game and enthusiastic. And when they stood in line under their tattered colors, their regiments were not larger than companies."

From Front Royal to Port Republic, Taylor's men marched 225 miles in twenty-one days, fought in three major battles, four actions, and numerous skirmishes, and preyed on Union supply trains and depots. In almost every engagement, Taylor and his Louisianans were first into the fight. Because of their marching ability and disregard for enemy fire, they became Stonewall's terrible swift sword. Taylor's own swift sword was Rob Wheat's Louisiana Tigers Battalion. When the Tigers were not looting a fallen enemy, they led the charges and held the rear guard. In the famous Valley Campaign, Taylor's Louisiana brigade suffered more casualties than any other in Jackson's army. Jackson paid the Louisianans the highest of compliments when he called them "my iron brigade." In Civil War lore, they remain "Stonewall's Iron Brigade."

★ ★ ★

BATON ROUGE, MAY 28—Short on rations and unable to contend with the cannons on the bluffs at Vicksburg, Farragut decided to return to Baton Rouge with Williams's troops. He left six gunboats at Vicksburg and went back down the river with the *Hartford* and *Kennebec*, accompanied by transports carrying the infantry.

Before Baton Rouge was secured, James B. Kimball, chief engineer on the *Hartford*, dumped his dirty laundry into a rowboat and, accompanied by four of his men, began rowing to shore to find a washwoman. Shotgun blasts from several partisan rangers hiding on the riverbank greeted them, wounding Kimball and two of the soldiers. The others rowed frantically back to the *Hartford* and informed Farragut of the ambush. The admiral ordered the gunners on the *Hartford* and *Kennebec* to open fire—not on the offending rangers but on the city.

Shells screamed in the air, exploding and crumbling storefronts. Citizens panicked, running through the streets away from the waterfront. Others sought shelter in backyard storm cellars. When the shelling finally ceased, remarkably there were only six casualties—three dead and three injured—all women and children. The city was a shambles, especially the buildings along the waterfront. Three out of four structures in Baton Rouge had been damaged. The elegant old Roman Catholic church sustained heavy damage, as did the Harvey House Hotel. The stately State Capital Building was pocked with scores of shot holes.

When the firing stopped, a contingent of citizens rowed out to the *Hartford* and pleaded with Admiral Farragut not to destroy the city. They explained that those who fired on the Union rowboat were guerrillas over whom they had no control. Farragut responded by sending General Williams and his troops ashore to "protect" the city against the guerrillas. Williams did so by proclaiming martial law and prohibiting anyone to leave or enter the city without a written pass.

★ ★ ★ ★

9

★ ★ ★ ★

In the Jaws of the Beast

NEW ORLEANS, JUNE 20—The man they called "The Beast" fit the image conjured by his nickname. Benjamin Butler had a large head that seemed out of proportion with his body and a face unblessed by classic features. Butler was cockeyed, prompting his enemies to say he had a good eye and an evil one. The eyes looked out from beneath drooping lids in a way that unnerved those meeting him for the first time, and a large lump beside the "evil eye" distorted his features. He smiled frequently, even when angry. Nervous by nature and brusque in manner, he was an autocrat by training and instinct. And, even when he tried to be charming, one had the impression that behind that smile lurked sinister motives.

Butler arrived in New Orleans with the intention of becoming a benevolent ruler. Within weeks he had emerged as an unashamed despot. He blamed New Orleans, not himself, for the transformation. Because of its conglomeration of cultures, the city was a many-headed hydra that could be controlled by the sword but not subdued. He was defied at every turn and the more people he imprisoned, the more defiant the citizenry became.

Upon assuming control of the city, Butler declared martial law. He set up a military court system, placed the city's newspapers under strict censorship, and ordered citizens to renounce their loyalty to the Confederacy and renew allegiance to the United States. He began seizing the homes and property from families of those serving in the Confederate military. The seizures quickly spread to anyone suspected of Southern sympathies. Those who resisted were beaten into submission with rifle butts.

When it came to the looting of confiscated homes, Butler allowed no competition. His troops were forbidden to engage in the practice and those who disobeyed the order were court-martialed or imprisoned. His own collection of silverware and other valuables from the city's finer homes soon earned him the nickname "Spoons" Butler.

He had church services monitored to be sure ministers did not express sympathy for the Southern cause in their sermons. Violators were arrested and their churches closed. Butler ordered the city's clergymen to conduct special services to pray for President Lincoln and other officials of the United States government, including himself. Ministers who refused were arrested, put in irons, hustled aboard ships, and sent to northern prisons. Butler closed the schools and requested that abolitionist friends back in Massachusetts send him teachers and Northern textbooks so that the children of New Orleans might be properly educated.

His heavy hand fell especially hard on the banks and their depositors. He forbid the circulation of Confederate bonds and notes and refused to allow depositors to retrieve their funds from the banks. Only United States Treasury notes or gold and silver could be used as legal tender. Many of the city's wealthy became paupers overnight. Although most of the banks were quickly bankrupted, Butler ordered them to remain open.

With the descent of fifteen thousand troops on New Orleans, food supplies, already scarce, became critical. On May 9, President Lincoln lifted the blockade against New Orleans, allowing the importation of food. Butler used the food supplies as leverage to force compliance with his edicts. Many families openly sympathetic to the South or known to have members serving in the Confederate Army were denied food. George Denison, the Federal customs collector, wrote to his mother: "Thousands in this city are almost starving for food and well dressed men and women beg bread from Uncle Sam's boys to keep themselves and children from starving."

Shop owners were forced to keep their places of business open, even at the expense of going bankrupt. Soldiers frequently "purchased" items without paying for them. Butler established The Relief Commission, ostensibly to provide food for the needy. Millions of dollars were extorted from local businessmen to fund the relief effort and millions disappeared in a maze of corruption presided over by Butler's brother, Andrew.

Even the assets of the foreign consuls of the city did not escape Butler's clutches. He seized $716,196 from the French consulate, claiming it was money the Confederate government had paid for supplies purchased from France. He seized the Netherlands' consulate and placed it under guard, charging its diplomats with hiding Confederate assets. Butler ordered the seizure of the Prussian ship *Essex* and removed gold bullion from it, claiming it belonged to the Confederate government. More than three thousand hogsheads of sugar scheduled for export were taken from British, Greek, and French citizens. The homes of foreign citizens suspected of being sympathetic to the Confederacy were raided. When British Counsel George Coppell protested, Butler placed him under house guard for lack of cooperation. Protests from foreign governments flooded Washington and Butler was ordered to return seized assets and stop the harassment of foreign residents. By then, many of those assets had simply disappeared.

Of all citizens resistant to the occupying force, the women of New Orleans were the most defiant. Many of them deliberately tried to get arrested by insulting and even spitting on Yankee soldiers. Their intent was to raise the ire of the men of New Orleans, which included hundreds of paroled Confederate soldiers, in the hope of inciting a rebellion. Butler responded on May 15 by issuing his infamous General Order No. 28:

> As the officers and soldiers of the United States have been subjected to repeated insults from the women (calling themselves ladies) of New Orleans, in return for the most scrupulous noninterference and courtesy on our part, it is ordered that hereafter

when any female shall, by word, gesture or movement, insult or show contempt for any officer or soldier of the United States, she shall be regarded and held liable to be treated as a woman of the town plying her avocation.

The order, which effectively reduced the city's women to be treated as harlots by Union soldiers, drew immediate protests from Richmond. From Texas to Virginia a new wave of Confederate volunteers emerged, anxious to fight for the honor of Southern womanhood. When Mayor Monroe confronted Butler over the "women's order," Butler issued the following statement: "John T. Monroe, late mayor of the city of New Orleans, is relieved from all responsibility for the peace of the city, and is suspended from the exercise of any functions, and committed to [prison at] Fort Jackson without further orders."

Sent to Fort Jackson with the mayor were Police Chief John McClellan and Judge Kennedy. Rather than sign an oath of allegiance to the United States, members of the city council resigned en masse. A committee of Union men, including speculators and commodities brokers who accompanied Butler to New Orleans, was named to run the city. Fort Jackson soon overflowed with political prisoners, making it necessary to open a second prison at Fort Burton and a third on Ship Island.

By the summer of 1862, protests from outraged government officials and individuals from New Orleans and around the world flooded Lincoln's desk. The president had had enough. He had wanted to pacify the people of New Orleans and bring Louisiana back into the Union—not subjugate its citizens and inspire resistance. And, considering all of the headaches created by the Trent Affair, the last thing Lincoln wanted was to further antagonize the British. He sent Reverdy Johnson to New Orleans to investigate charges against Butler by the foreign consuls. He also sent emissaries to set up a judicial system to replace the military courts that had become little more than the executioners of Butler's edicts. As a result of Johnson's investigations, all assets and materials seized from consulates and foreign citizens were returned and British Consul Coppell was reinstated. Butler protested, pointing out that some Southern sympathizers had lived in New Orleans for twenty or thirty years, yet still claimed French and British citizenship—including people who had never been to France or England. In defiance of Johnson, Butler issued an order stating that anyone who had resided in New Orleans for five years was a citizen of the United States and must sign an oath of allegiance. Washington promptly overturned the order.

A second army descended on New Orleans with Butler—one made up of brokers and speculators anxious to turn a profit by shipping contraband cotton, sugar, and salt to Northern ports. Some came with written grants signed by Lincoln and Stanton, permitting them to engage in such commerce. Butler had a degree of control over such activities in New Orleans but, as his troops moved into the countryside and began seizing contraband commodities, disorder and corruption prevailed. To regulate the traffic in contraband goods, Butler called on the organizational talents of the most corrupt speculator of them all—his brother, Andrew. By late summer of 1862, not even a grain of sugar moved through the port at New Orleans without the approval of Andrew Butler— and nothing moved without paying for the privilege.

✶ ✶ ✶

MONROE, LOUISIANA, JUNE 20—Upon his arrival at Monroe, Major James Beard found himself in the capital of military disorganization. Raw recruits and soldiers filled the streets, and one was hard pressed to distinguish between them. As a result of recent recruiting, three thousand men camped in and around the town, most of them waiting to be formed into regiments. Reporting to Colonel Shelly, Beard was introduced to the Louisiana 13th Battalion. It consisted of six companies totaling 580 men. Unlike the units in Virginia, the uniforms varied, as were the weapons, and there was an obvious absence of discipline in the ranks. Beard was surprised to learn that this was considered the best unit in the Monroe district.

Two new regiments were being formed at Monroe—the 28th and the 31st. The 28th was under the command of Colonel Henry Gray who, like Beard, had been detached from duty in Virginia and sent back to Louisiana. His second in command was a young lieutenant colonel from Winn Parish named William Walker. Colonel Charles Morrison commanded the 31st. A cavalry company under Captain R. G. Harper and a four-gun battery of light artillery rounded out the military force at Monroe. Among the field officers at Monroe, only Beard had combat experience, and that was limited. Except for a few companies of militia and partisan rangers in South Louisiana, this was the army being assembled to defend Louisiana.

Presiding over the confusion at Monroe was Brigadier General Albert G. Blanchard, a man incapable of organizing the distribution of food and equipment, much less a battle plan. Before the war ended, he would join a long list of incompetent generals appointed by Jefferson Davis.

✶ ✶ ✶

VIENNA, LOUISIANA, JUNE 25—To detach himself and his men from the growing confusion at Monroe, and the ready availability of whiskey there, Colonel Gray marched his regiment thirty-five miles west to the little town of Vienna and set up a training camp well away from the influences of the city. Having worked with Mississippi militias as a civilian volunteer for the Confederate Army, Gray was a proficient drillmaster. More important to the task ahead, he proved to be a leader—trusted and respected by his men. The colonel had a total disdain for personal display. He wore civilian clothes, as did most of his men. Although he had a uniform, it was devoid of braid or insignia indicating his rank. His top aide was Lieutenant Colonel William Walker—the former sheriff whose easy manner made him popular with the men.

Gray arrived at Vienna with ten companies totaling 902 men—most of them farmers and herders from the sand hills of North Central Louisiana. More than fifty were over the age of thirty-five, and several of those in their forties. About 150 were still in their teens—some, like Fred Hood of Jackson Parish, as young as fifteen.

Gray drilled them relentlessly beneath a blistering summer sun. Following long marches that left them drained of energy, he ordered the columns to form quickly into battle lines. The men responded well to Gray's regimen. They were hard men, tempered to toughness by hard lives. No exercise devised by the colonel could exceed the physical demands of plowing stump-filled new ground.

The men had no weapons at Vienna. They drilled with picket fence slats and tree branches simulating rifles. The more artistic used whittling knives to create remarkable replicas of rifles. There was no firing practice because they had no ammunition for the few muskets at the camp.

Typical of the recruits was Private Joseph Benjamin Hammonds, who owned a farm in Claiborne Parish near the Arkansas line. He was a thirty-one-year-old father of three small children, and his wife was pregnant with a fourth. He had just put in a crop that spring and at that time had no intention of joining the army. But on April 13, he went to church in the little town of Lisbon where Marcus Cheatham was holding a rally to recruit men for a company. Inspired by Cheatham's rhetoric and caught up in the excitement of the moment, Hammonds signed on, as did several of his neighbors. Mrs. Hammonds, upset by the decision, relented when Cheatham gave her his personal assurance that he would keep a watchful eye out for the well-being of her husband. At Monroe, the Claiborne Parish boys became Company D in the 28th Louisiana Infantry Regiment. They called their company the Claiborne Invincibles and elected Marcus Cheatham their captain.

* * *

ASHLAND, VIRGINIA, JUNE 27—Dick Taylor awakened that afternoon to the distant rumble of artillery. He was lying on a pallet on the floor of an abandoned farmhouse. He tried to sit up but was overcome by pain and a spinning sensation in his head. "Tom!" he called. "Sit me up and bring me a cup of strong coffee." Although in a state of near delirium, he realized that his men were in a great battle and he was not with them. The struggle for Richmond raged within earshot and he was lying on a pallet on the floor of an empty house in Ashland, unable even to sit up by himself. With Tom supporting him, he drank his coffee. "Bring the ambulance around," he said. "I must get to the fight." Tom gave him a strange look. His master surely was out of his mind this time. But Tom went out to find the ambulance driver.

The Valley Campaign had become legend. The genius of Stonewall Jackson was being compared to that of Napoleon, but the campaign had taken its toll on Dick Taylor. The day and night marches, the stress of almost daily combat, and sleeping on the ground in near-freezing nighttime temperatures had resulted in a severe case of influenza that sapped his strength and aggravated his arthritis.

After the battle at Port Republic, Taylor took leave to go to Richmond and check on his family back in Louisiana. At the War Department, he found several letters from Mimi, Governor Moore, and Duncan Kenner. He learned that Mimi and the children had fled to Baton Rouge and then to Opelousas with the governor. They were living with friends of the governor at a plantation on the Atchafalaya River near the little town of Washington. From Kenner, he learned that Fashion Plantation had become a campsite for Yankee troops.

On June 20, Taylor left Richmond and caught up with his brigade at Gordonsville.

He found a tired, dejected, and sullen Stonewall Jackson there. Stress and lack of sleep had dulled the fire in Jackson's eyes. Unknown to Taylor, there was another reason for Stonewall's uncharacteristic despondence. He later learned that Jackson had requested an army of forty thousand to invade Pennsylvania and march on Washington, D.C. He assured Davis, Lee, and Joe Johnston that, given such a force, he would relieve Richmond in a matter of days. With an enemy one hundred thousand strong outside the Confederate capital, Lee would have no part of Jackson's plan. With Davis's approval, Lee ordered Jackson to Richmond to help defend the capital. It was a worn and reluctant Jackson who moved his army toward Richmond in the June heat.

For weeks, Taylor had lived with arthritic pain, but during the march from Gordonsville to Ashland he developed a fever to compound the agony that racked his limbs. The fever weakened him to the point that he abandoned the saddle to ride in an ambulance. On Wednesday, the twenty-fifth, Jackson's army reached Ashland, twelve miles north of Richmond. That night Taylor was cheered by news that General A. P. Hill, with only three divisions, had driven General Fitz John Porter's corps of thirty thousand Yankees from Mechanicsville. Taylor received word that his brigade would move out with Ewell's division the following day to reinforce Hill in pursuit of Porter. On Thursday morning, Taylor's agony was such that he could not mount his horse. Ewell ordered him to rest and placed Colonel Isaac Seymour in temporary command of the brigade.

Taylor intended to rest for the night and catch up with his troops the next day. However, he could not sleep that night and it was near dawn when he finally fell into a state more akin to unconsciousness than sleep. He was startled awake that afternoon by the thunder of the artillery duel to the east. At Taylor's insistence, Tom and the driver helped him into the ambulance and tried to make him comfortable as they set out toward the sound of the battle. They met an officer who informed Taylor that a big fight was underway at Gaines Mill, and his Louisianans were in the thick of it.

Near sunset Taylor came upon an encampment of several hundred wounded Confederates at Cold Harbor. Among them was Brigadier General Arnold Elzey, who informed him that Ewell's division had suffered heavy losses in the day's fighting. With the help of Tom and the ambulance driver, Taylor struggled onto his horse and headed toward the battle. He recounted the scene he witnessed as he moved along the line searching for his men: "It was a wild scene. The battle was raging furiously. Shot, shell, and ball exploded and whistled everywhere."

Darkness was falling when he found his brigade pinned down in a swamp by a superior Union force pouring shot and shell down on it from an elevated breastworks. The moans and cries of wounded men mingled with the whiz of canister and rifle balls cutting through the underbrush, as the jarring thump of artillery shells showered them with mud and limbs torn from trees. Taylor inquired as to the location of Colonel Seymour.

"The colonel is dead, sir," he was told. "He was kilt in the first charge."

Taylor was visibly shaken by news. He later wrote: "I had a wretched feeling of guilt about Seymour who led the brigade and died in my place."

"Then where is Major Wheat?" he asked.

"He's dead too, sir."

This seemed unreal to Taylor. He had always imagined the warrior giant immune to destruction. Although their personalities prevented them from becoming personal friends, they shared a mutual respect that transcended friendship. When in camp, one never visited the campfire of the other. But in battle, it was as if they were of a single mind. A glance or the wave of a hand was as effective as a page of written orders. Not once had Rob Wheat failed him.

Taylor looked at the men around him, hopelessly pinned down by a rain of rifle fire and exploding shells. Still they fought—desperately loading and firing their rifles at a smoke-shrouded enemy; such magnificent men, these sons of shopkeepers and planters, these Irishmen from the docks and Cajuns from the little shacks that lined the Bayou Teche. The brigade that proudly marched into the valley with crisp new uniforms and polished bayonets gleaming in the sun had been reduced to little more than a regiment in numbers. The uniforms were soiled and ragged, and blood streaked the bayonets. Still they fought. Seymour, Wheat, Aaron Davis—while Louisiana was being overrun, her most gallant sons were dying in the Virginia hills a thousand miles from home, and there was nothing Dick Taylor could do about it.

★ ★ ★

DELTA POINT, LOUISIANA, JULY 24—In mid-June, Ben Butler sent General Williams with three thousand troops to Vicksburg, not to attack the stronghold, but to complete an ambitious engineering assignment. Looking at his maps, Butler decided the best way for boats to bypass the guns on the bluffs at Vicksburg was to redirect the channel of the Mississippi River. He proposed to cut a canal across a narrow neck of land on the Louisiana side of the river. On paper it seemed a simple enough task. The distance was only a mile and a quarter. His engineers figured a ditch just six feet across and five feet deep would suffice to divert the river. Once the Mississippi currents began to flow through it, they predicted the rushing waters would gouge out a channel wide and deep enough to float the largest warship. To occupy the garrison at Vicksburg while this work took place, Butler sent Farragut and his warships back up the river. This time Porter accompanied him with his mortar boats.

Williams began work on the canal on June 27, and soon discovered that his men were not up to the task. Before a ditch could be dug, they had to cut down a forest of giant trees and dig stumps and roots out of the ground. The men quickly wilted under the Louisiana sun in temperatures that one officer swore "reached 115 in the shade."

Williams dispatched "press patrols" to round up slaves from nearby plantations to do the work. Within days, twelve hundred contrabands were brought to the work site. Having been promised freedom for themselves and their families in exchange for labor, the slaves worked in a jovial mood. Meanwhile, exposed to the harsh elements, a large number of Williams's troops soon fell ill with malaria.

As the men labored on the ditch, the water level in the river began to fall. Williams ordered them to widen the channel and dig deeper to get lower than the level of the river. But even as they worked, a crisis arose. Williams was rapidly running out of food for his troops and labor force. He sent soldiers up and down the river to confiscate food from plantations, but the soldiers found that many of the plantation owners had fled with their livestock and those slaves who had not been impressed.

Troops and slaves were put on short rations. The slaves began to fall out from dehydration, and a variety of illnesses depleted their ranks as well as those of the soldiers. By July 11, the slaves were nearing completion on a ditch that had grown to eighteen feet across and thirteen feet deep when the sides began collapsing and tons of mud filled the opening. Undaunted, Williams abandoned that project and started a new ditch. By then he had run out of quinine, and fifteen hundred men, half of his army, were on sick call. With nothing to eat but small rations of salt pork and moldy hardtack, and no water to drink except that from the river, the slaves began to suffer heatstroke. Burial details for soldiers and slaves became a daily ritual.

Meanwhile, Farragut and Porter fared no better. Similarly reduced to short rations and river water, and without quinine, their sailors were dying of malaria at an alarming rate. Also near depletion was the supply of coal and ammunition. Their guns and mortars having proved ineffective against the cannons on the bluff, Farragut announced that he was returning to New Orleans.

On July 24, with his supplies exhausted, Williams loaded his soldiers aboard troop transports. Accompanied by Farragut's warships and Porter's gunboats, the armada steamed down the river, abandoning the Vicksburg campaign. Also abandoned were the impressed slaves. Until the last possible moment Williams promised them that they and their families would be taken to New Orleans. Instead, they were left standing on the levee, watching the last of the boats disappear down the river.

General Williams arrived at Baton Rouge on July 26 with orders to occupy the city. Local citizens were routed from their homes to make room for a procession of sick soldiers borne from the waterfront on litters and in wagons and ambulances. Butler's channel had cost almost four hundred lives, none felled by a rifle ball.

The State Capitol Building, where Louisiana declared independence, sat shell-pocked and gutted by fire during Union occupation of Baton Rouge.

Louisiana State University Archives

Richard Taylor, hero of Mansfield.
Mansfield Battlefield Museum

Henry Gray, commander of the 28th
Louisiana Infantry.
Mansfield Battlefield Museum

James Beard, killed in the charge of Gray's
Brigade at Mansfield.
Mansfield Battlefield Museum

Ned Beard, who accompanied his brother
James's body home after the war.
Mansfield Battlefield Museum

Roberdeau Wheat, commander of the
Louisiana Tigers Battalion.
Louisiana State University Archives

Camille Polignac, a French soldier of fortune
who won the respect of the Texas cavalry
under his command.
Mansfield Battlefield Museum

Alfred Mouton, leader of the charge that
broke the Union line at Mansfield.
Mansfield Battlefield Museum

Frederick Hood, who joined the 28th
Louisiana Infantry at age fifteen.
Courtesy of Keith Canterberry

Tom Green (*left*) and an unidentified Texas cavalryman (*right*) typical of
the wild horsemen under his command.
Library of Congress

Louisiana Governor
Thomas O. Moore.
Opelousas, Louisiana, Museum

Edmund Kirby Smith,
commander of forces west of
the Mississippi River.
Mansfield Battlefield Museum

John Pemberton,
failed defender of Vicksburg.
Library of Congress

William T. Sherman, president of
the Louisiana Military Seminary
before the outbreak of the war.
American Heritage Collection

Benjamin Butler, commander of
Union-occupied New Orleans.
Library of Congress

Admiral David Porter, who
almost lost his Union fleet on
the Red River.
National Archives

Admiral David Farragut, whose
fleet conquered New Orleans.
National Archives

Nathaniel P. Banks, defeated
commander of Union forces at
Mansfield.
Library of Congress

Louisiana African-American military officers served with distinction in the Union Army until General Banks had them purged because white troops refused to salute them.
Louisiana State University Archives

P. B. S. Pinchback, an African-American Union officer in the Louisiana Native Guards, later became the nation's first black governor, serving briefly as Louisiana governor during Reconstruction.
Library of Congress

Hand-to-hand fighting between black troops and Texas Cavalry at Milliken's Bend.
Louisiana Department of Tourism

Giant mortars hurled 225-pound shells into Fort Jackson, reducing its interior to rubble.
Library of Congress

This statue of the Virgin Mary, which overlooked the nuns and orphans during the shelling of Donaldsonville, still stands today, minus the right-hand fingers lost to a shell fragment.
From Fort Butler 1863, *courtesy of William A. Spedale*

The aftermath of Union bombardment of Port Hudson provided testament to the misery suffered by Confederate defenders during the siege.
National Archives

A Baton Rouge family and slaves look through the remains of their home, destroyed by Union warships. Two-thirds of the structures in Baton Rouge were damaged in the bombardment.

Louisiana State University Archives

★ ★ ★ ★

10

★ ★ ★ ★

The Holy Ghost

FORT JACKSON, AUGUST 1—Below the ramparts he once defended, William Seymour found himself ensconced in a damp, makeshift prison at the base of the walls of Fort Jackson. Unaccustomed to such primitive accommodations, he sweated profusely. The humidity was stifling, causing the shirt he had been wearing for four days to stick to his body as if held by plaster. With darkness, the mosquitoes descended. At first he tried to swat them, but finally conceded defeat and let them have their way. He was at the very depths of despondency. A week earlier he was informed that his father was dead—killed in battle at a place called Gaines Mill, Virginia. Now he had lost everything—home, holdings, bank account and, worst of all, his father's newspaper. Lying there, he had time to reflect on the worth of things and concluded that a single mosquito net would be worth a fortune. He also wondered if the satisfaction of defying old Ben Butler had been worth the price.

With the surrender of Fort Jackson, Seymour, technically a civilian volunteer, was sent back to New Orleans to be paroled. As a condition of the parole, he signed an oath of allegiance to the United States government. He did so under a threat that refusal would result in imprisonment and confiscation of his property. He was ordered to continue publication of the *Commercial Bulletin* under strict rules of censorship.

Upon General Butler's arrival in New Orleans, he declared martial law. Contained in that order was a censorship proclamation, bringing the city's newspapers under his control. Editors of the various New Orleans newspapers, known for their fierce independence and irreverent reporting, reacted by meeting to determine a course of action. They selected a committee of three to meet with Butler for clarification of the rules under which they were to publish. Seymour assumed the role of spokesman for the committee. In his memoirs he described the meeting with Butler: "The interview was quite an interesting one, many spicy things having been said on both sides, but we got little or no satisfaction from the old 'Beast.'"

Seymour asked Butler what an editor should do if his general order was in conflict with accepted international rules of war or the laws of the United States government. Butler's face flushed. He pounded the desk and, according to Seymour, "raged like a mad bull."

"I am the military governor of this state—and the supreme power!" Butler shouted. "You cannot disregard my order, sir! By God, he that sins against me sins against the Holy Ghost!"

In that case, Seymour asked him, what would happen if he simply stopped publishing the *Bulletin*.

"In that case I will seize it and make it a Union newspaper," Butler snapped.

Seymour left the meeting with little doubt that he had created a dangerous enemy in the "Holy Ghost" of New Orleans. But he vowed to continue publishing the *Bulletin* rather than allow it to become an outright propaganda vehicle for Butler.

Two days after the meeting, Federal troops stormed into the *Daily True Delta* and closed it down after the editor failed to publish one of Butler's proclamations. The newspaper immediately reopened with Federal soldiers performing editorial duties and publishing it as an official organ of the Union. A week later, the *Crescent* was closed and, shortly thereafter, the French newspaper *Estafette du Sud* was raided and put out of business. Fully aware that he might be next, Seymour walked a delicate editorial tightrope, trying his best to report legitimate news without offending the Union censors who perused every word. He succeeded only until July 28.

On the 27th of that month, I rec'd a confirmation that my dear Father had been killed in battle in Virginia. On the next morning, I published a biographical sketch of him to which my commercial editor, Mr. J. C. Dinnies, made an addition; in the last paragraph [he] declared that Father, in the Florida, Mexican and Confederate wars, had been actuated by the purest and most patriotic of motives—a sense of duty. Butler pretended to find something very treasonable in this expression.

That afternoon, a Butler staff officer, accompanied by twenty-five soldiers, stormed into the offices of the *Bulletin* and arrested Seymour and Dinnies. They were shackled, taken to the U.S. Customs House and placed under guard. The following morning, members of Butler's staff pointed out that Seymour's arrest was illegal because the warrant contained no charges. Butler replied that his offense was violation of parole. When General Godfrey Weitzel observed that there must be a charge before a parole violation could take place, Butler exploded: "I do not care if I am acting under law or not," he said. "I intend to put Seymour in prison and I order you to do so immediately."

The next day Seymour and Dinnies were transported down the river and imprisoned at Fort Jackson. Upon his arrival, Seymour was amazed to discover that he and Dinnies had so much company. "It seemed to me that half of New Orleans was there ahead of me," he wrote.

✱   ✱   ✱

BATON ROUGE, AUGUST 5—The citizens of Baton Rouge were jarred from sleep at dawn by the thunder of cannons and the rattle of musket fire. On the north side of town, people looked out of their windows to see rebel soldiers racing through yards and leaping over fences. Those living near the State Capital grounds opened their doors to see Yankee soldiers running through the streets and officers on horseback dashing about. Distant rebel yells and sporadic volleys of gunfire were punctuated by the crash of exploding shells.

Upon realizing that a battle was raging in their midst, the citizens panicked. Mothers herded their children into backyard storm shelters. Others fled, terror stricken, running aimlessly through the fog- and smoke-shrouded streets with toddlers in tow. Highland Avenue became clogged with people and soon the River Road out of town was choked with men, women, and children in wild flight. Many were shoeless and still in their nightclothes. The wails of children mingled with shouts, curses, and prayers even as the sounds of the battle in their city grew in intensity.

The rebel attack on Baton Rouge was part of a well-planned Confederate strategy to wrest control of a one-hundred-mile section of the Mississippi River from the Union. The fortunes of war had turned at Vicksburg. Not only had the Federal fleet failed to silence the rebel guns on the bluffs, it was unable to stop the ironclad *Arkansas*, which was loose on the Mississippi River below Vicksburg and a threat to any Union vessel it encountered.

With the Union retreat from Vicksburg, Secretary of War George W. Randolph saw the next logical move as obvious. If his forces could recapture Baton Rouge it would give the Confederacy control of two vital points on the Mississippi and provide a corridor through which goods and supplies could flow from Louisiana, Texas, and Arkansas to states east of the river. Within that corridor, the Red, Atchafalaya, and Ouachita rivers came together and flowed into the Mississippi, providing conduits for the salt, sugar, grain, beef, produce, turpentine, and forage desperately needed by the Confederacy. Such a corridor also would provide access to manufactured goods and arms from Europe by way of Mexico. To accomplish all of this General Van Dorn received orders at Vicksburg to attack Baton Rouge. He assigned General John Breckinridge to lead the campaign, but gave him only four thousand men to accomplish the task. Meanwhile, Van Dorn retained a force of some twenty thousand troops in Northern Mississippi.

In the heat of one of the worst summers on record, Breckinridge and his army traveled by rail to Camp Moore, Louisiana. Because of the limited number of cars available, they transported only a small amount of food and supplies. As the army, composed of regiments from Tennessee, Alabama, and Mississippi, rested at Camp Moore, dysentery swept through the ranks. Even with the addition of the 2nd Louisiana Infantry at Camp Moore, Breckinridge was left with only about three thousand effectives. His reduced army trekked thirty-five miles in two days in a stifling heatwave with little water, mercifully arriving at the Comite River late on Tuesday, August 4. At 11 P.M. Breckinridge received word that the *Arkansas* would arrive at Baton Rouge early the following morning to attack Union gunboats and support the rebel assault. Having subsisted on short rations for days and marching through the heat and dust of a region in the throes of a drought, it was a weary army that moved out at midnight to cover the final ten miles to Baton Rouge. Many of the men lacked shoes and some had stripped naked to the waist to contend with the heat. By the time they reached the outskirts of Baton Rouge, so many men had fallen ill Breckinridge was left with only about twenty-eight hundred troops, no more than a light brigade. One Tennessee regiment had only forty-five men fit for combat. On the opposite side, General Williams was no better off with only twenty-five hundred effectives. However, he had superior artillery and, more important, the firepower of five Union gunboats sitting at anchor beyond the levee.

At first light, the Confederates advanced through a heavy fog that cloaked their movements. With only 150 men and three field pieces, Lieutenant Colonel Thomas Shields circled unseen around the Federal left flank and opened fire on the camp of the 14th Maine. The rebel ranks charged, igniting a desperate battle that swayed back and forth through the heart of the city. Fog clung to the ground, limiting visibility and resulting in both sides firing on their own troops.

As Confederate units ran out of ammunition, they rushed forward with bayonets and engaged in bitter hand-to-hand fighting. After three hours of close-quarter combat the Federal troops were in retreat, when General Williams came to the front and tried to rally his men. A musket ball through the chest killed him instantly. Almost at the same instant General G. T. Roberts of the 7th Vermont was felled by a severe wound in the neck. Colonel N. A. M. Dudley replaced Williams as commander, but by then his forces had become disorganized. He collected enough men to mount a brief counterattack that was beaten back, and Dudley's forces fled toward the river.

At about ten o'clock the gunboats opened up on the rebels, forcing them to seek shelter. Breckinridge ordered a withdrawal beyond the range of their guns. His troops, thoroughly exhausted, hungry, and thirsty, sought out water wells and cisterns, and availed themselves of rations abandoned at the Federal campsites. Wagons and carriages carted away the wounded, but since the Confederates had no picks or shovels to dig graves, the dead of both sides littered the streets of the city.

Through the early afternoon, Breckinridge paced and watched the river, anxiously waiting for the arrival of the *Arkansas*. At four o'clock, a messenger arrived to inform him that the giant ironclad rested against the banks of the river four miles above Baton Rouge. Its engines had failed and could not be repaired. As night fell on the battered city, Breckinridge ordered his men to burn all supplies and equipment at the Federal campsites that could not be carried away and to withdraw back to the Comite River. There they set up an outpost at the Pratt Farm, five miles from Baton Rouge. Rather than pursue them, the Federals seemed satisfied to let them go.

In the short but bloody battle, the Union had lost 383 men: 84 killed, 266 wounded, and 33 captured. Confederate losses were estimated at 80 dead and more than 300 wounded. The following day, slaves set to the task of removing the bloated, blackened bodies and burying them. They then were put to work building earthen breastworks in anticipation of a second attack by the rebels. As they worked, a massive explosion sounded up the river. The crew of the *Arkansas* had blown up the stranded gunboat to prevent it from being captured.

In the days that followed, Union troops exacted revenge by ransacking Baton Rouge. Fine furniture from Europe adorned the tents of enlisted men. Officers dined beneath moss-draped oaks on ornately carved tables, draped with expensive linens and set with the finest china from Paris. Great four-post beds were chopped up and used for cooking fires and expensive armoires littered the streets.

General Butler, fearful that the Confederates' next attack might be directed at New

Orleans, sent orders for the troops at Baton Rouge to return to the Crescent City. At the same time, he ordered Colonel Paine to "burn Baton Rouge to the ground." Several officers protested, pointing out that there was a large orphanage, a home for the deaf and disabled, an insane asylum, and the state penitentiary in the city and it would be inhumane to burn the entire town. At the urging of his staff, Butler rescinded the order. However, he seemed delighted to learn that Baton Rouge had a penitentiary. He ordered the inmates released and conscripted into the army.

Before departing, the soldiers went on a second rampage of looting, this time in search of anything valuable they could take with them—souvenirs, books, paintings, silver, jewelry, and art objects. Slaves camped outside the city were brought into town and instructed to point out where their masters had buried valuables. Those who hesitated to do so were threatened with death. Across the city, backyards were pocked with holes. Anything that could not be carried away was destroyed. Portraits were slashed, mirrors broken, dresses shredded, books burned along with piles of furniture. Molasses, available in large quantities at the waterfront, was smeared on walls and poured on floors. Even General Butler got into the act by proxy. He ordered the removal of a giant statue of George Washington from the Capital grounds and had the books in the State Library crated. He sent the statue to the Patent Office in Washington and kept the books for himself.

Before the war, Baton Rouge had been city with many fine homes and impressive public buildings. Large oak trees lined its streets, making it one of the most beautiful cities on the river. By the time the transport vessels departed with Butler's troops, the great trees had been felled to provide clear fields of fire and the city skyline was barren except for the blackened buildings. More than a third of the homes had been destroyed by fire, and burned-out buildings lined the downtown streets. The State Capital Building was a soot-laden shell. Most citizens did not return to Baton Rouge until after the war, and many never came back at all.

* * *

DONALDSONVILLE, AUGUST 9—"Sister Mary! Sister Mary! Come see! Come see!" The excitement in the voices of the children on the playground caused Sister Mary Gonzaga to rush to the door of the orphanage. "Sister Mary! Look!"

Beyond the levee, silhouetted against the morning sun, Federal warships were dropping anchor. Their gunports were open and there was frenzied activity on the decks. In town, people filled the streets and fled along the bayou levee. Even as Sister Mary watched, fire and smoke belched from one of the vessels, followed by an explosion that sent a section of roof flying from the bakery building downtown. Like an alarmed mother hen, Mary Gonzaga began shooing the children into the orphanage.

The Ursline Convent-Orphanage was part of a complex that included the Catholic Church, its rectory, dormitory, and school. As the other nuns slammed and locked the heavy wood shutters and secured doors, Sister Mary herded the children into the central hallway of the convent's living quarters. There they huddled at the feet of a statue of the Blessed Virgin Mary. One by one the nuns arrived to hover protectively over them. Outside, the sound of exploding shells and crash of cannonballs slamming into wood and brick built to a crescendo, drowning out their prayers.

A shell exploded in the front yard, blowing open the door, shaking the walls of the building, and sprinkling the hallway with bits of plaster. They could hear shell fragments and brick and debris raining on the roof and the sound of slate shingles falling to the ground. Following a second nearby explosion, a large iron shell fragment whizzed down the hallway and over the heads of the children, struck the outstretched hand of the statue, and slammed into the wall. In her writings, Sister Mary provided an account of what happened next:

> In another interval a terrible crash was heard in the apartment in back—a classroom. A cannon ball had struck the window shutter, shattering it and the sash to pieces; such was its apparent form, had it gone forward it must have pierced the door leading into the passage immediately back of the sisters and orphans kneeling before the statue. The shock was so great that the corners of the desks were wrenched from the hinges and all of the pictures were thrown and shattered to pieces on the floor. But wonderful to relate, the cannon ball, as if pushed by an invisible hand, fell outside of the window near the wall.

As the nuns and orphans huddled in the convent hallway and townspeople fled the city with their belongings bundled in sheets, Admiral David Farragut stood on the deck of the *Hartford* and surveyed the carnage. Shot and shell rained on the downtown business district fronting the river, slowly reducing its buildings to rubble. Cannonballs fell on rows of framed houses, splintering walls and blowing roofs into the streets. Some of the gunners amused themselves by taking potshots at the great plantation homes lining the bayou beyond the city. Shells ripped into the house at Le Petit Versailles Plantation, severely damaging the structure. Above the city, as cannonballs began striking the great house at Laura Plantation, its elderly mistress, Nannette PrudHomme, stood on the upper verandah and screamed at the warships: "You can't do this! My father fought with George Washington in the Revolution!"

★ ★ ★

Few in Donaldsonville had taken seriously David Farragut's threat to destroy their city. If they had known of the admiral's mind-set as his fleet steamed down the river that morning, they would have thought otherwise. He was frustrated and angry. After months of effort, he had not subdued the guns on the bluffs at Vicksburg. He had lost a mortar boat and gunboat at Vicksburg, and a second gunboat at Baton Rouge. Several of his warships were heavily damaged, half of his men were sick with malaria, and he was out of quinine. The crews on some of his ships besieging Vicksburg had been reduced to a diet of salt pork and hard biscuits, and their drinking water came from the river.

Further, despite the fact that his gunboats had repulsed a Confederate attack on the Federal garrison at Baton Rouge, General Butler ordered a pullout of the troops there, leaving the city to the rebels. In four frustrating months since the fall of New Orleans,

Farragut had failed to fulfill his promise to clear the Mississippi River of rebel resistance. Confederate batteries remained intact on the bluffs at Vicksburg and Port Hudson, and roving bands of guerrillas, with their little horse-drawn six-pounders, harassed his ships from the banks of the river. Adding insult to injury, Secretary of War Gideon Welles had ordered him to return his warships to the Gulf of Mexico and leave it to Porter's gunboats to continue the fight for control of the river. It was a brooding Farragut who anchored his warships before the old river town at Donaldsonville that morning.

Strategically located at the convergence of Bayou Lafourche and the Mississippi River, Donaldsonville had served as the state capital of Louisiana in the 1830s. The emergence of Baton Rouge diminished its importance over the years, but in 1861 it remained a booming river port with a population of thirty-five hundred. Having existed for more than a century, Donaldsonville was a city of ornate downtown buildings and elegant old homes. There were more than fifty stores and shops in town, two banks, manufacturing plants, waterfront warehouses and wharves, hotels and boarding houses, an opera house, and one of the most influential newspapers in the state. The ethnic makeup was almost as diverse as that of New Orleans. Late-arriving English, German, and Italian shopkeepers and bankers conducted much of the commerce of the city, but the wealth of the region flowed from the French Creole sugar and cotton plantations lining Bayou Lafourche. Some of the state's wealthiest families lived along the bayou, although they spent much of their time at second homes in New Orleans—especially during the season of festivals and grand balls.

The anger that unleashed the firestorm on Donaldsonville had been building in Farragut for weeks. The bluffs near Donaldsonville provided any number of locations where partisan rangers could conceal themselves and fire on Union warships and transports moving along the Mississippi River. The rebels planted their cannons, fired a few rounds, and disappeared into the forests before Union gunboats had a chance to respond. Tiring of the game, in late July Farragut sent a party ashore under a flag of truce with a warning to city officials: "From this date . . . every time my boats are fired upon, I will burn a portion of your town," he threatened. His emissaries also warned that the admiral would destroy every plantation on the Mississippi River six miles below and nine miles above the city if the guerrilla activity persisted.

The people of Donaldsonville had no more control over the guerrillas than did Farragut. Several bands of partisan rangers participated in the sport, some coming from as far away as Thibodaux. The attacks were uncoordinated and involved little planning. The rangers took orders from no one, not even the governor, and random firing on the ships continued.

On August 6, Farragut anchored the *Hartford* at Donaldsonville and sent a party ashore under a flag of truce to meet with the mayor and civic leaders. They were informed that the admiral was on his way to Baton Rouge and that he would return in three days. "At that time Donaldsonville will be destroyed," the Union representatives told the mayor. "You have three days to evacuate your citizens."

For two days a steady stream of humanity and animals moved out of Donaldsonville. Women, old men, children, and slaves formed long columns. Wagons, buggies, and every type of conveyance was loaded with goods ranging from furniture to chicken coops. Cows and pigs were herded out of town into the countryside. However, as many as half of the inhabitants did not leave, convinced that the threat was not real. The doubters would regret their skepticism.

★ ★ ★

As the firing slowed, then ceased, Sister Mary looked around the convent. Pictures, vases, lamps, furniture, and plaster littered the floor. Cautiously, she ventured outside. Although damaged, the church and rectory still stood but, around her, the city was in ruins. Row upon row of familiar shops and homes had simply disappeared. Rubble filled the streets, and along Front Street hardly a structure was left standing. As she watched, men in uniforms appeared on the levee and began moving into the downtown area. Some were armed with rifles, others carried torches. They set those homes and buildings still standing or only partially destroyed on fire. Within minutes a pall of black smoke blanketed the town. On Railroad Avenue, only one house was spared, a large, two-story, owned by Solomon Weinschenck that the troops occupied for a command post.

When a young officer approached the orphanage with the announced intention of using the bell tower as an observation post, a bristling Mother Superior, Sister Maria Clara, met him in the doorway. "You will enter this building over my dead body!" she told him. She then proceeded to give the officer a dressing-down more severe than any he might receive from a military superior.

That afternoon Sister Maria Clara wrote a scathing letter of protest to Ben Butler in New Orleans, decrying the wanton destruction and Admiral Farragut's disregard for the lives of citizens and those of the nuns and orphans. As word of the atrocity spread north the Catholic Church demanded an explanation from the government. On August 18, Admiral Farragut tried to head off criticism when he sent the following message to Secretary of Navy Welles:

> Sir, I regret to inform the department that at the town of Donaldsonville they have pursued a uniform practice of firing upon our steamers passing up and down the river. I sent a message to the inhabitants that if they did not discontinue this policy, I would destroy the town. The last time I passed up to Baton Rouge in support of the army, I anchored about a mile from Donaldsonville and heard them fire upon our vessels. In the latter case they made a mistake and it was so quickly returned that they ran away. The next night they fired on the St. Charles. I therefore ordered them to send their women and children out of town, as I certainly intended to destroy it on my way down the river and I fulfilled my purpose to a certain extent. I burnt down the hotels and wharf buildings; the dwelling house and other buildings of a Mr. Philip Sandy, who is said to be a captain of the guerrillas. He fired upon our men, but they chased him off. We also brought off ten or twelve of his slaves and supplied ourselves with cattle and sheep from his place.

Farragut neglected to mention that his warships had destroyed far more than a few wharves and hotel buildings. He had leveled hundreds of homes and businesses, destroying or damaging three out of four structures in the city. Also missing from Farragut's report was an explanation of why it was necessary to destroy a city in order to chase off a single rebel guerrilla.

Under pressure from Washington, General Butler sent a letter of apology to Sister Maria Clara. Although Butler had authorized the bombardment, the tone of his letter placed the blame on Farragut:

> Madame: I had not information until the reception of your note that so sad a result to the sisters of your command had happened from the bombardment of Donaldsonville. I am very, very sorry that Rear-Admiral Farragut was unaware that he was injuring your establishment by his shells. Any injury must have been entirely accidental. . . . No one can appreciate more fully than myself the holy, self-sacrificing labors of the Sisters of Charity. To them our soldiers are daily indebted for the kindest offices. Sisters of all mankind, they know no nation, no kindred, neither war nor peace. . . . I regret that any harm should have befallen your society of sisters.

WINNFIELD, AUGUST 10—Although far removed from the fighting, the town of Winnfield came under siege that summer—not by an invading army but under the ruthless rule of Howard "Dog" Smith. A few weeks after William Walker turned in his badge and left for Monroe with his company of volunteers, a posse of armed men rode into town. Trotting along beside the lead horse were two of the largest dogs the citizens of Winnfield had ever seen. The men stopped at the hitching rail before the courthouse and went inside where the leader presented a set of documents to the Clerk of Court. The papers purported to appoint Howard Smith the sheriff of Winn Parish and authorized him to organize a "home guard" for protection of the citizens. The credentials bore the forged signature of no less an authority than Jefferson Davis.

Assuming law enforcement duties, "Dog" Smith made up his own laws. He enforced them with his posse of hardcase deputies. However, Smith's dogs, named Rock and Ruler, struck at least as much terror in the hearts of the citizenry as did his henchmen. Smith required every man in the parish either to serve in the home guard or to pay an "exemption" fee. The fee seemed to be whatever the citizen could afford. Those who refused to pay saw their homes mysteriously catch fire in the middle of the night. Several mysterious murders in the parish also served to inspire compliance.

Smith's men secretly encouraged slaves to run away from their masters. He then offered to track them down with his dogs, for a fee. Soldiers who came home on leave were arrested as deserters or evaders. Smith destroyed their papers and turned them over to authorities in Monroe for one-hundred-dollar bounty fees. Those who tried to flee were tracked down by Rock and Ruler.

Within weeks of Howard Smith's arrival, Winn Parish residents were living under a lawless reign of terror with business places and citizens being robbed. Those who spoke out against the sheriff were subject to having their homes burned. One citizen who was not intimidated, however, was William T. Barnett. He secretly organized a group of men to oppose Smith. One by one Smith's deputies were intimidated by threats into deserting him. When Smith awoke one morning to find Rock and Ruler slain, he decided it was time to move on. He disappeared as quickly as he had arrived, and a local poet penned a verse: "Old Rock and Ruler are dead and gone, / And left old Howard blowing his horn."

A grateful Winn Parish Police Jury appointed William Barnett to serve as the sheriff and restore order until an election could be held.

* * *

WASHINGTON, LOUISIANA, AUGUST 20—It was well before daylight when Mimi Taylor heard a rapping on the brass door knocker, followed by the low drone of voices downstairs. Slipping on a housecoat, she went down the hallway to the landing to see who might be calling at such an inconvenient hour. In the dim light of the foyer, she saw a man in uniform standing with his back to the stairs. She first thought that the governor had sent soldiers to move them to yet another location. Slowly the visitor turned, and Mimi's breath caught in her throat. Tears streaming, she descended the stairs and threw herself into the arms of her husband, Dick Taylor. For months she had suppressed her emotions for the sake of the children. Now, all of the pent-up anxiety and uncertainty released in her sobs. She was reluctant to release her grip on him, even when he tried to tilt her chin to look at her face.

When she did look up, it seemed to her the man she was clinging to was far different than the one who departed Fashion Plantation. The boyish face had lost its youth. The smug little half-smile was missing—the one that always made her believe he was enjoying some secret amusement. The face looked tan, and the carefully crafted beard had grown full. His body, once a bit overweight, was lean beneath the uniform. Even when he smiled down at her with affection, there was something different about the eyes—as if they held secrets he could not share.

* * *

Following the Seven Days' struggle for Richmond, Taylor spent almost a month at the capital recuperating from his illness. On July 24, President Davis summoned him to his office. Upon seeing Davis, Taylor had the immediate impression that the responsibility of command was taking its toll on the man. Davis's face was pale and drawn, and a weariness that had not been there before had crept into his voice. "I need you back in Louisiana," Davis told him.

With Richmond safe from imminent attack, Davis had found it increasingly difficult to ignore the demands of Governor Moore in Louisiana. Butler's troops daily ranged further from New Orleans, pillaging homes and stealing cotton and sugar, livestock and food stores. Porter's gunboats landed troops to prowl the banks of South Louisiana's rivers and bayous, forcing Louisianans to abandon their homes and businesses. Many citizens had fled across the Sabine River into Texas. Meanwhile, word arrived that Farragut's gunboats had shelled an undefended Baton Rouge, causing civilian casualties and damaging much of the city, including the capital building.

While sympathetic to the plight of the people, Davis had a more pragmatic reason for sending Taylor to Louisiana. Porter's gunboats and Farragut's warships had gained control of the lower Mississippi River except for the corridor between Vicksburg and Baton Rouge. "You will go to Louisiana, assume command of Confederate forces, and organize a defense of the state," Davis told him. "But above all, you must keep the river corridor open. Without it we are cut in two." With Taylor's new responsibilities came a promotion to major general.

Even as Davis spoke, Taylor's ever active mind was toying with other possibilities. Would Zachary Taylor be content simply to defend a territory? What would Stonewall Jackson do? Taylor concluded that, presented the opportunity, those men would set their sights on retaking New Orleans.

Upon leaving Davis's office, Taylor met with George Randolph, who only recently had replaced Judah Benjamin as Secretary of War. Taylor was gratified to find in Randolph one who shared his conviction that, regardless of what happened in Virginia, control of the lower Mississippi River was essential if the Confederacy was to survive. Randolph noted that Benjamin Butler had only fifteen thousand untested troops defending New Orleans. He and Taylor formulated an ambitious strategy to liberate the city and presented the plan to Davis. They pointed out to the president that, at some point, the South must attempt to wrest back territory taken from it. To recapture New Orleans not only would weaken the North's will to continue the fight, it would make England and France more inclined to recognize the Confederate government. With Davis's approval, Randolph gave Taylor authority to detach troops from Texas, Mississippi, and Alabama for a two-pronged, east-west attack on New Orleans.

Taylor departed Virginia with mixed emotions. Although excited by his new assignment and anxious to see Mimi and the children, he was saddened at the thought of leaving his brigade. The officers of the 9th Louisiana Regiment signed a formal request to accompany Taylor to Louisiana: "You have made soldiers of us. Wherever you go, we desire to go and let your destiny be our destiny," it read. However, Lee was reluctant to let a single soldier leave Virginia for other theaters—much less a regiment.

At age thirty-six, Dick Taylor was a rising star in the Confederate Army in spite of his health problems. His promotion made him the youngest major general in the army and one of only four not to attend West Point. But in Taylor's estimation nonattendance at West Point was an asset rather than a liability. Except for Jackson, Ewell, and a few others, he held West Pointers in low esteem. He had seen enough combat to conclude that most West Pointers made excellent drillmasters but generally lacked imagination and initiative in the absence of specific orders.

The person most upset at Taylor's assignment to Louisiana was Stonewall Jackson. He had grand ambitions that included Taylor. Jackson had recommended Taylor's promotion to major general two months earlier. And he still had not given up on a plan to invade Pennsylvania. It was Jackson's intention to place Taylor in command of a division in a new, expanded army. Upon learning that he was losing Taylor, Jackson protested to Davis. The president was less than truthful when he told Jackson that one of Taylor's primary responsibilities in Louisiana was to recruit troops for Virginia. Davis assured Jackson that those new recruits would be assigned to him.

Yet another general had plans for Taylor's talents. Braxton Bragg, commander of the Army of Tennessee, had badgered Davis for months to assign Taylor to him as his chief of staff, but Davis had ignored the request. Traveling south by rail, Taylor stopped in Chattanooga to see his old friend. Upon surveying the disorderly state of affairs there, he wrote: "I felt no regret at the refusal of authorities to assign me to duty with him." What Taylor found was a demoralized army of forty thousand commanded by a general who had essentially isolated himself from his men and officers' corps.

He found Bragg physically drained, emotionally unstable, and at war with his own officers. Bragg's irrational behavior had made him universally hated among the rank and file. Because he could not get along with the officers assigned to him, Bragg had transferred, demoted, and court-martialed several of his subordinates. Almost daily, President Davis and Secretary Randolph received letters from disgruntled officers requesting transfers and criticizing Bragg's behavior. Likewise, letters from Bragg routinely landed on Davis's desk with complaints of incompetence and insubordination among his men. His patience exhausted, Davis finally ignored all such correspondence, yet in spite of the obvious chaos in Bragg's army, he refused to consider relieving the man whose artillery had saved him at Buena Vista. Taylor left Chattanooga haunted by the image of Braxton Bragg sitting alone in his office, planning an invasion of Kentucky. Denied Taylor's services, and unable to get along with anyone else, Bragg had become his own chief of staff. "From that hour, I had misgivings about General Bragg's success," Taylor later wrote.

On his trip south, Taylor also visited Pierre Beauregard and found the hero of Fort Sumter grievously ill, his handsome features drawn and his once-dark hair turned mysteriously gray. Taylor could not conclude whether the abrupt change in hair color was a result of stress or Beauregard's inability to acquire Parisian cosmetics at the front. Beauregard informed Taylor that he was being assigned command of a new department that included the Carolinas and Georgia. He asked Taylor to consider a young French officer when organizing his staff in Louisiana. The officer was a colonel who had been assigned to Bragg's staff and was desperate to be transferred. His name was Camille Polignac.

On August 19, 1862, for the first time in sixteen months, Taylor set foot back on Louisiana soil. He and Tom Strother were ferried across the Mississippi and landed near the mouth of the Red River. They traveled all night on horseback, arriving at the little town of Washington at about 4 A.M.

The commotion caused by his arrival awakened the children, who greeted him with hugs. He marveled that Dixie had grown from toddler to boyhood during his absence, and the girls seemed to have become proper young ladies. After greeting his father, six-year-old Zack ran to his room and minutes later reappeared, proudly wearing a uniform of Confederate gray complete with tiny leggings and insignia. Carefully examining the uniform, Taylor allowed that he would be proud to have an officer so finely attired in his army. He ate breakfast with Mimi and the children and visited with them until noon, then left for a meeting with the governor at Opelousas.

At a temporary state capital set up in a private home, Taylor was warmly greeted by Moore but soon received a rude awakening. There was no Confederate Army for him to command in Louisiana. Moore noted that two newly formed Confederate regiments and a battalion were training at Monroe and Vienna, but there were less than twelve hundred weapons available for three thousand men there, and most of those were shotguns. Besides, the governor informed him, those regiments had been assigned to the defense of Vicksburg by Richmond and were not available to Taylor. Other than a few state militia companies, the only defenders of Louisiana were partisan rangers who had formed into small guerrilla bands. These "partisans" were generally out of control, the governor admitted, and more inclined to steal food and livestock from citizens than to harass the enemy. Moore estimated that, including state and local militias and partisan rangers, he had no more than three thousand men available. Those, he told Taylor, were scattered about the state and most were armed with personal weapons, ranging from shotguns to ancient muskets and pistols, making it difficult to supply ammunition for them. The governor pointed out that General Breckinridge had troops across the river at Port Hudson, but they were assigned to the defense of the river.

The governor said that the 18th Louisiana Regiment, commanded by Alfred Mouton, was being sent back to Louisiana from Corinth, Mississippi, but was not expected for another three weeks. A skeleton unit that had been badly bloodied at Shiloh and decimated by disease, the 18th could muster no more than three or four hundred men.

Before leaving Richmond, Taylor had asked Randolph to assign as many regiments of Texas cavalry to Louisiana as was practical. He learned to his disappointment that only one light battalion numbering some three hundred Texas riflemen under Major Edward Waller was being sent to him. When Taylor asked Moore how many Louisiana militia companies were fully armed and prepared for immediate service, the governor slowly shook his head. "Two," he said.

Tired and discouraged, Dick Taylor finally went to bed that night after being up for more than thirty hours. His army consisted of 300 poorly armed Texans and two militia companies that had never seen combat—a total of perhaps 450 men. The grand plans for the conquest of New Orleans, so neatly mapped on Randolph's desk back in Richmond, could be tossed out the window. New Orleans would have to wait. First he must build an army. And in order to do that he needed a quick victory to inspire confidence in the people and bring in recruits.

* * *

DES ALLEMANDS, SEPTEMBER 4—As sunlight slowly penetrated the moss-draped oaks surrounding the isolated little railway station at Des Allemands, Federal sentries were startled to discover two companies of rebel infantry in a battle line across the tracks from their encampment. A quick volley from the rebels sent the Yankees scurrying for their rifles. They were attempting to form ranks when the thunder of pounding hooves and high-pitched rebel yells came from the rear. Waller's horsemen, screaming and firing wildly, fell immediately upon them.

Under attack from front and rear, the Federals quickly surrendered. Waller placed some two hundred prisoners under guard, then led a detachment five miles down the railroad tracks to Boutte Station. A small contingent of Union troops there promptly surrendered. In one day, two Union outposts within twenty miles of New Orleans had fallen to the rebels. With the raids, the Confederates gained control of the Western Railroad that linked New Orleans with Brashear City and Berwick Bay. Along with prisoners, they captured two field pieces, almost two hundred rifles, ammunition, food stores, and several wagons full of booty looted from nearby homes and churches. With the raid, Dick Taylor had dropped his calling card at the doorstep of New Orleans.

* * *

Upon assuming command, Taylor spent a week traveling through what was called the Attakapas country—the Cajun French heartland of South Central Louisiana. There, along the Bayou Teche, Cajun shacks lined the banks beside grand plantation homes owned by Americans and Englishmen. While these "foreigners" generated wealth from the region's vast sugar cane and cotton fields, the free-spirited Cajuns lived off the bounty of the bayous—hunting, trapping, fishing, and celebrating the simple joys of living in their moss-draped paradise with its traditional Saturday night *fais do do* house parties. North Louisiana had been drained of its manpower. But in this region of the state, many men of military age remained. Taylor knew from experience that the Cajuns made good soldiers. In Virginia, they were among the most ferocious fighters in his brigade. If the Cajun fighter had a weakness, it was his occasional disregard for danger. In his memoirs, Taylor offered this analysis of the Cajun soldier: "A home loving, simple people, few spoke English; fewer still had ever moved ten miles from their natal *cabanes*; and the war to them was a liberal education. . . . They had all the light gaiety of the Gaul and, after the manner of their ancestors, were born cocks of the walk."

Taylor talked to planters, politicians, militia leaders, and those living in the bayou shacks. He found a population with no means to defend itself and resigned to defeat. "We are prisoners in every sense of the term," a militia commander told him. "If we were to attempt exercising any military authority, we would be arrested and our families harassed. Where is our protection to come from?"

Taylor had answered that question by dispatching Waller's Texans and the two companies of militia infantry from New Iberia to Des Allemands. Word of the victory swept through South Louisiana and spread north, and with each retelling, the battle became more significant. "This trifling success, the first since the loss of New Orleans, attracted a great deal of attention and the people rejoiced," Taylor wrote. He further endeared himself to the people by returning much of the loot recaptured from the Yankees. "Books, pictures, household furniture, finger rings, breast pins and other articles of feminine adornment and wear attested [to] the Catholic taste and temper of these patriots [the Yankees]," he wrote. Meanwhile, volunteers began showing up for induction at camps from Thibodaux to Ville Platte.

* * *

DES ALLEMANDS, SEPTEMBER 10—"The Texans are coming back and they're walkin'!"

The announcement emptied tents, and curious Cajuns lined the railroad tracks to witness the unusual sight of walking Texans. There was a standing joke among the Louisianans that a Texan would not go to answer nature's call without riding his horse, even if he had to saddle him first. But, sure enough, approaching the camp a group of grim-faced Texans walked slowly along the railroad grade. They were a pathetic sight— sweat-soaked, clothing torn and caked with mud, some carrying boots slung over their shoulders while others appeared to have lost their footwear. A few lugged muddy saddles. Far down the tracks, more men could be seen walking along the edge of the Des Allemands swamp.

"Hey, cher! What happen to you, huh?"

"Had to take to the swamp to git away from the Yankees."

"Where you hoss?"

"Had to leave 'im."

"Ah, mon amis. What you do now?"

"I'm goin' back to Texas to git me another horse. I'll be damned if I'll let the Yankees take my horse and git away with it."

Just four days after the Confederate capture of Des Allemands, a terrible blunder reduced Taylor's cavalry to infantry. He had returned north to set up his headquarters at Alexandria and, in his absence, authorized Waller's restless Texans to raid Federal encampments along the west bank of the Mississippi River above New Orleans. Taylor instructed Waller to strike quickly and get out before the enemy had a chance to send large numbers of troops against him. The purpose of the raid was not military conquest but to keep Butler off balance and force him to withdraw raiding parties that were harassing citizens along the banks of the Mississippi. Taylor warned Waller that he would be operating in a dangerous locale where he might become trapped by swamplands if he was not careful. To prevent such an occurrence, he assigned several scouts familiar with the area to accompany the Texans.

For three days, from Boutte Station to the River Road, Waller's cavalry uprooted rails and burned bridges, a railroad station, and several transport steamboats. Unchallenged, the Texans were feeling invulnerable when, on Tuesday, September 8, they camped on the Old River Road, three miles north of St. Charles Courthouse, and some thirty miles above New Orleans.

Meanwhile, General Butler, angry at having the railroad cut and his waterways' shipping lanes disrupted, dispatched the better part of four regiments up the river on transports, accompanied by the gunship, *Mississippi*. A portion of the 21st Indiana and 9th Connecticut regiments landed below the Texans and the 14th Maine and 4th Wisconsin above them. Hemmed in by a gunboat on the river and trapped by a combined force of three thousand Federal troops, Waller's three hundred Texans briefly exchanged fire, then fled into the nearby swamp.

Less than two hundred yards into the morass they encountered thick vines, cypress knees, and soft mud beneath water that was thigh-deep in places. There they abandoned horses, saddles, and supplies. Their only consolation was that the Northern troops were not inclined to pursue them. Slogging through mud and swatting mosquitoes, Waller's men finally managed to reach Boutte Station shortly after daylight on Thursday. From there they walked down the railroad tracks toward their base at Des Allemands.

In his report of the action, Union Colonel James McMillian noted that the Federals took fifty prisoners, three hundred horses, two rebel flags, one French flag, four light field pieces, and several shotguns and pistols.

Even more humiliating than the military setback was the ribbing the Texans received from the Cajuns at Des Allemands. C. C. Cox, Waller's adjutant, wrote of the incident: "This left our little band of heroic Texians [sic] in a bad plight and our humiliation and discomfiture in the presence of the victorious Kageans [sic] was most mortifying. Now we are on foot, dismounted and degraded to the infantry service."

Two days later a repentant Colonel Waller showed up at Taylor's office in Alexandria with a request that he be allowed to send a small detachment of his men back to Texas to secure more horses. Taylor finally consented, reasoning that the Texans' aversion to foot travel probably would result in a rash of desertions anyway. A month later, a herd of horses was driven across the Calcasieu River at Lake Charles, providing the Texans with new mounts. According to Cox, the arrival of the horses was "greeted with great joy and celebration" by his Texas comrades.

* * *

At Alexandria, Taylor received disturbing news of wanton destruction along the River Road. A militiaman sent to accompany Waller as a scout described the destruction left by the Yankees:

> It was one continual scene of desolation and sadness—nearly every place on the route had been despoiled and plundered—even to the huts of the poorest Creoles. [At Fashion Plantation] the officers entered the house. It was a complete wreck, the furniture smashed, the walls torn down, pictures cut out of their frames while . . . scattered over the floor lay the correspondence and official documents of the old general while president of the U.S.

In a letter home, a Vermont private provided a graphic description of the Yankee occupation at Fashion Plantation:

> It is the most splendid plantation that I ever saw. I wish you could have seen the soldiers plunder this plantation. The slaves were forced to help them ransack the house and barns. [The spoils included] hundreds of bottles of wine, eggs, preserved figs and peaches, turkeys, chickens and honey in any quantity. . . . The camp is loaded down with plunder—all kinds of clothing, rings, watches, guns, pistols, swords and some of General [Zachary] Taylor's old hats and coats, belt-swords and, in fact, every relic he had is worn about the camp. . . . Nothing is respected.

Not mentioned in the private's inventory of things taken were 130 horses and mules, 200 head of sheep, several hundred head of cattle, and hundreds of hogsheads of sugar.

Herded along with the cattle were 175 Fashion slaves—men, women and children—officially seized as contraband of war since their owner was branded a traitor. They were taken to a camp at Algiers where they joined almost 40,000 other contrabands being held in squalid, prisonlike conditions. Unable to feed and care for this mass of humanity, Butler and his staff grappled with the question of what to do with them even as sickness swept the camp, killing hundreds. Martin Gordon, Taylor's brother-in-law, who still lived in New Orleans, received a letter from William Hawkins, the house servant at Fashion, pleading with him to "get word to Mars Dick that we are dying of disease and starvation. Thirty have died today."

In October 1862 General Butler finally devised a solution to the contraband slave problem. For months he had resisted pressure from Washington and his own officers to form black regiments in the U.S. Army. The situation at Algiers finally forced his hand. He issued orders for the strongest young men to be inducted into the army—not to fight but to perform manual labor. Those who would not volunteer were to be conscripted under the new Federal Conscription Law. At the same time, Butler placed abandoned and confiscated plantations along the river under Federal overseers and sent the older men, women, and children contrabands back to work the fields. The general's brother, Andrew, directed this enterprise from behind the scenes, prepared as always to reap any profits.

★ ★ ★

NEW ORLEANS, SEPTEMBER 15—Under the Butler regime, opportunists flocked to New Orleans like vultures but no one touched a carcass without the permission of the man they called "The Colonel." Andrew Butler was not a colonel. He was not in the military and, in fact, had no official capacity. Unencumbered by such restraints, he was free to wheel and deal as he pleased. But Andrew had an advantage over other speculators. His brother was the "Holy Ghost" of New Orleans.

One of the first things General Butler did upon assuming control of New Orleans was to forbid the public sale of liquor. Seeing an opportunity, Andrew promptly bought up all of the liquor stocks in the city at greatly reduced prices. He then convinced his brother to lift the ban and made a fortune selling whiskey. The scheme worked so well it was repeated twice more during Butler's rule.

Andrew had cattle brought in from Texas and flour imported from the North. He established a monopoly on all groceries, breadstuffs, medicines, and staples arriving in the city and reaped huge profits from the inflated prices he charged the U.S. Army as well as the residents of New Orleans. He took over a bakery seized by the general. All other bakeries in the city were promptly closed, leaving Andrew with a monopoly on every loaf of bread sold in New Orleans.

In physical appearance, Andrew Butler did not appear threatening or intimidating. He was fat and jovial, quick to laugh, and constantly glad-handing the people around him. However, word quickly spread that if one wanted a favor from the general he must go through "The Colonel." For a fee, Andrew could see to it that certain property was not confiscated by the army. He could get criminal charges dropped and prisoners paroled. He became a debt collector for Northern businessmen who claimed they were owed money when Louisiana seceded. Although many of these "debts" were disputed, Andrew seized property, took a rake-off on collections, and once the properties were sold, pocketed what was left.

For a share of profits, Andrew could secure passage through Union lines for speculators selling food, medicines, and clothing to the Confederate Army. Large quantities of cotton and sugar seized from plantations by Federal troops were "auctioned off" in New Orleans with the only bidder being Andrew Butler. He carefully controlled the quantity and prices of shipments of cotton and sugar to New York and Boston. A bale of cotton purchased for as little as thirty dollars in Louisiana could bring as much as seven hundred to nine hundred dollars at the port in Boston. To avoid paying shipping costs, cotton and sugar often were labeled as "ballast" for government transports returning to the East Coast.

Nine riverboats, intended for military use, were placed at Andrew's disposal for the transportation of confiscated goods and produce. Using this fleet, he soon established a lively trade with the enemy across Lake Pontchartrain. Armed with a pass signed by his brother and escorted by a company of Federal soldiers, Andrew traveled into enemy territory where he traded foodstuffs, medicines, salt, and cloth for cotton and sugar. Friends of Andrew also profited handsomely. In one case a speculator named D. D. Goicouria of New York paid two dollars a sack for six hundred sacks of salt. Four hundred sacks were sold to the Confederate Army in Mississippi for twenty-five dollars each. The other two hundred sold to individuals for thirty-six dollars a sack. Andrew collected five dollars per sack just for securing a permit clearing the cargo for shipment. Goicouria openly boasted that, with the help of his friend, "The Colonel," he made a profit of more than two hundred thousand dollars in just four months.

The clandestine dealings of General Butler and his brother were common knowledge in Washington. George S. Denison, a treasury agent assigned to New Orleans, filed numerous complaints with Secretary of the Treasury Salmon P. Chase. Shortly after his arrival in New Orleans, Butler was caught red-handed playing the speculation game. Noticing that the transport ships that brought his troops to Louisiana were about to return empty and that thousands of hogsheads of sugar were sitting on the docks, the general decided to "rent" the ships. He shipped the sugar to his business agent, Robert S. Fry Jr., in Boston.

However, General Butler made a terrible mistake, paying the government for shipping costs. That alerted the U.S. quartermaster general, who promptly seized the goods and had them sold at auction. Butler was paid for his "expenses," which included a five-dollar-per-hogshead payment to Andrew for handling the deal, and the rest of the money went to the Treasury Department. Butler received a sharply worded rebuke from Secretary Chase warning him not to take advantage of his "military command to engage in mercantile speculation." Butler had learned his lesson. He turned such matters over to Andrew, who was much more adept than himself at circumventing the law.

★ ★ ★

NEW ORLEANS, SEPTEMBER 27—In late September, General Butler wrote a letter to Secretary Stanton stating his intention to induct a "colored" regiment into the United States Army: "I shall have within ten days a regiment, 1,000 strong, of Native Guards (colored), the darkest of whom is about the complexion of the late Mr. [Daniel] Webster." On September 27, 1862, the first regiment of the Native Guards was mustered into the service for three years, becoming the first officially sanctioned regiment of black soldiers in the Union Army.

During the fall of New Orleans, the mayor had assigned the Native Guards Militia to help maintain order along Esplanade Avenue. When Federal troops entered the city, Charles Sauvenet, one of the black freedmen who organized and served as officers in the Native Guards, ordered his men to hide their uniforms and rifles, most of which were hidden at the same Convent School where the regiment was organized. In early September, some members of the unit became concerned that the stash of military gear might be discovered, resulting in punishment for officials at the school. To prevent such an occurrence, Sauvenet and four of his officers went to Butler to officially surrender and hand over their weapons. Butler was impressed by the bearing and intelligence of the officers, noting of Sauvenet, "he was a translator in the Provost Court of German, Spanish and French." In a letter to Stanton, Butler expressed disappointment at his efforts to recruit white troops in New Orleans and stated: "I shall call on Africa to intervene."

The decision was an abrupt about-face for Butler. Just three months earlier General John Phelps had attempted to form three armed regiments of black troops at Fort Carrollton between New Orleans and Baton Rouge. Butler refused to allow it, prompting an angry Phelps to resign from the army and return home to Vermont. During his standoff with Phelps, Butler expressed an opinion that it was "ludicrous in the extreme" to arm blacks because "they are afraid of firearms." To Stanton, he wrote, "I am inclined to the opinion that John Brown was right in his idea of arming the negro with a pike or spear instead of a musket, if they are to be armed at all."

Unable to acquire adequate reinforcements from Washington, Butler decided to solve his manpower problem with black troops. In the Native Guards, he had a regiment already formed, complete with an officers corps. However, only about one half of the original Native Guards volunteered for service in the Union Army. A mix of conscripts and additional volunteers filled out the regiment. Two additional regiments were organized, their ranks completed with conscripted contraband slaves. Although Butler approved issuing arms to the Native Guards 1st Regiment, he had no intention of placing its troops in combat. In addition to rifles, the men were armed with shovels, picks, and axes. Their first assignment was to repair the rails and bridges of the railroad between New Orleans and Brashear City.

★ ★ ★

SIMMESPORT, OCTOBER 7—Frustrated at every turn in his attempts to acquire men and supplies, a hopeful Dick Taylor anxiously awaited the arrival of Brigadier General Alfred Mouton. Through the efforts of Randolph in Richmond, the Louisiana 18th and Crescent infantry regiments had been detached from the Army of Tennessee and sent back to Louisiana. Taylor also succeeded in getting two small artillery batteries released to him—Semmes's and Ralston's batteries.

Otherwise, his pleadings for troops from other theaters produced no results. General Theophilus Holmes at Little Rock, Governor John Pettus of Mississippi, and General John Pemberton at Vicksburg all turned him down. Holmes, commander of the Trans Mississippi Department, had the authority to assign troops from Arkansas and Texas to Taylor, but he refused to do so. Called "Old Granny" because of his wrinkled appearance and lack of initiative, Holmes's refusal to cooperate with fellow officers would soon get him fired. Pemberton, only recently appointed to replace Van Dorn as commander of Mississippi forces, had thirty thousand men in and around Vicksburg. He responded to Taylor's request for troops by suggesting instead that Taylor send troops to him. A more sympathetic reply was received from Governor Pettus—but no men or materials. Thus, it was with a great deal of anticipation that Taylor greeted Mouton, the son of his old friend Alexandre Mouton, upon his return to Louisiana with two infantry regiments.

Even as Mouton's men disembarked on Louisiana soil, the Cajun spotted Taylor in his black greatcoat, smoking a cigar and watching the exercise. A broad smile spread across his face and he came over with hand extended, then, remembering protocol, snapped a salute. Taylor's memories of Alfred were of a carefree young man in his twenties. The man before him had the insignia of a brigadier general on his jacket and wore a heavy beard that did not fully cover a terrible scar across his cheek.

"How many men do you bring me, General Mouton?"

"The 18th and Crescent," Mouton said. "Four hundred effectives."

"Do you mean four hundred in the 18th?"

Mouton gave him a quizzical look. "In both regiments," he said. Seeing the disappointment on Taylor's face, he quickly added, "but they know how to fight, sir."

Indeed, they knew how to fight. Mouton's men had occupied Pittsburg Landing on the Tennessee River a full month before the Battle of Shiloh and received their combat baptism in a three-hour firefight with two Union gunboats. They had riddled the vessels with rifle and artillery, killing seventy of the enemy, wounding almost a hundred and sending the boats fleeing back up the river. On the first day at Shiloh, the 18th was part of the Confederate left flank that drove General Sherman's division back three miles on that side of the field. At one point Mouton's regiment charged into the concentrated fire of three Federal regiments. In spite of being struck in the face by a rifle ball, Mouton led his men almost to the muzzles of the enemy guns before being forced to fall back for lack of support. In a matter of minutes, more than two hundred of his men lay dead or wounded on the field.

Following the Confederate retreat from Shiloh, the 18th fought in several engagements that summer in the struggle for the rail center at Corinth. In addition to heavy battlefield casualties, many of Mouton's men died in a plague of diseases that swept through the ranks of the Army of the Mississippi. Of the more than 900 who left Vermillionville for service in Mississippi that spring, only 250 returned to Louisiana that fall. The Crescent Regiment accompanying Mouton was even more decimated. A regiment in name only, it had no more than 150 men—no more than two small companies.

✱ ✱ ✱

Jean Jacques Alfred Mouton emerged from the devastation of Shiloh as a hero and a goat. He was a hero to his men and to the folks back home where the newspapers praised his bravery. However, his superior officers labeled him as reckless, and General Bragg claimed Mouton was incapable of handling large numbers of men. It was a reputation not fully deserved, resulting from a self-serving report by General Preston Pond in the wake of Shiloh. The charge of the 18th Regiment at Shiloh was one of many mistakes on both sides of the field in a battle described by some as little more than a bloody brawl between two armed mobs. Pond had ordered the ill-fated charge that proved so costly to the 18th. Mouton claimed he was following a direct order when he attacked the Federal position, but Pond's report indicated that Mouton attacked prematurely and should have waited for support from the Louisiana 16th and Crescent regiments before ordering the charge. The controversy left a stain on Mouton's reputation among his superior officers, if not his official record.

Knowing the Mouton family as he did, Taylor refused to accept Bragg's assessment of Alfred Mouton's ability. He descended from two famous and wealthy old Acadian families—the Moutons and Rousseaus. After attending St. Charles College at Grand Coteau, he graduated from West Point in 1850 and was commissioned a lieutenant in the U.S. Army. He served only briefly before resigning and returning to Louisiana to become a planter, engineer, and surveyor. He was the assistant building engineer during construction of the New Orleans, Opelousas & Great Western Railroad, which linked the Crescent City with Berwick Bay and South Central Louisiana.

In 1854, he married Philomene Mouton, his second cousin. The marriage produced five children in seven years. He remained active in the local militia throughout the 1850s, and with the firing on Fort Sumter, helped organize a company at Vermillionville that was incorporated into the 18th Regiment. Because of his station and background, Alfred was promoted to colonel and placed in command of the regiment.

Taylor saw in Mouton a fighter—the kind of terrible swift sword he himself had been to Stonewall Jackson in the Valley. He placed him in command of all troops in South Louisiana—by now totaling some twenty-five hundred men, most of them untested militiamen and unruly partisan rangers. Mouton was instructed to set up his headquarters at Thibodaux, organize the troops, and defend the Bayou Lafourche region. Taylor then set out for Vicksburg to confer with Pemberton. Ostensibly, his mission was to arrive at a strategy for protection of the river corridor between Vicksburg and Port Hudson. His real purpose was to talk Pemberton into loaning him a regiment to bolster his army in Louisiana.

✱ ✱ ✱

LABADIEVILLE, OCTOBER 28—Informed of General Mouton's presence in the Lafourche region, General Butler dispatched a force of five thousand men supported by gunboats to trap and destroy his little army. He sent General Weitzel with four thousand troops to the blackened ruins of Donaldsonville at the upper end of Bayou Lafourche. Another one thousand men were dispatched along the partially destroyed Western Railroad at the southern end of the bayou. Accompanying this unit was the 1st Native Guards Regiment, assigned to repair the rail line and rebuild its burned-out bridges. Gunboats and troop ships went to Berwick Bay to be stationed along the Atchafalaya River and cut off Mouton's escape via the railroad.

Butler had several reasons for wanting to destroy Mouton's army quickly. He knew of Mouton's popularity in the area and feared that, if left alone, he would attract recruits. The location of Mouton's headquarters at Thibodaux, in the heart of the rich Bayou Lafourche region, was particularly upsetting to Butler. Before being occupied by the rebels, his troops had freely raided the area to provide beef, sugar, produce, salt, and other goods for New Orleans. Butler also wanted to restore the railroad between Des Allemands and New Orleans and reclaim Berwick Bay, a notorious smuggling hub for the rebels. However, the most important reason for ridding the Lafourche of Mouton was that Butler was under orders to capture Port Hudson and then assist General Grant in taking Vicksburg. Butler had only fifteen thousand troops at his disposal. If he sent the bulk of that force upriver to attack Port Hudson, New Orleans would be vulnerable to a back-door assault by Mouton. Knowing the aggressive natures of Taylor and Mouton, Butler had no doubt that, given the slightest opportunity, they would attack New Orleans.

On October 25 Mouton had barely settled into his headquarters at Thibodaux, with his militia units still scattered from New Iberia to Des Allemands. He was supervising the construction of a pontoon bridge across Bayou Lafourche when he received word that Weitzel had landed troops at Donaldsonville and was marching toward him. Gathering as many men as he could, he chose to make a stand near the little town of Labadieville, ten miles above Thibodaux.

Weitzel's army came marching in battle formation down both sides of the bayou, forcing Mouton to split his force to avoid being flanked. He deployed the newly formed Louisiana 33rd Infantry Regiment and a small company of Terribone militia, totaling 628 men on the west bank of the bayou along with 150 horsemen from the 2nd Louisiana Cavalry and Semmes's artillery. On the other bank he placed the 18th and Crescent infantry regiments with 390 men, along with 100 cavalrymen and Ralston's artillery—a total force of 1,268 men, plus cannoneers.

As Weitzel's troops on the east bank came into view, Captain George Ralston's artillery opened up and Mouton's veterans in the 18th and Crescent put down a galling fire that stopped the Union advance. Weitzel's forces remained pinned down until Ralston's battery ran out of ammunition. Mouton then retreated a mile down the bayou to make another stand.

At 4 P.M., as Weitzel's men on the opposite bank crossed a cane field, they came under fire from the 33rd Regiment and Semmes's artillery. Recognizing that he faced a larger force on that side of the bayou, Weitzel sent men to confiscate mules and slaves from a nearby plantation to lay a pontoon bridge across the stream. Reinforcements raced across the bridge to overwhelm the Confederates on that side of the bayou. Under heavy fire for the first time and armed with inferior weapons, some of the militia troops fought well while others fled.

Using guerrilla tactics, Mouton contended for every foot of territory, sending his cavalry to harass the enemy flanks while his infantry came forth to fire quick volleys, then disappear back into the woods. Pushed back to Thibodaux, he gathered what supplies his troops could transport and ordered the rest burned. He retreated to the railroad at Lafourche Crossing, loaded his supplies and men aboard a waiting train, burned the station, uprooted rails, and set out for Berwick Bay.

With his cavalry trailing the train, Mouton and the remnants of his little army reached the Atchafalaya River the following morning. As they crossed Berwick Bay to safety, they saw smoke from the stacks of Union gunboats steaming up the channel from the Gulf to cut them off.

The gunboats had arrived too late. Because of his hit-and-retreat tactics, Mouton's casualties were light—less than 50 killed and wounded, compared to 20 killed and 74 wounded for the Yankees. However, 138 rebel troops on the west side of the bayou were taken prisoner—men Mouton could ill afford to lose. Another acute loss was that of Ralston, his artillery officer, killed in the action. Still, Mouton and his little army had escaped Butler's trap and would live to fight another day.

★ ★ ★

VICKSBURG, OCTOBER 29—Unaware of Mouton's defeat at Labadieville, Taylor met with Lieutenant General John Pemberton in Vicksburg to discuss a cooperative means to expedite the shipment of goods across the river. In addition to directing Louisiana's military affairs, Taylor had spent two months dealing with the logistics of purchasing and shipping supplies to Mississippi. Of the effort he wrote, "It was of vital importance to control the section of the Mississippi River receiving the Red and Washita [Ouachita] rivers as I undertook to supply Vicksburg and Port Hudson with corn, forage, sugar, molasses, cattle and salt."

Salt was especially important because it was used to cure and preserve meat, and it was in short supply throughout the Confederacy. Upon assuming his command, one of the first things Taylor did was establish a mining operation at Avery Island in the coastal region of the state where a giant dome of pure rock salt rose out of a vast swampland. He also set up a meat-packing plant and a tannery nearby at New Iberia.

After only a few minutes of conversation with Pemberton, Taylor had misgivings about the defender of Vicksburg. That was the time required for Pemberton to reveal himself as a man of shallow intellect and imagination and someone, Taylor feared, incapable of dealing with the responsibility thrust upon him. "I began to doubt President Davis's wisdom in appointing such an apparently ordinary artillery officer to a pivotal command like Vicksburg," Taylor later stated. "Davis should have known all about it . . . and yet he made a pet of Pemberton."

Taylor went to Vicksburg with expectations that he might secure the loan of an infantry regiment. He soon discovered that Pemberton's obvious lack of military expertise might be matched by his arrogance. Taylor pointed out that he desperately needed a veteran infantry regiment to supplement his small army of untested militias. Such a move, he said, would allow him to contend with Butler and relieve pressure on Vicksburg and Port Hudson, as well as to expedite the delivery of supplies. In a condescending manner, Pemberton told him that nothing happening in Louisiana was as important as maintaining a strong defense at Vicksburg. Pemberton did not grasp that Vicksburg's survival depended on what happened in Louisiana.

* * *

Upon being informed of Mouton's retreat from Thibodaux, Taylor made arrangements to return to Louisiana. Meanwhile, he sent instructions for Mouton to establish earthen breastworks on either side of Bayou Teche, some eight miles above Berwick Bay at Bisland, and concentrate his forces there. Taylor was familiar with the locale. He had scouted the region and remembered the spot as ideal for defense. A dense swamp protected one flank and grassy marshlands the other. An enemy attacking Bisland from Berwick Bay would have to commit to a frontal assault against entrenched troops. With proper fortifications, a small army could hold off a large one at Bisland.

The only problem with the location was the danger of becoming trapped. A single, narrow road followed the winding course of Bayou Teche north through Franklin and New Iberia to Vermillionville. Taylor knew he would have to be vigilant for any attempt by the Yankees to attack him from the rear. But he had made up his mind to fight at Bisland and was willing to take the risk.

* * *

NEW YORK, NOVEMBER 8—While Mouton prepared to defend the lower Teche, and Taylor dealt with the politics of trying to build an army, decisions were being made in Boston, New York, and Washington, D.C., that would have a profound effect on Louisiana. Hounded by daily howls of outrage resulting from Ben Butler's behavior in New Orleans, Lincoln finally replaced him with Nathaniel P. Banks. The loudest protests against Butler came from foreign governments, whose citizens in New Orleans were routinely maltreated, and from New England's textile barons, who had to deal with the duplicitous Andrew Butler to obtain cotton for their looms. Banks was a logical choice to replace Butler. Not only was he respected among New England's politicians, he was a diplomat. Even more important, he understood the textile business.

Nathaniel Banks, the son of a textile baron, began his career in a Massachusetts mill and became so proficient at operating the equipment he was called "The Bobbin Boy of Waltham." The name stayed with him during his campaign for governor of Massachusetts. He served three terms as governor, was elected to the U.S. House of Representatives, and became its speaker. Handsome and meticulous in dress and manner, he was a mellow-voiced, spellbinding orator who did his best to be all things to all men on any political issue. He had ambitions to become president, and many in New England who followed his career assumed that, someday, he would achieve that goal.

Originally, Banks was supposed to go to Texas, not New Orleans. Following his rude introduction to Stonewall Jackson in Virginia, Banks was assigned by Secretary of War Stanton to return east and raise an army for the long-awaited invasion of Texas. With headquarters at New York, Banks's campaign for volunteers resembled a crusade more than a recruiting drive. Men who signed up were promised bonuses and ownership of the farms they conquered in Texas. To inspire them, images of beautiful plantation homes appeared on recruiting billboards. To help matters along, Stanton appealed to the governors of the New England states to send to Banks "all troops in your state not otherwise appropriated." By the end of October, Banks had gathered almost thirty thousand recruits—men who would become the 19th Army Corps. An article in the October 30 issue of the *New York Times* had high praise for Banks's expedition.

Once the state [Texas] is possessed, the work contemplated by the government is but begun. What is that great territory worth to the Union if it is again to be remanded . . . to the traitor owners who monopolize the lands? . . .

Texas needs to be colonized as well as captured. New England and the middle states must furnish the new population for Texas. . . . Industrious, practical, enterprising, liberty-loving men will follow him [Banks] with enthusiasm, help him win back the vast empire of Texas, and to found beneath the genial skies there not one state only but half a dozen states.

However, the *Times's* grand vision of a Texas populated by right-thinking New Englanders would have to wait. On November 8, the White House made a sudden shift in policy. Banks was given command of the Department of the Gulf and assigned to New Orleans, replacing Ben Butler. His new orders, issued by General-in-Chief Henry Halleck read as follows: "The President regards the opening of the Mississippi River as the first and most important of all our military and naval operations, and it is hoped that you will not lose a moment in accomplishing it."

There was sound political reason for the policy shift. In the congressional elections on November 4, the Democrats won stunning victories in Indiana, Ohio, and finally, in Lincoln's own state of Illinois. Along with the election returns, Lincoln received a wake-up letter from an angry Governor Oliver Morton of Indiana. It emphasized that the midwestern states were being strangled economically by closure of the Mississippi River. The letter also contained a veiled threat that the western states might cease supporting the war effort if the river was not opened to commerce.

As Banks's armada departed New York harbor, its destination was kept secret. Thirty thousand New England soldiers boarded ships thinking they were going to Texas, where rich homesteads and confiscated estates waited for the taking. They were well out to sea when they learned they were going to New Orleans.

★ ★ ★

NEW ORLEANS, DECEMBER 24—On the eve of Christmas, the people of New Orleans received an early gift. That morning, General Butler and his wife boarded a ship bound for New York. During the night, several personal crates were placed on board. Butler carried with him a case that he refused to let out of his grip. After shaking hands with Admiral Farragut, he made his way up the gangplank. As the boat pulled away from the dock and headed downstream, the *Hartford* and several shore batteries fired a parting salute.

For New Orleans, the rule of The Beast was over.

★ ★ ★

At Butler's office, Banks and his staff found numerous empty files. The letters file was gone, as was a *Special Order Book* and a *Special Permits Book*. Those records that remained were so muddled that an accounting of financial affairs was impossible. In a letter to his wife, Banks described what he called "the stealing" he found under the auspices of Ben Butler, and its consequence.

> They have stolen everything they could lay their hands on. There has been open trade with the enemy. . . . This state could have made and ought now to be thoroughly for the Union and against the Confederate States. Instead of that they have been robbed of their silver forks and spoons, jewelry . . . silver plate, pictures, books, carriages, horses, houses, plantations and negroes, not for the benefit of the government but for individual plunder. . . . I am glad that I have no desire for individual plunder.

Within days after Ben Butler left New Orleans, Banks received a note from the general's brother, Andrew, and his associate, C. A. Weed, a speculator well connected with top officials at the Treasury Department: "Dear Sir: If you will allow our commercial program to be carried out as projected previous to your arrival in this department, giving the same support and facilities as your predecessor, I am authorized on your assent to place at your disposal $100,000." The bribe offer was blatant, devoid of even a hint of subtlety. Banks turned it down. No longer able to wheel and deal with impunity, and having acquired a fortune, Andrew left New Orleans a few months later.

Within days of his arrival, Banks released hundreds of political prisoners, reopened churches and newspapers, and restored many private homes to their owners. He set up a food distribution program for the needy and opened up trade between the commodities brokers in the city and plantation owners who pledged allegiance to the United States. He ordered elections for public officials, including one for two congressmen to represent the state in the nation's capital.

By the close of 1862 Nathaniel Banks, the politician, was the most popular man in New Orleans. Remaining to be seen was whether Banks, the general, would be equally successful in subduing the small Confederate army in South Louisiana.

✮ ✮ ✮ ✮ ✮ ✮ ✮ ✮ ✮ ✮ ✮ ✮ ✮

1863

Mud and Blood

And heavy with his armor,
And spent with changing blows;
And oft they thought him sinking,
But still again he rose.

"HORATIUS"

THOMAS BARINGTON MCCAULAY

11

Battle for the Bayous

NEW ORLEANS, JANUARY 14—Nathaniel Banks saw many parallels in Louisiana to his experience in the Shenandoah Valley. In order to move against Port Hudson and Vicksburg, he knew he must secure his western flank by chasing Taylor's army from the lower Teche. Failure to do so would leave New Orleans vulnerable to a back-door assault by Taylor, jeopardizing the Port Hudson operation just as Stonewall Jackson's threat against Washington compromised McClellan's Richmond campaign. An officer on Banks's staff sized up the situation: "The Teche country was to the war in Louisiana what the Shenandoah Valley was to the war in Virginia. It was a sort of back alley, parallel to the main street [the Mississippi River] and one side or the other was always running up or down the Teche with the other side in full chase after it."

On January 14 Banks sent General Weitzel with forty-five hundred troops and four gunboats to the Teche with orders to clear out the enemy before proceeding north to capture Fort Burton on the Atchafalaya River. If Fort Burton could be subdued, shallow-draft gunboats would be able to steam, unchallenged, all the way to the mouth of the Red River, sealing off that vital waterway.

To oppose Weitzel, Mouton had only twelve hundred troops and the Confederate gunboat *Cotton*, anchored in Bayou Teche. Since Mouton had not completed his breastworks at Fort Bisland, he moved part of his troops downstream to a favorable location just above Lynch's Point where the Teche and Atchafalaya converge. There Captain Edward W. Fuller positioned the *Cotton* for battle in a spot where the Teche narrowed such that two boats could not pass side by side. Meanwhile, Mouton lined both banks of the bayou with sharpshooters in rifle pits to support the gunboat.

Lieutenant Commander Thomas L. Buchanan had four well-armed gunboats to contend with the *Cotton*—the *Diana, Estrella, Kinsman,* and *Calhoun*. In a pitched battle they might have easily overwhelmed the Confederate steamer. But the *Cotton's* position forced Buchanan to send his gunboats against her in single file. He sent the *Kinsman* and *Estrella* forward as supporting Union artillery opened up on the *Cotton*. Confederate Lieutenant B. F. Winchester, in command of Faries Battery, responded with six field pieces, including two captured twelve-pound bronze howitzers that slowed the advance of Weitzel's infantry.

As the *Kinsman* came into range, its crew was pinned to the deck by rebel sharp-shooters while shell after shell from the *Cotton* tore into it—five hits in all. Under an intense fire that threatened to disable his vessel and decimate his crew, Captain Wiggins tried to maneuver his craft back down the stream out of range of the rebel riflemen. As he did so, the stern of the gunboat struck a rebel torpedo, sending a shudder through the massive vessel and making it impossible to control.

The *Kinsman* drifted past the *Estrella* even as that vessel came under fire from the rifle pits. Winchester's artillery and shells from the *Cotton* tore into the gunboat, forcing the captain to retreat back downstream. Commander Buchanan, aboard the *Calhoun*, ordered the captain of the *Estrella* to resume his attack on the Confederates, but he refused. "Rifle pits line the bank!" he shouted back to Buchanan. The commander was furious. "Then move out of the way and I will go!" he yelled. As the *Calhoun* steamed up the bayou and Buchanan stood on deck looking through his spyglass a minié ball struck him in the temple, killing him instantly. Rifle fire soon swept the decks of the *Calhoun*, killing and wounding several crewmen. Under heavy fire, the pilot ran the craft aground.

The captain of the *Diana* sent an urgent message back to Weitzel: "Buchanan dead. *Calhoun* aground. If rifle pits are not cleared out in five minutes the *Calhoun* will be lost." Weitzel sent three infantry regiments forward, accompanied by cavalry and backed by an artillery barrage. Charging up both banks of the bayou the Union infantry chased the rebel snipers from their pits. As the Yankees encountered the main Confederate force, a brief but bloody firefight produced casualties on both sides.

The suddenness of the attack caught the crew of the *Cotton* by surprise. Captain Fuller ordered the springs cut and desperately tried to maneuver his gunboat back up the bayou. Enemy rifle fire and artillery riddled the vessel, killing and wounding a large number of crewmen. Naval Lieutenant Henry Stevens, the *Cotton's* gunnery officer, fell, mortally wounded. As bullets shattered the pilothouse, Captain Fuller sustained wounds in both arms. Still he managed to back the gunboat out of range of the enemy guns, by using his feet to turn the pilot wheel.

Safely beyond range of the Yankee guns, the Confederates removed the dead and wounded from the boat. Among the severely wounded was Fuller, who was taken six miles upstream to Franklin for treatment. Meanwhile, Lieutenant E. T. King assumed command of the *Cotton* and steamed back down the bayou to renew the battle. By then the Federals had concentrated their forces and the *Cotton* had to retreat once more under heavy fire. As dusk settled on the bayou, Mouton inspected the gunboat. The damage was so extensive he decided to sacrifice it to obstruct the waterway. King, who had a sentimental attachment to the *Cotton*, strongly objected. He insisted the vessel could be repaired. However, Mouton realized that if nothing was done, both the Teche and Atchafalaya could be lost. To effectively block the waterway, he selected a location where the Teche was especially narrow. There was only one problem with the spot: It was within 150 yards of Weitzel's campsite.

All guns, ammunition, and everything of value was removed from the *Cotton*. Under cover of night, King silently guided the drifting gunboat to within sight of the white tents of the Federal encampment. He plowed the bow into an embankment and allowed the stern to swing around until the 250-foot vessel was positioned across the channel.

Holes were cut in the bottom. Fires were set and the boat sank quickly and soon burned to the waterline. Union sentinels realized what was happening only when they spotted flames leaping from the deck. By then, King and his skeleton crew had boarded a skiff and escaped back upstream.

Daylight confirmed Weitzel's worst fears. The smoking hull of the *Cotton* blocked the bayou in such a way it could not be easily removed. Since Weitzel would be deprived of the protection of his gunboats if he pursued the rebels, he decided not to renew the attack. He withdrew the badly battered gunboats to Brashear City and, with most of his troops, returned to his headquarters at Thibodaux. In his report to Banks, he described the engagement as a victory. But it was Mouton who held the Teche.

★ ★ ★

KINGSTON, FEBRUARY 5—When the dogs started barking, Kate Beard went to the door to see who was coming to visit. Approaching the house were three riders. She recognized Alonzo first and then Ned and her husband James. Calling to Mary to "come quick," she rushed outside to greet them. After almost two years of separation from his wife and daughter, James Beard had returned to Auburnia.

Although he had been back in Louisiana for nine months, this was James's first opportunity to see his family. After joining Shelley's Battalion, he was assigned to duty at Richmond, Louisiana, a little town on the Vicksburg-Monroe Railroad, more than two hundred miles from Kingston. From there he went to Rosedale, just fifteen miles from Union-held Baton Rouge. There he protected citizens in the Bayou Grosse Tete region from forays by enemy troops looking to loot area homes. Although no major battles occurred in the region, James took part in several skirmishes that came with enough frequency to prevent his taking a leave of absence. From Rosedale, the battalion marched north to Simmesport and went into winter camp. Finally taking leave, James rode the 200 miles to Kingston in just four days to be certain he would arrive in time for his daughter Corinne Gayle's birthday.

His brief stay at Auburnia was a happy one. The child who waved good-bye on the levee at Shreveport was a precocious three-year-old who made no pretense of her affection for her father. James was able to see old friends who dropped by to inquire about the well-being of their sons and husbands in Virginia. The visit was cut short by news that his battalion was being transferred to South Louisiana. Several weeks after his departure, a letter from Kate informed James that Corinne Gayle might soon have a little brother or sister.

★ ★ ★

FORT DE RUSSY, FEBRUARY 24—Darkness had fallen and sleet rattled on an eggshell sheet of ice covering the ground when a courier arrived at Taylor's Alexandria headquarters. The Union gunboat *Queen of the West* had entered the Red River and Fort DeRussy was under attack. Taylor realized that if the *Queen* got past DeRussy, all that stood between her and Alexandria was a lightly armed ram named the *Webb*—no match for the Union gunboat.

Taylor ordered Tom Strother to saddle his horse. Shivering against gusting winds, Taylor rode through the night, covering the thirty miles to Fort DeRussy by daylight. He feared what he might find, but as he approached the earthen embankments beside the Red River, all seemed it order. Then he spotted the *Queen of the West*, lying disabled against the opposite bank, riddled with shot, steam still rising from her ruptured boilers. He could not suppress a shout of joy and relief. His novice cannoneers had stopped the *Queen*.

Taylor's concern was fueled by a total lack of confidence in fixed river fortifications as a defense against gunboats. He had concluded that horse-drawn cannon supported by infantry was most effective at stopping gunboats in the narrow channels of Louisiana's bayous. But in this instance, the troops at Fort DeRussy proved more than adequate to the task. The fort's cannons had disabled the *Queen*, and several of her crewmen sat in sullen silence under guard on the river bank. Upon inspecting the damaged gunboat, Taylor sent word for the *Webb* to come down the river and tow the captured vessel to Alexandria for restoration. Good fortune had provided Taylor with a gunboat.

Even as the *Queen* was being repaired, word arrived that the Union gunboat *Indianola* had fought its way past Vicksburg and was loose in the corridor. Taylor decided to send the *Queen* and the *Webb* to engage the *Indianola*. "To attempt the destruction of such a vessel as the *Indianola* with our limited means seemed madness; yet volunteers for the work promptly offered themselves," he wrote. The volunteers came from the ranks of the men at Fort DeRussy, none of whom had naval experience. He assigned Major Joseph Brent to command the expedition.

On February 24 Brent located the *Indianola* midway between Natchez and Vicksburg. Attacking under cover of darkness, he sent the *Queen*'s steel-plated bow ramming through a coal barge and into the side of the *Indianola*. Almost immediately the *Webb* sliced through a coal barge on the other side, striking the Union gunboat. Surprised by the suddenness of the attack, crewmen aboard the *Indianola* raced to their guns. Avoiding cannon fire, the *Queen* circled and crashed into the ironclad's paddle box, collapsing its armor. As the *Queen* disengaged, the *Webb* came on under a full head of steam and struck the same spot, ripping a hole in the hull. Within minutes the *Indianola*, one of the most powerful gunboats in the Union fleet, was sinking and its crew clamoring to be saved. "Thus we regained control of our section of the Mississippi," Taylor wrote, "and by an action that for daring will bear comparison with any recorded by Nelson or Dundonald."

Once more Confederate shipments flowed uninterrupted across the Mississippi—but only for a few days. The loss of the *Queen of the West* and sinking of the *Indianola* proved a wakeup call for Union strategists. Farragut and his warships were recalled from the Gulf of Mexico and sent upstream to attack Port Hudson. Two of his ships managed to run past the fort and once more patrolled the corridor. Meanwhile, in New Orleans, General Banks put domestic and commercial matters on hold, and with his staff, began planning a campaign to capture the river strongholds at Port Hudson and Vicksburg. He intended to take Port Hudson, clear Louisiana of enemy forces, and invade Texas before the summer was over. But first, he must take care of an old foe from Virginia—Dick Taylor.

* * *

FORT BISLAND, MARCH 12—While Taylor fought a desperate cat-and-mouse war of survival in Louisiana, the laconic "Granny" Holmes was content to remain idle in Little Rock. With a great deal of gratification, Taylor received word that Holmes was being relieved as commander of the Trans Mississippi Department. And he was pleased to learn that his replacement would be Lieutenant General Edmund Kirby Smith. Taylor had served briefly under Smith in Virginia before being assigned to Ewell. He assured his staff that President Davis's appointment of Smith was "an excellent selection." Unknown to Taylor, Smith's selection had little to do with merit or grand strategy but resulted from a feud between Smith and Bragg during their ill-fated invasion of Kentucky. Thus, Davis solved two problems when he finally fired the incompetent Holmes and replaced him with Smith. In Richmond, it seemed a good option. The department had a competent field general in Taylor, and Smith's strong suit was administration. The teaming of the two seemed only logical.

With spectacles worn low on his nose, Kirby Smith looked more like a scholar than a warrior. He was only thirty-eight years old, but a receding hairline; a reserved, aloof manner; and the scholarly spectacles made him appear older. Unknown to Taylor, his new commander also possessed a stubborn streak, disguised behind a perpetual smile and cajoling manner.

A Florida native and West Point graduate, Smith was a veteran of the Mexican War and had served in the West Texas Indian wars. In Virginia, he proved to be an adequate if not outstanding brigade and divisional commander and was considered one of Davis's pet generals. Given command of the District of East Tennessee, he was assigned to Bragg's army for the invasion of Kentucky in the fall of 1862. Even as they engaged the enemy, he and Bragg clashed repeatedly over strategy. Bragg's complaints to Richmond finally resulted in Smith's transfer to the Trans Mississippi theater.

At Taylor's suggestion, Smith transferred the department's headquarters from Little Rock to Alexandria. Smith also prevailed upon Davis to assign Brigadier General Henry H. Sibley's Texas Cavalry Brigade to Taylor. Sibley's men had seen hard fighting in West Texas and New Mexico and driven Union troops out of Galveston. The prospect of having a detachment of experienced cavalry to bolster his small army bolstered Taylor's spirits, and he anxiously traveled from Alexandria to Fort Bisland to inspect his new troops. He found them lounging about in a camp that "defined disorganization." He was disappointed at the size of the force, which totaled only about thirteen hundred men. He had expected two thousand. However, numbers did not concern him as much as what he perceived to be a total absence of discipline.

The forty-six-year-old Sibley had a reputation as a notorious alcoholic and loose disciplinarian. There had been so many complaints about his fondness for spirits and the resulting behavior that he was summoned to Richmond to answer charges of dereliction of duty. Faced with the possibility of losing his command, he promised Davis and Secretary of War James E. Seddon that he would give up the bottle. Upon meeting Sibley, Taylor noted that the general had reneged on his pledge. However, Sibley was known as a fighter, and Taylor decided to reserve judgment on the man.

While searching the camp for an old acquaintance from the Mexican War named Tom Green, it occurred to Taylor that Texans seemed to have little respect for rank—be it corporal or major general. He came upon a major sitting beneath a shade tree dealing a Mexican card game called "monte." Neither the major nor the card players rose as he approached and, in fact, paid little attention to his arrival.

"Can I deal you in, Gen'ral?" the major drawled.

"You can put down the cards and stand at attention!" Taylor snapped. The major stood and endured a tongue-lashing while his grinning men watched. Other than providing amusement for the troops, Taylor observed that the bawling-out seemed to have little effect. "It was a scene for that illustrious inspector Colonel Martinet to have witnessed," he wrote.

* * *

COCHRAN PLANTATION, MARCH 28—Hidden in the woods on the banks of Grand Lake, Colonel Henry Gray and three hundred troops from the 28th Louisiana watched smoke rising from the stacks of a Union gunboat beyond Cypress Island. As he predicted, the gunboat appeared to be headed in their direction. He alerted the men to ready themselves for action. Nearby, another three hunded men, most of them dismounted Texas cavalrymen, waited with several light field pieces.

Aboard the gunboat *Diana*, Captain Thomas Peterson was a man on a mission of revenge. Assigned to reconnoiter the shores of Grand Lake above Berwick Bay, he intended to level the plantation home of the widow Cochran who, he believed, had tried to lure him into an ambush the day before. Peterson had docked the *Diana* at Cochran Plantation to take on a load of sugar. However, as his men began loading barrels on the boat, the sugar deal went sour. Instead of payment, the widow received only a promise of payment. As an argument developed, one of Colonel Gray's patrols happened on the scene and began firing on the *Diana*. Peterson had beat a hasty retreat with only twenty hogsheads of sugar in the hold. After seething overnight, he concluded the widow had betrayed him and decided to return and teach her a lesson. Gray, figuring the gunboat would return to the plantation, arranged a reception.

As the *Diana* rounded the island and moved into the channel of the Atchafalaya River, Captain Peterson spotted the Texans' artillery battery on the shore and ordered his forward guns to open up on it. He was not prepared for the intensity of the rebel response. A hurricane of rifle balls, canister and cannonballs from the Louisiana and Texas troops slammed into the gunboat, killing or wounding most of those on deck. Captain Peterson staggered from the pilothouse clutching his chest: "Great God!" he shouted. "They have killed me!" His lifeless body tumbled onto the deck. The engine's escape pipe was riddled with holes, and scalding steam filled the spaces below deck where the men had fled. Forced back onto the deck, now slippery with blood, they were cut down by Gray's men, who were firing as fast as they could reload. A flag of surrender finally was raised. Of the 150 men on board—including 70 soldiers from New York and Connecticut and some 30 contrabands—33 were dead or wounded, including seven officers.

The excited rebels rowed out to the boat in sugar coolers and took control of the vessel. Among the loot found on board was a fiddle. A Texan grabbed it and began playing a version of *Dixie* that was a horrible assault to the ears. His fellow rebels agreed that the screeching notes were just punishment for their Yankee prisoners.

When the sun set across Berwick Bay that evening, Richard Taylor acquired another gunboat for his small but growing fleet.

* * *

For the men of the 28th Regiment, the assault on the *Diana* provided their introduction to combat. Until then their only fight had been against the clouds of mosquitoes at Milliken's Bend on the west bank of the Mississippi River. After training at Vienna, Colonel Gray had marched his troops to Monroe for assignment. Upon reviewing the 28th, General Blanchard told his staff to arm them with shotguns because he did not want to waste rifles on such a motley-looking group. To Henry Gray's credit the unit's reputation as the "Rag Tag 28th" later became a symbol of pride rather than shame.

Leaving Monroe, the regiment spent almost four months guarding the Vicksburg-Monroe Railroad at Milliken's Bend, during which time several men were lost to malaria and other diseases. In November Gray received orders to take his unit to Fort Bisland, almost three hundred miles to the south. Ill-prepared for a winter march of such duration, the men were worn out when they reached Avery Island and camped there for several weeks to recuperate before pushing on to Bisland.

At Franklin, the men learned that the town had an authentic French tailor from Paris. As a joke on their colonel, they had the Frenchman make a gaudy jacket, trimmed with fancy gold braid and buttons. At a ceremony arranged by the men, Gray accepted the jacket and thanked them. However, he continued to wear his old frayed and faded jacket even as the new one remained hanging in his quarters. To constant inquiries after his fancy Parisian jacket, Gray had a standard reply: "I prefer to admire it rather than wear it."

The 28th finally arrived at Fort Bisland in February and found duty there somewhat boring until fate inspired Captain Peterson to guide the *Diana* into their gunsights that afternoon.

* * *

BRASHEAR CITY, APRIL 12—By late March, Nathaniel Banks had decided to crush the pesky Taylor with one mighty blow. An opportunity to do so presented itself when word reached him that Taylor had concentrated his army at Fort Bisland. Twice Weitzel had failed to expel the rebels from the Teche region, blaming the marshy terrain and insufficient manpower. Banks would not make that mistake. By April 10 he had moved three divisions of his 19th Army Corps, totaling fourteen thousand men, to Brashear City, just nine miles from Bisland. He ordered another four thousand troops from Baton Rouge to cross Grand Lake and attack Taylor from the rear.

Sitting at the western edge of Tiger Island, overlooking Berwick Bay, Brashear City was a natural staging point for a major campaign. Protected from enemy attack by the bay on one side and marshes on the other, it was accessible to Federal gunboats from both the Gulf of Mexico and an inland network of streams and lakes. Brashear City had good port facilities, warehouses for supplies, an adequate water supply, and a rail connection to New Orleans. By the second week of April the town had become so crowded with troops that an Indiana private predicted that if one more soldier set foot on the island it would sink into the swamp. It also was crowded with mosquitoes. Lawrence Van Alystene, a New Yorker, wrote home: "If I had a brigade of men as determined as these Brashear City mosquitoes, I believe I could sweep the Rebellion off its feet in a month's time."

Banks arrived at Brashear City on the night of April 8, his first opportunity to go into the field since his arrival in New Orleans. Before leaving the Crescent City he had to deal with a multitude of problems left in the wake of the Butler brothers' departure. By necessity, his initial battles were political, commercial, and organizational. He was under instruction to set up workable city and state governments in New Orleans and to expedite the flow of cotton and sugar to the commodities-starved East Coast. Banks also faced the task of organizing a dysfunctional army. The thirty thousand troops that accompanied him from New York had received virtually no training and its command structure was only loosely organized. Of the ten thousand troops he inherited from Butler less than half had seen combat, and he questioned the loyalty of the officers' corps.

In addition to those problems, almost daily he received pressure from Washington to move against the rebel garrison at Port Hudson. Banks intended to do just that—but on his own timetable. Not only would he silence the guns at Port Hudson, he planned to march on Vicksburg and capture that city as well—something Williams, Grant, and Farragut had not been able to accomplish. Once the Mississippi River was secured, he had plans to invade Texas and subdue Louisiana before winter rains set in. He figured the man who opened the Mississippi River and conquered Texas would make a formidable presidential candidate in 1864. On the eve of opening his spring campaign, all that stood in the way of his ambitions was a small rebel army behind earthen embankments only nine miles away.

Banks planned not to simply defeat Taylor but to strike him front and rear and destroy his army. To cut off any chance of retreat, General Culiver Grover and four thousand troops from Baton Rouge boarded transports on the Atchafalaya River and proceeded to Grand Lake. Grover's objective was Franklin. From there a single, narrow road flanked by swamplands provided the only escape route for Taylor's army.

At first light on April 11, a Saturday, Banks sent twelve thousand troops under Weitzel and General W. H. Emory across Berwick Bay. Supported by gunboats, they spread out on both sides of Bayou Teche and began moving north toward the waiting guns of Fort Bisland.

★　★　★

FORT BISLAND, APRIL 12—Taylor was bound to fight at Bisland. He had promised the people living in the region he would do so. His total force numbered less than five thousand men, one thousand of those deployed at Franklin to harass Glover and prevent him from landing his troops and crossing the Teche. Included in that detachment was the 2nd Louisiana Cavalry under Colonel W. S. Vincent. That left Taylor with only four thousand men at Bisland, including Sibley's Texas cavalry.

By traditional definition, Bisland was not a fort, but it was good ground for a fight. Located on a narrow ridge rising out of the swamps, the bayou flowed down its middle. The cypress swamps of Grand Lake on the east and the grass marshes of Vermillion Bay to the west protected Taylor's flanks. The strip of land to be defended was little more than a mile across, and most of it was planted in sugar cane. Mouton's men, along with slaves impressed from nearby plantations, had constructed a line of breastworks stretching across the strip and built redoubts on both sides of the bayou. The Confederates on the west side were well entrenched. There, some two thousand men waited, including Sibley's horsemen and Colonel Gray's untested 28th Infantry. On the east side of the bayou, Mouton had the 18th and Crescent regiments and assorted other units totaling about fifteen hundred men. Another three hundred troops under Colonel Arthur P. Bagby were stationed down the bayou at Lynch's Point as an advance guard. Mouton had not completed the breastworks on the east side, and his men worked feverishly to raise the height of the embankments even as the Federals approached. Taylor had thirty-nine pieces of assorted artillery, including two twenty-four-pound cannons salvaged from the *Cotton* and the thirty-pound Parrott on the *Diana,* which he stationed out of sight around a sharp bend in the bayou. His strategy was to entice Banks into a full frontal assault, where a concentrated fire could cut up his infantry. Once Banks was driven into retreat, Taylor figured he would turn and deal with Grover at his rear.

At mid-morning, Taylor sent the Texans out to harass the enemy. They raced out of a patch of woods, hitting an advance unit of Union infantry with such suddenness they almost picked off Banks before his horrified staff hustled him to safety. While the attack stymied the advance on that side of the bayou, on the other side, Colonel Bagby's three hundred troops met the onslaught of three Yankee regiments. Under heavy fire, Bagby's men were pushed back toward the breastworks. As the Federals moved forward, their advance formations alone outnumbered Taylor's entire army.

By three o'clock, shells from the Federal gunboats began falling around the rebel breastworks. Just after four o'clock, the long lines of the advance units of Banks's infantry could be seen coming through the cane fields. A Confederate soldier with a lyrical flair described the action when Taylor's artillery opened up on them: "They were advancing with cavalry, artillery and heavy columns of infantry. . . . Thirty-nine pieces of artillery on our side opened the ball at half past four o'clock p.m.; four thousand muskets supported the music from behind our breastworks."

The Confederate barrage sent Federal infantrymen scurrying for cover in drainage ditches that crossed the fields. Within minutes, Banks brought up his artillery and a mighty battle of big guns began. With several twenty-four-pound Parrotts in their arsenal, the Federal cannoneers held an advantage. Taylor had only three guns to equal them—the twenty-four-pounders from the *Cotton* and the *Diana's* Parrott. Several soldiers from Winn Parish Company K, under the command of Captain Darling P. Morris, had been assigned to the big gun on the *Diana*. Entering the fray, they employed a strategy that mystified the Yankees. The gunboat emerged from behind the cover of foliage at a bend in the bayou, fired, and quickly retreated from sight. There was a simple solution to the mystery. With ropes secured to the stern, the rebels let the boat drift beyond the bend and fire its guns, then quickly pulled it back.

With so many artillery pieces confined to such a small area, the concentration of fire became intense on both sides of the field. A Union surgeon vividly described the scene:

> All over the field, the thunder of artillery blended into one continuous roll. For an hour and a half, while lying in the ditches, the men were subjected to the deafening roar of one of the severest and most remarkable artillery duels of the war. A thousand Fourth of July celebrations were concentrated into a second of time. The air was rent with solid shot and grape. A haze filled the atmosphere from the smoke of discharged guns and bursting shells . . . while falling missiles cut down the cane and threw up showers of dirt.

As explosions chewed up Mouton's breastworks and redoubts, the men clung to the ground, more than a few praying for deliverance from the hell that had descended on them. Their prayers were answered when darkness settled on the bayou and the cannonading slowly ceased. Casualties on both sides were moderate, considering the intensity of the duel.

Taylor expected an all-out assault at dawn. Taking no chances, he sent a staff officer to New Iberia to begin removing supplies and ammunition stored there. He rode the twelve miles to Franklin that night to confer with Colonel Vincent on the progress of Grover's troops. Vincent informed him Grover was still on Grand Lake and had not landed. Taylor sent a messenger to Avery Island, where ninety men from Clack's Battalion were guarding the salt works, and ordered them to go to Franklin and support Vincent.

He returned to Bisland after midnight and learned that the Federals were using gunboats to transfer men across the bayou, apparently to attack his left flank. Confident Mouton could hold that side, Taylor decided to beat Banks to the punch and sent word to Sibley to attack the enemy's weakened left flank at first light. Captain Oliver Semmes was told to bring the *Diana* down the bayou to lend support. Having ridden twenty-five miles that night, an exhausted Taylor instructed Tom to wake him at five o'clock and then retired to his cot.

* * *

FORT BISLAND, APRIL 13—On Monday morning, a heavy fog blanketed the landscape as the *Diana* moved into position to support Sibley's attack. Taylor patiently waited for the sound of battle on his right. There was only silence. He sent a messenger to see why Sibley had not attacked and learned that the Texans were still sitting behind their barricades because of the fog. Taylor was furious. Having lost confidence in Sibley, he called off the assault. Meanwhile, Banks also seemed in no hurry. It was almost ten o'clock when his artillery opened up and his troops formed battle lines and began moving forward.

On the west side of the bayou the soldiers of the 28th hunkered behind their embankments as the earth shook beneath them and shells screamed above. At the hellish height of the bombardment, they witnessed a remarkable sight. Through the smoke a lone figure in a black greatcoat walked along the breastworks calmly rolling a cigarette. As grape and shell fragments whizzed about him, he stopped to light the cigarette, then resumed his walk as if taking a casual Sunday stroll. Sixteen-year-old Fred Hood was awestruck when the figure, seeming more apparition than man, stopped before him.

"What is your name, soldier?" Taylor yelled above the din of the battle raging around him.

"Frederick Swint Hood."

"Are you ready to shoot the Yankees when they come across that field, Private Hood?"

"Yes, sir!"

"That's good."

Taylor later recalled the moment in his memoirs:

The troops on the right of the Teche were raw and had never been in action. As shot and shell tore over the breastworks behind which they were lying, much consternation was exhibited, and it was manifest that an assault, however feeble, would break a part of the line. It was absolutely necessary to give the men some morale; and, mounting the breastwork, I made a cigarette, struck fire with my briquet, and walked up and down smoking.

Emboldened by the seeming invincibility of his commander, Captain Robert H. Bradford of the Jackson Parish Volunteers stepped forward. "If I can borrow your glasses, Gen'ral, I'll see what the Yankees is up to," he said.

Taylor continued his narrative:

Near the line was a low tree with spreading branches, which a young officer, Bradford by name, proposed to climb so as to have a better view. I gave him my field glasses, and this plucky youngster sat in his tree as quietly as in a chimney corner, though the branches around were cut away. These examples, especially that of Captain Bradford, gave confidence to the men who began to expose themselves, and some casualties were suffered in consequence.

When the Federal charge finally came, the men of the 28th braved the artillery barrage to lay down a heavy fire, as did the dismounted Texans fighting beside them. As the battle raged, Colonel Tom Green of the Texas Cavalry became concerned that his flank might be overrun. He sent word to Taylor that his corner was "getting hot" and he was taking casualties. "Tell the colonel that to my knowledge there are no cool places on the line," Taylor told the courier. "If there was one, I would be there."

Across the bayou, on Mouton's extreme left flank, it was even hotter than on the right. There he had only five hundred men holding off five Union regiments. In one charge the Federals came so close that Mouton ordered his men to fix bayonets, but rifle fire and the Parrott on the *Diana* finally drove the enemy back. That was as close as Banks would come to breaching the rebel defense.

The Confederate Parrott had become an irritant to Banks. Determined to silence her, he had his gunboats and land artillery concentrate their fire on the *Diana*. At about two o'clock, Taylor received word that the *Diana* had been disabled. He immediately went to check on the gunboat: "She was lying against the bank under a severe fire. The waters of the bayou seemed to be boiling like a kettle. . . . An officer came to the side of the boat to speak to me, but before he could open his mouth a shell struck him and he disappeared."

Semmes braved the fire to come ashore and report to Taylor that a shell had penetrated the railroad steel protecting the vessel's hull and exploded in the engine room, severing a steam line and damaging a boiler. Several of his men were killed and others scalded by the steam. "Can you move her?" Taylor shouted above the roar of exploding shells. Semmes said he would try. "Then take her out of this fire and see if she can be repaired."

Unknown to Taylor, at five o'clock that afternoon Banks received word that Grover was landing troops near the Porter Plantation, just north of Franklin. Grover advised that he had driven off the rebel cavalry opposing him and would move against Taylor at daylight. Convinced he had trapped Taylor, Banks broke off the fighting, intending to finish the job on Tuesday.

As darkness settled on the battlefield, Taylor assessed his situation. Instead of the frontal assault he would have preferred, Banks had attacked his flanks, preventing him from concentrating his fire. He had managed to hold his position but at a cost of more than 450 casualties, almost all resulting from the artillery barrage. Federal losses were less than 300. At nine o'clock a courier brought Taylor news that Grover's troops had landed behind him. Colonel Vincent had delayed the landing by racing his cavalry up and down the Grand Lake shoreline, exchanging fire with Union gunboats protecting the troop transports. Muddy roads prevented him from moving his artillery to the eventual landing site in time to stop Grover. The Union troops finally had disembarked from their boats and waded almost one hundred yards to land.

Outnumbered more than four to one with the enemy now front and rear, Taylor wondered what Stonewall might do—or Zack Taylor. Stonewall, he concluded, would attack Grover, just as he had done Fremont in the Shenandoah. Taylor ordered his men to begin loading wagons and prepare the artillery for movement. By midnight, his cargo train was headed up the bayou road, trailed by Sibley's cavalry and Mouton's infantry. When the Federals stormed Fort Bisland at daylight, they found it deserted.

* * *

FRANKLIN, APRIL 14—While a disappointed Nathaniel Banks stood on the rebel breastworks at Bisland, twelve miles to the north—at a place the natives called Irish Bend—Taylor was preparing a surprise for Grover. There, some four hundred rebels spread in a thin line across a narrow strip of solid land wedged between Bayou Teche and a marsh. Taylor hoped to hold Grover's army in that bottleneck conveniently provided by nature until the last of his wagons were safely across the Bayou Yokely bridge north of Franklin. Into this strip marched Union Colonel Henry Birge's brigade, led by the 25th Connecticut Infantry. It was greeted by a volley of rifle fire from rebels hidden in the cane rows. More startled than damaged, the Union troops fell back, seeking cover. A Connecticut soldier described the ensuing firefight in his diary: "The Confederate musket fire rattled through the dry stalks like hail against the windows."

At the moment the fighting began, Gray arrived with the 28th, his men having loaded supplies half the night and marched the other half. Taylor posted them in a battle line behind a strip of moss-draped cypress trees on his left flank. Meanwhile, more Federal troops slogged their way across the field, still muddy from recent rains. They were startled by the scream of a shell followed by a jarring explosion in their midst. The *Diana* had dropped her calling card. Chugging up the Bayou, enveloped in steam escaping from her patched pipes, she began lobbing thirty-pound rounds onto the field as fast as the Winn Parish boys could reload. At the same time, two small cannons manned by the St. Mary's Volunteers were brought forward and opened up on the Connecticut troops at close range. Caught by surprise, Colonel Birge and two of his staff officers had their horses blown from beneath them. Taylor, his ranks having swelled to more than twelve hundred, chose that moment to order an attack.

Colonel Gray led his men out of the woods and into the cane field. Since many of his troops were armed with shotguns, he closed to almost point-blank range with the enemy before giving the order to fire. The New York 159th had the misfortune to be crossing the field when the rebels suddenly appeared on its flank and unleashed a murderous blast of buckshot and buck and ball. Within seconds, 115 men of the regiment lay dead or wounded in the cane rows. The devastation caused by the volley left the men of the 28th in awe of their own destructive power and taught them a valuable lesson. If armed with a short-range weapon, one must quickly close ranks with the enemy in order to effectively shoot him. Although the 28th suffered few casualties in the charge, the action drew a barrage of Union artillery that did inflict damage. Most notable among those wounded by flying shrapnel was Colonel Gray and Captain Bradford, the young man who had impressed Taylor by sitting in a tree under fire. Their wounds proved minor, and both remained in action and retained their commands. Asked by Major William Walker if he was all right, Gray affirmed that he was fine but Eleanor would be mad as hell when she saw what the Yankees had done to his coat. A soldier commented that perhaps now he would wear the fancy jacket given to him by the troops. "I am afraid I left that one back at Bisland," the colonel smiled. "I am sure some Yankee will appreciate it."

Even as Grover rushed reinforcements forward at Irish Bend, Banks sent troops up the Teche Road in pursuit of the retreating rebels. Mouton personally directed the rear guard. Being familiar with the area, he led his men along off-road trails and paths. Snipers harassed the Federals along the main road and, occasionally, Mouton's troops emerged in force, sending a volley into the advancing enemy and disappearing back into the woods.

By noon, with his artillery and supply wagons across the Yokely Bridge and Grover's artillery engaged in a duel with the crew of the *Diana*, Taylor saw an opportunity to withdraw his troops. His plan called for the *Diana* to cover the retreat until Mouton was ready to cross the bridge, at which time the crew was to set fire to the gunboat and escape with the rear guard. By now Taylor was thoroughly disgusted with General Sibley's seeming inability to carry out orders. He sought out the cavalry commander and personally instructed him to cover Mouton's men and the crew of the *Diana* until they crossed the bayou, at which time he was to set fire to the bridge, assume the rear guard, and prevent straggling by the infantry. Sibley, thinking all troops were across the bridge, fired it prematurely. As Mouton arrived with his rear guard, he was stunned to see the bridge in flames. He and his men sprinted through the inferno, barely getting across before the structure collapsed. Several members of the 28th Regiment were not so fortunate. They were trapped on the wrong side of the bayou and captured. Aboard the *Diana*, Captain Morris and Semmes set fire to the gunboat and, upon discovering that the bridge was destroyed, fled into a nearby swamp. They, along with several of their men, were quickly captured by the Federals.

When informed of Sibley's mistake, Taylor launched into a tirade and swore to his staff he would have him court-martialed. Not only did Sibley fail to organize an attack on the Union flank on Monday, he remained in his tent all day, well away from the fighting. Although he claimed to be ill, Taylor suspected he was drunk. Put in charge of evacuating the cargo and munitions wagons from Bisland that night, Sibley delegated the responsibility to a subordinate, then returned to his tent to sleep. Ordered to evacuate the wounded by wagon and ambulance, Sibley loaded them on an old steamer at Pattersonville. As the boat chugged up the bayou on Tuesday morning, the Yankees stopped it and took almost two hundred prisoners. Taylor's troops were approaching New Iberia when he received word that his men were straggling. Riding quickly to the rear, he found troops scattered and disorganized and Sibley's cavalry nowhere to be seen. As a result, some of his soldiers had fallen behind and were captured by the Federals. Later, when Sibley showed up, still claiming to be ill, Taylor relieved him of command and placed Tom Green in charge of the cavalry brigade.

The forty-eight-year-old Green was a genuine Texas hero. He had fought with Sam Houston at San Jacinto and achieved legendary status as an Indian fighter and Texas Ranger. He served as an officer under Zack Taylor in the Mexican War and had distinguished himself more recently in the West Texas and New Mexico campaigns. For the remainder of the Confederate retreat, Green proved himself an outstanding field commander. He and his Texans slashed at Banks's flanks and delayed the Union cavalry in its pursuit of the slow-moving rebel wagons.

Determined to save his army, Taylor pushed his columns unmercifully until they had left the Yankees several miles behind. Colonel Arthur W. Hyatt of Mouton's staff described the forced march in his journal: "A regular race with the enemy. Feet sore, dust intolerable. . . . When we halt, we squat ourselves down, no matter where—in the sand, in the mud,—anywhere and our only hope is that the halt will last fifteen minutes. At night you fall down too tired to be careful of selections and go to sleep, without taking off clothes, shoes or cap."

On April 15, as the rebel army trudged wearily through Mouton's hometown at Vermillionville, Taylor gave him a promotion. He was placed in command of all troops south of the Red River. When Gray offered his congratulations, Mouton replied that he would have enjoyed the promotion more without the presence of sixteen thousand Union troops at his heels.

* * *

NEW IBERIA, APRIL 16—By the time Banks's army entered New Iberia on Wednesday, it resembled a mob more than a military force. The Federals had pillaged virtually every home along the Teche, leaving many in ashes. Although the destruction seemed not to concern Banks, it appalled one of his brigadiers, who made the following observation in his official report:

> The scenes of disorder and pillage on these two days march were disgraceful to civilized war. Houses were entered and all in them destroyed in the most wanton manner. Ladies were frightened into delivering their valuables into the hands of soldiers by threats of violence to their husbands. Negro women were ravished in the presence of white women and children. These disgusting scenes were due to the want of discipline in this army, and to the utter incompetence of regimental officers.

However, the men in the ranks paid little attention to those officers who tried to stop the rapes and looting. A soldier in the New York 114th Regiment wrote in a letter, "Oftentimes a soldier can be found with such an enormous development of the organ of destructiveness that the most severe punishment cannot deter him from indulging in the breaking of mirrors, and pianos, and the most costly furniture. Men of such reckless dispositions are frequently guilty of the most horrible desecrations."

Union troops descended on New Iberia like locusts, many of them drunk on liquor taken from the cabinets of plantation homes along the Teche. Entering homes and businesses, they stole anything of value and destroyed the rest. Residents who protested were beaten with rifle butts. Soldiers looted the Catholic Church, taking its sacred vessels and statues. Some draped themselves in the robes of the priest and danced in the street.

At the home of a family named Borel, everything of value was taken, including all of the food in the smokehouse and pantry. The troops also took Borel's plowhorse, his only means to support his wife and children. Spotting General Banks nearby, Borel approached him and tried to explain that, without his horse, his family would starve come winter. Banks responded, "The horse is no more your property than the rest. Louisiana is mine and I intend to take everything."

The Union cavalry occupied the city cemetery, turning it into a horse corral. Because of underground water levels in South Louisiana, above-ground vaults traditionally were used to bury the dead. These vaults seemed to fascinate Northern troops, who proceeded to open them. While families of the deceased looked on in horror, remains were pulled from the vaults and scattered about. Metal coffins were used as watering troughs for horses.

Harris Beecher, who later wrote a regimental history of the 114th New York, provided a description of the Federal pursuit of the rebel army from Franklin to Vermillionville:

> It was a miserable march for both sides. Foot soldiers limped along on raw, blistered feet. Suffocating clouds of dust turned faces into masks of grime and sweat. Hour by hour, the columns became more and more scattered and confused. Federal soldiers began grabbing anything they could ride—horse, mule or milk cow. . . . Huge plantation carts, drawn by diminutive donkeys were loaded down with lazy soldiers. In one instant, some officers were laid out full length in a hearse, smoking their pipes while an ugly mule and a ragged Negro driver were conducting them along the road. A soldier was being drawn by a comrade on a hand cart. Wheelbarrows even came into use. An elegant *barouche* [carriage] conveying some officers with cigaretts [sic], was drawn by a novel team composed of a cow and mule. Skeleton buggies, family carriages, doctors' sulkies, wagons, all brought into requisition to complete the amusing but sad picture.

Banks finally issued an order to forbid looting. He did so not out of compassion for the besieged locals but because it was slowing his pursuit of Taylor. Soldiers in the rear, finding nothing left to steal in the line of march, were ranging miles from their columns to plunder homes. The rank and file generally ignored his order. To inspire compliance, Banks had a looter ceremoniously shot. However, the demise of the unfortunate example had little effect on the men.

* * *

VERMILLIONVILLE, APRIL 18—On Thursday, April 17, General Banks sent the following report to General in Chief Henry Halleck in Washington:

> We have pursued the enemy closely more than 50 miles; we have destroyed the *Queen of the West* and have compelled him to destroy *Diana* and *Hart* [a Confederate ram scuttled by Mouton]. . . . We have taken eleven guns, one steamer, over a thousand prisoners, and large quantities of ammunition, camp equipage and quartermasters stores and destroyed his salt works below New Iberia; his infantry has dispersed over the prairies and in the woods, so that the people and Negroes tell us nothing but cavalry and artillery passed beyond New Iberia.

Banks's wishful report on the condition of the rebel army was far from accurate. Even as he wrote it, Taylor's troops were in Opelousas, twenty-five miles away. He had lost some four hundred men to capture, not the one thousand claimed by Banks. Although there had been desertions by South Louisiana soldiers who could not resist the temptation to visit their homes, Taylor still had twenty-five hundred men in ranks and another fifteen hundred mounted. The desertions did not disturb him. He had seen the men slip away before, and return when it was time to fight. By necessity, the disciplinarian in Virginia had become the tolerant commander in Louisiana. Here he was fighting a different kind of war with a different kind of soldier. What was important was that he still had the core of his army intact and had salvaged virtually all of his artillery, ammunition, and twenty-seven wagons of stores and supplies. Also fanciful was Banks's claim to have destroyed the Avery Island salt mine, an impervious dome of rock salt.

Upon the rebels' arrival at Opelousas, they found a frenzy of activity that bordered on panic. The governor had departed with the local militia, and as word of Yankee atrocities spread, residents were fleeing the city with their belongings in wagons, carts, and carriages. Many plantation owners sent their slaves west to Texas and drove their herds into the hills. Taylor was relieved to learn that Mimi and the children had left for Alexandria with the governor and his entourage. Moore intended to establish the state capital at Shreveport where Kirby Smith was setting up his headquarters.

Word that Admiral Porter waited at the mouth of the Red River with several gunboats caused concern at Alexandria and Shreveport. In a communiqué to Taylor, Smith expressed a fear that Banks might sweep up the entire length of the Red River Valley and lay siege to Shreveport. In spite of Taylor's assurance that Banks's objective was Port Hudson and not Shreveport, Smith took no chances. He ordered Major General John G. Walker's Texas Division from Arkansas to protect Shreveport.

Taylor correctly surmised that Porter's gunboats were clearing the lower Red River to accommodate the troop ships that would transport Banks's army to Port Hudson. Realizing that Fort DeRussy did not have the firepower to stop a fleet of gunboats, Taylor sent word for the men to remove the guns and temporarily abandon the stronghold.

At Opelousas, Taylor split his force. He did so because there was not enough young spring grass to provide forage for both the cavalry horses and the mules pulling his artillery and supply wagons. He sent Green and Mouton with some two thousand men to the west to find better foraging and instructed Green to circle back to strike Banks's rear and threaten his communications and supply lines when the opportunity presented itself.

★ ★ ★

SHREVEPORT, APRIL 28—Taylor arrived in Alexandria on Friday, April 24, to be greeted by Mimi and the children. She had refused to leave for Shreveport, choosing to wait for her husband. They spent a night together before Taylor put his family on a steamer with other refugees bound for Shreveport. "It was a moment of sad farewell," he wrote. The sight of the children standing at the rail waving to him would become a cherished and haunting memory.

On the trip upriver, there was an outbreak of scarlet fever on the steamer. All of the Taylor children contracted the disease. Mimi was swept up in a hellish world of coughing and crying children as she mopped fevered brows and prayed. That first night on the river, Little Zack's face flushed crimson and his skin became so warm it pained her to touch it. He died the following day, just two weeks before his sixth birthday. In a letter to her niece, Mimi described her heartbreak: "My little man Zack was manly to the last. I thought my heart would break when I saw that dearest little face covered with death's icy hand, [and] when those beautiful bright eyes closed forever . . . I felt as if I had lost all in this world."

Soldiers on the steamer built a tiny coffin. A young woman who had married just before departing Alexandria donated part of her wedding dress to line the coffin. The small body, dressed in the uniform Zack had so proudly modeled for his father, was placed inside. When the boat arrived in Shreveport, the body was taken to a church where Confederate officers stood watch overnight. In Taylor's absence, Kirby Smith made arrangements for the funeral. Taylor did not learn of his son's death until the day after his burial.

Mimi and the other three children, all terribly ill, were taken in by a Shreveport family. Ulger Lauve and his wife risked their lives and those of their own children to help nurse the Taylor children. Clarice Hewitt, who had fled her family's plantation on Bayou Lafourche, became a good friend to Mimi on their journey north. She did her best to comfort Mimi and assist with the nursing.

Three weeks later, Taylor was near Vicksburg when he received word that his second son, Dixie, also had died.

*　*　*

ALEXANDRIA, MAY 8—As the Union Army entered Alexandria on Friday, May 8, a committee of city leaders met with Banks. Having heard of the devastation left in the wake of the Union army in South Louisiana, they petitioned Banks to spare their city from the kind of looting and burning that had taken place elsewhere. But the general was not in a magnanimous mood that day. "Believe it, gentlemen, as if you heard God himself speak it. I will lay waste to your country so that you will never organize and maintain another army in this department."

Although several hundred bales of cotton were seized by the Northern army at Alexandria, the city avoided the kind of wanton looting that devastated New Iberia, Vermillionville, Opelousas, and scores of smaller towns. It was spared, not out of sympathy for the population, but because of time restraints. Almost immediately upon their arrival, Banks and his staff began loading troops on transports bound for Port Hudson, and Banks sent another glowing account of his expedition to Halleck: "We have destroyed the enemy's army and navy, and made their reorganization impossible. . . . Among the evidence of our victory are 2,000 prisoners, two transports and twenty guns taken and three gunboats and eight transports destroyed."

Far from being destroyed, however, the main body of Taylor's army was camped forty miles away at Natchitoches and Tom Green's horsemen continued to harass Union troops below Alexandria.

In response to Halleck's concern over reports that the property of foreign citizens was being confiscated, Banks responded that many persons claiming to be French or English were actually U.S. citizens. Banks responded to Halleck's questions regarding reports of looting by assuring him that he was doing everything possible to stop the practice: "One soldier has been shot to death for plundering and pillaging, and some others are being tried for the same offense, who will doubtless have to suffer the same penalty. The temptations to plunder and pillage have been so strong and the disregard of reiterated orders forbidding it such that severe measures were indispensable."

However, the men might have been taking their cue from the "official" looting taking place under the sanction and blessing of their commander. In a subsequent report, Banks noted that he had seized "20,000 beeves, mules and horses [and forwarded them to] Brashear City, with 5,000 bales of cotton and many hogsheads of sugar." In the same report, Banks reported yet another capture: "I ordered the arrest of ex-Governor Mouton, who occupied the gubernatorial chair in 1845 and subsequently. . . . It seemed important that such a man should at least be quiet. I have therefore ordered him to New Orleans in the custody of the provost marshal general."

Governor Mouton had fled his stately home in Vermillionville only to be overtaken by a detachment of cavalry at Opelousas. He had plenty of company on the trip to New Orleans. On May 5, Captain Howard Dwight of Banks's staff had been ambushed and killed, and Banks promptly ordered the random arrests of one hundred male residents of Opelousas in retaliation for the slaying. Banks directed that the men be imprisoned in New Orleans as hostages until local residents handed over the "assassin" of Captain Dwight. The prisoners, some of whom were in their seventies, never identified the guilty party and remained in prison.

Meanwhile, at Vermillionville, Governor Mouton's family became prisoners in their own home. While the bottom floor of the mansion was occupied by Federal officers, the family was confined, under guard, on the upper floor.

★ ★ ★

PORT HUDSON, MAY 27—If ever nature provided a perfect location to be defended from attack, it was Port Hudson. The picturesque little town sat on a sixty-foot bluff on the east side of the Mississippi, overlooking a sharp bend in the river. On its landward side, steep hills plunged into a network of deep ravines created by centuries of rainfall cascading down the inclines. Port Hudson was a shipping outlet for a large agricultural region. A railroad connected it to the booming town of Clinton, twenty miles away. A network of well-kept roads funneled cotton and produce to its docks from a dozen small towns and numerous plantations lining the river. The town's most prominent feature was its collection of warehouses, all newly constructed at great cost. A dozen retail businesses, several saloons, and two large hotels surrounded by some fifty houses completed the town.

Pierre Beauregard originally suggested Port Hudson as a good site for a fort. When Breckinridge withdrew from Baton Rouge, he chose to set up a camp there and brought troops up from Camp Moore to bolster his small force. General W. N. R. Beall arrived in the fall of 1862 to supervise construction of a fort on the site. Taking advantage of the rugged natural terrain, he had built a series of earthworks in a defense line some three miles long around the heights. The earthworks, protected by built-in rifle pits, averaged twenty feet thick, with ditches ten to fifteen feet deep in front. On hillsides below the earthworks, trees were felled across gullies, creating a tangle of branches to slow the enemy under the guns of the fort. On the north side of the works, where Thompson Creek emptied into the Mississippi River, a dense swamp protected the fort. In this enclosure, shaped like an irregular horseshoe, seven thousand rebel soldiers waited for the attack that was sure to come. From the bluffs above the Mississippi, nineteen pieces of artillery looked down on the river channel waiting for Farragut's warships.

The commander at Port Hudson was General Franklin Gardner, a New Yorker with unique ties by marriage to the Mouton family. He came to Vermillionville by virtue of his friendship with Alfred Mouton and married his sister, Marie Celestine Mathilde Mouton. Meanwhile, the widowed governor married Gardner's sister, creating an unusual situation in which Gardner's sister became Alfred's stepmother.

Gardner's father, Charles Gardner, had an outstanding military career, rising to adjutant general of the U.S. Army and, upon his retirement, became a prominent writer with deep involvement in New York politics.

At age twenty, Franklin graduated from West Point in the class of '43—the storied class that produced fifteen Civil War generals. When Louisiana seceded, he left the U.S. Army to command an infantry regiment in the Confederate Army. He distinguished himself in the fighting at Shiloh, earning a promotion to brigadier general. He led a brigade in Bragg's invasion of Kentucky and emerged a major general. He had a reputation as a ferocious fighter and for being stubborn to a fault. As Banks closed in on him with thirty thousand troops, he ignored an order from General Joseph Johnston to abandon the fort. To do so, he concluded, would doom Vicksburg and surrender the entire length of the Mississippi River without a fight. Gardner informed his staff that he would not become the general who gave up the Mississippi River.

★ ★ ★

By May 23, Federal troops from Alexandria, New Orleans, and Baton Rouge had converged on Port Hudson. By May 26, Farragut's warships and Palmer's gunboats stood ready to lend support to Banks's ground forces. Banks intended to make quick work of Port Hudson and then move on to Vicksburg. His strategy was simple: Pound the Confederates into submission with artillery then overwhelm them with superior ground forces.

At daylight on Wednesday, May 27, the Union army and navy unleashed a massive artillery bombardment that leveled buildings, destroyed cannons, and mowed down men and livestock. The rebels hunkered in rifle pits and holes dug into the earthworks as an inferno of shot and shell turned the little town to rubble. At mid-morning, with banners waving and bayonets gleaming in the sunlight, the Union infantry advanced in wave after wave.

Reaching the rugged terrain of the hillsides, the lines became disorganized as they crossed ravines and made their way through the tangle of felled trees. The rebels, most of them armed with old smooth-bore muskets loaded with buck and ball, crouched in their rifle pits, holding their fire. They waited until the Union troops were within forty yards, then stood and fired in volley. A storm of lead slugs and buckshot ripped into the Union's advance units. An infantryman described the devastating result:

> [As we approached] the long line of [Confederate] rifle pits there was no sign of life. I looked to the right and saw the long line of blue advance, with flags waving in the gentle breeze. I turned my eyes to the silent rebel rifle pits. Suddenly above them appeared a dark cloud of slouched hats and bronzed faces; the next moment a sheet of flame. I glanced again to the right; the line of blue had melted away.

Time after time the Federals charged the breastworks in piecemeal attacks, only to be repulsed by Confederate fire. In one sector a regiment reached the rifle pits and engaged in hand-to-hand combat before being driven back. Union troops finally took refuge in the gullies and behind fallen trees. The rebels dragged cannons to the edge of the breastworks and discharged round after round into those positions until Federal riflemen began picking off the cannoneers, forcing them to retire. Within an hour of the beginning of the assault, blue-clad dead and wounded littered the hillsides.

Meanwhile, on the extreme left of the rebel defense, an "experiment" was taking place with tragic consequences. There Brigadier General William Dwight Jr. sent two regiments of Native Guards against the strongest sector of the Confederate line. Dwight, only thirty-one years old, was a notorious alcoholic who had been kicked out of West Point for his drinking and "association with obscene women." Placed in command of three regiments of black troops, he had decided on his own "to test the Negro question." In a letter to his family on the eve of the attack, he wrote, "I am going to storm a detached work with them. You may look for hard fighting, or for a complete run away. The garrison [rebels] will of course be incensed and fight defiantly. The negro will have the fate of his race on his conduct. I shall compromise nothing in making this attack for I regard it as an experiment."

Considering the terrain on that side of the field, what happened could hardly be considered an "experiment." The rebels held such an advantage that Banks had no intention to attack the position. Later, when informed that the Native Guards had assaulted the position, Banks expressed surprise that Dwight had ordered it.

To approach the rebels on that side of the field, the troops had to traverse an open swamp at the base of steep bluffs under a crossfire by Confederate rifles and artillery. Dwight never even bothered to reconnaissance the terrain before sending his troops into battle. His only preparation for the assault was to get drunk before breakfast. Having given the order for the 1st and 2nd Native Guards regiments to advance on the stronghold, he sat beneath a tree with a bottle of whiskey and left it to Colonel John A. Nelson to command the men. As the Native Guards formed lines in a willow grove at the edge of the swamp, two field pieces were brought forward to support them. When the lines advanced, the cannoneers fired a round into the defense works. Six Confederate cannons responded, killing two artillerymen and several horses. The others fled, leaving their field pieces, and the Native Guards remained to fend for themselves.

When the fully exposed regiments advanced within four hundred yards of the bluffs, hell descended upon them. In addition to shot and shell, the rebels had cut up railroad iron in one-foot lengths to load their cannons. Color Sergeant Anselmas Planciancois, whose outgoing personality made him popular among the men, proudly carried the banner of the 1st Regiment forward. In stunned disbelief, the men saw half of his head blown away. Captain Andrew Cailloux had part of his left arm blown off. The mangled arm dangling at his side, he urged his men forward, only to be killed by a rifle ball.

Once they came in range, rifle fire from behind the earthworks swept the field, opening gaps in the ranks. The concussion of exploding shells sent mud and debris flying through the smoke. The whiz of shrapnel and whine of musket balls filled the air, punctuated by the sickening thud of metal striking flesh. The Native Guards fell back in confusion, slogging through the mud and staggering into the willow grove, some dragging their wounded comrades. In a matter of minutes, the 1st Regiment had sustained 150 casualties, including two officers killed and three wounded.

When Colonel Nelson reported the failed attempt to Dwight, the brigadier became angry and ordered another attack. Nelson protested but Dwight was adamant and Nelson dutifully returned and ordered Lieutenant Colonel Henry Finnegass to prepare for another assault. Finnegass refused, pointing out the obvious—that even if his men made it across the open swamp, it would be impossible to scale the bluffs. Jarred to his senses by the simple truth of the logic, Nelson told the colonel to remain in the willow grove. He instructed Finnegass to have his men continue to fire their weapons so that Dwight would hear them and think an attack was taking place.

By noon Banks realized that his general attack had been repulsed, but he was not ready to give up. At two o'clock he massed troops for an attack on the Confederate center. He intended to concentrate enough troops and artillery to punch a hole in the Confederate defense. From their elevated earthworks, the rebels watched in awe as line after blue-clad line formed up on a large, open plain appropriately named Slaughter's Field. Many of them later recalled that it was an amazing sight to behold. A Confederate soldier captured the awe mixed with concern among his fellow rebels:

> It was a magnificent sight, but the great odds against us looked appalling as our line was weak, averaging about one man every five feet, and no reserve force. Of one thing we felt sure and that was that our men would do all that it was possible for us to do. Every company officer, as far as I could see, stood in line with his men, musket in hand. Varied were the expressions on the faces of the men. Some were serious and silent. Others joked and danced or sang short snatches of song but there was an intense earnestness about all.

Once within range, Confederate artillery tore into the Union ranks. Among the first to fall was General T. W. Sherman, who was coordinating the attack. The bone in his right leg shattered, he was dragged from the field even as two of his staff officers were killed and another severely wounded. His troops came under intense musket fire and fell by the scores as they tried to scramble over and around the branches of the fallen trees below the rifle pits. The artillery bombardment set underbrush on fire and flames swept through the ravines, driving Federal troops into the open and into the fire of the riflemen. At 5:30 P.M., Banks called off the attack.

When dusk mercifully settled on the battle-scarred hillsides below the defense works, more than two thousand Federal soldiers lay dead or wounded. Confederate casualties were less than three hundred. For all of the blood spilled that day, Banks had accomplished little—a few buildings destroyed, moderate casualties on the rebel side, and several Confederate cannons put out of action. Most of that damage had taken place in the first few minutes of the Federal artillery bombardment.

That night a member of the 4th Massachusetts Infantry recorded in his diary "a scene I will never forget." He wrote, "On the operating tables were the victims, whose shrieks of agony [were] partially deadened by chloroform. . . . Seeing the doctors with sleeves rolled up, splashed with blood, here a pile of booted legs, there a pile of arms, was more trying than the horrors of the battlefield."

The next morning Gardner agreed to a one-day truce to allow Banks to retrieve his dead and wounded. Even as bodies were pulled from ravines and from the tangled branches of the felled trees, General Banks sent a message to New Orleans, ordering more troops to Port Hudson.

*　*　*

MONROE, JUNE 4—In late May, Dick Taylor was in a state of deep despondency over the loss of his sons. Moody and reclusive, he remained in his quarters for extensive periods. However, in early June he received a bit of intelligence that energized him. Word arrived that Federal troops were being rapidly withdrawn from South Louisiana to reinforce Banks at Port Hudson. One report indicated that no more than one thousand troops remained in and around New Orleans, with another two or three thousand scattered in camps from Berwick Bay to Donaldsonville.

The moment for which he had waited had arrived. New Orleans would never be more vulnerable. With the recent arrival of Walker's Texas Division in Shreveport, Taylor figured he could put together a formidable army of seven thousand battle-tested veterans, capable of sweeping through South Louisiana, cutting Banks's supply lines and capturing New Orleans. If he could retake New Orleans and hold it even briefly, Banks would be forced to abandon the siege at Port Hudson, freeing the rebel garrison there to march north and cut Grant's supply line at Port Gibson. Grant would be trapped between Gardner, Pemberton, and Johnston, and cut off from his gunboats on the river. An attack on New Orleans, Taylor believed, would bring in thousands of volunteers trapped in the Crescent City without a means to resist the Federal occupation. He presented his strategy to Kirby Smith and was stunned when Smith turned it down.

Instead of a South Louisiana expedition, Smith ordered Taylor to assist Pemberton in the defense of Vicksburg by attacking Grant's supply lines at Milliken's Bend on the west bank of the Mississippi. Taylor pointed out that Pemberton had thirty thousand troops sitting under siege in Vicksburg capable of contending with Grant if he would only use them properly, and Joe Johnston had another twenty thousand men in Southern Tennessee and Northern Mississippi if Pemberton needed relief. He suggested that, instead of Pemberton letting his troops sit in trenches and face starvation, the war effort would be better served if he went out and fought Grant. "The solution to the problem is to withdraw the [Vicksburg] garrison, not reinforce it," he insisted. Unswayed, Smith sent Taylor the following message:

> I know your desire is naturally great to recover what you have lost in lower Louisiana; and to push on toward New Orleans; but the stake contended for near Vicksburg is the Valley of the Mississippi and the Trans-Mississippi Department; the defeat of General Grant is the *terminus ad quem* of all operations in the west this summer; to its attainment all minor advantages should be sacrificed.

Smith's belittling of a New Orleans campaign as a "minor advantage" angered Taylor, who saw the Crescent City as the Union's Achilles' heel. By threatening Washington, Jackson had relieved Richmond and assured a Confederate victory. Taylor had no doubt that a threat against New Orleans would similarly relieve Port Hudson and Vicksburg. He pointed out to Smith that, even if he cut Grant's lines at Milliken's Bend, his men would not be able to hold a position on the west bank of the river because of the presence of Union gunboats. Unmoved, Smith told Taylor that orders to reinforce Pemberton came from the "highest command" in Richmond. The high command, Taylor knew, was Secretary of War James A. Seddon, an ally of both Smith and Pemberton, but a man in whom Taylor had no confidence at all. "To go two hundred miles and more away from the proper theater of action [New Orleans] in search of an indefinite *something* was hard," Taylor wrote, "but orders are orders."

* * *

MILLIKEN'S BEND, JUNE 7—Kirby Smith wanted Taylor to attack two Federal camps across the river from Vicksburg—at Milliken's Bend and Young's Point. From the outset, Taylor considered the operation an exercise in futility and waste of resources. He knew Walker's Texans could carry the camps, for they were lightly manned. Holding them would be another matter as an armada of Federal gunboats on the river north of Vicksburg protected them. Unlike Vicksburg, which was protected by steep cliffs, the Louisiana side of the river was low and flat. With the river at a high level, the gunboats would virtually be able to look down the throats of his men.

Taylor set up a headquarters at Richmond, several miles west of Milliken's Bend, and conferred with Walker on a plan of attack. Intelligence reports indicated there were only one thousand Federals at Milliken's Bend, and several hundred of those were black troops who had been issued rifles only two weeks earlier. The Union force at Young's Point numbered no more than two or three hundred. To assure surprise, Walker suggested that he split his force and assault both positions at the same time. Taylor agreed with the plan, emphasizing that the camps should be carried quickly before gunboats arrived to provide cover.

At daybreak on Sunday, June 7, fifteen hundred Texans under Brigadier General Henry McCulloch caught the garrison at Milliken's Bend eating breakfast. The attack quickly sent the disorganized Federals fleeing behind a levee from which they began firing sporadically on the Texans. McCulloch decided the quickest way to dislodge the enemy was with bayonets. He ordered a charge and the rebels rushed forward, yelling like demons and shouting "no quarter." As the Texans poured over the levee, one of the most brutal struggles of the war took place. Many of the black troops, having received little or no instructions, were unfamiliar with their rifles and, after firing a single shot, did not reload. As the Texans descended on them, they instinctively began using their rifles as clubs. Having been told by white officers that they would be shot if captured, the black troops fought with desperate resolve. A Union officer wrote of them, "To their credit, they never flinched but made a desperate resistance. . . . So it came to thrusting at each other with bayonets, clubbing muskets, and dashing each other's brains out. It was a horrible fight, the worst I was ever engaged in—not even accepting Shiloh."

The curses of combatants and screams of the dying and wounded filled the air in a brief but bloody brawl. As rebel numbers overwhelmed the defenders a terrible slaughter began. Black soldiers attempting to flee were shot in the back. Wounded men were bayoneted even as they tried to surrender. In the official report of the battle, Union casualties erroneously were listed at 101 killed and 285 wounded. However, another account noted that in just one 300-man black regiment, 128 were killed. The death rate in relation to wounded was staggering. Heavy Confederate losses testified to the viciousness of the struggle—44 killed and 130 wounded, twelve percent of the brigade. The Federal death toll might have climbed higher if not for the appearance of two Union gunboats. They arrived shortly after 8 A.M. and began shelling the rebels, forcing a withdrawal beyond the range of their guns.

Although the Union force was routed, at the end of the day Federal troops still held both Milliken's Bend and Young's Point. Brigadier General James Hawkes, finding three gunboats anchored at Young's Point chose not to attack. Grant's supply lines remained intact. Receiving the news, Taylor was disappointed but not surprised. "As foreseen, our movement resulted, and could result, in nothing," he wrote.

In the wake of the day's fighting, Taylor found himself in a dilemma when Walker presented him with fifty black prisoners and two of their white officers. Upon hearing rumors that Taylor was holding black prisoners, Smith sent the following message: "I hope this may not be so, and that your subordinates . . . may have recognized the propriety of giving no quarter to armed negroes and their officers. In this way we may be relieved from a disagreeable dilemma."

Taylor, who had no intention of executing fifty-two prisoners, sent a terse reply to Smith's veiled suggestion that execution might be a solution to the "disagreeable dilemma." "Then I respectfully ask instructions as to the disposition of these prisoners," he wrote, placing the burden of responsibility squarely on Smith. Unsure of the latest policy regarding the handling of black prisoners of war, Smith contacted his friend Seddon at the War Department. Seddon informed him that President Davis wanted black prisoners "considered as deluded victims [to be] treated with mercy and returned to their owners."

If it accomplished nothing else, Milliken's Bend finally clarified the Confederate policy regarding "no quarter" for black prisoners of war. Early in the conflict the War Department had approved a request by the army to execute ex-slaves who took up arms against the Confederacy. President Davis quickly rescinded that policy, leaving it up to the individual states "to prosecute them [ex-slaves in uniform] for inciting insurrection." As a result, several states, including Louisiana, passed laws approving the execution of black prisoners of war. Davis, fearing that England and France would react negatively if such executions took place, finally came up with the more lenient policy. Taylor did not even wait for a reply from Smith. He sent the white officers to Shreveport to await exchange and turned the black captives loose, instructing them to go home.

* * *

SHREVEPORT, JUNE 10—"My sweet little Dixie lingered for three weeks," Mimi Taylor wrote to her niece, Wilhelmine, in a letter dated June 5. "Nothing, scarcely nothing, was left of him. It was enough to soften the hardest heart to witness the sufferings my sweet little man went through the last 24 hours of his short, happy life."

Another three weeks passed after the death of Dixie before Taylor was able to join his family at Shreveport. Although Mimi tried to present a brave front for her husband, the strain of her experience showed. She appeared weary, as if her very spirit had been used up. Taylor found Louise and Betty still weak from their illness, but apparently recovering. The beaming smiles that lit their faces at the sight of their father was a moment he cherished.

Taylor spent little more than an hour with Mimi and the children. "Poor husband," Mimi wrote. "It nearly breaks my heart when he speaks of those dear, departed angels. He tries so to console and comfort me when the blow has fallen as heavily on him."

Mimi would not recover from the tragedy. At age twenty-nine, the impulsive girl had become a woman who suffered lengthy bouts of depression. In his memoirs, Taylor wrote little of his own feelings following the death of his sons. "It was well perhaps that the absorbing character of my duties left no time for the indulgence in private grief," he noted in one passage. However, his writings reflected an evolving bitterness dating from the tragedy—and a renewed determination to punish an enemy he held responsible.

Upon leaving Mimi and the girls, Taylor visited the graves of Zack and Dixie. With heavy heart, he left the little cemetery and proceeded downtown for a dreaded meeting with Kirby Smith.

* * *

By early June, as the spring rains ceased and the summer sun bore down, the heated animosity between Dick Taylor and Kirby Smith paralleled the increasingly sultry discomfort of the Louisiana countryside. Two rumors fueled Taylor's growing mistrust of his superior. An Alexandria newspaper reported that Smith intended to replace Taylor with "a senior officer" who would bring reinforcements into the state. The officer Smith had in mind was John B. Magruder, commander of Confederate forces in Texas. According to the article, Smith intended personally to take to the field and command the troops while Magruder handled matters at headquarters. Confronted by Taylor, Smith denied the report and blamed Major Eustace Surget, Taylor's adjutant at Alexandria, for starting the rumor. Smith had instructed Surget to counteract "these misstatements," assuring him that "I have General Taylor's best interests at heart."

The second rumor asserted that Smith was prepared to abandon Louisiana and Texas and lead an expedition to liberate St. Louis. Governor Moore expressed outrage that Smith, a native Missourian, would place the welfare of St. Louis above that of Louisiana. The source of the controversy was a letter written by Smith to Seddon in which he stated: "The movement into Missouri is the *terminus ad quem* of all my hopes. Complete success on the Mississippi will, I trust, enable its realization."

Confronted by the governor, Smith had denied any intention to abandon Louisiana but affirmed his desire to retake St. Louis if Vicksburg and Port Hudson could be held. The governor sent a letter to President Davis, criticizing Smith and extolling Taylor's accomplishments. "We owe it to him [Taylor] that the state is not now entirely overrun and occupied by the enemy." In his reply, Davis ignored criticism of Smith and said he was glad the governor was pleased with Taylor's performance. From the tone of Davis's letter, Moore discerned that the president of the Confederacy had lost touch with happenings in the Trans Mississippi Department. Informed of Smith's plans for an invasion of Missouri, Taylor thought the idea ludicrous. Missouri and Northern Arkansas were firmly in enemy hands, and Federal gunboats controlled the river beyond Vicksburg. In his writings Taylor noted that Smith "seems to devote much of his mind to the recovery of his lost empire, to the detriment of the portion yet in his possession."

Against this backdrop of mistrust the two met in Shreveport. Having prepared himself for a confrontation, Taylor was surprised by the friendly nature of Smith's greeting. His superior was full of praise for his efforts and apologetic for past differences. Smith denied any intention of replacing Taylor in the field and showed him dispatches sent to Richmond praising his handling of the troops. Smith gave Taylor permission to proceed with his South Louisiana campaign, explaining that his earlier refusal to approve it was due to extreme pressure from Richmond and not his personal desires. Rather than abandon Louisiana, Smith said he would bring Parson's Cavalry from Arkansas to harass Grant's supply lines, freeing Walker's Texas Division for service under Taylor. Finally, Smith emphasized that their personal destinies, as well as that of the Trans Mississippi, depended on a cooperative effort. Taken aback, Taylor could only agree with his superior.

12

The Mosquito Fleet

ALEXANDRIA, JUNE 14—Arriving back at his Alexandria headquarters, Taylor began concentrating his forces for the long-delayed strike into South Louisiana. He ordered Walker's division to Bayou Teche for an assault on Brashear City, but two days later, received a dispatch from Shreveport countermanding the order. Reneging on his promise to Taylor, Smith had decided to keep Walker's troops in North Louisiana. Upon receiving the news, Taylor gave his staff another impromptu demonstration of his remarkable ability to curse in multiple languages.

Deprived of Walker's division, Taylor was left with no more than 3,500 men, including Green's cavalry, Mouton's infantry, and a 650-man cavalry brigade under James P. Major, only recently arrived from Texas. Still, he was determined to proceed with an invasion of South Louisiana. He came up with a bold plan that, if successful, might not liberate New Orleans, but surely would scare the hell out of Nathaniel Banks. He would sweep down Bayou Lafourche, overrunning the lightly manned Federal outposts along the waterway. At the same time, a force would head down the Teche to capture the Union fort at Brashear City, even as his artillery attacked Banks's supply transports on the Mississippi River.

For the strategy to succeed, he would have to disguise his numbers to give Banks's staff the impression that a large force threatened New Orleans. Therefore, he took a chance that would have made his fellow gamblers at the Boston Club proud. He split his little army for a complicated, three-pronged assault designed to put him at the doorstep of New Orleans before Banks could stop him. Taking a page from Stonewall Jackson's book, the plan existed only in the mind of Dick Taylor. He did not reveal it fully to his staff or even his field commanders. And he certainly did not reveal it to Kirby Smith.

★ ★ ★

BRASHEAR CITY, JUNE 23—On June 19, Taylor had sent Major's 650 horsemen on a sweeping, 150-mile raid through the Bayou Lafourche region, the objective being to secure the railroad connecting Brashear City with New Orleans. Another 300 troops under Major Sherod Hunter were to row across Grand Lake to Tiger Island and attack the Federal fort at Brashear City from the rear. They spent two days at New Iberia collecting anything that would float to transport the men—boats, skiffs, rafts, and even sugar coolers from nearby plantations. Hunter's troops named their little armada "The Mosquito Fleet." Meanwhile, Taylor's main force, totaling some two thousand men, proceeded down the Bayou Teche Road, arriving at Berwick Bay in the middle of the night on the twenty-second. Taylor told Green to unlimber his artillery and begin bombarding the fort at Brashear City at first light.

★ ★ ★

Instead of awakening to the gentle strains of reveille, the two thousand Union troops at Brashear City awoke to the sounds of exploding artillery shells. They scrambled to their gun emplacements and returned the fire across the bay. The Federal officers felt secure in their star-shaped earthen fortress, confident the surrounding swamps and waterways protected them from a ground assault. The early morning bombardment they regarded as nothing more than a rebel attempt at harassment.

Green's artillery barrage was the signal for Hunter to attack the fort from the rear, at which time Taylor's main force would quickly cross the bay in assorted watercraft for a frontal assault. But Hunter was not on the scene. He and his men were bogged down in knee-deep mud, still almost five miles from their objective. After paddling twelve miles across Grand Lake, the men of the Mosquito Fleet had become lost in the swamps, where they wandered about aimlessly for most of the night. By daylight they were a sorry sight. Having slogged, stumbled, and fallen in the muck, many were covered with mud from head to toe.

As the sound of the artillery duel intensified, Hunter urged his men on through the morass. About seven o'clock they emerged in an open field where hundreds of white tents stood in rows before them. Some of the men recoiled at the sight of so many enemy troops. The Yankees were equally startled by the sudden appearance of what appeared to be a large Confederate force virtually in their midst. Hunter cursed and cajoled his hesitant troops into an irregular battle line, pointing out that they had no option but to fight.

Left with little choice the Texans fired a volley and charged the camp with fixed bayonets and demonic rebel yells. The sight of an army of screaming, mud-covered swamp monsters bearing down on them proved too much for the Federals, inspiring some to break ranks and run without firing a shot. The sporadic fighting was over in minutes. By the time Taylor and the main force made it across the bay, Hunter and his boys had seventeen hundred prisoners under guard and were already looting the commissary. Another three hundred Yankees had fled into the swamps. A Federal soldier remembered his captors as, "the most ragged, dirty-looking set of rascals I had ever seen. The only thing uniform among them was dirt—shirts, pants, skin being all of a fine mud color. . . . [But] on the whole they were a good-natured, jolly set of country boys." With the discovery of a large store of Yankee whiskey, they quickly became even jollier. "It was a scene of wildest excitement and confusion," Taylor wrote. "The sight of such quantities of loot quite upset my hungry followers."

Green rounded up some three hundred cavalrymen and set out to secure the railroad east of Brashear City. Some of the Texans had adorned themselves in brand-new uniforms from the Union supply depot. Fortified with bottles of whiskey and with sacks of fine Yankee cuisine tied to their saddle horns, they rode along the tracks in fine spirit. In the distance, they heard a train engine building steam. Galloping toward the sound, the Texans saw a train loaded with blue-clad troops pulling quickly away. They gave chase, but the train steadily outdistanced the horsemen. Stubbornly, Green continued the pursuit.

Meanwhile, Taylor assessed his own "loot." Included were twelve heavy artillery pieces, five thousand new rifles, large quantities of ammunition, and $2 million worth of supplies. However, his most treasured prize was the western terminal of the railroad, key to the control of South Louisiana and his doorway to New Orleans. His most pressing question now was where was Major's Cavalry?

Unknown to Taylor, Major's wild Texans had rampaged some thirty miles down Bayou Lafourche, scattering Federal troops in lightly manned outposts before them. A Yankee prisoner described how they descended on his camp "with double-barreled shotguns and border rifles cracking like champagne corks . . . and yelling like Comanches." Also fleeing before them were scores of Northern overseers from confiscated plantations and thousands of ex-slaves conscripted to work the fields, many of them wearing Union Army uniforms.

For Major's men, supplied with captured whiskey, the raid became a nonstop party of fighting, looting, and celebrating. The same night Colonel Hunter slogged through a muddy swamp, Major's troops were throwing a drunken party near Thibodaux, during which they sang their own version of *Dixie,* including a refrain about marching to New Orleans. Somewhat miraculously, on the morning of June 24, Major's brigade was exactly where it was supposed to be. As Green pursued the Yankee troop train, he was surprised to find it halted at the Bayou Boeuf bridge below Thibodaux, blocked by Major's cavalry. Sitting on the grade beside the train were more than four hundred prisoners.

* * *

The success of the lightninglike Confederate strikes caused jubilation among Southern loyalists in South Louisiana and concern among the occupiers of New Orleans. General Emory, sent an urgent plea to Nathaniel Banks at Port Hudson for troops to reinforce the city. Banks responded that he found news of the loss of Brashear City "incredible." Emory, trying to impress on Banks the urgency of his request, quickly responded: "You need no longer be incredulous."

Leaving a small detachment at Brashear City, Taylor ordered Mouton to occupy Thibodaux and sent Green and Hunter to the Mississippi River to sweep Yankee outposts from the west bank. There they set up artillery on the bluffs and began shelling Banks's supply boats. Taylor made a quick trip to Alexandria, where he had access to telegraph communications and sent a message to Kirby Smith detailing his successes. "[Because] results of great interest can be accomplished . . . I have ordered Major General Walker's Division to proceed immediately to Berwick Bay," Taylor wrote. Smith reacted with a terse reply countermanding Taylor's orders: "I shall order Walker's Division to you whenever operations about Vicksburg will permit." To his staff, Smith expressed doubt that Taylor had accomplished all of the successes he claimed.

Although upset, Taylor was not surprised. He promptly returned to South Louisiana, determined to press on to New Orleans with his small army. Though outranked, Dick Taylor was at least equal to his commander in sheer stubbornness.

✶ ✶ ✶

ÐONALDSONVILLE, JUNE 28—On the afternoon of June 27, Yankee pickets in a tree line beside a cornfield just south of Donaldsonville heard horsemen coming up the bayou road. When the lead elements of Green's Texas Rangers came into view, the Yankee pickets dutifully fired a volley and fled toward their camp. However, they found a line of grim-faced rebel cavalrymen blocking their escape. The pickets dropped their weapons and raised their hands.

Within minutes, Tom Green reined his horse before the captives. He did not have the time or inclination to waste men guarding prisoners. "Take off your clothes," he instructed. Puzzled and embarrassed, the captives complied while the grinning Texans hooted and made crude comments. "Go and tell your ranking officer I have come to take his fort and he would best surrender," Green told them. Glancing apprehensively over their shoulders, the naked men began walking along the corn rows. A gunshot in the air inspired them to begin running, the sharp leaves of the cornstalks whipping their bodies as they sprinted across the field toward the bayou. When the disrobed pickets stumbled into camp at Donaldsonville, their bodies were covered with nicks, cuts, and bruises. At first their fellow soldiers were more amused than concerned, but that changed when informed that Tom Green and his cutthroat Texas Rangers were just down the road and headed their way. The news inspired a quick exodus behind the walls of Fort Butler.

✶ ✶ ✶

Fort Butler sat on high ground across Bayou Lafourche from the blackened ruins of Donaldsonville. A substantial fortification of brick and masonry, it was built in the shape of a half star with three points protruding from the front and sides to accommodate artillery redoubts. Its back rested against the levee of the Mississippi River, where the gunboat *Princess Royal* sat at anchor like a protective mother hen watching her brood. Because of high water, the guns of the *Princess* sat at almost the same elevation as the fort. Around the front and sides of the fort, a moat sixteen feet wide and twelve feet deep followed the contours of the walls. Six twenty-four-pound siege guns covered a broad plain in front of the fort.

Because of the presence of the gunboats and uncertainty as to troop strength, General Mouton had suggested to Green that he not attack the fort until Taylor returned from Alexandria to assess the situation. Mouton's instructions were for Green to set his artillery on the bluffs below Donaldsonville and stop the river steamers out of New Orleans from supplying Banks at Port Hudson. However, as he approached Donaldsonville, Green received intelligence from local residents that convinced him the fort had a weakness. He was told that only the levee and stockade walls made of logs protected its rear. This intelligence proved to be wrong. A wide ditch and a wall of brick and masonry recently had been added at the back of the fort. Green also was led to believe that no more than two hundred or three hundred men occupied the facility, including convalescing wounded from Port Hudson. Green commanded a force of fifteen hundred seasoned cavalrymen, and the temptation to attack Fort Butler proved too strong for the combative Texan to resist.

On the afternoon of the twenty-seventh, he sent an emissary to the front moat to demand an immediate surrender. Colonel J. D. Bullen of the 28th Maine, the commanding officer, refused the offer. He lined his men on the parade plain, gave a passionate speech, pointed to the U.S. flag, and shouted, "It shall hang there as long as there is a man of you left to defend it." Waiting several hundred yards away, Green heard a loud cheer rise from the fortress. He did not know that, including eight companies of the Maine regiment, convalescents who were able to fight, and 250 black troops, there were almost 600 defenders inside the walls.

To negate the advantage of the gunboat guarding the fort, Green decided on a night attack. At two o'clock on the morning of June 28, Captain Oliver Semmes's artillery opened up on the fort. The gunboat *Princess Royal* and the guns of the fort immediately responded.

Jarred from their sleep, the sisters and orphans of the Catholic Convent crowded the windows to witness a spectacular pyrotechnic display reflected in the waters of Bayou Lafourche. Soon they heard high-pitched rebel yells mingled with the sound of exploding shells.

Green sent Colonel Major and his 2nd Cavalry Brigade in a frontal assault across the plain to distract the defenders while units under Major Denman Shannon and Colonel William Hardeman, totaling some two hundred men each, assaulted the stockade walls flanking either side of the fort between the levee and the river. Green planned to swarm both sides of the fort, enter it from the rear, and subdue the defenders before daylight exposed his men to the cannoneers on the *Princess*. Green figured that once his men were over the levee and inside the fort, the gunboat crews would not dare fire for fear of hitting their own troops.

Commander M. B. Woolsey positioned the *Princess Royal* near the levee. Although his gunners could not see the attacking rebels they could hear their yells and began firing twenty- and thirty-pound shrapnel and nine-inch grapeshot toward the sounds. The storm of lead, fired almost point-blank into troops attacking the north wall, took a heavy toll. Shannon's men responded with rifle fire that killed and wounded several crewmen, cleared the decks, and temporarily silenced the guns of the *Princess*. As the battle raged, the gunboats *Kineo* and *Winona* arrived on the scene and returned the fire from Semmes's batteries.

Armed with axes, the Confederates desperately chopped holes in the stockade walls, while others were boosted over the top. At the south wall, rebels waded through waist-deep water and made their way around the stockade. Once inside, the Texans stormed over the levee only to discover that they were not inside the fort. Blocking their way was a deep ditch and yet another wall. Even worse was the realization that they were trapped between the gunboats and an enemy on parapets firing down upon them. Taking refuge in the moat and clinging to the sides of the wall, the rebels began a desperate struggle. They fired their weapons until they ran out of ammunition then, dislodging bricks from the wall, hurled them at the enemy. Soldiers on the parapets threw them back, setting off a bizarre battle of flying bricks.

Assessing the situation, Colonel Joseph Phillips realized that the only way his men could save themselves was to take the parapets with bayonets. Urging the men to follow, he and Major Alonzo Ridley scrambled up the wall. Miraculously, they reached the top, swinging their swords in the face of the defenders. A rifle ball killed Phillips and sent him tumbling back down the incline past his men. Finding himself alone, Ridley lowered his sword and surrendered. Witnessing the fate of their officers, the men retreated to the bottom of the moat out of the line of fire. The artillery soon fell silent and, at 3:45 A.M., sporadic rifle fire slowly ceased. The cries and moans of the wounded mingled with the crackle of burning barracks and the chug of the gunboats's engines. Flames inside the fort cast an eerie glow against the smoke hovering over the waters. The battle was over, and Fort Butler remained in Federal hands.

The first light of dawn revealed evidence of the night's brutality. Dead and wounded littered the battered walls and grounds around the fort. Rifles, swords, axes, and cartridge pouches were scattered about. Along the parapets, outlined by smoke rising from the fort, men stood in rows, silently surveying the chaos. In the moat at the rear of the fort, more than 100 Confederates, many of them wounded, huddled beneath white flags of surrender. Aboard the *Princess*, Commander Woolsey surveyed his battered vessel. The gunboat had been struck more than 20 times by Semmes's artillery, and several of his crewmen were dead and wounded. Confederate casualties were heavy—50 killed, 114 wounded, and 107 captured out of 1,000 engaged. However, many of the wounded did not survive. Bullen reported the burial of 69 Confederates and noted that he sent 124 prisoners down the river to New Orleans. Of the defenders, Colonel Bullen reported only eight killed and fifteen wounded. However, that total was believed to be grossly understated and probably reflected only the casualties in his own regiment.

In his long and illustrious military career, Tom Green had encountered his first defeat. In his official report, he stated:

> All of my guides assured me that when we got through the stockade between the levee and the river we had an open way into the fort. . . . We were not repulsed and never would have been until we found after getting into the stockade there was yet another ditch to cross with no means whatever at hand to cross it. There never was more desperation displayed than was shown by our men engaged in this assault.

Informed of the defeat, General Mouton was outraged that Green had ignored his advice and lost so many men in what he considered a senseless attack. But when he complained of Green's "reckless decision," Taylor refused to discipline the Texan. "We can only assume that if the enemy is before Tom Green, he is going to attack him," he told Mouton.

The morning after the battle, Green sent an emissary under a white flag to the fort, seeking permission to retrieve and bury his dead. Colonel Bullen refused. He ordered the dead buried in mass graves.

Colonel Bullen did not have time to savor his victory. His fort remained under siege by Green. It was a miserable existence for the men inside the fort, since most of their tents and a large quantity of supplies had been destroyed by fire. Meanwhile, Semmes lined his artillery along the bluffs below Donaldsonville and temporarily shut off the transportation of supplies to Port Hudson as well as Fort Butler. For a time, at least, Dick Taylor, not Nathaniel Banks or Ulysses Grant, controlled the lower Mississippi River. Taylor had ambitions to control even more. Still bent on taking New Orleans, he ordered Mouton to secure the railroad beyond Lafourche Crossing and sent Green's cavalry down the west bank of the Mississippi toward St. Charles Station.

★ ★ ★

Following the battle, Colonel Bullen got into a confrontation with some of his black troops over work detail assignments. The black soldiers complained that they were doing all of the work while the white soldiers sat idle in camp. Since they had fought as bravely as the white troops, they thought this unfair. Animosity between the colonel and the black troops escalated. On the night of July 5, Colonel Bullen confronted several black soldiers who had managed to locate some whiskey. As Bullen berated them, a soldier raised his rifle and shot the colonel dead. Private Francis Scott, a member of the Native Guards, was arrested. Wounded at Port Hudson, he had fought bravely in the defense of Fort Butler. Now he was placed in double irons and sent to New Orleans where, a few days later, he was executed.

★ ★ ★

BRASHEAR CITY, JULY 4—On Independence Day, an exultant Dick Taylor sent the following report to Trans Mississippi Headquarters at Shreveport:

> The railroad has been repaired and the first train passed to Thibodaux today. The Telegraph soon will be in operation from Bayou des Allemands to New Iberia and I hope to find wire to extend the line to Alexandria. The events since my last report are as follows: On the 24th, we drove the enemy from Raceland Station so rapidly that he abandoned four field pieces. On the 28th the advance on the railroad reached Bayou des Allemands where the enemy abandoned another field piece. On the 1st, we held Boutte Station, 29 miles from New Orleans. I am now pushing for the Barataria Canal, behind which the enemy have been routed. [At this point in his report, Taylor described Green's ill-fated attack on Fort Butler before continuing.] A column has been pushed down the river below Saint Charles Court House some 20 miles from New Orleans, finding no enemy. Colonel Major is on the river, 10 miles from Donaldsonville with six rifled guns and expects to prevent the transports from passing. One of my scouts has returned from the city with journals up to the 1st. The city is greatly excited. Enemy have worked night and day to remove negroes and

stores from Algiers to the other side. . . . If any opportunity, however slight, offers, I will throw myself into New Orleans, and make every effort to hold it, leaving my communications to take care of themselves.

That same day, General W. H. Emory, commander of the defense force in New Orleans, sent a desperate plea to General Banks at Port Hudson:

My information is that the enemy are 13,000 strong and they are fortifying the whole country as they march from Brashear [to New Orleans] and are steadily advancing. I respectfully suggest that, unless Port Hudson be already taken, you can only save the city by sending me reinforcements immediately and at any costs. It is a choice between Port Hudson and New Orleans. . . . There are at least 10,000 fighting men in this city and I do not doubt from what I see that these men will, at the first approach of the enemy within view of the city, be against us to a man.

Emory would be saved, not by Nathaniel Banks, but by John Pemberton. Even as Taylor and Emory wrote their reports on July 4, the sublimely incompetent Pemberton was surrendering the Confederate bastion at Vicksburg and its thirty thousand Confederate troops to Ulysses S. Grant.

Also unknown to Taylor and Emory, another disaster had befallen the Confederacy just one day earlier at a little town in Pennsylvania named Gettysburg. Frustrated and feverish with dysentery, Robert E. Lee had ordered an ill-advised charge against a concentrated enemy position atop a hill called Cemetery Ridge. George Pickett sent three brigades totaling eleven thousand men up the hillside and watched as they were cut apart by eighty Federal field pieces. Only a few managed to reach the crest. Having twenty thousand men killed and wounded in just three days, by July 4 Lee's army was straggling back to Virginia. The disaster at Gettysburg and debacle at Vicksburg were twin disasters from which the South would not recover.

DONALDSONVILLE, JULY 13—On July 6, Banks had received Emory's desperate plea for forces and, for the first time, considered that the stubborn resistance of Gardner and his garrison might cost him New Orleans. He had thrown his legions against the fortifications at Port Hudson three times, only to be repulsed with heavy casualties. In fact, Banks had lost five thousand troops, killed, wounded, and missing trying to take the stronghold. Another four thousand had been hospitalized by sunstroke and a variety of diseases, including malaria, and almost five hundred of those had died. The demoralized soldiers in some regiments, who had been held beyond their enlistment periods, were near mutiny. Taylor had a stranglehold on the river below him, cutting off his supplies. But Banks stubbornly refused to abandon the siege and planned one final, all-out assault on Port Hudson.

The attack was to take place July 7, but as Banks waited for the weather to clear that morning, word arrived that Vicksburg had surrendered. He received the message with relief and disappointment. He had lost his race with Grant to become the conquering hero of the Mississippi River Valley. But, without Vicksburg, he knew Port Hudson was at last bound to fall.

Banks dispatched emissaries to inform Gardner of Vicksburg's fate, finally convincing the Confederate commander by sending him the official report from Grant. That night, Gardner met with his officers behind Port Hudson's shell-pocked embankments. Cut off from communication with the outside world, Gardner and his staff knew nothing of Taylor's South Louisiana campaign or that Confederate troops were on the outskirts of New Orleans. They only knew that Grant's army was now available to join Banks's. Supported by Farragut's gunboats, such a force would easily overrun their little garrison. Or the Yankees might simply continue the siege and starve them out.

Gardner's men had withstood sixty days of bombardment by Union gunboats and forty-eight days under siege by Banks's army. They were existing on a diet of weevil-infested peas, molasses, mule meat, and an occasional boiled rat. The water wells were dry, so when rainwater was unavailable, drinking water had to be hauled up from the river. They were also low on ammunition, and it was doubtful enough remained to stop another general assault. Gardner sent word to Banks that he was ready to talk terms. On July 8, the ragged, sunburned defenders of Port Hudson stacked their arms, and the flag of the United States was raised above the battered hillsides they had so bravely defended.

On July 10, Taylor learned of the surrender of Vicksburg and Port Hudson. The following day, he was told that thousands of Federal troops from Port Hudson were being unloaded from transports at Donaldsonville. The scales of fate had tilted against him. Instead of attacking New Orleans, Taylor now faced the danger of having his army cut off by a vastly superior foe. He sent word to Green to harass the enemy at Donaldsonville while Major removed his artillery from the banks of the Mississippi and Mouton withdrew troops from Brashear City.

When Union columns under Weitzel and Grover moved out from Donaldsonville to reclaim Bayou Lafourche, Green did more than harass them. Still smarting from his defeat at Fort Butler, he attacked the Union columns with such ferocity Weitzel sent word to Banks that he needed reinforcements. He told Banks he was facing an army of twelve thousand. In reality, he was under attack by fourteen hundred Texas Rangers.

On July 13, Weitzel had six thousand troops strung out over several miles when Green's Texans hit the advance units of his army six miles south of Donaldsonville. Green drove Weitzel's army all the way back to Donaldsonville, where the Federals took refuge behind the walls of Fort Butler and under the cover of Union gunboats. In addition to inflicting heavy casualties, Green captured Weitzel's artillery and munitions wagons. Rumors that the Texans were not taking prisoners caused panic in some Union regiments, and as they scattered before the rampaging Texas horsemen, they became easy prey. Taylor, who was there to witness Green in action, described what happened in the final rebel attack on Weitzel's disorganized forces: "The gallant, noble Green, dismounting from his horse, placed himself at the head of his old regiment, captured the enemy's guns and drove his forces into the fort."

A Confederate soldier described the brutal result of Green's "no quarter" assault: "I passed over the battlefield [and] saw Yankees lying in every direction . . . [and] I saw all manner of wounds, but most of the Yankees were shot through the head."

Green's attack stopped Banks cold at Donaldsonville. Convinced he was under mul-tiple attacks by a large Confederate force, Banks began pulling troops out of Donald-sonville and rushed them downriver to defend New Orleans. If he had committed those men to securing the Lafourche region, most of the rebel army in South Louisiana would have been cut off. The miscalculation allowed Taylor time to withdraw Mouton's small army from the outskirts of New Orleans and Brashear City. At Berwick Bay, tons of weapons, supplies, and ammunition were loaded on carts and wagons and sent north to New Iberia. Many of Mouton's men left Berwick Bay wearing captured Union uniforms. What the rebels could not transport, they dumped in the bay, including the large siege guns from the fort at Brashear City. Among the discarded loot were thousands of stiff, white collars that were standard issue with the uniforms worn by the troops of Banks's 19th Army Corps. Taylor later wrote a letter to Banks, inquiring about these unusual items. "My men have boiled, baked and fried them and still complain that they cannot eat them," he wrote.

★　★　★

BRASHEAR CITY, JULY 22—A reluctant Dick Taylor ordered the abandonment of the lower Teche. The day after Mouton's troops moved out of Brashear City, Federal troops arrived aboard steamers to once more occupy the town. Just days earlier Taylor's artillery had controlled the lower Mississippi, and his infantry was within sixteen miles of New Orleans. The only Federal force large enough to resist him was pinned down be-hind earthworks at the Barataria Canal. Given two or three days more, Green's cavalry would have galloped through the streets of New Orleans, virtually unopposed. "A few hours more and the city would have been wild with excitement," Taylor wrote. He had performed miracles with his little thirty-five-hundred-man army, but to no avail. Be-cause of ill-conceived decisions by others, the states west of the Mississippi River were now cut off from the rest of the Confederacy.

Taylor blamed Kirby Smith and John Pemberton for the disaster. Although he re-frained from criticizing Smith directly in his official reports, he expressed bitterness to-ward his commander in conversation with his adjutant, Eustace Surget. "The plan I had arranged for an attack on New Orleans fell through as soon as I was advised that Walker's Division would not join me," Surget quoted him in his writings. Until his death, Taylor was convinced that if Smith had given him Walker's division, he would have taken New Orleans in early June, sealed off the Mississippi River to Federal ship-ping, and relieved Port Hudson and Vicksburg. According to Surget, news that Pember-ton had surrendered thirty thousand troops on the Fourth of July physically sickened Taylor and, for the first time, he talked of resigning. "I am fatigued and jaded beyond de-scription," he told his aide. The loss of his sons lay heavy on his heart, and he felt an al-most irrepressible need to be with Mimi. Living in the field had aggravated his arthritis and he suffered severe headaches. He rarely slept more than two or three hours at a time, and Tom Strother fretted over his eating habits.

Many in the South believed Pemberton, a northerner, might be guilty of betrayal.

Why else would he surrender Vicksburg to Grant on the Fourth of July? Why would he allow thirty thousand men to remain behind their breastworks and be captured rather than fight their way out? But Taylor attributed the blunder to the shallow character of the man, not betrayal. Returning from his April meeting with Pemberton, Taylor had suggested to his staff that Davis might have done better to randomly select a private out of the ranks to command Vicksburg. Finally he blamed Davis's poor judgment in selecting generals. Davis and Seddon, he believed, had become so detached from the reality of field activities that their judgments could no longer be trusted.

Taylor was especially bitter at Kirby Smith. The commander of the Trans Mississippi had surrounded himself with a bloated staff of budding bureaucrats at Shreveport. With little to do other than attend social functions and engage in petty politics, Smith's staff demanded constant reports from the field. Smith spent more time writing dispatches to Richmond, trying to endear himself to the high command, than he did devising military strategies for the defense of Louisiana. Most disturbing to Taylor were rumors that Smith had become heavily engaged in the clandestine trading of cotton with the enemy.

★ ★ ★ ★

13

★ ★ ★ ★

"Gen'ral Polecat"

IN THE WAKE of his retreat from South Louisiana, a rising dissension in the ranks of his army compounded Taylor's problems. Some of the Texas troops wanted to go home—especially those in Walker's division. By the time Smith finally released the division to join Taylor, it had virtually ceased to be a viable fighting unit. Camped for weeks in the sun-baked Mississippi River bottomlands across from Vicksburg, a third of Walker's troops were sick and the rest near mutiny. Captain Elijah P. Petty wrote, "There is great dissatisfaction in the army here. . . . Men are insubordinate and I would not be surprised if this army was comparatively broken up. Men say that they will go home and let the Confederacy and the war go to hell."

As Taylor pulled his troops out of the lower Teche, desertions spread like a fever. Even Tom Green's Texas Rangers became discouraged and tired of fighting. Some wanted to go back to Texas to defend their home state. Others just wanted to see their families. Dissension reached a crisis when some of Green's troops defied their officers and went on a drunken rampage in New Iberia. The 28th Regiment had to be dispatched from Vermillionville to put down the mutiny. As a result of the incident, Taylor issued orders for his officers to shoot deserters on the spot, after which Captain Petty noted: "The desertion furor has about ceased, the prospect of being shot having deterred some."

Because of unrest in the ranks, it was the worst possible time to introduce a new brigadier to the men—especially one like the dapper, smartly dressed, and grandly named Camille Armand Jules Marie, Prince de Polignac. Taylor formed five light regiments of newly arrived dismount Texas cavalry into a brigade under Polignac's command—the 15th, 17th, 22nd, 31st, and 34th, totaling some seven hundred men. Almost immediately a contingent of officers visited Taylor and bluntly asserted, "We ain't gonna take orders from no damned frog-eatin' Frenchman." He assured the Texans that Polignac was an outstanding officer and asked them to reserve their judgment until he had an opportunity to lead them in battle. "Then if you want me to replace him, I will do so," he said.

Since the Texans could not pronounce his name, they referred to their new commander as "Gen'ral Polecat." Some of the men even held their noses when he passed by.

Polignac went about his business, giving no outward indication that he was even aware of the insults.

* * *

Drawing on his experience in the Shenandoah campaign, Taylor ordered Mouton to shift his forces constantly to deceive Banks into believing he faced a larger army than was the case. Four of Polignac's five regiments were mounted and Mouton kept them constantly on the move, adding to unrest in the ranks of the Frenchman's brigade. Taylor loosed Green to strike the enemy any time the opportunity presented itself. As Federal units moved forth to probe Confederate strength, Green's horsemen attacked them, adding to the perception that the rebels had a large force in South Louisiana.

Meanwhile, Taylor moved his captured supplies and munitions north beyond the reach of the enemy. In remote barns, he set up forage stations at various locations for the cavalry and supply depots for the infantry in the event he was forced to retreat. Telegraph wires were repaired between his headquarters and Shreveport. Intelligence sources told him large numbers of Federal troops were concentrating at Brashear City, and Taylor predicted another Union campaign against him before winter weather set in.

* * *

NEW ORLEANS, SEPTEMBER 4—By late August both Ulysses Grant and Nathaniel Banks were under pressure by Lincoln to occupy Texas. France had taken over Mexico as a protectorate, and Lincoln was afraid the French might try to reclaim the long-disputed territory between the Neches and Rio Grande rivers. The possibility that the French Army might even join Confederate forces in Texas deeply concerned the president.

In late August, Grant came down from Vicksburg to confer with Banks on strategy. However, they discussed very little strategy as Mrs. Banks scheduled a series of appearances for the Hero of Vicksburg, and his visit evolved into a continuing celebration. Grant's fondness for spirits compelled him to participate in a succession of parties, dinners, and grand balls.

Grant personally considered an invasion of Texas a waste of time. He wanted to concentrate all available forces on the conquest of Mobile and Atlanta, believing the capture of those Southern strongholds would end the war. However, he knew that Lincoln and Halleck would not release Banks's forces to him until Texas and Louisiana were secured. To assist Banks in that endeavor, Grant ordered the 13th Army Corps from Vicksburg to New Orleans to bolster Banks's depleted forces.

Banks and Grant decided to concentrate twenty thousand troops under General William B. Franklin in the lower Teche region to pin down Taylor while staging a surprise attack on the Texas coast. The target was Sabine Pass at the mouth of the Sabine River, which divided Texas and Louisiana. From Sabine Pass, a railroad ran south along the Gulf Coast, providing a supply conduit for a Union army to attack Houston and Galveston. Once a beachhead was established, and shallow-draft gunboats patrolled the

Sabine River, Banks intended to send Franklin's army across Southwest Louisiana into Texas, cut off rebel supply routes, and starve Shreveport into submission.

On the morning of September 4, twenty-two troop ships carrying six thousand men escorted by five gunboats left New Orleans for Sabine Pass. All that stood between them and their objective was a small mud fort at the mouth of the river, and a few light field pieces under the command of a nineteen-year-old lieutenant who had never seen combat. On the same day the boats departed, a drunken General Grant fell from his horse on a street in New Orleans and was injured severely enough to be confined to his quarters under a doctor's care for several days, a possible portent of the disaster about to befall the Union invasion fleet.

* * *

SABINE PASS, SEPTEMBER 7—On the morning of September 7, four Union gunboats opened fire on the mud fort, still not completed, rising out of the marsh grass near a point where the Gulf of Mexico joins Sabine Lake. The response from the fort caught the attackers by surprise. Cannonballs from the fort began striking the lead gunboats with an accuracy that stunned the captains. Within minutes, fifty crewmen were killed, scores wounded, two gunboats lay crippled near the entrance to the lake, and survivors were scrambling to shore with their hands raised in surrender. Stunned by the loss of the gunboats, Navy Lieutenant Frederick Crocker ordered the three remaining boats to retreat out of range. Unsure of the strength of the rebel defenders, the troop transports turned around and return to New Orleans. If Crocker had known the makeup of the defense force he might have acted otherwise. It consisted of forty-three soldiers and six cannons.

* * *

Among the prisoners at Sabine Pass was Lieutenant Henry Dane, commander of one of the Union gunboats. When he asked to see the commander of the fort, his captors pointed to a slender young man who looked more like a schoolboy than a military officer.

"The commander of the fort was a modest, retiring, boyish-looking, Irish lad nineteen years old," Dane later wrote. "I could not refrain laughing in his face when he was introduced to me as Lt. Dick Dowling in command of the fort. 'Are you the shaughran [sic] who did all of that mischief?' I asked. 'How many men and guns did you have?'"

"We had four thirty-two-pounders and two twenty-four-pounders and forty-three men," was his reply with a blush.

"And do you realize what you have done?" I asked.

"No," he said frankly, "I do not understand at all."

"Well sir, you and your 43 men, in your miserable little mud fort in the rushes have captured two gunboats, a goodly number of prisoners, many stands of small arms and plenty of good ammunition and all of that you have done with six pop guns and two smart Quakers. And that is not the worst of your boyish tricks. You have sent three Yankee gunboats, 6,000 troops and a general out to sea in the dark."

Defeated at Galveston and ignominiously turned back at Sabine Pass, Nathaniel Banks was rapidly running out of options for the conquest of Texas.

★ ★ ★

WASHINGTON, LOUISIANA, OCTOBER 24—By late September, Dick Taylor was fighting a war on two fronts: a large Union army sat before him, and Kirby Smith and his Shreveport brain trust lurked at his back. Within the same week, he received conflicting dispatches from Shreveport instructing him to move his army first to Texas, and then to Arkansas and, finally, to stay where he was. Smith warned him not to engage the enemy, writing: "You as well as myself know our means are too limited to risk any general engagement without some reasonable chance of success." By then, Taylor was ignoring the daily dispatches from Shreveport. He was more concerned by an obvious buildup of Federal troops along the lower Teche.

In addition to Banks's 19th Army Corps, elements of the 13th Corps joined General Franklin at Berwick Bay. The news worried Taylor because the 13th was made up of seasoned Midwestern troops who had fought in Tennessee and at Vicksburg. Combining the 19th and 13th gave General Franklin thirty thousand troops in South Louisiana, and Taylor had only about five thousand effectives to oppose him.

By September 27, Taylor had concentrated most of his units near Opelousas. Ignoring Smith's dictates, he sent the combined forces of Mouton and Green to attack a Federal outpost at Morganza, some forty miles to the east. On September 29, the Confederates struck during a driving rainstorm, catching the one thousand defenders by surprise. The rebels took 450 prisoners and sent the remaining bluecoats fleeing into a nearby swamp. At his Opelousas headquarters, Taylor carefully questioned the captured officers in an effort to learn Banks's intentions. Shreveport speculated that Franklin might be preparing to march west through the swamplands of Southwestern Louisiana, cross the Sabine River, and invade Texas. However, that assessment came from dated information based on Union success at Sabine Pass. Taylor's interrogations convinced him Franklin intended to march north toward the Red River Valley and Shreveport.

Franklin's advance units moved out on October 1 and, two days later, occupied New Iberia without opposition. However, as Union troops proceeded north toward Vermillionville, they came under attack by Green's cavalry. A series of quick strikes left the Federal forward elements bloodied and confused. Upon occupying Vermillionville, the Union troops exacted revenge by once more looting homes and businesses and terrorizing those inhabitants who had not fled.

When it rained for several days and Franklin's army did not move, an impatient Taylor sent a raiding party to hit the telegraph station at Vermillionville. On October 13, Colonel Oran Roberts and a small band of horsemen circled behind Federal lines, surprised guards at the station, and rode off with secret dispatches between Franklin and

Banks. The messages confirmed Taylor's suspicion that Franklin intended to proceed up the Red River Valley and place Shreveport under siege. Among the dispatches, an appeal by Franklin for Banks to send him more cavalry revealed a weakness in the Union Army. It was composed almost entirely of infantry, making it easy prey for Green's hit-and-run brand of warfare. Taylor sent a message to Smith stating his intention to attack the Union Army in South Louisiana. True to his character, Smith immediately sent a dispatch placing the onus of possible defeat squarely on Taylor's shoulders: "Difficult as you may find it, you must restrain your impulses as well as the desires of your men. The Fabian policy is now our true policy. In the present state of the public mind, a defeat to your little army would be ruinous in its effects. When you strike, you must do so only with strong hopes of success."

Taylor was more than willing to accept the responsibility. As the Union Army moved north, slowed by muddy terrain, poor foraging caused Franklin to spread his ranks, presenting an inviting target for Green. His cavalry struck with such frequency and effect that Franklin wired Banks for reinforcements, stating that he was facing an army of twenty-five thousand. He complained of the constant harassment by rebel cavalry: "They hover on all sides . . . producing an annoyance the severity of which cannot be appreciated unless it be felt." A Union soldier observed: "Our generals, who made war according to rule, were disgusted with the irregular tactics of the Confederates who played swordfish to the whale." Franklin tried to correct the imbalance in his ranks by converting infantry to cavalry. Instead of properly-trained cavalry, however, he simply placed several regiments of foot soldiers on horseback, inept for the task ahead.

As Franklin's massive army crawled north along the Vermillionville-Opelousas Pike, Taylor was laying a trap for him. Three miles north of the little town of Washington lay an open field flanked by woods. Taylor had ridden past the place many times, observing that it was good ground for an ambush. He entrenched his infantry there and hid his cavalry and artillery in the woods. He sent forth Colonel Roberts with a cavalry regiment to engage the forward elements of Franklin's army and lure it into the trap.

As the Confederates waited in the woods, they saw approaching across the plain "a well-dressed, matronly looking lady" on horseback. Reining her mount before the men, she gestured and shouted: "The Yankees are over there. Come on and whip them." Waiting in ambush, the men looked at each other and then to their officers, who instructed them to stay put. The sound of distant gunfire indicated that Colonel Roberts's cavalry had engaged the enemy. "Are you going to go whip them or not?" the lady berated them. "Come on!" She turned the horse about and rode at full speed toward the sound of the gunfire, disappearing into the tree line.

Within minutes, Roberts's cavalry appeared on the road, with Union forces in close pursuit. When they came within range, six batteries of Confederate artillery opened up, turning the field into a holocaust of flying metal.

Quickly unlimbering their cannons, the Yankees responded. Camille Polignac led his men from the woods. Standing in his stirrups and saber held aloft, he rode his horse down the line in front of his men. "Follow me! Follow me!" he shouted. "You call me Polecat. Now I will show you whether I am Polecat or Polignac." With that, he rode into the smoke and thunder of exploding shells. A cheer went up from the men as they rushed forward. Major's cavalry, Gray's brigade, and Walker's division also charged out of the woods, striking the blue-clad ranks before they could form a battle line. The forward Yankee regiments were driven back into those in the rear.

Hearing the thunder of artillery at his front, General Franklin rode up to assess the situation. Having experienced only hit-and-run cavalry attacks, he was surprised to find a major battle unfolding. Seeing widespread confusion in his ranks and fearing a rout, Franklin quickly organized a rear guard and ordered a withdrawal to Opelousas. In minutes, he was in retreat, having left more than one hundred dead and wounded on the field.

The horselady in elegant dress was not seen again. The men assumed she came from one of the plantation homes in the region. Her identity unknown, she remains a legend in Civil War lore.

★ ★ ★

BAYOU BOURBEAU, NOVEMBER 3—If Franklin thought retreat would save him from Tom Green's cavalry, he was wrong. When it came to hanging on the heels of a retreating enemy, Taylor was as stubborn as the stock dogs on his plantation, and he sent Green and Major to harass the Federals. Franklin's foot soldiers converted to cavalry went out to contend with the Texans. Inevitably, however, they used their mounts to flee at the first appearance of Green's wildly screaming horsemen.

On the afternoon of November 2, Green's scouts reported that several infantry units and a regiment of cavalry comprising Franklin's rear guard were camped along Bayou Bourbeau, some eight miles below Opelousas. Green was informed that the guard was strung out down the bayou and appeared vulnerable to attack. Although under orders from Taylor simply to pursue and harass the enemy, Green decided to strike in force. He borrowed the 11th, 15th, and 18th Texas regiments, along with three artillery batteries, and on the morning of November 3, with some three thousand men, he hit Franklin's rear guard with a vengeance.

The guard was made up of Midwestern veterans from the 13th Corps under the command of Brigadier General Stephen Burbridge. Caught by surprise, the Yankees quickly formed a battle line and, just as quickly, split apart. Lieutenant Colonel James E. Harrison of the 15th Texas described what happened next: "We drove them back one mile and a half to their main encampment before which was a deep ravine and here they made a desperate stand. A shout and a rush [and] then our rifles told on their routed, confused masses."

Harrison's troops plunged so far into the enemy ranks, they were attacked from the rear by Union cavalry. Instead of reacting as if entrapped, Harrison turned his troops around and ordered a charge. The Union horsemen were so startled by the maneuver, many of them fled. "[It was] a scene of wild confusion. Men tumbling from horses, screaming. Others throwing up their hands for mercy. Horses running over the field without riders."

Informed of the collapse of his rear guard, an alarmed General Franklin ordered artillery to the rear to lay down a barrage that finally stopped the Confederate advance and prevented what was rapidly developing into another rout. When the smoke cleared, Burbridge had lost more than 650 men—154 dead and wounded and 500 captured, including 30 officers. Confederate casualties were 125 dead and wounded. Franklin had had enough. He ordered his army withdrawn beyond Vermillionville to New Iberia where it went into winter camp. In his report to Banks he described the battle at Bayou Bourbeau as a victory, to which a staff officer responded, "A few more such victories would not leave us many men." An officer in the 13th Corps observed: "If we had a general with as much spunk as a mouse, we would have turned about and whipped them soundly. This was the first time the 13th Army Corps ever turned its back."

Meanwhile, the men of Polignac's brigade no longer held their noses when he passed. They stopped calling him "Gen'ral Polecat." They taught him how to play "monte" well enough that he won more often than he lost, and they discovered that he could drink bad whiskey with the best of them and cuss better than most. From then on, any soldier from another unit who dared make a disparaging remark about Camille Polignac was likely to find himself in a fistfight with one of his men.

★ ★ ★ ★

14

★ ★ ★ ★

A March through Winter Hell

PINEVILLE, DECEMBER 16—The winter storm descended on Henry Gray's brigade with a fury unlike anything he or his men could recall. Having crossed the Red River on cotton barges and flatboats the day before, they were moving up the Pineville Road when a cold drizzle began falling. The flannel uniforms of those without slickers became soaked, causing them to shiver as they sought shelter beneath a canopy of towering pine trees. What began as a gentle rustling of pine needles high above suddenly became an explosion of wind and rain as a mighty storm slammed into the forest. Large limbs snapped like kindling and fell among the men. Great pines, more than one hundred feet tall, bent under the force of the howling winds until their tops almost touched the ground. Trunks splintered, popping like gunfire, and trees fell, crashing like thunder. Felix Poche recalled the horror of the moment in his journal:

> The thunder roared, lightning struck all around us and immense pines . . . fell by the hundreds. I learned several persons had been hurt. . . . Soon the ground was covered with water . . . wagons unable to pass. . . . Thus those poor soldiers were drenched to the skin, shivering with cold, starving and dead tired after a march of fifteen miles, having nothing with which to cover themselves, and spent a miserable night as near to the fires as best they could.

Twenty-four hours passed before the men, cold and hungry, were able to clear the road, so that supply wagons could reach them with food and blankets. It was a sorry beginning for a journey that had begun with great promise.

Several days earlier, word that Mouton's division was being sent to Monroe was greeted with cheers, especially in the ranks of the 28th Regiment. Many of the men would be marching through their home parishes for the first time since their enlistments. Some had not been home for a year and a half, and all were anxious to see their families.

By now the rag-tag boys from the North Louisiana pine hills were jaded by months of fighting and constant marching. Seeing them at Vermillionville in late September, an observer described the 28th as appearing "tired and broken down." But individually, they were as tough as leather, conditioned by nature's elements while living daily with death and discomfort. In the past six months, they had distinguished themselves in battles at Mansura, Fordouche, and Washington with a dozen skirmishes in between.

As the men shouldered their gear and moved out on the morning of the seventeenth, they had no way of knowing they were embarking on a "fools' errand" orchestrated by Smith's Shreveport brain trust. They were destined, they would learn, not for the comforts of winter camp at Monroe, but for the marshy banks of the Mississippi River near the Arkansas border, 250 miles away. Secret arrangements had been made to smuggle a shipment of guns and ammunition from Mississippi to Louisiana, and Mouton's Division had been assigned to protect it. The men set out that day, little knowing that nature was about to deliver a blow even more cruel than the storm they had just survived.

* * *

WINNFIELD, DECEMBER 22—A muddy and miserable army was strung out over several miles as it entered Winn Parish that chilly morning. The men of the 28th knew they were home when small clusters of civilians began appearing beside the road to greet them. Cries of joy rang out as women recognized the sun-browned faces of sons and husbands behind scraggly beards and, one by one, the men broke ranks to embrace them. At small crossroads communities, women, children, and old men gathered to cheer them, and many a soldier, hardened by the bloody harrows of war, could not hold back his tears.

They camped that night four miles south of Winnfield. The campsite soon swarmed with wives and relatives pleading with officers for overnight passes. More often than not, they were granted.

* * *

MONROE, DECEMBER 28—On Christmas Eve, yet another howling norther had descended, pelting the marchers with sleet and covering the pine hills with ice. Without tents and short on blankets, the troops took shelter in a pine thicket in eastern Jackson Parish near the little community of Hoods Mill. In spite of the storm and plunging temperatures, men whose homes stood within overnight walking distance silently stole out of camp to spend Christmas with their families. His home being nearby, it can be assumed that Private Frederick Swint Hood was among those who slipped out of camp. Officers, knowing most of the absentees would return within days, simply looked the other way. Those who remained in camp built roaring fires, and as darkness settled, there was laughter, loud talk, and singing beneath the ice-draped pine trees. In his journal, Poche made note of the festivities: "Tonight, despite the bad colds suffered by the men, it was easy to realize it was Christmas Eve by the shouting and noise in the regiments."

The men moved out on Christmas Day and made it to Monroe on the twenty-sixth. They crossed the Ouachita River on flatboats on the twenty-seventh, and the following day were encamped at Colony Church on Bayou Desiard when yet another storm swept across the North Louisiana landscape. "It rained and later it snowed and the ground froze," Poche wrote. "One can well understand the misery and suffering of our poor soldiers without tents and practically no fire."

Colonel Hyatt gave an even more graphic description of the misery visited upon the men: "[Everything] frozen over and the boys sliding on ice. . . . The ground too cold to lie down. Pitiable at night to see them nodding around campfires with only one blanket. This is soldiering, this is."

In a little over two months, Mouton's division marched more than 350 miles through one of the worst Louisiana winters on record. Starting from their camp on the Sterling Plantation near the Fordouche battlefield in Point Coupee Parish on December 5, they slogged through mud, ice, and snow to Plantersville, Arkansas, arriving there on January 12, 1864. It was all for nothing. The Union Army stopped the shipment of guns and ammunition they were sent to escort before it reached the river. The division was ordered back to Alexandria to rejoin Taylor's army in winter camp. For many in the 28th Louisiana, the brief passage back through their North Louisiana homeland would be the last time they saw their families and their beloved pine hills.

* * *

ALEXANDRIA, DECEMBER 30—After spending Christmas with his family in Shreveport, Dick Taylor returned to his duties more focused and relaxed than his staff had seen him in months. Although his troops were in winter camp, he was far from idle. He had moved his headquarters from Opelousas to Alexandria and now began preparations for the Union offensive he was sure would come with the spring. He sent wagons out to strip the landscape of forage that might feed the enemy's horses. He sent Colonel Vincent and his 2nd Louisiana Cavalry to scour the countryside for deserters and conscript evaders. They brought in more than a thousand men, swelling the numbers in his army to more than six thousand. Many of the evaders protested, claiming they needed to stay at home to protect their families from gangs of jayhawkers roaming the countryside. Depredations by outlaws had increased in recent months, especially in the remote Sabine River region of Western Louisiana. Taylor dispatched Vincent's cavalrymen to hunt them down and hang or otherwise execute the leaders, a task at which the men became highly proficient.

Although there was confusion in Shreveport as to General Banks's intentions, they were clear to Taylor. With the coming of spring, the Union Army would come up the Red River supported by an armada of gunboats. That is what his spies in New Orleans told him, and he had no reason to doubt the intelligence.

In the grip of one of the worst winters on record, the opposing armies were content to remain in their camps, and except for an occasional clash by cavalries, all was quiet along the Louisiana bayous. Franklin had twenty thousand troops encamped between New Iberia, and Brashear City. The only Union activity of note in the Trans Mississippi Department that winter took place hundreds of miles away on the Texas Gulf Coast.

Having failed to occupy Galveston or Sabine Pass, Banks sent five thousand troops to Brownsville at the southern tip of Texas. The invasion force gained a precarious toehold on an island there, and small detachments, supported by gunboats, were sent up the coast to occupy beachheads at Aransas Pass and Corpus Christi. However, those forces posed little threat to the rest of Texas and had little effect on Louisiana other than to deprive Taylor of Tom Green's cavalry. An excited John Magruder, anticipating additional strikes along the Gulf Coast, demanded that all of the Texas units in Louisiana be returned to him. Smith sent him Green's Texas Rangers but retained Walker's division in Louisiana. Taylor protested the loss, pointing out that the real threat to Texas was a Red River invasion in the spring. Smith promised him that if the Red River Valley was threatened, Green's Texans would be returned.

As the weather cooled, so did the heated acrimony between Taylor and Smith. A new cordiality between the two resulted, in large measure because of increasing criticism of Smith's tactics from other sources. In November, an article in the *Louisiana Democrat* blasted Smith, labeling him too incompetent to command the Trans Mississippi and demanding his resignation. Meanwhile, Governor Moore had sent letters to President Davis, urging Smith's removal and Taylor's elevation to command of the Trans Mississippi. Instead of firing Smith, Davis wrote back to the governor congratulating himself for having the good judgment to assign Taylor to Louisiana.

Under fire by the governor and the state's newspaper editors, Smith plunged into politics. He convinced Henry Watkins Allen, a popular legislator and twice wounded war hero, to run against Governor Moore in the November election. Allen, bearing a facial scar from a rifle ball at Shiloh and with both legs shattered by an artillery round that blew his horse from beneath him at Baton Rouge, defeated Moore without even campaigning. Having dealt with Governor Moore, Smith turned his attention Dick Taylor.

By now Taylor was the most popular figure in Louisiana so, instead of opposing him, Smith sought to mend fences. He sent the following report to the War Department: "[Taylor] is cautious, yet bold; always prepared for and anticipating the enemy; concentrating skillfully upon his main force, holding it in check, and crippling its movements; promptly striking his detached columns, routing and destroying them . . ."

Meeting with Taylor, Smith showed him a copy of the report as evidence of his confidence in him. Taylor was not fooled by Smith's sudden show of friendship. He later remarked to his staff that, upon reading the report, he thought Stonewall Jackson himself had been resurrected and sent to Louisiana, somehow assuming his name in the process. Four days later, Taylor learned the real reason for Smith's plaudits. The commander sent him a letter expressing concern over the criticism he had received in the latest issue of *The Democrat*. He urged Taylor to use his influence to suppress such attacks since "they go abroad with the impression of your sanction." Smith ended the letter by assuring Taylor that the assaults on his character by others would not affect "the cordial relations existing between us."

Taylor knew he could not change the public's negative perception of Smith but he wrote a letter to *The Democrat* stating that he supported him. He did not want Smith's job and the headaches inherent in its politics and bureaucracy. When Banks came north in the spring, Taylor wanted every available soldier from Texas and Arkansas to stop him. Kirby Smith was the one person who could release those troops.

★ ★ ★ ★ ★ ★ ★ ★ ★ ★ ★ ★ ★

1864

Dark and Bloody Ground

Suzanna, Suzanna,
When it comes my time,
won't you bury me near
That old Red River line.

ANONYMOUS

★ ★ ★ ★

15

★ ★ ★ ★

"I Shall Hold All I Can"

WASHINGTON, D.C., JANUARY 1—With the dawning of the election year 1864, few in the North expected Abraham Lincoln to be reelected president—not even Lincoln himself. The successes of the previous summer at Gettysburg and Vicksburg were distant memories in the minds of the Northern public. Rosecrans's defeat at Chickamauga that fall tempered expectations that the war might end. Troops had to be pulled out of Virginia and Mississippi to relieve the Army of the Cumberland. In spite of Northern victories at Chattanooga and Missionary Ridge, the Union Army remained bogged down in Tennessee with its supply lines stretched and under attack by Joe Wheeler and Nathan Forrest. In Arkansas and Missouri, General Joe Shelby's Confederate cavalry seemed to roam at will. In the East, Lee's Army of Northern Virginia, although reduced to less than forty thousand men, was far from subdued. Beyond the Mississippi River, after two years of fighting, the rebels still held 90 percent of Louisiana, Southern Arkansas, and all of Texas. The people of the North were growing weary of a war it seemed would never end.

There also seemed to be no end to those seeking to take Lincoln's place in the White House. Foremost in line was George B. McClellan, the discarded general who had become the peace candidate and darling of the Democrats. He pledged to quickly negotiate an end to the war if elected. Several members of Lincoln's cabinet harbored presidential ambitions, Salmon Chase and Edwin Stanton among them. In the field, political generals like Ben Butler and John Fremont remained alert for any opportunity that might propel them into the White House. And in New Orleans, Nathaniel Banks had not given up on his dream to march down Pennsylvania Avenue to the cheers of the multitude.

Lincoln repeatedly had urged first Butler and then Banks, to hold elections in Louisiana and organize a state government there. He saw in Louisiana a model for benevolent repatriation. Lincoln believed reentry of Louisiana into the Union with the same voting rights and privileges as the states in the North might inspire other Southern states to cease resistance. With a presidential election on the horizon, establishing a Union-backed government in Louisiana became even more vital to Lincoln. It was a potential electoral state—as were Texas and Arkansas. The only thing standing in the way was Shreveport, which Lincoln saw as the Confederate keystone supporting the region. Without Shreveport, three Confederate states would collapse, allowing a mother lode of electoral votes to tumble into the Republican column come November.

Deprived of the economic might of New Orleans, Shreveport had become the commercial and industrial hub for the Trans Mississippi Department, and East Texas was its breadbasket. Once under Union control the Red River, usually navigable for six to eight months of the year, would provide a supply conduit from New Orleans to within shouting distance of the Texas border, and lying between Shreveport and Marshall was an abandoned railroad that, once completed, could supply a large army operating in Texas.

Until now, Lincoln and General-in-Chief Henry Halleck had left military and political matters in Louisiana to Banks's judgment. Having had his nose bloodied by Dick Taylor's hit-and-run tactics, Banks was reluctant to expose his army to a 250-mile march through the heart of Louisiana with Tom Green's cavalry waiting to ambush him at every turn in the road. He had chosen instead to send one failed mission after another to the Texas coast on the premise that, if he controlled Texas, Louisiana and Arkansas must fall. However, by 1864 it was clear, even to Banks, that Texas would not be conquered from its beaches.

Sitting on Henry Halleck's desk in Washington was a two-year-old plan for an invasion of Texas via the Red River Valley of Louisiana. Ironically, it had been drawn up by Lincoln's old nemesis, George McClellan. Halleck had favored the plan for some time. Now he convinced Lincoln to commit the resources to make it work.

While Halleck's goals were purely military, Lincoln's were tinted by political and commercial considerations. Halleck wanted to destroy a growing military-industrial base developing along the Red River, halt agricultural production in East Texas, and cut off supplies coming into the department from the French in Mexico. Lincoln, on the other hand, felt increasing pressure from the New England textile barons to supply more cotton for their idle looms. There were rumors that as many as three hundred thousand bales of cotton were stacked on levees and in barns, sheds, and warehouses along the length of the Red River Valley. Lincoln also remained under pressure from New England's more vocal abolitionists to conquer Texas and open the state to colonization.

The French presence in Mexico presented yet another problem. Although neutral, France's government was openly sympathetic to the Confederates. Vital goods flowed freely from France into Texas via Mexico in exchange for cotton. In addition to cutting off that trade, Lincoln wanted to establish a strong military presence in Texas to discourage the French from forming a military alliance with the Confederacy. There were rumors the Confederacy might cede disputed territory between the Neches and Rio Grande rivers back to Mexico in exchange for French military support. If that happened, Lincoln worried that the United States might find itself at war with France as well as the Confederacy.

On January 6, Halleck sent word to Banks that the president thought he should proceed up the Red River, capture Shreveport, and invade Texas. To reinforce Banks's army, ten thousand of General Sherman's crack troops would be withdrawn from Meridian, Mississippi, and sent to Louisiana to spearhead the campaign, placing forty-one thousand men under Banks's command. Halleck suggested a two-pronged assault on Shreveport. As Banks marched on the city from the south, Major General Frederick Steele would come down from Little Rock with another fifteen thousand troops from the north. The Red River Campaign would be supported by virtually the entire Mississippi River fleet—twenty-two gunboats and forty transports under the command of Admiral David Porter. On paper it was a plan drawn for success—one that even Nathaniel Banks could not foul up.

★ ★ ★

SHREVEPORT, JANUARY 7—When Samuel Casey of Kentucky served in the U.S. Congress, he befriended a young Illinois congressman named Abraham Lincoln. Upon his departure from public office, Casey became one of the most successful cotton brokers on the Mississippi. Late in December 1863, Casey went to Washington to seek a favor from his old friend. Following a meeting with Lincoln, he departed the Oval Office with the following document signed by the president:

> All Military and Naval commanders will please give to the Hon. Samuel Casey, of Kentucky . . . protection and safe conduct from Cairo to Red River, and up said river and it's [sic] tributaries, till he shall pass beyond our Military lines, and also give him such protection and safe conduct, on his return to our lines, back to Cairo with any cargoes he may bring; and on his safe return from beyond our lines with said boats and tows, allow him to repeat once or twice if he shall desire.

Beneath the order of protection, Casey signed an agreement in which he promised not to carry contraband into Confederate territory. He also pledged not to take boats assigned to him by the military beyond the enemy lines: "[Until I have] secured the personal pledge of Gen. Kirby Smith, given directly by him to me, that said boats and tows shall without condition, safely return to our military lines."

The order of protection tucked in his case, Casey arrived at Vicksburg on New Year's Eve and was met by a young Louisianan from Shreveport named John B. Shepherd. The following day they crossed the river and left on horseback for Shreveport, escorted by Confederate cavalry. Six days later, Casey was ushered into Confederate Headquarters at Shreveport and greeted by Kirby Smith. By Casey's own description, he found the headquarters "a rather flourishing commercial center."

Casey negotiated a deal with Smith whereby he purchased twenty thousand bales of cotton at one hundred dollars a bale. He paid for the goods in sterling exchange notes and made arrangements for the cotton to be shipped through Confederate lines to New Orleans. The bales, although dusty and grimy from sitting in warehouses for years, would bring up to nine hundred dollars each on the docks at Boston.

The Casey deal was not the first completed by Smith. He had been carrying on a thriving export-import business for some time, ostensibly to support the war effort. At first the avenue of trade went through Mexico. However, Banks's occupation of Brownsville had restricted that route, necessitating the evolution of a thriving, clandestine trade with the enemy that, if not officially sanctioned, was permitted by the turning of heads in Richmond and Washington.

* * *

For some time, Dick Taylor had been aware that certain planters in Confederate territory were selling cotton to speculators representing Northern interests in New Orleans. One of those speculators was his own brother-in-law, Martin Gordon. In the early years of the war when many farmers were desperate for currency, Taylor had allowed them to transport their cotton through his lines to be sold. At the same time he urged planters to stop planting cotton and grow produce and forage to feed not only their families and livestock, but the army and its stock as well. The planters paid little heed and continued to grow and store cotton on the theory that they would reap huge profits at the end of the war. By January 1864 desperation had been replaced by outright greed among many of the planters. The country was overrun with speculators on both sides, and clandestine trading with the enemy became rampant. One broker, Benjamin F. Camp, part owner of the *New York Tribune* and a friend of Ben Butler and Treasury Secretary Salmon P. Chase, boldly sent his agents through North Louisiana canvassing planters. He reported to Chase that five hundred to seven hundred planters were willing to sign the Union loyalty oath and exchange their cotton for supplies and minimal payments. Camp predicted he could acquire up to one hundred thousand bales, turning a profit of $40 million in gold. He magnanimously offered to sell the gold to the Treasury Department to build up its bullion reserve.

By early 1864 Taylor's patience had worn thin. Northern brokers wandered, seemingly at will, into Confederate territory, doling out small deposits for cotton stores and promising full payment once the Union controlled North Louisiana. "The possession of any large amount of cotton will in the end destroy the patriotism of the best citizen," Taylor wrote to Smith. He had no way of knowing that Smith had taken the process a step beyond the planters and was selling cotton directly to agents of the United States government. Upon hearing rumors that Smith was dealing with the enemy, Taylor took action.

In preparation for the coming invasion, he began purging the countryside, from Opelousas to well above Alexandria. He was determined to leave nothing in Central Louisiana for an invading Union Army to seize. Taylor sent his cavalry to confiscate horses, mules, and wagons and clean out corn cribs and haylofts. He issued orders "to burn all cotton, baled or in seed, within the enemy's reach." Citizens were warned that Central Louisiana soon would become a battlefield. They were urged to abandon their homes until the war was over. As chimneys of smoke from cotton fires filled the skies, howls of protest echoed in the streets of Shreveport. When Smith protested to Taylor, he was assured that only private cotton was being burned to keep it out of the hands of the Yankees. Taylor informed his superior that no cotton belonging to the Confederate government was being destroyed. On that basis, Smith could do little to stop the destruction.

★ ★ ★

ALEXANDRIA, FEBRUARY 28—Dick Taylor's mood was no less gloomy than the skies outside his office window that Sunday morning. The bone-chilling dampness that accompanied February in Louisiana had aggravated the arthritis. Correspondence from Shreveport littering his desk had inflamed his temper. Bombarded by memos and conflicting orders, he had grown tired of playing bureaucratic games with the headquarters staff. The completion of Fort DeRussy above Simmesport was the latest obsession in Shreveport. Taylor had resisted rebuilding the fort, pointing out that it would not stop the Union fleet and was vulnerable to an attack by the enemy's infantry. He long ago had concluded that building fixed fortifications against gunboats was a waste of time and resources. "Should the enemy advance in heavy force we would inevitably lose the guns and material at DeRussy," Taylor wrote to Smith. Still Smith insisted on a quick completion of the facility, as if a few earthen embankments and a half-dozen cannon were the salvation of North Louisiana. Unable to impress slaves for the work, it fell to Taylor's troops to do it at a time when they should have been preparing for combat instead of laboring with picks and shovels. He sent Walker's division to complete the task, apologizing to the general: "If you can complete DeRussy, so as to get it off my hands, it will be a great relief to me," he told Walker.

Taylor faced even greater problems. His army was down to six thousand men—hardly enough to contend with the thirty thousand troops he expected Banks to send against him with the clearing of the weather. Some of the new conscripts had deserted, and he lacked the cavalry to hunt them down and return them to camp. He petitioned Smith repeatedly to return Tom Green's cavalry division to Louisiana, but General Magruder insisted on keeping it in Texas and Smith seemed reluctant to order the transfer. In January, when it became apparent that the target for a Union invasion was the Red River and not the Texas coast, Taylor warned Smith that, without Green's division, Shreveport could not be defended. He even offered to relinquish his command to Magruder if Green's troops were brought back to Louisiana. Smith rejected Taylor's offer to step aside, and Green remained in Texas.

By February 28, Taylor's frustration progressed to anger. He sat at his desk and wrote a letter to Smith requesting a sixty-day leave of absence. Still unwilling to publicly criticize Smith, he cited his health as the reason for the request. Upon receiving the correspondence on March 4, Smith was stunned. He immediately wrote back, refusing to grant Taylor a leave: "You know there is no one to take your place, even temporarily, without great injury to the cause. The Dept. cannot do without you. . . . Please write frankly and let me know what the problem really is. . . . [I will] explain or remedy any action that might prove disagreeable."

Smith closed the letter "with feelings of friendship." There was only one remedy for Taylor's dissatisfaction and Smith knew it. That same day, he telegraphed Magruder, ordering him to send Green's division to Louisiana. Upon receiving news that Green's troops were being released to him, Taylor's health seemed to improve and he withdrew his request for a leave.

The decision came not a moment too soon. Even then, an armada of twenty-two gunboats under the command of Admiral Porter was preparing for a Red River expedition, and forty transports were being loaded in New Orleans and Vicksburg with men and materials. Ten thousand battle-hardened troops from Sherman's legions were at Vicksburg, prepared to descend on Louisiana. Eighteen thousand men under General Franklin were preparing to move up from New Iberia, accompanied by a thousand wagons filled with supplies and ammunition. And, at Little Rock, General Steele had another fifteen thousand troops. Hard-pressed to supply such a large force in the field, however, he decided to take only seventy-five hundred men to Shreveport, assuming that would be enough to accomplish his objective.

* * *

NEW ORLEANS, MARCH 2—General William T. Sherman arrived in New Orleans on March 2, fully expecting to command the Red River campaign. Having lived in Central Louisiana, he was familiar with the region. Sherman also assumed that his troops would spearhead the invasion, making him a logical choice for the assignment. Both Halleck and Grant thought Banks would ask Sherman to lead the expedition. But, upon meeting with Banks, Sherman realized that Banks himself intended to command the campaign—after he wrapped up a few political matters in New Orleans. Michael Hahn had just been chosen the Union governor of Louisiana in an election orchestrated by Banks, and a gala inauguration was planned by Mrs. Banks.

Sherman wrote in his memoirs:

> General Banks urged me to remain over the 4th of March to participate in the ceremonies. He explained they would include a performance of the 'Anvil Chorus' by all the bands of his army, and during the performance the church bells were to be rung and cannons were to be fired by electricity. I regarded all such ceremonies as out of place at a time when it seemed to me every hour and minute were due to the war.

Sherman did not stay for the ceremonies. He left by boat for Vicksburg the next morning, wanting no part of an expedition led by Nathaniel Banks.

* * *

As Sherman departed New Orleans, General Grant was on his way to Washington, D.C., having been summoned by President Lincoln. Grant had opposed the Red River campaign from its inception. He wanted instead to combine Banks's forces with his own, march on Mobile, and then capture Atlanta, a strategy that he thought would hasten an end to the war. But once Lincoln committed to a Red River invasion, Grant reluctantly went along. He agreed to lend Banks the ten thousand troops from Sherman's army but demanded that they be returned to him as soon as Shreveport was in Union hands. Grant was apprehensive of Banks's decision to personally take command in the field but had little choice in the matter since Banks outranked him, not only in seniority but political influence in Washington. In fact, Grant had no control over matters west of the Mississippi River. However, that was about to change. Upon his arrival in Washington, Lincoln promoted him to lieutenant general and named him general-in-chief over all U.S. forces, replacing Halleck.

* * *

SIMMESPORT, MARCH 12—For days David Porter had impatiently paced the deck of his flagship, the *Black Hawk*, and studied reports of water levels in the lower Red River. His fleet was anchored in Old River, some twenty-five miles above where the Red entered the Mississippi. Finally, he figured the waters in the Red had risen high enough to accommodate his gunboats. Near nightfall on March 11, the first of the troop transports from Vicksburg with Sherman's soldiers on board began arriving, four days behind schedule. There were twenty-seven transports in all, twenty-one of them packed with soldiers from their hurricane decks to boiler rooms. The others carried supplies, ammunition, and forty field pieces. Sherman had placed his best subordinate in command of the troops—a crusty old brigadier named Andrew J. Smith.

Darkness was settling on the river when Smith went on board the *Black Hawk* to confer with Porter. If possible, he was even more impatient than the admiral to get started—anxious to complete quickly what he considered a minor mission, so that he could get back to the serious business of taking Mobile. His initial objective was Alexandria, some sixty miles to the north by land, and more than three times that for Porter's gunboats via the winding river. Alexandria had the docks and warehouses necessary to supply Smith's army in its march to Shreveport. All that stood between him and Alexandria was a lightly defended little mud fort named DeRussy. It was decided that Smith would land his troops at Simmesport the following morning, march some thirty miles overland, and attack the fort from the rear while Porter's gunboats came up the Red and bombarded DeRussy from the river.

Even as A. J. Smith met with Porter that night, some of his troops went ashore to loot and burn a nearby plantation. They returned with hogs, chickens, cured meats from the smokehouses, and valuables from the dwelling. Upon his return from the *Black Hawk*, instead of disciplining the men, Smith expressed amusement at their initiative. His approval of the raid set the tone for what would become one of the most destructive campaigns ever conducted by an invading army.

* * *

Early on the morning of the twelfth, Confederate scouts at Simmesport looked on in disbelief as a seeming endless line of steamboats, escorted by gunboats, churned past Turnbull's Island and began disgorging troops at the little river port town on the Atchafalaya near the mouth of the Red River. Even as they disembarked, the soldiers began looting and burning nearby homes.

By the time news of the landing was relayed to Dick Taylor in Alexandria, estimates of Union troop strength at Simmesport had become exaggerated to fifteen thousand men—half again the actual number. Taylor's New Orleans intelligence network, usually reliable, had failed him. With his attention focused on Franklin's movements in South Louisiana, the enemy invasion at Simmesport caught him by surprise. He was unaware that Sherman had committed troops to the campaign until they were on Louisiana soil. Still, he did not believe the numbers being reported to him. Especially disturbing to Taylor was a message from General Walker stating that he was pulling his forces back before overwhelming odds. Walker suggested that Taylor consider abandoning Alexandria noting, "Fort DeRussy must fall as soon as it is invested . . . which would enable the enemy to throw his whole force up the Red River as high as Alexandria."

Walker had thirty-eight hundred troops in the region, most of them located at Yellow Bayou just north of Simmesport. Without issuing a direct order, Taylor urged Walker to attack immediately: "Close, sharp, quick fighting is our game. . . . Any severe check to the head of their column would probably break up this expedition. [We must] take more than ordinary hazards. . . . The loss of our guns at DeRussy and the occupation of Alexandria by the Federals would be a great disaster."

But it was Walker, not Taylor, who was in the field, faced with a momentous decision. He had three choices. He could attack or fall back and attempt to defend the fort. Or he could retreat across the Bayou Du Lac bridge and save his division to fight another day. If he chose one of the first two options, he risked entrapment and the destruction of his army. Weighing on Walker's decision was the fact that part of his cavalry was across the river and unable to support his infantry. Since the Du Lac bridge afforded his only avenue of escape, he wisely chose retreat, leaving DeRussy to the mercy of A. J. Smith's army and Porter's gunboats.

* * *

FORT DE RUSSY, MARCH 14—As the Yankee columns moved north, stretching for miles along the narrow roads that wound between swamps and bayous, they captured a dozen or so Confederates who had lingered to herd mules and oxen. Those were the only rebels seen during the entire march toward DeRussy. Crossing Bayou de Glaise, the troops emerged from the swamps on a beautiful prairie. A Yankee officer was inspired to describe the scenery in a letter to his wife:

> Ascending a slight elevation we suddenly emerged in one of the most beautiful prairies imaginable. High table land, gently undulating, watered by exquisite lakes, occasional groves, the landscape dotted with tasteful houses, gardens and shrubberys. This prairie, called Avoyelles, is settled exclusively by French *émigres,* many of whom, as our army passed, sought shelter under the tricolor of France.

The Federals marched through the old French Creole town of Marksville at noon, treating the inhabitants who remained for the show to a rowdy rendition of *Rally Round the Flag Boys.* The song was accompanied by the boom of cannons to the east. Just three miles away, the defenders of DeRussy's and Porter's gunboats engaged in a duel of heavy guns. By late afternoon A. J. Smith had maneuvered some five thousand troops of the 3rd Division into a battle line and gave the order to charge. DeRussy was built to defend the river, not a back-door infantry attack, and as predicted by Taylor, the fort fell in minutes. Directed by General Joseph Mower, the attackers swept over the earthworks and overwhelmed the three hundred defenders. Union losses were only thirty-eight killed and wounded, several of those victims of errant shells from Porter's boats.

From the *Black Hawk*, Admiral Porter noted that the operation resembled a parade ground drill rather than a battle. He compared the rebels' resistance to "the antics of Chinamen, who build canvas forts, paint hideous dragons on their shields, turn somersets [sic] . . . and then run away at the first sign of an engagement." He congratulated A. J. Smith on his conduct of the operation and predicted a quick completion of the campaign with the capture of Alexandria and Shreveport. "I do not think the rebels will fight until their backs are to the Gulf of Mexico," he told Smith.

* * *

ALEXANDRIA, MARCH 15—Informed of the fall of DeRussy, Taylor was more philosophical than disturbed. "Thus much for our Red River Gibraltar," he told his staff. He issued orders for an immediate evacuation of Alexandria and sent a messenger to urge Green's Texas Rangers to proceed to Natchitoches with all possible haste.

Taylor worked through the night, personally supervising the evacuation of Alexandria. Cannons, munitions, supplies, and all government property were loaded aboard steamers and sent up the river to Natchitoches. That morning, one of the boats ran aground on the treacherous rapids above the city and Taylor ordered its cargo transferred to other boats. As he watched the work progress, word came that Porter's gunboats were approaching and he ordered the steamer burned. Even as flames consumed the vessel, Taylor saw the first of the gunboats arrive at the city docks. He reined his horse westward and soon caught up with his staff and headquarters company. Some twenty miles from Alexandria, they met Mouton's division and camped for the night. Taylor had managed to salvage everything from Alexandria except three field pieces, left behind due to an oversight.

* * *

As Porter steamed up the river toward Alexandria, he was accompanied by General Mower's 3rd Division. A. J. Smith retained several brigades at DeRussy to destroy the fort. The men spent three days digging out and burning giant wooden beams and trying to level the earthworks. In the middle of the night, the general decided to hasten the work by setting fire to the fort's magazine. Having misjudged the amount of explosives present, the result was spectacular. The troops encamped beside the fort were jarred awake by a thunderous explosion. A soldier described the scene in his memoirs: "I knew what it was in an instant, for I could see shells bursting high in the air, the whole heavens seemed to be on fire, pieces of timber and hard lumps of earth were falling in camp and even beyond. Men were running for life to the woods."

Two soldiers were killed by the falling debris and scores wounded. For a time, A. J. Smith was the most unpopular man in his own army, hissed at when he approached the men in the ranks.

* * *

JONES PLANTATION, MARCH 21—Carroll Jones, a wealthy, free black man, owned a large farm some thirty miles west of Alexandria on the road between Opelousas and old Fort Jessup. Because his place stood on high ground and was accessible by good roads, Taylor used his barns as a storage depot for supplies and forage. Here he waited for Walker's division and Vincent's cavalry to catch up with the remainder of his army. For Walker's Texans, the 125-mile march from Bayou de Glaize was a grueling experience. Captain Petty described the forced march in his journal: "For five days and nights I never pulled off my over coat or shoes, but slept with all on. We marched day and night and lived on coarse cornbread and poor beef. . . . Weary and footsore . . . [but] our deeds will be remembered for years."

With the arrival of Walker's troops on March 18, and Vincent's cavalry on March 19, Taylor had drawn together a force of almost seven thousand men. Mouton's light division, composed of two brigades commanded by Camille Polignac and Henry Gray, totaled some twenty-three hundred men. Walker's Texas division numbered thirty-eight hundred, and Vincent's cavalry about four hundred, some of them recent conscripts.

Taylor noted in a report that the cavalry appeared "jaded" and their horses worn out. For weeks, Vincent's horsemen had been chasing jayhawkers, rounding up conscript evaders, and harassing Franklin's army in South Louisiana. Still, they were all he had. He dispatched them to Bayou Rapides to delay advance units of the Federal army coming out of Alexandria.

* * *

ALEXANDRIA, MARCH 21—Some of General Mower's troops went up the river on transports, but most marched along the Cheneyville Pike, finally arriving at Alexandria on March 16. They found the city sitting peacefully under the guns of Porter's ironclads. They also found Porter's men scouring warehouses and the countryside for cotton. The soldiers themselves had little interest in cotton and went instead on a rampage of looting and destruction. Smashing windows and kicking in doors, they entered business establishments, took what they wanted, and upon departing threw goods into the streets. Private homes were pillaged, and the inhabitants were threatened with torture if they did not give up their valuables. Pantries were ransacked for delicacies. What was not taken was often destroyed.

Entering one dwelling, soldiers found a black woman and demanded to know the location of her master. She replied that she was a free woman and insisted that she owned the house. The intruders said they knew black people were not allowed to own houses in Louisiana and, therefore, she must be lying. After taking anything of value they could find, the men used horses to pull down the walls, reducing her house to a pile of rubble.

The remainder of A. J. Smith's troops arrived in Alexandria on the nineteenth to join in the looting. The following morning, a Sunday, those citizens who remained in town awakened to the rumble of more than two thousand cavalrymen riding down Main Street, advance elements of General Albert Lee's cavalry arriving from South Louisiana.

On Monday, General Mower left Alexandria with six regiments of infantry and a brigade of cavalry bent on extracting revenge for an attack on one of his patrols. Thanks to information supplied by a jayhawker who had infiltrated the rebels, Mower not only knew where the enemy horsemen responsible for the attack were camped, he knew their countersign.

Late that afternoon, a storm blew in with large hailstones accompanying a driving rain. Instead of seeking shelter, Mower pushed his men on through the storm toward a place named Henderson's Hill, some twenty miles above Alexandria. Located at the confluence of two bayous, Henderson's Hill rose out of a flooded swamp. Some three hundred of Colonel Vincent's 2nd Cavalry had taken refuge there, wrapped in slickers and cursing the elements. As night fell and the rain continued, some of the pickets returned to camp while others sat hunched beneath slickers and blankets, more intent on staying warm and dry than being alert to danger.

Guided by the jayhawkers, Mower's men made their way through the swamps along narrow, muddy trails, their movements shielded by the storm. They crept up the rain-drenched hillside, gave the countersign, and were upon the pickets before they could sound an alert. The Yankee soldiers were in the rebel camp before Vincent's men could organize a resistance. After brief fighting, Mower took 250 prisoners, captured almost as many horses and a four-gun battery. Some of the rebels escaped by riding their mounts down the steep hillside and through mud that was almost belly-deep to their horses.

The Union coup was a terrible blow to Taylor. Deprived of two-thirds of Vincent's cavalry, he had lost his eyes and ears at the worst possible time. Until Green arrived, he would have to rely on dismount cavalry from Polignac's regiments and Walker's division, depriving him of infantry. Taylor blamed himself for the debacle at Henderson's Hill. Noting the number of new conscripts among Vincent's men, he admitted to his staff that he should not have assigned them to work so near the enemy. "In truth [they were] too ill-disciplined for close work," he said. "They found their fires more agreeable than out-posts." The next day, he ordered a retreat up the Fort Jessup Road to Beasley's Crossing, another of his supply depots. In a report to Shreveport, he noted: "I am therefore com-pelled to fall back . . . and wait until I can effect a junction with General Green."

Taylor's strategy was simple. Once Green joined him, he planned to select good ground and defeat Banks. But he would not risk a major battle until he had sufficient cavalry to assure success.

In the wake of the disaster at Henderson's Hill, Taylor finally received good news from Shreveport. In addition to Green's division, Kirby Smith had ordered two addi-tional regiments of cavalry from Texas to Louisiana. He also announced he was bringing General Churchill's four-thousand-man infantry division from Arkansas to assist in the defense of Louisiana. In a dispatch, Smith inquired if Taylor could hold Natchitoches until reinforcements arrived. Taylor's reply was noncommittal: "I shall hold all I can."

* * *

ALEXANDRIA, MARCH 26—Arriving in Alexandria by riverboat on March 24, General Banks was horrified by what he found. Instead of preparing for a campaign up the river, Admiral Porter's sailors were scattered over the countryside seizing contraband cotton, and A. J. Smith's soldiers were rampaging through the city, terrorizing the citizenry. The horde of cotton speculators accompanying Banks howled in protest at the sight of transports and barges loaded with cotton bales emblazoned with the letters "USN." Among those howling the loudest was Lincoln's old friend, Samuel Casey.

Confronting Porter, Banks ordered all cotton confiscated by the Navy turned over to him for assignment to the U.S. Treasury Department. Porter flatly refused, insisting the bales were prizes of war and property of the U.S. Navy. He pointed out that navy regulations permitted such seizures and provided for compensation to his officers and men once the cotton was shipped to Chicago and sold. After promising his men prize money, Porter said, he could not go back on his word without creating discipline problems. The thought of all of that cotton going to Chicago instead of New York and Boston was more than Banks could tolerate. He informed Porter that the transport vessels were technically under his command and he would not allow their use by the navy to ship cotton. Porter said he would confiscate barges from the local docks to haul his cotton.

Even as the two commanders argued, the cotton speculators fanned out across the nearby hills, frantically searching for any cotton overlooked by the navy. What they found was a large amount of unginned cotton sitting in barns and sheds. They urged Banks to confiscate gins in the region to bale the cotton.

The cotton controversy quickly degenerated into a competition between the sailors and Banks's soldiers. The army was ordered to escort speculators into the countryside and protect their private acquisitions. According to dictates from Washington, the speculators were limited to the acquisition of privately owned cotton, for which they had to compensate the owners. Meanwhile, the army itself could confiscate only that cotton owned by the Confederate government. The navy, unencumbered by any restrictions, held a decided advantage. Porter's men ignored all rules, seizing private cotton where they found it, claiming everything was Confederate cotton, and marking bales with the letters "CSA-USN." A standing joke in Alexandria was that the letters stood for "Cotton Stealing Association of the United States Navy."

In addition to the cotton flap, a problem posed by A.J. Smith's troops confronted Banks. He was under orders to pacify the population, conduct elections, and set up local governments in the cities he occupied but at Alexandria he found that many residents had fled to avoid harassment by Smith's soldiers, and those who remained cowered behind locked doors. Banks's solution was to get the Midwestern legions out of town as quickly as possible. He ordered Smith to draw supplies for his forces and proceed to Cotile Landing, a hamlet on the Red River some eighteen miles north of Alexandria. On March 25, Smith's three divisions prepared to leave town while Banks's army was arriving from South Louisiana.

General Franklin's 19th and 13th corps entered the city with flags waving and bands blaring. The procession went on most of the day of the twenty-sixth, and by nightfall soldiers filled the streets. Banks proclaimed that Alexandria was in permanent possession of the United States government and issued an order requiring all citizens to sign an oath of allegiance to the Union. People who refused were subject to having their properties confiscated. He scheduled an election for April 1 for local officials as well as delegates to an upcoming convention in New Orleans to form a new state constitution, part of Lincoln's reconstruction plan for Louisiana. Banks opened a recruiting office and offered large bounties to men who joined the Union Army. Some 150 men signed up, many of them anti-Confederate jayhawkers who arrived in town in large numbers from the Sabine River region. Most of the local men who joined did so under the threat of Union seizure of their homes if they refused.

The jayhawkers, described by one citizen as a "bunch of cutthroats," were formed into a mounted unit called the Louisiana Scouts. Instead of scouting, they were set loose on the countryside to wreak vengeance on Confederate sympathizers. According to one citizen's account: "They patrolled the country adjacent. They scoured it, visiting upon individuals their vengeance and vindictiveness. . . . In remote parts of the parish they burnt dwellings of those who were supposed to have been active in pointing out or in aiding in arresting [Confederate] conscripts."

By the time Banks settled political matters in Alexandria, he was more than a week behind his own schedule for capturing Shreveport. The delay did not go unnoticed elsewhere. On March 26, just when Banks seemed to be gaining control of the local situation, he received a disturbing letter from Ulysses Grant, new general-in-chief of the Union Army. Grant informed him that he must return General Sherman's ten thousand troops to Mississippi by the middle of April if they were not directly engaged in the taking of Shreveport at that time. Under any circumstance, they were to be returned by May 1 to participate in campaigns against Mobile and Atlanta.

The ultimatum jolted Banks to action. He immediately began making logistic arrangements to move thirty thousand troops, one thousand supply wagons, and trains of artillery more than a hundred miles to Shreveport. Other than harassment by enemy cavalry, he expected no serious Confederate resistance until he reached Shreveport. Some members of his staff speculated that the rebels might not defend Shreveport, but retreat to Texas to consolidate their forces before making a stand.

Banks faced two obstacles that prevented an immediate departure from Alexandria. The first was the election scheduled for April 1. The second was David Porter's reluctance to take his gunboats up the river.

In normal years, water in the Red River began rising in early December and reached its highest level by March. That year, the water did not start rising until February and the river was much lower than expected. The most treacherous part of the Red was just above Alexandria. There, twin rapids several hundred feet apart created a danger for boats ascending the river. When the water was high it flowed over the rock formations with barely a ripple, allowing riverboats to traverse them easily. But in the last week of March 1864, the water still moved swiftly over the shallows, creating a hazard for river pilots.

Porter liked to boast that he could take his gunboats "anywhere the sand is damp." Now he expressed concern that if he took his gunboats up the river, he might not be able to navigate them back past the rapids. Still Banks persisted and, whether convinced by the general's arguments or inspired by reports of large amounts of cotton waiting in the upper reaches of the Red, Porter at last agreed to go.

★ ★ ★

PLEASANT HILL, MARCH 30—From the beginning, it was Dick Taylor's intention to stop Banks before he got to Natchitoches—a beautiful, old French town of elegant homes and ornate downtown buildings located near the confluence of the Cane and Red rivers. But on Monday, March 28, with Tom Green's Texas Division a week overdue, he received word that the Union Army had reached Cotile Landing in force. In fact, General Albert Lee had arrived at the little river hamlet south of Natchitoches with five thousand Union cavalry, trailed by A. J. Smith's ten-thousand-man army. General Franklin, with another fifteen thousand infantry, was only a day behind Smith. The news dashed any hopes Taylor had of saving Natchitoches. In fact, the Federal occupation of Cotile Landing threatened to cut him off from Shreveport. Reluctantly, Taylor ordered his army to withdraw north to Pleasant Hill, where he had yet another supply depot. At the same time, Taylor sent his depleted cavalry to keep an eye on Union movements at Cotile Landing and burn cotton along the river road north of Natchitoches.

Just as Stonewall Jackson had done in Virginia, when retreating Taylor always kept his cargo wagons and artillery miles ahead of the army. The separation assured the retention of his supplies, munitions, and heavy guns in the event of an attack. While sound militarily, the policy deprived his men of the few comforts usually associated with camp life—like tents, blankets, fresh meat, and cooking pots.

As Taylor watched his ragged columns move out along the Fort Jessup Road, he saw clearly that his army must soon fight or disintegrate. He did not have the resources to sustain indefinitely a six-thousand-man army on the move. Supplies were low, and the men had been on short rations for days. Forage for the animals also was becoming a problem. He repeatedly asked Kirby Smith for provisions and received only excuses. In the absence of Green's cavalry, he asked Smith to send him the Louisiana 4th Cavalry Regiment operating in Eastern Louisiana. His pleas were answered by promises but no horsemen from the east.

Meanwhile, the men had grown weary of "skedaddling from the Yankees" and grumbled discontentedly. Some of the men, jaded by two years in the field, were ready to fight or go home. An officer in the 18th Regiment captured the mood in a letter: "During this march we have not [had] a single tent and when it rains, which is frequently, the case [is] we have to lay and take it. We have nothing but bull beef, corn bread, dirty clothes and sore feet."

In a letter to his wife, a Texan in Walker's division summed up the attitude of many of the men and expressed dismay at news that the Texas state government was rationing food for families there: "The men are literally starving here. A great many are talking of leaving the field. . . . When times get so that your women and children are to be put on half rations . . . it will be time for us to wind it up."

During Taylor's withdrawal from Beasley's Crossing to Pleasant Hill, he received a letter that sent him into a rage. The missive came from Duncan Kenner, his brother-in-law who also was a Confederate congressman. Kenner informed him that Churchill's Infantry Division, totaling four thousand troops, had arrived from Arkansas but was being held in Shreveport by Kirby Smith. Kenner wrote that when he asked Smith why the troops were not being sent to reinforce Taylor, Smith replied that, "Taylor is waiting for Green and does not want the extra troops."

Taylor immediately sent a letter to Smith informing him that, although he was waiting for Green, he still needed all the men he could get: "I scarcely [can] conceive how this could be interpreted into a declaration that I did not want reinforcements. I certainly would have been the first commander possessing ordinary sense who voluntarily declined reinforcements while retreating before a superior force."

He let Smith know that if Churchill's division had been made available to him he would have fought Banks at Natchitoches. Taylor protested Smith's seeming lack of concern and ended the letter with a tone of defiance: "When Green joins me, I repeat, I shall fight a battle for Louisiana, be the forces of the enemy what they may."

Smith's response served only to irritate Taylor further. The general claimed to be was holding Churchill's division at Shreveport in case it was needed to contend with General Steele in Arkansas. Upon reading the letter, Taylor wondered aloud to his staff that if Churchill was needed in Arkansas, "then what in hell is he doing in Shreveport?" He penned a blistering reply to Smith:

> I respectfully suggest that the only possible way to defeat Steele's movement [in Arkansas] is to whip the enemy now in the heart of the Red River Valley. [Then, he suggested, full attention could be given to Steele.] Had reinforcements come forward I could have fought a battle for the department today. To decline [troop] concentration when we have the means, and when the enemy is already in the vitals of the department, is a policy I am too obtuse to understand.

Upon his arrival at Pleasant Hill on Wednesday, more bad news awaited Taylor. Green would not arrive in Louisiana for another ten days. Magruder had delayed the release of Green's division while an unconcerned Smith sat idly in Shreveport and allowed it to happen. Taylor's staff bore witness to a tirade of profanity. He could forgive bad judgment in a superior, Taylor said, but not deception. In that moment of anger, he made a decision. He would not allow Banks to proceed further. If the Union Army reached Shreveport it would all be over. Given time for Steele's troops to come down from Arkansas, the Federals could concentrate forty-five thousand troops at Shreveport. Taylor resolved to fight the battle for Louisiana in the pine hills, with or without Green, Churchill, or Kirby Smith. He lamented the fact that he had retreated so far and had allowed the Union Army to destroy so much of the heartland of Louisiana. "We have given up too much already," he told his staff. "Like the man who has admitted the robber into his bed-chamber instead of resisting him at the door, our defense will be embarrassed by the cries of wives and children. I shall never cease to regret this error."

★ ★ ★

ALEXANDRIA, MARCH 31—Lieutenant Charles Washington Kennedy hated rats. He had developed a dislike for the repulsive creatures aboard the transport ship during the journey from New York harbor to New Orleans. The sound of them scurrying about in the dark and running across his legs as he lay in his bunk had cost him many a sleepless hour, so he was relieved upon being assigned a room in one of Alexandria's finer homes. A member of the 156th New York Volunteers, he had arrived with General Banks's army at Alexandria the previous morning and spent the day supervising the unloading of supplies from the river transports into a dockside warehouse. Having worked well into the night, he had no time to secure a place to stay, leaving him little choice but to spend the night in the warehouse. Unfortunately, the facility had been used to store grain and flour, attracting a colony of rodents. Instead of sleeping, the lieutenant spent the night listening to rats scurry around in the darkness and chasing them away from his pallet on the floor.

Upon completing his duties on Sunday, Kennedy retired to his assigned room. Although he was tired, he sat at a desk in the bedroom and wrote a long letter to his wife back in Kingston, New York, as he did faithfully every Sunday evening:

My Dearest Katey:

In my last letter I said that I was afraid I would be unable to be as regular as usual in my weekly correspondence, but Sunday evening has come around again and, though I am two or three hundred miles from where I was last Sunday, I am still in comfortable quarters and able to write as usual. . . . We left Baton Rouge about 10 o'clock Friday morning and did not reach this place til day-break yesterday.

We found General Banks here with nearly thirty thousand men, by far the largest army I have ever seen since I have been in service. The town was full of soldiers, wagon trains loading up with supplies, officers and mounted orderlies galloping about in every direction but the town looked just as Baton Rouge did when we first occupied it. Til the stores and houses were shut up and hardly one of the inhabitants to be seen (sic) in the streets. The 16th and 17th Army Corps marched out the day we arrived. They were Western men who came down the river from Vicksburg, good for fighting but awfully rough. The inhabitants were in a sad state of tribulation while they remained here. They committed all sorts of outrages, ransacking stores and dwelling houses and carrying off whatever they took a fancy to and destroying more than they took.

I have got a first rate warehouse for my stores and for my quarters have had a nicely furnished room assigned to me by Lieutenant Colonel Neafie. . . . My room is just as it was when the owner left it, everything in its place and a great deal more comfortable than even our quarters in Baton Rouge. Am I not lucky? I have a nice bed with clean, white sheets (fancy?) and it does look so tempting that I don't know how I have managed to keep out of it long enough to write you. . . . Love to all of the little ones and kisses from Papa and to yourself, all that you know I feel for you.

Good-bye Dearest Wife,

Your Own Charley

∗ ∗ ∗

PLEASANT HILL, APRIL 2—Camped on the outskirts of Pleasant Hill, another soldier penned a letter to a wife named Kate. It was brief and obviously written in haste. Upon completing it, James Beard summoned a young soldier and instructed him to deliver the missive to his wife at Auburnia. In addition to serving as a courier, it was Beard's way of sending the boy out of harm's way. There was a tone of confidence, mixed with caution in the letter:

> We expect reinforcements to arrive in time to make a successful stand here. I do not have any fear of our being able to whip the scoundrels here, having the advantage of a good position and the army *wants* a fight. The best of spirits pervades the entire army. . . .
>
> If we have to fall back towards Shreveport from here, tell your pa it is my advice for him to send off all of his Negro men and such women as Lucy. I am so glad that there is a prospect of our going no higher than this. It would disturb me so much to be forced to retreat and leave you behind.
>
> Kiss the children for me and give love to all the family. Good-bye Darling and may God bless and protect you and my little ones.

When he wrote those words, James Beard had no way of knowing that his four-month-old son, Charlie Edward Beard, had fallen ill with a fever and died five days earlier.

∗ ∗ ∗

GRAND ECORE, APRIL 2—Although Porter's fleet had several low-draft ironclads that could easily ascend the rapids at Alexandria, the commander was determined to lead the expedition with the *Eastport*, one of his largest and most powerful gunboats. Against the advice of his pilots, on March 26 he sent the *Eastport* churning up the river and, as they predicted, it became stuck on the rocks, blocking the channel. As Banks looked on in dismay, the navy spent two days trying to free the *Eastport*. Finally, on March 28, a slight rise in the river proved sufficient for the gunboat to break free and cross the shallows. That same day, Franklin's army began marching out of town toward Natchitoches.

Five more days were required for Porter to get another twelve gunboats and thirty transports across the shallows. Seven deep-draft gunboats and ten transports remained left at Alexandria, requiring Banks's men to use mules and wagons to transfer cargoes from the steamers below the rapids to those above.

At Cotile, A. J. Smith's troops boarded the transports and went on up the river to

Grand Ecore, a small port town two miles above Natchitoches. Some two thousand of Smith's soldiers accompanied Porter's fleet further up the river while eight thousand waited at Grand Ecore to rejoin Banks's army. Albert Lee's cavalry proceeded by land to Natchitoches, and Franklin's infantry, marching eighty miles in four days, joined him there on April 1. Traveling by boat, Banks arrived at Natchitoches the next day, having concluded his political duties in Alexandria—including staging an election for local officials and a delegate to a constitution convention in New Orleans.

At Natchitoches, Banks made two quick decisions, involving the route he would take and the disposition of his forces. Two roads ran out of Grand Ecore. One followed the winding banks of the Red River north to Campti, Blair's Landing, Coushatta, and eventually to Shreveport. The other went west to Crump's Corners before turning north through the towns of Pleasant Hill and Mansfield, then on to Shreveport. Assured that the latter was a much better road than the one that followed the river, Banks chose it. He also chose to send Lee's cavalry ahead, followed by Franklin's infantry, with A. J. Smith's forces bringing up the rear.

By circumstance more than design, the troops borrowed from Sherman to spearhead the campaign had ended up at the back of his column. However, at that point, Banks was far more concerned with getting his army moving than its order. Only two weeks remained before Grant would demand the return of Sherman's men and he intended to occupy Shreveport by then.

So anxious was Banks to get to Shreveport, he did not consider the risk of leaving the protection of Porter's fleet with its 150 heavy guns. His jayhawk scouts assured him the small rebel army in his path was demoralized and posed no threat. Banks departed Grand Ecore convinced the Confederates would not fight before Shreveport. He sent a message to Washington stating that he would be in Shreveport within the week. "I then will pursue the enemy into the interior of Texas for the sole purpose of dispersing or destroying his forces."

SABINE CROSSROADS, APRIL 5—In the gray light before sunrise, a solitary figure in a black greatcoat sat on his horse on an open hillside. In the quiet before daybreak, Dick Taylor surveyed the ground he would defend. It was a wheat field on the Moss Plantation, unplanted that spring because its owner had moved away.

The enemy would emerge from the woods on the Pleasant Hill road, his cavalry in advance. The Yankees would ride to the crest of the hill before seeing his batteries guarding the road. They would see his infantry and horse drawn up in a V, the battle line stretching more than a mile along the edge of the forest. The field of battle was one thousand yards long and eight hundred yards across, covered with dried stubble from the previous year's crop and clear of obstruction, except for a few trees lining a ravine that ran down its middle.

He would give the Yankees the high ground because the low offered a better defense. As the enemy regiments came out of the forest, they would deploy behind a rail fence on the south side of the field. If he could lure Banks into an attack, the enemy lines would be in full view of Taylor's batteries and rifles for the entire distance across the field. If it became necessary for him to attack Banks, a slight rise in the sloping hillside and the trees along the ravine would temporarily shield his lines crossing the field. Satisfied, Taylor turned his horse and rode back to the little woodland town of Mansfield, two miles distant, to assemble his officers.

* * *

Tom Green's cavalry division began arriving on April 4. The men drifted into camp, one regiment at a time, seemingly in no particular hurry. First to arrive was Colonel Xavier Debray's regiment. When Taylor began upbraiding him for being ten days late, the fiery Frenchman snapped back, pointing out that his men had traveled 250 miles encumbered by a wagon train hauling supplies for Taylor. Taken aback by Debray's feisty response, Taylor smiled and extended his hand. "Well, I see you are not a politician," he said in French. Debray, pleased at being addressed in his native language, informed Taylor that Green would arrive with the last of the division within two days.

The next day when Colonel Walter Lane rode into town at the head of his Texas regiment, he spotted the general sitting on his horse waiting to greet them. "Boys, I am glad to see you," Taylor said, nodding politely as the Texans rode by. After spending months moving from one winter encampment to another and seeing little action, the Texans seemed happy to be back in Louisiana. One shouted, "Hey Gen'ral! We've come back to save you boys agin." Another later wrote, "We were, if anything, overjoyed at the prospects of returning to Louisiana with our favorite chieftain [Green] to our favorite General—Taylor."

Having made up his mind to fight, Taylor paid little attention to Smith's almost daily warnings against engaging the enemy. However, a message from Shreveport on the fourth, stating that Churchill's troops would continue to be held in reserve, sparked Taylor's anger sufficiently for him to send a reply. To relieve Smith's fear of Steele, Taylor offered to go to Arkansas and whip him, then return to Louisiana and whip Banks, noting that, though impractical, any plan of action would be better than none: "Action, prompt, vigorous action is required. While we are deliberating the enemy is marching. King James lost three kingdoms for a mass. We may lose three states without a battle."

The tone of Taylor's letter alarmed Smith. He did not believe Taylor could defeat Banks in a major battle and feared the army would be destroyed in an attempt. Smith's strategy was to delay Banks and Steele as long as possible, tying up their armies so that they could not be used east of the Mississippi River. If circumstance dictated, he was prepared to give up Shreveport and retreat to the interior of Texas. Smith decided to go to Mansfield and impress upon Taylor the need to avoid an all-out battle.

* * *

PLEASANT HILL ROAD, APRIL 6—If this was the good road, Albert Lee told his staff, he would hate to see the bad one. He was deep in the pine-clad hills south of Pleasant Hill when he encountered a substance unlike anything he had seen. The red clay covering the rutted road seemed to embody every bad element of mud, but multiplied several times. Pelted by intermittent rain for two days, it was as slick as grease, yet clung to wagon wheels and horses' hooves like glue, building up great globs that had to be scraped off with boards and tree branches. More frustrating was the fact that there was no consistency to the stuff. In some places progress was akin to wading in molasses. In others the clay was as hard as a rock and so slick the horses could barely maintain their balance.

The very nature of the terrain made Lee nervous. The narrow road was hemmed in by dense forest, a primeval wilderness with pine trees so large two men could not reach around them. The forest floor was covered with thick underbrush, laced together by networks of muscadine, scuppernong, and wild grape vines, making it virtually impenetrable. Unlike the heavily populated river deltas, here Lee and his horsemen rarely came upon a field hewn from the forest and a rough-board house with outbuildings.

Topping each hill, Lee spied rebel horsemen sitting on their mounts on the crest of the next one, watching him. An attack by cavalry in this rugged terrain did not concern him, but he did worry that he was vulnerable to an ambush by infantry. By then the column of men, wagons, and artillery was strung out for miles. Three hundred supply wagons and artillery trailed Lee and his five thousand cavalrymen. Next came General Franklin's fifteen thousand infantrymen, followed by another seven hundred wagons with twelve hundred troops of the Native Guards acting as teamsters and guards. At the rear, a full day's march back was A. J. Smith and his eight thousand troops. If attacked, Lee realized, he would not have infantry support because General Franklin's troops were blocked by the cavalry's supply wagons. Lee sent a message to Franklin suggesting that the cavalry's wagons be moved to the rear, allowing the infantry to move up directly behind his horse soldiers. Franklin refused, noting that it was Lee's responsibility to take care of his own wagons.

As the Union cavalrymen approached Pleasant Hill, they encountered several refugees. When questioned, the locals told Lee that General Taylor was amassing a big army at Mansfield, some twenty miles to the north. Lee's staff officers scoffed at the report. "I recollect this distinctly," one of them wrote later. "They said the rebels were boasting that here was the place they were going to bury the Yankees."

Although others were skeptical that the rebels would fight a pitched battle, Lee was not so sure. He was at Washington five months earlier when Taylor lured he and Franklin into the ambush and drove the army back to Bayou Bourbeau. He recalled crossing a bridge south of Washington and wondering why the Confederates had not burned it as they had others. Only after the ambush did Lee realize that the intact bridge was part of Taylor's trap. Now he noticed that none of the bridges on the Pleasant Hill road were burned. He appealed once more to Franklin to bring his infantry forward and, again, his request was refused.

★ ★ ★

MANSFIELD, APRIL 6—Kirby Smith arrived in Mansfield at noon on Wednesday and Taylor escorted him four miles north of town to inspect the troops camped on a farm. With the arrival of the last of Tom Green's Texas Rangers that morning, Taylor had assembled eighty-eight hundred men and some forty field pieces. After reviewing the troops, the general and commander returned to Mansfield for a conference.

Smith told Taylor there was no need for a general engagement with Banks, that simply by tying up his army in Louisiana he was providing a valuable service to the Confederacy. "Otherwise, these troops would be used against our brethren east of the Mississippi," Smith said. He further stated that he was considering weathering a siege at Shreveport or, perhaps, even withdrawing into Texas to concentrate a larger army before fighting the Yankees.

Taylor bristled at the suggestion, pointing out that if Shreveport fell so would all of Louisiana and Arkansas, and the troops from those states would desert in droves. "Besides," he said, "from the interior of Texas we could give no more aid to our brethren east of the Mississippi than from the Sandwich Islands." Unmoved by Taylor's arguments, Smith instructed him not to engage Banks without written orders. Smith then returned to Shreveport to attend a gala ball being given in his honor that night.

★★★★

16

★★★★

Mansfield

WILSON'S FARM, APRIL 7—Near Sabine Crossroads on Thursday afternoon, Taylor heard the rumble of heavy gunfire from the south and spurred his horse toward the sound of a battle. He had gone only a few miles when he met about fifty Texas cavalrymen galloping up the road, obviously running from the fight. At the sight of their grim-faced commander in his trademark black greatcoat, they reined in their horses. Before Taylor could berate them, one yelled: "Gen'ral! If you won't cuss us, we'll go back with you and fight 'em!" Amused that his reputation had spread to apparently new recruits, Taylor nodded.

Some four miles north of Pleasant Hill, Taylor led his little band of recants into a clearing where Tom Green and several of his regiments were locked in a heated battle with part of Albert Lee's cavalry. Most of the Yankees had abandoned their horses to fight on foot, due to the roughness of the terrain. By contrast, Green's horsemen dashed in and out of the woods, striking the enemy where he was most vulnerable. "Putting in my little re-enforcements, I joined [Green] and enjoyed his method of handling his wild horsemen," Taylor wrote.

As more Union regiments struggled up the road and entered the fight, Green found himself outnumbered and ordered a withdrawal. He fell back some five miles to Caroll's Mill where he paused to set an ambush that sent several pursuing blue coats tumbling from their saddles. By the time Lee rushed reinforcements forward, Green and his men had disappeared.

Riding back toward Mansfield, Green turned to Colonel Augustus Buchel, who had just seen his first combat in Louisiana: "We haven't had much show yet, Colonel, but we will give them hell tomorrow," Green promised. His statement would prove prophetic.

★ ★ ★

That night, Taylor attended a ball arranged by the ladies of Mansfield for his officers. During the evening, several women appealed to him not to let the Yankees destroy their town. "To do that, ladies," he assured them, "Banks would first have to pass over my body." The ladies seemed greatly impressed by such gallantry. Taylor left the party early, returning to his quarters about nine o'clock. He sat at his desk and wrote the following carefully crafted message to Kirby Smith: "I respectfully ask to know if it accords with the views of the lieutenant-general commanding, that I should hazard a general engagement at this point, and request an immediate answer, that I may receive it before daylight tomorrow morning."

Taylor waited another hour before sending for a courier, ensuring that Smith would not receive the letter until well after the deadline for a reply. With the message, he had taken matters into his own hands and provided himself a defense in the event of a court-martial. He sent another courier to Keatchie with written orders for General Churchill to proceed to Mansfield at first light with his entire force. Anticipating a busy day ahead, Taylor instructed Tom Strother to awaken him before daylight and retired for the night.

Others wrote letters that night as a rumors of an impending battle spread through the ranks. One was Captain Elijah P. Petty of Walker's division who penned a missive to his wife in Texas: "If I am to die for my country, I hope it will be in a blaze of glory that will shine upon my wife and children."

* * *

As Albert Lee attempted to set up camp for the night at Carroll Crossing, he received a message from Franklin ordering him to move farther up the road to allow room for his troops. Leery of yet another ambush, Lee proceeded cautiously for four more miles and finally camped just six miles from Sabine Crossroads.

Near nightfall, he was visited by Colonel John S. Clark, an officer on Banks's staff who came to inquire about the action at Wilson's Farm. Clark reported finding Lee "much depressed and apprehensive" that his inexperienced cavalry might be mauled by the rebels before Franklin could bring up reinforcements. Clark returned to Pleasant Hill and suggested to Franklin that it might be wise to at least send a brigade of infantry forward to support Lee. By now, Franklin had become irritated by Lee's repeated requests and flatly refused. Clark left Franklin's tent and went to see Banks. Although Banks expressed doubt that the rebels would oppose Lee in force, he ordered Franklin to send two brigades forward the next morning. Instead of two brigades, Franklin sent only one—the 1st Brigade of the Fourth Division under Colonel Frank Emerson. With only about twelve hundred men, it was the smallest brigade in Franklin's army.

* * *

MANSFIELD, APRIL 8—Lieutenant Colonel William Walker began rousting the men of the 28th Regiment from their tents at six o'clock Friday morning, instructing the captains to prepare for a march. For four days, they had been living a life of relative ease in the scenic hills north of Mansfield, enjoying the hospitality of local residents and savoring the contents of smokehouses, potato bins, and pantries still untouched by war. The ladies of Mansfield had brought food to the camp and patched tattered jackets, and girls from the female academy gave a musical recital that drew a great deal of praise.

As the ranks began to take shape in the half light, there was the usual grumbling questioning the sanity of superiors until the men saw mounted officers begin to gather near the Mansfield Road. There had been talk for days that this was where they would fight the Yankees. General Kirby Smith and Dick Taylor had visited the camp on Thursday, and the sergeants had passed among the troops inventorying ammunition on Friday. Saturday was spent drilling and forming battle lines. Now the men were about to find out if they were in for a fight or another long march. If the officers beside the road went south it was fight—to the north meant more marching toward Shreveport.

Gray's brigade moved out first with William Walker and his 28th in the lead. Colonel Leopold Armant's 18th and James Beard's Consolidated Crescent followed. The three regiments made up Gray's brigade—a brigade in name only because there were only about eleven hundred men in the ranks. Falling in behind them was Polignac's brigade, made up of five undersize regiments of dismount Texas cavalry numbering about twelve hundred men. Together, these units made up General Alfred Mouton's thin but grandly named 2nd Division of the Trans Mississippi Department. In reality its strength was no more than that of a small brigade. Behind Polignac came General John G. Walker with his thirty-eight-hundred-man Texas Division, composed of dismount cavalry and infantry.

As the soldiers approached the road, any doubt about their destination was settled. The officers turned south—toward Mansfield and the enemy.

Wagon traffic, heading north out of harm's way, was heavy along the narrow road, delaying the arrival of the division in Mansfield until mid-morning. Any remaining doubt that they were in for a major battle was dispelled upon entering the town. Ambulances stood waiting in rows. Women carried bundles of sheets that would be stripped into bandages. The medical staff scurried about, trailed by women and old men carrying cots and blankets, preparing the churches and larger downtown buildings to receive wounded.

Three miles beyond Mansfield, the soldiers spotted several mounted officers clustered near the intersection at Sabine Crossroads. Taylor in his dark greatcoat stood out, as did Henry Gray, mounted on the massive Caesar. The boys of the 28th were directed off the road, and Colonel Walker led them behind a rail fence that ran along the edge of a forest of towering pine trees. Beyond the fence, a field stretched to a distant tree line on their left and to a swamp on the right. In front, the open field sloped upward beyond a gully to a tree line a half mile away. Somewhere on the other side of those trees, they knew a Yankee army was marching toward them.

Shortly before noon, the distant sound of gunfire came from beyond the tree line, indicating that Tom Green's cavalry had engaged the advance units of the enemy. Soon the Texas horsemen were seen dashing back and forth across the crest of the hill. The sporadic fighting had been going on for some time when a force of about fifty riders broke out of the tree line and came down the hill at a gallop. At first the men behind the fence thought it was Confederate cavalry. But when the horsemen came to within a hundred yards, they realized they were Federals. The 18th Regiment opened fire, sending several riders and horses crashing to the ground. The others wheeled their mounts around and raced back across the field in a hail of rifle balls.

The smoke from the volley had not cleared when General Mouton appeared on his horse, dashing down the line in front of the brigade waving his hat. Stopping before his old regiment, he shouted: "Louisiana has drawn first blood today! The victory is ours!" From the line rose a cheer that sent chills along the spines of the men.

Also near the action was General Taylor—so close in fact that a Yankee bullet had struck his horse, causing a superficial wound. He rode down the line congratulating the Louisianans. "We fight for Louisiana today," he shouted and the men responded with yet another cheer.

* * *

Albert Lee's horse soldiers were kept busy that morning as they moved north on the Mansfield-Pleasant Hill road. The rebel cavalry struck them repeatedly, firing quick volleys and then disappearing before reinforcements could be brought forward. Unable to ride through the woods with the skill of the Texans, most of Lee's men dismounted and spread out, threading their way through the forest underbrush in an attempt to flush out the rebels before they could strike. They then had to go back to retrieve their horses, wasting valuable time. One mounted company raced off in pursuit of an elusive group of rebel horsemen, later returning to report that while crossing a field they were fired on by a large concentration of Confederate infantry.

The news concerned the cautious Lee, but there was little he could do except press on. He was somewhat encouraged when Colonel Landrum joined him at mid-morning, but disappointed that he did not bring another infantry brigade to the front. Landrum had merely come forward to assess the situation for Franklin.

About noon, Lee's troops came upon an abandoned enemy camp where corn cakes and bacon were spread out on logs and stumps, indicating a hasty departure. A few hundred yards more and Lee and Landrum emerged into a clearing. Before them was a line of Confederate cavalry on a hill. As Lee watched, the enemy horsemen retreated, almost casually, toward a distant tree line. Lee suggested to Colonel Landrum that he secure the crest of a hill to their right with his brigade. Upon reaching the top of the hill, Lee found his worst fears realized. Spread out before him in a scenic valley was a Confederate battle line—infantry and cavalry formed in an inverted V, stretching for more than a mile end to end. Plainly visible were artillery batteries, covering the road. The rebels were drawn up for a battle, and for every man he could see, Lee feared there might be two waiting in the woods. He immediately dispatched a courier to the rear with an urgent message to send reinforcements.

* * *

Remarkably, in a matter of days, Dick Taylor had managed to piece together a formidable army to oppose Banks. It included approximately three thousand infantry, twenty-eight hundred dismount cavalry converted to infantry, and three thousand cavalry—all drawn up in a battle line and supported by forty field pieces. Unlike many of Banks's troops, most of these were hard men, veterans toughened by two years of fighting, forced marches, and living with the elements. In reserve, Taylor had several companies of quickly assembled militias—some two hundred or three hundred untrained old men and boys who would be of little use in a pitched battle. His hidden ace was the forty-four-hundred-man division under Churchill he had usurped without Kirby Smith's knowledge. It would be nightfall before Churchill's troops completed the march from Keatchie, too late to participate in the day's battle, but just in time to provide a substantial reserve if things went badly.

Opposing him was a poorly organized army of thirty thousand men and ninety field pieces strung out over twenty miles. Although Taylor had no way of knowing it, A. J. Smith's eight thousand veterans were just reaching Pleasant Hill—still a full day's march from Mansfield.

Anchoring the center of the Confederate line on the east side of the road was Mouton's division. To Mouton's left, protecting the Confederate flank, was Tom Green's beefed-up cavalry division with brigades under the command of Major, Bagby, and Lane. Also placed under Green's command were the 2nd and 7th Louisiana cavalry regiments and three regiments from General Bee's division. To Mouton's right was General Walker's Texas Division with brigades under Randal, Waul and Scurry. General Hamilton P. Bee, with two regiments of Texas cavalry, held the extreme right, his flank protected by a swamp. Nettles's Valverde Battery and McManas's Texas Battery covered the field east of the road.

As the rebels watched the Yankee infantry deploy at the top of the hill, Union cannons opened up. The rebel batteries responded, and an artillery duel was soon underway. As the Yankee gunners gauged distance, shells crashed and exploded in the limbs of the pine trees high above the men. Giant limbs fell to the ground, causing the soldiers to scramble out of the way. Finding their position uncomfortable, several Cajuns from the 18th Regiment crawled on hands and knees into the field to lie prone behind a slight rise. From there they began sniping at Union officers. The enemy responded, setting off a brisk firefight. A tendency by the Yankee riflemen to overshoot their targets resulted in the men behind the rail fence receiving a heavier fire than did the skirmishers in the field for whom it was intended. The men of the 28th Regiment crouched behind the fence as bullets struck the rails and clipped twigs around.

Banks was at Ten Mile Bayou conferring with Franklin when a courier arrived with Lee's urgent request for reinforcements. With Banks's approval, Franklin instructed General Ransom to accompany a second brigade to the front to relieve Emerson and evaluate the situation. Banks decided he also would go to the front to see what was happening. "If there is no heavy fighting, I will return," he told Franklin. "There will be no heavy fighting," Franklin assured him.

Passing Ransom's troops on the way, Banks arrived at Sabine Crossroads about 1:30 P.M. and found a long-range artillery duel and a spirited firefight in progress—but no general battle. He asked Lee for his assessment of the situation. "I told him that we must either fall back immediately or we must be very heavily reinforced." Banks ordered him to retain the position and he would have reinforcements sent forward. He then dispatched the following note to Franklin:

The commanding general desires me to say that the enemy are apparently prepared to make a strong stand at this point, and that you had better make arrangements to bring up your infantry and to pass everything on the road. The general will send again when to move. He thinks you had better send back and push up the trains [of artillery], as manifestly we shall be able to rest here.

The note illustrated Banks's inability to grasp the situation. He saw the field at Sabine Crossroads as a place for his troops to rest for the night after dispersing the Confederates. But lest it be eternal, Banks's men would find no rest at Mr. Moss's wheat field.

★ ★ ★

As the afternoon wore on, the field officers of Gray's brigade circulated among the troops, inflaming the emotions of the Louisianans by circulating a rumor that the high command in Shreveport planned to abandon the state without a fight.

"Shall we abandon Louisiana?"

"No!" came the thundering reply.

"Will we fight for Louisiana?"

"Yes!" they shouted.

Caught up in the excitement of their own creation, the brigade's officers held a meeting and decided to go into battle mounted on their horses as an inspiration to the men. It was a decision that would cost many of them their lives.

As the field officers sat talking behind the battle line in the woods, a stray minié ball struck the ground within inches of Colonel Armant's arm, throwing dirt onto his new uniform. The commander of the 18th Regiment, known for his dapper sense of fashion, calmly stood and brushed the dirt away.

"I may be killed today," he said. "But I'll be damned if I let them soil my jacket."

★ ★ ★

By mid-afternoon, Albert Lee was breathing easier. He had managed to bring superior artillery to the front and held the advantage of high ground. He had secured his left flank with Dudley's Cavalry Regiment, and Landrum was rapidly deploying fresh troops behind a rail fence on the right. By three o'clock, he had more than five thousand men and four artillery batteries in place when he was visited by one of General Banks's staff officers.

"The general wants you to move forward immediately and take Mansfield," the officer told him. Dumbfounded, Lee assumed there must be a mistake. The officer assured him the orders came directly from Banks. Lee rode back to personally talk to the commander. "The orders are correct," Banks told him. "I want to move against the enemy and drive him beyond Mansfield."

Lee protested, pointing out that the visible strength of the Confederates was superior to his own force and there was no way of knowing how many troops might be waiting in reserve beyond the forest wall. "I told him," Lee later wrote, "that we could not advance ten minutes without a general engagement in which we should be most gloriously flogged. I told him I did not want to do it." According to Lee, Banks seemed confused by his assessment, but he called off the attack and sent a staff officer to the rear to bring up more troops.

* * *

Taylor had ridden up and down his lines, conferring with his officers and offering encouragement to the men. His forces were perfectly positioned to repel an attack. The center was manned by veteran riflemen who would stand firm. His artillery batteries covered the field. A swamp protected his right side and he outflanked the enemy on the left. With admirable restraint, considering Taylor's small measure of that virtue, he waited for Banks to make the first move. He knew well Banks's own reputation for impatience and anticipated an attack at any moment.

For almost two hours Taylor waited, watching nervously as the Yankees deployed more men. By four o'clock, the last of that small measure of patience was drained. The sun was nearing the tree line across the road where General Bee's horsemen waited in the shade. No more than three hours of sunlight remained. Even now, he knew a messenger might be riding from Shreveport with an order for him to withdraw. The enemy forces were rapidly deploying and he estimated that the opposing force at the crest of the hill soon would equal his own.

Although Taylor did not know the numbers, the Federals had brought seventy-nine hundred men to the front. He did know that if he waited longer, Banks would have a superior force in place. His gambling instinct overcame caution—the same instinct that inspired him to dash across a burning bridge at Front Royal and to hold his own against the best whist players at the Boston Club.

Beside the road at the edge of the forest, a cluster of officers had gathered, waiting for him. Mouton, Gray, and Polignac were there with Randal and Walker. Taylor rode over to join them. He raised his field glasses and surveyed the enemy position.

"What shall we do, sir?" Polignac asked him.

"Little Frenchman," Taylor calmly replied, "I am going to fight Banks here if he has a million men."

He watched as several more skirmishers from the 18th Regiment emerged from the forest and made their way into the open field. By now Colonel Armant had sent most of his regiment forward to reinforce the skirmish line, and the firefight was growing in intensity.

"It appears your Louisianans are anxious for a fight, Mr. Mouton," Taylor observed.

The Cajun rose in his stirrups and drew his sword. "They are, sir!"

"Then they may advance and engage the enemy," he said.

Having set the attack in motion, Taylor rode to a slight elevation beneath a large tree, a lone figure in a black greatcoat. He hooked his right leg over the saddle horn, calmly lit a cigar, and waited for the battle to unfold.

Down the line, the call went out: "Colors to the front! Companies forward!" Mouton, with sword held aloft, reined his horse before Gray's brigade. "Throw down that fence, boys!" he shouted. "Charge across that field and drive the enemy into the woods"

There was a roar as the men came forward and the wooden rails were tossed aside. Taylor had envisioned a steady advance by the entire left wing of his V. Once the enemy was fully occupied on that side of the field, he intended to strike hard, en echelon, with Walker and Dudley on the right and overrun the Federal artillery batteries beside the road. What happened next surprised him as well as the enemy.

To the men of the rag-tag 28th, an order to advance was interpreted as an order to charge. They began running across the field. There was a method to the seeming madness of their racing toward self-destruction. Although most now carried muskets, they were weaned on shotgun warfare and conditioned by experience to quickly close with the enemy in order to shoot him.

The rapid advance of the 28th startled its own officers, who had to wheel their horses around and catch up with the men. In an effort to keep pace, the 18th broke into a run, then the ranks of the Consolidated Crescent. Not to be left behind, Polignac urged his Texas brigade to pick up the pace. Mouton, too, spurred his mount to a gallop, criss-crossing the field, and urging all onward. It was a wild charge—ragged and undisciplined, and certainly not worthy of a chapter in a West Point textbook.

Four Union artillery batteries and the rifles of five infantry regiments opened up on the irregular rebel line. The barrage churned the earth, filling the air with dirt and shrapnel. Rifle balls whined through the ranks of the sprinting men. Lieutenant Colonel Franklin Clack of the Crescent Regiment was no more than a hundred yards into the field when an explosion sent him and his horse crashing to the ground. Horribly wounded, he bled to death where he fell.

Lieutenant Colonel William Walker was riding at the head of the 28th Regiment when a minié ball struck him in the stomach. Sliding from the saddle, he fell hard upon the ground. The former sheriff of Winn Parish knew immediately that he had sustained a mortal wound. Although in agony, he propped himself painfully on an elbow so that he could see the battle.

Considering the intensity of the fire, the men of the 28th sustained remarkably few casualties in their dash to the safety of the ravine. Those of the 18th and Consolidated Crescent were not so fortunate. Enemy fire was even more intense on that side of the field. Men began to go down in clusters as Yankee artillery took a deadly toll.

To reach the enemy, the rebels had to cross an open field for more than a quarter of a mile before going down an incline into the ravine. Coming out of the ravine, they had to charge up an exposed slope for some three hundred yards to get to the Yankees behind the rail fence. Emerging from the smoke and flying debris of the battlefield, the men of the 28th raced down the incline into the protection of the gully. There they paused, gasping for breath. Behind them, the 18th and Crescent received the full concentration of enemy firepower. Great gaps appeared in the ranks of the 18th. Officers tumbled from their saddles as they came within effective range of Union rifles. A soldier in the 48th Ohio later wrote: "Their field officers, being mounted, were picked off as fast as they came in range." As bullets whined around him, Colonel Armant urged his men steadily forward, wincing each time he heard the dull thump of a rifle ball striking one of his men. His horse jumping nervously beneath him, he virtually herded them into the ravine before, he feared, they would all be killed.

By now the cannons of the Chicago Mercantile battery, well behind the Federal lines, had joined the thunderous chorus of Yankee artillery and found the range of the Consolidated Crescent Regiment. Joining the guns of the 5th U.S. and 6th Missouri, the Mercantile gunners sent a hellish barrage raining down on the Crescent, bringing it to a halt in the open field. James Beard realized he must get his men moving once more or his entire command would be wiped out. He spurred his horse through the holocaust, grabbed the regimental flag from the color bearer, and urged the men to follow him. Almost instantly, a bullet struck him, knocking him from the saddle. Riding at the heels of his brother's mount, a horrified Ned Beard dismounted, ran to his brother's side and dragged him several yards to the protection of a small log.

Seeing his commander fall, Major Mercer Canfield took up the banner and carried it forward until he, too, was killed. Private Louis Hall saw both Beard and Canfield go down. In his memoirs he wrote: "I had not gone far before Maj. Canfield fell and I immediately after tumbled, shot through the knee, which shook me up considerable." Hall went on to describe how he spotted a log and crawled toward it seeking protection. There he found Ned Beard clutching the limp body of his brother, shaking him and begging him to speak. "But the colonel was dead," Hall wrote.

Colonel Gray, riding Caesar, had made it to the ravine when he realized the Crescent Regiment remained pinned down in the open field. He sent his brigade inspector, Lieutenant Arthur Martin, to rally the men. Martin had barely picked up the Crescent banner before falling, mortally wounded. Next to grasp the flag was Captain Seth Field of Company A, who was literally fighting at his doorstep that afternoon as Mansfield was his hometown. Only that morning, he had broken ranks to hold his baby and kiss his wife. "There ain't no Yankee bullets made for me," he assured her before mounting his horse and catching up with his company. Lifting the flag on the battlefield, the young captain was struck repeatedly and managed to advance only a few feet before sinking to the ground, his body riddled with bullets.

No less than seven men carried the regiment's colors across the field that day. Each was either killed or seriously wounded. Finally, Captain William Claiborne Jr., grandson of the first governor of Louisiana, rallied the men and got them moving forward. Eyes wide with shock, gulping for breath, those of the Crescent fortunate enough to have survived finally staggered into the ravine. While others crouched, out of the line of fire, Captain Claiborne stood there, calmly surveying the enemy position as bullets whizzed around him. His men urged him to take cover, some risking their lives to tug at his coattails. "Leave me be, boys," he shouted above the din. "If I am going to die, I prefer to do it standing up." All three field officers and nine captains in the regiment were killed or seriously wounded that afternoon. Claiborne did not receive a scratch.

While Claiborne stood defiantly against the whistling rifle balls, an officer noticed Sergeant Benjamin Wall of Clinton, Louisiana, sitting against the bank, calmly reading a book. "What are you doing, sergeant?" the officer asked. "Sir, I am reading my Bible," he replied. "I expect to be killed in a few moments."

With the 18th and Crescent regiments still under heavy fire, Colonel Gray realized they must have relief or be destroyed. He rode into the midst of the 28th regiment. In his official report, he wrote: "I immediately gave the order to the Twenty-eighth Regiment to charge over the fence upon the enemy's line. This was done instantly, in good order. . . . The Crescent Regiment and the Eighteenth, thus relieved, moved forward to take their places in line." However, Colonel Gray's abbreviated description hardly reveals the full story.

Having caught their breath, the men of the 28th responded to Gray's order with a loud rebel yell that could be heard well down the line and by the enemy. They charged out of the ravine and up the slope, screaming wildly, bayonets leveled. They were no more than two hundred feet from the rail fence when it seemed to explode in a sheet of flame. Volleys from the 19th Kentucky and 48th Ohio regiments staggered the line and brought it to a halt. At the urging of General Mouton, the 18th and what remained of the riddled Crescent also charged from the ravine. They were met by a devastating fire from the rifles of the 130th Illinois and 48th Ohio. In his journal, Poche compared the effects of that volley to the violent storm the men had endured at Pineville: "The balls and grape shot crashing about us whistled terribly and plowed the ground and beat our soldiers down even as a storm tears down the trees of a forest."

In a matter of seconds, more than 200 men were cut down—an estimated 55 killed and 150 wounded by those volleys alone. One of the wounded was Poche. Seeing the popular captain go down, two members of the 28th Regiment tried to pull him back to the safety of the ravine. "Just leave me, boys!" he told them. "Go back to your company." Poche survived his wounds. The two soldiers who tried to save him were killed. Also killed in the charge was Sergeant Benjamin Wall who had prepared himself for that eventuality by reading his Scriptures.

As Colonel Armant led his regiment out of the ravine, his horse was shot from beneath him. Although injured, he continued to lead his men toward the fence. He was within one hundred feet of the Federal line when struck by a rifle ball. Still he moved forward, urging his men onward.

Seeing the 28th stalled and vulnerable, Major W. F. Blackman rode his horse to the front and snatched the regimental banner. "Follow the colors, boys!" he shouted as he guided his horse through the ranks toward the enemy. Bullets whistled about him, ripping his jacket and twice wounding his horse. A Union soldier later estimated that more than two hundred shots were fired at Blackman, at almost point-blank range. Miraculously, he was not hit. The men responded by charging the rail fence, by now almost completely concealed by smoke. Most of those in the 28th had crossed the field without firing their weapons. Now they unleashed a volley virtually in the faces of the Federals. The buck and ball and buckshot charges ripped into the 19th Kentucky and 48th Ohio. The startled Federals staggered back, scores of dead and wounded falling at the fence. Some dropped their weapons and fled, causing others to panic. The men of the 28th tore down the fence and poured through in pursuit.

As the soldiers of the 18th and Crescent charged from the ravine, they received one final volley of rifle fire from the 130th Illinois. At the front of his ranks, Colonel Armant went down mortally wounded—his new jacket perforated by rifle balls.

By now, General Polignac had arrived at the fence with his Texas regiments. The

Illinois troops, overwhelmed by numbers and seeing their comrades in the 48th Ohio and 19th Kentucky in disorderly retreat, fell back toward the woods only to find scattered elements of the 28th regiment already there, taking prisoners. All three regiments of Gray's brigade had become disorganized. However, Polignac's brigade advanced in line, driving the enemy before it. Colonel Gray described the action in his report:

> This part of the brigade [the 28th] advanced to the lane occupied by the enemy battery [Chicago Mercantile], fired on and killed many of the horses. At this time the brigade, somewhat broken in consequence through the wood and securing of prisoners, was . . . protected by the advance of the brigade under Brigadier General C. J. Polignac, which opportunely brought up, and fighting courageously, contributed materially to the success of our troops.

With three regiments routed, the Union defense came apart. By now Taylor's forces were engaged from one end of the field to the other. When Taylor saw Gray's brigade charge out of the ravine, he ordered General Walker's division and Bee's two regiments of cavalry forward. While Walker's Texans braved an artillery barrage and advanced along both sides of the Pleasant Hill road, Bee's wildly yelling horsemen hit the Union's left flank, driving back Colonel Dudley's 2nd Illinois Cavalry. On the other end of the Confederate line, Green's twenty-five hundred Texas cavalrymen thundered across the open field and caved in the Union's right flank. Walker's Texas regiments bore down on the 67th Indiana and 23rd Wisconsin infantry regiments, overrunning them before they had a chance to retreat. "They came like a cyclone . . . yelling like infuriated demons," a Union soldier wrote. Union General Thomas Ransom ordered General Charles Stone to pull his Ohio regiments out of the line and reinforce the left flank. When Stone got to that side of the field, he sent a message back to Ransom. "There is no left flank."

The 6th Texas Battalion along with the 12th, 13th, and 14th Texas regiments captured the guns of Ormand Nims's Massachusetts Battery and turned them on the fleeing Yankees. Seeing the horses of the Chicago Mercantile being shot by the rebels, the officers of the 1st Indiana battery quickly hitched horses to caissons and tried to save their field pieces. But as they fled, they found the road blocked by the cavalry's supply wagons. Some of the teamsters, witnessing their troops in retreat, had cut the traces and ridden the mules to safety, leaving wagons sitting in the road. The artillerymen had little choice but to abandon their field pieces, still hitched to the horses.

As the rebel cavalry collapsed the Federal flanks, hundreds of troops were trapped with Confederates at front and rear. While some attempted to flee, others surrendered. Near the woods General Mouton saw some thirty Union troops being fired on, though it appeared they were trying to surrender. He ordered his men to cease firing and secure the prisoners. The sight of a rebel general sitting on a horse in their midst proved too tempting an opportunity for some of the Federal soldiers. Several of them grabbed up their weapons and fired. The dashing Cajun warrior tumbled from his saddle, killed instantly. His men were so enraged they shot the offenders as well as several innocent prisoners before officers managed to stop the slaughter.

★ ★ ★

As hordes of Union troops fell back in panic and confusion, General Franklin arrived with General Cameron at the head of thirteen hundred troops from the 3rd Division of the 13th Corps. Cameron quickly deployed his men in a second defense line stretching across the road. Cavalrymen from Dudley's regiments and the 3rd Missouri organized to strengthen his left flank, swelling the numbers in the reserve line to about two thousand. As they fought a desperate battle for survival, Lieutenant Colonel Lorenzo Thomas of the Missouri artillery battery imparted some words of dubious encouragement to his frantic soldiers. "Try to think that you are already dead and buried," he shouted. "That way you won't have any fear of dying."

Although Cameron's line withstood the first assault by the rebels, Franklin quickly recognized that he was outflanked on both sides and could not hold the position. He sent word back to General Emory to bring up the 1st Division from the 19th Corps and form a third battle line. The messenger had barely departed when the 28th Louisiana and elements of the 18th and Crescent charged Cameron's right flank, driving it back.

The unlikely hero of the charge was a small-town store clerk from Vernon. Lieutenant Edward Kidd of Company C of the 28th Regiment, seeing confusion in the ranks, looked around for a superior officer to give him orders. Informed that he was the only officer left, Kidd rallied elements of the 18th and 28th and led a desperate charge into the Federal line. In bloody hand-to-hand fighting, the rebels collapsed Cameron's flank, setting off yet another rout. John Russell, a Northern newspaper man who had the misfortune to wander into the battle at that moment, described what happened: "Suddenly there was a rush, a shout, the crashing of trees . . . and scamper of men. I turned to my companion to inquire the reason for this extraordinary proceeding, but before he had the chance to reply, we found ourselves swallowed up, as it were, in a hissing, seething, bubbling whirlpool of agitated men."

Colonel Landrum, a veteran of many vicious battles, described the fighting in this sector as, "the most desperate I ever saw." General Franklin's horse was shot from beneath him and the general received a wounded in the thigh, a musket ball shattering the bone. Watching the rout unfold, General Banks rode forward, shouting: "Form a line here, men! I know you will not desert me!" But the troops ran past him, leaving guns and knapsacks scattered in the road. Members of Banks's staff had to hustle the general to the rear as he barely avoided being overrun by the onrushing rebels.

★ ★ ★

As Dick Taylor rode across the battlefield, watching his troops rout the last of the Federal regiments, a messenger on a horse lathered with sweat caught up to him. Unfolding the dispatch, Taylor could not suppress a wry smile. The message was from General E. Kirby Smith, ordering him to avoid a general engagement with Banks's army. "Too late, sir," Taylor said, more to himself than to the courier. "The battle is won."

★ ★ ★

Well to the rear, General Emory was bringing the 1st Division up the Mansfield road at double quick when he was met by men running toward him. There were only a few at first but soon desperate men clogged the road. Private Harris Beecher with the 114th New York described the scene:

> Still thicker and denser came the frightened crowd . . . men without hats or coats, rushing past in every possible manner. Men without guns or accouterments, cavalry-men without horses and artillerymen without cannon, wounded men bleeding and crying at every step, men begrimed with smoke and powder—all in a state of fear and frenzy, while they shouted to our boys not to go forward for they would all be slaugh-tered. . . . The road was almost blocked up with wagons, caissons, mules and run-away horses, while negro [sic] teamsters and cavalrymen were driving directly through our ranks.

Unable to move forward, Emory deployed his men some three miles from the battle-field, along the banks of a small creek at a place called Chatman's Hill. On the heels of the fleeing soldiers of Cameron's division came the rebels. Euphoric in victory and disor-ganized in their pursuit, they were surprised when Emory's riflemen opened up on them. They scrambled for cover, and an intense firefight soon filled the little valley with smoke and the whine of bullets ripping through underbrush. As dusk settled on the woods Confederate reinforcements from Walker's division arrived, accompanied by Dick Tay-lor. Since the creek provided the only source of water for miles, he considered it vital to secure it. Several charges by the rebels were repulsed before they finally succeeded in driving Emory's troops away from the stream. When it became too dark to see, the crack of rifle fire slowly faded and ceased.

Waiting in the woods in the darkness, the Yankees heard the sounds of a celebration at the creek. In the distance, bugle calls sounded, calling cavalry units together. Captured supply wagons rumbled along the road toward Mansfield. And the wounded cried out for water, unavailable because the rebels held the creek.

Unsure of Confederate numbers and concerned that he would be overrun at day-light, Emory suggested to Banks that he withdraw to Pleasant Hill and join A. J. Smith's troops. At about ten o'clock, Banks reluctantly gave the order to retreat. Under the cover of night, the men stumbled through the forest, made their way out to the road, and walked the sixteen miles back to Pleasant Hill.

The Battle of Mansfield was over.

Dick Taylor's assessment of the day's fighting, reflected in his official report, illus-trated the totality of the victory: "Twenty-five hundred prisoners, twenty pieces of ar-tillery, several stands of colors, many thousands of small arms and 250 wagons were the fruits of victory. . . . Eight thousand of the enemy, his horse and two divisions of in-fantry had been utterly routed and over 5,000 of the 19th corps driven back at sunset."

Banks, who never lost a battle in a report, listed Federal losses at 2,235 out of 7,000 engaged, with 113 killed, 581 wounded, and 1,541 captured. However, those figures were for the action at Sabine Crossroads. Not reflected in the totals were casualties from Cameron's 1st Brigade or Emory's troops at Chatman's Bayou or those who did not survive their wounds. In reality, more than 13,000 Union troops were engaged in the day's fighting—including 7,900 under Lee and Landrum at Sabine Crossroads, 1,300 under Cameron, and 4,000 under Emory at Chatman's Bayou—and total casualties for the day probably exceeded 3,000, rather than the 2,200 reported by Banks.

Confederate success came at a high price. Of the estimated 1,000 casualties suffered by the rebel army that afternoon, more than 800 were sustained among the 2,300 men of Mouton's division. Gray's brigade suffered an estimated 410 casualties among its 1,100 men. More than twenty officers in the brigade were killed or mortally wounded—seventeen in the 18th and Consolidated Crescent regiments alone. All three regimental commanders in the brigade died on the field, never reaching the rail fence. All three field officers in the Crescent were killed. Two volunteer aides on Gray's staff were killed. Colonel William Walker was found still alive on the field that afternoon and taken to Mansfield. He died the following morning.

Dick Taylor, the gambler, had won the greatest wager of his life. Defying his commander and all odds, with boldness, luck, and a superior force at the point of attack, he had stopped Banks and thwarted Lincoln's plans for conquest of the Confederacy west of the Mississippi. It was as if the ghosts of Stonewall Jackson and Zack Taylor looked over his shoulder.

★ ★ ★ ★

17

★ ★ ★ ★

The Great Skedaddle

PLEASANT HILL, APRIL 9—With Chatman's Creek securely in Confederate hands, Taylor rode back to Mansfield to hurry General Churchill's divisions forward. He arrived there about midnight and found the Arkansas troops resting just outside town. Taylor had Churchill roust the men and get them moving once more. Having covered twenty-two miles that day, the men answered the order to move out with moans from the ranks.

Taylor arrived back at Chatman's Creek about three o'clock that morning to confer with Tom Green. Although unsure of Banks's numbers, they had a good grasp of his deployment. Their main objective was to prevent Banks's main army from linking up with Porter's gunboats some twenty miles to the east. Taylor knew a detachment of two thousand troops from A. J. Smith's division remained with the gunboats. He also knew that Porter could not proceed beyond Springfield Landing and the mouth of Loggy Bayou because the Confederate steamer *New Falls City* was scuttled there, blocking the river. With bow and stern buried into opposite banks, currents flowing over the sunken hull had created a massive sandbar. Even if the steamer was removed, it would require days to dredge a channel through the sand sufficient for Porter's gunboats to proceed to Shreveport. Taylor's intelligence also told him the gunboats were having a great deal of difficulty negotiating the river because of low water levels. He figured if he could defeat Banks's main army before it reached the river, he might then trap Porter's gunboats in the shallow waters above Grand Ecore. To prevent a linkup, Taylor had Green send a detachment of cavalry to Pierre Point to block a narrow road that connected Pleasant Hill and Blair's Landing on the Red River.

Just before dawn, the Confederates moved out in pursuit of Banks with Green's cavalry leading the way and Dick Taylor riding at his side. Behind them came Churchill's troops, Walker's Texans, and Mouton's division, now commanded by Polignac—12,500 men in all, by far the largest army Taylor had ever commanded. They found the road to Pleasant Hill littered with discarded rifles, knapsacks, cooking utensils, harnesses, and burned-out supply wagons. They came upon wounded soldiers sitting in the shade of the forest awaiting capture, and the dead curled up beside the road.

As they neared Pleasant Hill, smoke rose from blackened farmhouses and barns along the route. Women and children, eyes wide with shock and red from crying, stood beside the road telling Taylor how the Yankee soldiers had shot their farm animals and dumped them down the water wells. The destruction of water wells indicated to Taylor that Banks was in full retreat.

The Confederates came upon clusters of stragglers, walking slowly along the road. Others sat passively beside it. One such group, Zouaves from New York, wore the customary brightly colored pantaloons and fancy jackets. Their appearance provided a source of entertainment for the Texans, who had never seen such uniforms. The Zouave captives were greeted with whistles and catcalls. "The war must be about over if they're sendin' women in bloomers to fight us," a Texan taunted.

Just after nine o'clock, Green's scouts reported that the Yankees were forming battle lines at Pleasant Hill. As they approached the town, Taylor expressed surprised that the enemy seemed to be deploying in force. He knew that Banks's supply wagons and a large number of troops, including most of Lee's cavalry, were on the road to Grand Ecore. Taylor had expected nothing more than a rear-guard action at Pleasant Hill. However, the Federal lines clearly extended across the road and through the center of the village. Banks obviously intended to make a stand here.

At one o'clock Churchill's troops began arriving at a staging area two miles from town. Having marched forty-five miles in thirty-six hours, the men were worn out. Since it appeared that Banks was not prepared to attack, Taylor gave his infantry a two-hour rest. The men were awakened just after three o'clock and formed into ranks. Taylor sent Churchill's divisions, guided by the local sheriff, along a network of back roads and trails circling far to the right of the Union position. He deployed Walker's division and Green's cavalry squarely facing the enemy, with Majors and Bagby's cavalry on the extreme left. Polignac's division, decimated by the previous day's fighting, was held in reserve. Facing the rebels were 13,500 Union troops that included some 7,000 under A. J. Smith. Taylor's plan was to outflank the Union left, overwhelm it with Churchill's divisions, and then strike Banks's center with Walker's Texans and Green's cavalry, in echelon from right to left. Major and Bagby were to sweep around the left side and seal off the road to Blair's Landing. That would leave only one other avenue of escape available to Banks—the road to Grand Ecore. To block it, Green dispatched three regiments of cavalry to support Churchill. In the event of a successful attack on that side, the horsemen were to circle behind the enemy, block the Grand Ecore Road, and prevent Banks from retreating. Having deployed his forces, Taylor retired to the shade of a tree to give Churchill's troops time to get into position.

At 4:30 P.M. he sent orders for a twelve-cannon battery to commence firing as a signal for Churchill to begin the attack. That was the last thing that went according to Taylor's plan at Pleasant Hill.

Hampered by dense underbrush and a series of gullies, Churchill's troops were not in position to attack when the signal came. As the artillery batteries dueled, Walker and Green's men waited impatiently to move out for thirty minutes before they heard gunfire on their right, signaling that the Arkansas divisions had engaged the enemy. On cue

Walker sent his ranks forward. However, on the left side General Bee launched a premature attack. His horsemen rode across an open field into withering fire from the 24th Missouri Regiment. Men and horses went down in heaps, forcing Bee to withdraw. Meanwhile, on the other end of the Confederate line, General Churchill made a blunder that proved even more disastrous.

Disoriented as they emerged from dense woods, the Arkansas regiments attacked at the wrong angle. Instead of hitting the Union's left flank, Churchill's troops missed it altogether and assaulted the interior of the Federal line. The mistake left Churchill's own flank fully exposed. A. J. Smith, with three fresh regiments on that side, attacked the startled Arkansans.

Meanwhile, Walker's division and Green's cavalry fared much better. With a combined force of more than five thousand men, they drove back the center of the Federal line. Taylor, seeing Bee's cavalry repulsed on his left, rushed Polignac's division forward to reinforce Bagby and Major in that sector. However, hidden from Taylor's view by woods, a disaster unfolded on his right.

Churchill's troops on that side of the battlefield had missed their objective so badly that the 58th Illinois Regiment ended up behind them. Realizing his advantage, A. J. Smith attacked with the 89th Indiana and 119th Illinois regiments, while the 58th circled behind the rebel line. Taylor's right flank disintegrated under the assault.

In command of rebel forces on that side of the field, General Mosby Parsons was unable to rally his troops. His command split apart, some of his men retreating back into the woods while others were driven into the ranks of Walker's division. More than 400 rebels were cut off and forced to surrender.

Still unaware of the full extent of the disaster on his right, Taylor had the impression that he was winning the battle. In bloody hand to hand fighting, Green's dismounted cavalry and Walker's division caved the Union center, routing three regiments and cutting off the 32nd Iowa Regiment. But just when it seemed the enemy defense would collapse, Churchill's troops were driven back into the lines of Walker's division, causing confusion in the Confederate ranks. With Green advancing on the left and Walker forced to fall back on the right, the lines of the combatants began swinging around like a giant pinwheel.

Seeing Churchill's troops routed, an excited Nathaniel Banks rode up to A. J. Smith. "God bless you, general!" he shouted. "You have saved the army!"

As darkness settled and smoke from the battle-scarred little town drifted into the pine trees, the fighting ceased with no clear winner. Taylor called off the fighting when, in the half-light, Colonel Major's brigade and Walker's troops began firing at each other. The battle had lasted less than three hours. Two thousand six hundred dead and wounded lay on the field, testament to the viciousness of the fighting.

The two sides had entered the battle at almost equal strength—12,200 Union troops and 12,500 Confederates. (Three of A. J. Smith's regiments were present but not engaged. Including those units, Banks's force totaled 13,513.) Federal casualties were listed at 1,369 killed and wounded and 495 taken prisoner. Confederate losses were estimated at more than 1,200 killed and wounded. The Union Army also took 426 prisoners, left behind when Churchill's ranks collapsed—a total loss of more than 1,600 men on the Confederate side. Among the dead was Captain Elijah P. Petty whose wish that he go out "in a blaze of glory" had been fulfilled.

To his credit, Churchill assumed responsibility for the failure to achieve victory. "[Had I] extended a half mile to the right a brilliant success would have been achieved," he wrote in his report. Taylor blamed himself. In his memoirs, he noted that instead of sending Churchill on such a difficult assignment, he should have taken Polignac's division and personally led the attack against the Federal left. Of Churchill, Taylor later wrote: "A worthy, gallant gentleman . . . but unfortunate in war." To a subordinate he remarked: "He is a good man in the wrong profession."

★ ★ ★

The night of April 9, 1864, was one of horror at the little resort town in the Louisiana pine country. Because the fighting had continued into darkness, the wounded remained on the battlefield. Their cries and moans filled the night, including heart-rending pleas for a simple drink of water. However, the wells of the town had been drawn dry by Smith's troops and Lee's retreating horsemen. The sounds of that night would haunt those who survived it for the rest of their days. Dying men called out for their mothers. Some of the wounded cried, others cursed, and still others prayed. The night turned pitch black and a cold front moved through, plunging the temperature to an unseasonable low. The troops on both sides were without blankets. They sat where they had stopped fighting, shivering until their teeth chattered, unable to light fires and finding it impossible to sleep.

Taylor knew his army was physically exhausted. Walker's and Polignac's divisions were especially worn out after two days of marching and fighting that often included brutal hand-to-hand combat. Churchill's troops, having suffered heavy casualties, were demoralized by the day's events. Green's cavalrymen, on the move for three days, had not stopped to feed their horses. There was no way to anticipate what Banks would do come daylight. He might bring up reinforcements or continue to retreat back to the river and the protection of Porter's gunboats. Under any circumstance, Taylor did not expect him to resume his march on Shreveport. Banks's army was ill-supplied, without water, and had sustained a loss of almost five thousand men in two days.

Taylor also recognized that his own army needed not only rest, but reorganization. He had been low on ammunition when the battle began that morning, and now he was critically so. He sent his infantry regiments five miles to the rear to a small stream where they could light fires and get access to water. Most of Green's cavalry went to Mansfield to find forage for the horses. After resupplying his division, Green was to proceed to the Red River and attack Porter's gunboats. Taylor remained at Pleasant Hill with Bee and Debray's regiments and a battery of artillery just in case the Yankees resumed the fight in the morning. Near midnight he was awakened by the arrival of visitors. General Kirby Smith and an entourage of staff officers had ridden down from Shreveport to confer with him on strategy.

* * *

Across the way another consultation was taking place. General Emory, by now bleary from a lack of sleep, and General Franklin, his leg in splints, met with Banks to decide on a course of action. Conspicuously absent was the volatile A. J. Smith. Banks favored an immediate withdrawal to Grand Ecore, and the others agreed. Emory especially had had enough. His food supplies were depleted, his regiments lacked sufficient ammunition, he had sustained heavy casualties, and the Pleasant Hill wells were dry. Banks told them to prepare the troops for withdrawal.

Upon being told the army was going to retreat to Grand Ecore, A. J. Smith became enraged. One of his soldiers reported hearing "an outburst of curses loud and deep." After his staff calmed him, he went to confront Banks. Smith wanted to resume the fight. He said that he had never left wounded men on the field and to do so now would demoralize his army. But Banks refused to rescind the order. Leaving Banks's tent, Smith went to see Franklin. He told him that Banks was unfit to command and urged Franklin to take over. "I will back you," Smith promised. Franklin refused, saying that, although he had no confidence in Banks, he would not take part in a mutiny.

A. J. Smith rode out of town that night with the pleas of his wounded men ringing in his ears. A group of surgeons from his medical corps volunteered to stay behind and care for their wounded the next morning, though they were aware that they might end up in a Confederate prison. As Smith rode at the head of his troops, he openly cursed Banks, derisively referring to him as "Napoleon P. Banks." The comment amused his Midwestern troops, some of whom began shouting the unflattering nickname. As they marched, they sang a paraphrased version of *When Johnny Comes Marching Home* that included the line: "In eighteen hundred and sixty-four / We all skedaddled to Grand Encore." Each time they ended the ditty, the troops shouted in unison: "Napoleon P. Banks!"

Passing an abandoned farmhouse, several men broke ranks to set it on fire. A cheer went up as the flames lit up the night sky. Not to be outdone, another group torched the outbuildings. As the men marched, they began burning any structure that came into sight. Those in the rear ranks, feeling deprived, spread out looking for structures well off the road. Sheds, fences, and even outhouses were torched. Soon the night was lighted by a string of fires stretching for miles.

* * *

Kirby Smith did not receive word of Taylor's victory at Mansfield until four o'clock on the morning of the ninth. He expressed doubt that the report was accurate, telling his staff that Taylor had exaggerated his success. The arrival of a subsequent report from Governor Henry Allen, who had witnessed the battle, convinced him that Banks was indeed routed and that Taylor was pursuing him to Pleasant Hill. Smith left Shreveport at daylight, riding sixty-five miles before finding Taylor camped at Pleasant Hill.

The two men met at General Bee's campfire and discussed the events of the past two days over cups of coffee. Smith seemed especially friendly, inspiring Taylor to offered a quasi-apology for not keeping his commander better informed as to his actions in the field. Taylor's assessment was that Banks would retreat to the river to his supply boats and the protection of Porter's gunboats. He said he intended to keep pressure on Banks to prevent him from resuming his march on Shreveport.

Smith expressed concern that Shreveport faced a more immediate threat from General Steele's army in Arkansas. Taylor tried to convince him that Steele would not march on Shreveport without the support of Banks. Once Steele learned that Banks was defeated and in retreat, Taylor predicted he would go back to Little Rock.

Smith suggested that they discuss their options in detail the next day. He said he was returning to Mansfield and asked Taylor to meet him there. Taylor agreed to leave for Mansfield as soon as he took care of the wounded and assessed the situation at Pleasant Hill in the morning.

⋆ ⋆ ⋆

LOGGY BAYOU, APRIL 10—As the bow of the gunboat nosed around a bend in the river and David Porter saw the obstruction, he could not suppress a hearty laugh. Before him the scuttled *New Falls City* stretched across the breadth of the river, blocking his way. Painted in large letters on its side was an invitation for him to attend a ball in Shreveport. "Regrettably, I was unable to accept," he later wrote.

Porter set two tugboat crews to the task of removing the steamer. Meanwhile, he borrowed a horse and accompanied several officers, a half dozen cotton brokers, and a small contingent of infantry into the countryside to reconnoiter the area and look for cotton. They had traveled only a short distance when they spotted about thirty Confederate horsemen on a ridge. Porter immediately grasped the significance of their presence. "Banks has been defeated or we wouldn't see those men," he said. They quickly returned to the river, set out artillery, and posted pickets. At four o'clock, as the crews struggled to remove the *New Falls City* from the channel, Captain William Andres rode up with fifty men from the 14th New York Cavalry.

"Banks has been whipped and is in full retreat," he told Porter. "The general wants the fleet to return to Grand Ecore at once."

Porter knew instantly that he was in trouble. He had six gunboats, two tugs, and more than twenty transports in the upper end of the river. Between Loggy Bayou and Grand Ecore lay several stretches where the riverbanks sat higher than his pilothouses. Enemy infantry on those banks could sweep his decks with rifle fire, and he would be helpless to contend with them because his guns would not elevate that high. Along the waterway, dozens of locations provided hiding places for six-pounders to blast away at his boats. Compounding his situation, the narrow, twisting channel made it necessary for him to back his boats some twenty miles downstream before they could turn around at Coushatta Chute. Porter lined the upper decks of the gunboats and transports with cotton bales and posted riflemen and artillery field pieces behind them. He then instructed his pilots to begin backing their vessels down the twisting channel.

⋆ ⋆ ⋆

MANSFIELD, APRIL 12—Chaos had descended on Mansfield. Business buildings, churches, and private homes were filled with wounded men. Confederate and Yankee, with gaping wounds and mangled limbs, lay side by side on blood-stained piles of cotton. Northern and Confederate surgeons, groggy from lack of sleep, worked side by side, unmindful of patient allegiance. Girls from the female academy and women in blood-spattered aprons scurried about with bandages, sheets, and pillows. Ambulances and supply wagons created traffic jams along the main street. Food supplies in the town and surrounding countryside were running low. Although some prisoners were sent on to Shreveport, more than a thousand remained in the vicinity of Mansfield to be fed and cared for, and the little town was pushed to its limit.

It was welcome news when several wagons filled with medical supplies arrived in town. A small contingent of Yankee soldiers, concerned for their fallen comrades, had brought the wagons to Pleasant Hill. General Taylor graciously received them and sent them on to Mansfield. A volunteer described the scene at the little woodland town in her diary: "Oh what a dreadful sight. Our poor men just lying on the floor in cotton. And such an odor. Every private house is full. There are more than a thousand wounded."

Private Joseph Benjamin Hammonds of the Claiborne Invincibles lay among the wounded. He could look down and see a stump where his lower leg had been. The farmer from Lisbon with a wife and four children to support would never plow another furrow. After visiting him, Captain Marcus O. Cheatham wrote a letter to Sallie Hammonds: "It becomes my painful duty to write you that Mr. Joseph Hammonds rec[eived] a wound in the left leg below the knee which broke the leg so badly that is was necessary to cut it off below the knee. . . . He was wounded while in the front rank of the company among the foremost in the charge, fighting gallantly and bravely, doing his duty nobly."

In the midst of this frenzy of activity, Kirby Smith returned from Shreveport to meet with Taylor. The department commander instructed him to transfer his infantry divisions to Shreveport immediately in case they were needed to protect the city from an attack by Steele. Taylor protested, insisting once more that Steele did not pose a threat. He tried to convince Smith that such a move would squander a chance to cut off Banks's supply lines and destroy his army. Once Banks had been defeated, Porter's fleet would be vulnerable. Smith was unmoved by the argument. He instructed Taylor to send the divisions of Churchill, Parsons, and Walker to Shreveport—a total of eighty-five hundred men. Taylor was afraid that if he ever let those troops get out of his command he would not get them back. He also was tired of cooling his heels in Mansfield while Smith tried to make up his mind on a course of action. Left with little choice, Taylor volunteered to lead the army into Arkansas and defeat Steele if Smith would then allow him to return the army to Louisiana and deal with Banks.

Taylor did not realize that Smith already had decided on a course of action of his own. Masked behind glasses and a face devoid of emotion lurked a seething jealousy exceeded only by his ambition. Kirby Smith had decided that he, not Taylor, would lead the army into Arkansas. Smith had the benefit of intelligence to which Taylor was not privy. Steele, having received word of Banks's defeat, was in retreat. Bogged down by muddy roads, harassed by rebel cavalry, and short on supplies, he was fighting his way back to Little Rock. Smith intended to overtake Steele, defeat his weakened army, capture Little Rock, and march on St. Louis.

Smith instructed Taylor to wait at Mansfield until he received orders. Taylor waited there for three days before orders finally came for him to report to headquarters at Shreveport. Taylor assumed he was being summoned to command an invasion of Arkansas, but upon his arrival, he discovered that the army already had departed the city with Kirby Smith at its head. "I was further informed," Taylor later wrote, "that my presence with the troops was not desired, and that I would remain in nominal command at Shreveport."

Disgusted by the deception, Taylor left Smith's staff of bureaucrats his "nominal command," along with some choice expletives directed at their hero. He spent some time with Mimi and the girls while writing a carefully crafted report of the events leading up to the battles of Mansfield and Pleasant Hill and of Smith's actions afterward. He returned to Mansfield, vowing to have nothing more to do with the duplicitous Kirby Smith. He had made up his mind to resign his commission—but not before he dealt with Nathaniel Banks.

★ ★ ★

BLAIR'S LANDING, APRIL 12—As Porter's ironclads rounded a bend in the river, Tom Green signaled his gunners with a wave of the hat and watched as artillery rounds ripped into the fleet. Bales of cotton lining the decks were sent flying. Smokestacks crumpled as cannonballs shattered wheelhouses and steam burst from ruptured pipes. For two days, Green's horsemen had harassed Porter's fleet as it slowly made its way down the river under sporadic rifle fire from the banks. At Blair's Landing, Green finally managed to unlimber his field pieces, setting off one of the most unusual engagements of the war until that time—a running gun battle between cavalry and gunboats.

Porter's gun crews answered the fire, setting off one of the hottest close-range artillery battles of the war. So hot was the fire of the Confederates, the crew of the *Black Hawk* abandoned ship and the vessel had to be towed down the river to safety by the *Lexington*. Porter later said of his flagship: "There was not a place six inches square not perforated by a bullet." Thomas Selfridge, aboard the *Lexington*, later wrote: "The rebels fought with unusual pertinacity [sic] for over an hour, delivering the heaviest and most concentrated fire of musketry that I have ever witnessed."

As was his custom, Green had prepared for battle by consuming an inordinate quantity of whiskey. At the height of the battle, he noticed that some of his troops, recently arrived from Texas, seemed more concerned with the quality of their cover than with keeping enemy gun crews pinned down on the decks of their boats. "There's nothing to be afraid of!" he shouted, mounting his horse. To demonstrate, he rode recklessly along the bank, taunting the gun crews. Riflemen on the decks of the boats fired at him without effect. But, as he passed the gunboat *Osage*, a blast of canister intended for rebels in the woods struck him in the head, decapitating him. His horse, spooked by the smell of blood, spun about. To the astonishment of those who witnessed it, the body remained upright in the saddle for several seconds as if refusing to accept its fate before finally slumping to the ground. The blood-spattered horse obediently stood over its master, waiting for him to rise.

Rebel and Yankee alike were stunned. The Texans had seen their legendary commander tempt death with impunity so many times they simply assumed he was immune to destruction. The Yankees were awestruck by the sight of a headless body remaining upright in the saddle of a spinning horse. Slowly, the firing ceased. The last of Porter's battered fleet chugged downstream, leaving Tom Green's headless body resting beneath the moss-draped trees that lined the river bank.

* * *

GRAND ECORE, APRIL 15—Smoke from the fires of scores of burning farm buildings created a surreal, yellow glow in the sky as dusk settled on the river and Admiral Porter stood on the dock at Grand Ecore surveying his fleet. The transport vessels, unprotected by metal plating or chain armor, were a sorry sight. Rudders were shot away, and gaping holes yawned in the hulls. Smokestacks lay twisted on the decks. According to one crewman, the stacks that remained upright "looked like huge pepper boxes." Some of Porter's gunboats had fared little better. The *Black Hawk* had sustained more than forty hits by Confederate artillery on its way down the river. Four disabled transports were saved only by lashing them to the sides of other boats to keep them afloat. Porter felt lucky to get his battered fleet to Grand Ecore without the loss of a single vessel. On his way up the river, he had left a dozen transports and seven of his heavier gunboats, including the *Eastport*, at Grand Ecore. Extracting twenty boats from the narrow channel at Loggy Bayou had been a nightmare. Now he faced the task of getting a fleet of thirty-eight down the river to Alexandria, and he feared the nightmare was only beginning.

Upon his arrival at Grand Ecore, Porter was greeted by a scene of disorder bordering on pandemonium. Banks's soldiers were everywhere, milling about, without apparent direction or purpose. Cargo wagons, sutler's carts, and ambulances clogged the streets, adding to the confusion.

Proceeding to Banks's headquarters tent, Porter was surprised to find the general lounging in surroundings "rather opulent for field conditions." Banks wore a fine robe, a velvet nightcap, and fancy slippers. Porter found him reading a copy of *Scott's Tactics*, by Winfield Scott. Banks immediately launched into his own version of the Battle of Mansfield, describing it as a tactical withdrawal. He insisted that he had won the battle at Pleasant Hill and that he had withdrawn because of an absence of water. At that point, Porter could restrain himself no longer. He interrupted to remind the general that when he was at Sabine Crossroads, if he had marched six miles to the east, he would have come upon an entire lake.

Porter was not interested in Banks's assessment of events at Mansfield and Pleasant Hill. He had thirteen gunboats and twenty-five transports trapped between Grand Ecore and the rapids at Alexandria, and a treacherous channel with a potential ambush around every bend still stretched out before him. He announced his intention to withdraw his boats to Alexandria, where he could better protect them. All Porter wanted from Banks was an assurance that he would not abandon the fleet until it was safely below the rapids. Banks agreed to stay with the fleet. He speculated that, once there was a rise in the river, he and Porter might resume their campaign against Shreveport. Porter gave him a look of sympathy and excused himself. "I left the general under the delusion that he had won the battle of Mansfield, or Sabine Crossroads, or whatever name that unfortunate affair was known by," Porter wrote. Once outside the tent, he turned to an aide. "He should have read *Scott's Tactics* before he went to Sabine Crossroads," he said dryly.

* * *

GRAND ECORE, APRIL 16—In his haste to get his boats to Grand Ecore, Porter left two thousand of A. J. Smith's troops some twenty miles upstream at Campti. Fearing that these troops might be cut off by the rebels, Smith sent reinforcements to accompany them to Grand Ecore, delaying Porter's departure by a day. Smith's men returned on the sixteenth, leaving Campti in ashes.

With a sigh of relief, Porter finally watched the *Eastport* move out into the channel and head south toward Alexandria. It had gone no more than a few hundred yards when there was a terrific explosion beneath its bow. Weeks earlier the Confederates, knowing that the fleet eventually would return down the river, anchored six mines across the channel. They were placed too deep to strike the hulls of the transports, but lay just right to catch that of the deep-draft *Eastport*. Slowly, the massive gunboat went down, closing the channel and bottling up the remainder of the fleet behind it.

Determined to save the vessel, Porter had the *Eastport*'s guns removed. All unnecessary cargoes were dumped overboard, and two pumpboats began the task of removing water from the hull. Porter personally supervised the operation, occasionally pausing to scan the distant banks in case the Confederates might be lurking there.

* * *

ALEXANDRIA, APRIL 17—On April 13, as Lieutenant Charles Kennedy moved up the Red River with General Grover's 3rd Brigade, word came that General Banks's army had been defeated and was fleeing south. Grover immediately turned his troops around and returned to Alexandria, expecting an attack on the city at any time. Overnight, the complexion of the campaign had changed. The great army that marched north to conquer Shreveport and Texas suddenly found itself besieged. Upon his return to Alexandria, Lieutenant Kennedy penned his usual Sunday night letter to his wife. But this one was different. There was an element of panic in the lines:

> My dear Wife:
> . . . The Army has fought a great battle in which we suffered terribly though we finally drove the Rebs off. It has become very important, owing to the rivers falling so rapidly, that this place be held at all hazards and on this account we were sent back

into the city. I should not be surprised if the Rebels make a desperate effort to take it as it would compel General Banks to surrender, being unable to get any supplies. If they come we will do our best to keep them out as long as we can.

* * *

NEAR NATCHITOCHES, APRIL 19—It was a sullen and vengeful Dick Taylor who came down from Shreveport to renew his war on Nathaniel Banks's legions and Porter's iron monsters on the river. Not only had he lost his army, he had lost his strong right arm. News of the death of Tom Green affected him deeply. A genuine friendship that transcended mutual respect existed between the reckless frontiersman and the brooding intellectual. Green was almost childlike in his devotion to Taylor. Given an order, he was bound to carry it out against all odds. Taylor held boundless admiration for Green's courage and leadership qualities. Riding at the head of his wild Texans, Green had an uncanny ability to see an entire battlefield, anticipate the action of the enemy, and dispatch his troops accordingly. Although from different worlds, they were kindred spirits in combat—each inspiring the other to perform deeds beyond what either might have accomplished alone. Green, Mouton, William Walker, James Beard, Leopold Armant—the good ones were dying and Taylor had none to take their place.

Taylor was left with only forty-five hundred troops to contend with more than twenty-seven thousand Federals at Grand Ecore. A less stubborn man might have contented himself simply to harass the Union Army. However, adversity seemed only to strengthen Taylor's resolve. He was not content to harass Banks, he intended to destroy his army. He had witnessed Old Zack Taylor, deprived of half of his army, rout Santa Anna at Buena Vista. He had seen Tom Green, with no more than fifteen hundred horsemen, drive six thousand Federals behind the levee at Fort Butler. To Taylor, nothing was impossible as he studied his maps and analyzed his options.

His most critical problem was an absence of foot soldiers. His only infantry was Polignac's depleted division, which totaled no more than fifteen hundred men, even with replacements. His strength was in his cavalry. There he had three thousand men, most of them veteran fighters. He had more artillery than he did men to man the guns. He also had an abundance of ammunition, thanks to the capture of Albert Lee's supply train. Scattered about the state were another one thousand men in state and local militias that Taylor intended to utilize if he could incorporate them into his veteran units. It would not be easy. Some of those companies consisted of no more than a dozen men, and many of them were reluctant to leave their homes vulnerable to raids by jayhawkers.

To discourage Banks from resuming his campaign against Shreveport, Taylor had to convince him that he was under siege by a large army. To accomplish that, Bee, Wharton, and Major conducted a series of hit-and-run cavalry raids against the picket outposts at Grand Ecore. The ruse was successful enough for Banks to send a report to Grant that he was being besieged by an army of twenty-five thousand Confederates.

* * *

To read Banks's April 13 report to General Grant, one would assume he had whipped the Confederate Army and was withdrawing to Grand Ecore only to resupply and resume his advance on Shreveport. He was even so bold to suggest that Grant send him reinforcements. Grant was not fooled nor was Sherman, who demanded an immediate return of A. J. Smith's troops to Vicksburg. Banks refused to release the troops, citing a need to protect Porter's gunboats. For once Porter agreed with him. In a letter to Grant, Porter asked that Sherman's 16th and 17th corps be allowed to remain in Louisiana until he could extract his fleet from the Red River. Left with little choice, Grant agreed. In fact, Porter had no intention of going to Shreveport. If Banks had illusions of marching back to Shreveport, he would do it without gunboats.

Blaming others for his failures, Banks began purging the ranks of his officers. He fired General Charles P. Stone, his chief of staff. He dismissed Albert Lee and "Gold Dust" Dudley, sending them to New Orleans. As his new chief of staff, Banks appointed General William Dwight, who had commanded a division at Pleasant Hill.

Even as Banks withdrew from Pleasant Hill, he sent a message to General Grover at Alexandria, instructing him to bring another four thousand troops up the river to Grand Ecore as quickly as possible. At the same time, he sent word for General John McClernan to withdraw some five thousand troops from the Texas Gulf Coast and bring them to Alexandria. There McClernan was to assume command of Banks's 13th Army Corps.

Meanwhile, Grover's soldiers were experiencing an adventure just making it up the river from Alexandria aboard troop transports. At the most unexpected times, the underbrush along the riverbank exploded with fire, smoke, and rebel yells as showers of musket balls rained down on the decks. As casualties mounted, the men simply remained below deck, packed like cordwood in the muggy, stifling heat of the holes. They arrived at Grand Ecore just in time for Banks to inform them that they were going back to Alexandria.

★ ★ ★

RIGOLET DU BON DIEU, APRIL 21—When Banks agreed to stay with the fleet, he had no idea that David Porter would spend four days trying to salvage a single gunboat. On April 21, the *Eastport* finally was afloat—but only barely. The badly damaged gunboat began moving slowly down the river, even as work crews frantically tried to stem the flow of water into its bow. Porter hoped that the crippled vessel could be nursed to Alexandria for repairs.

With the fleet under way, Banks's legions began marching south out of Grand Ecore along the banks of the Cane River toward Cloutierville. Assigned to the rear guard, A. J. Smith's soldiers torched Grand Ecore before leaving the village. After their departure, not a building was left standing. Natchitoches, a picturesque old town sitting on the banks of the Cane River just four miles away, was spared a similar fate, not out of compassion, but because of the sudden arrival of Colonel Wharton's cavalry. Even as the inhabitants fled and the invaders doused downtown buildings with camphene, rebel horsemen rode into town and captured several of Smith's soldiers with torches in hand. Several fires were extinguished before they did extensive damage.

The retreating Union Army followed a road that traversed a narrow island some forty miles in length. The island, named Rigolet Du Bon Dieu, was formed between the channels of the Red and Cane rivers. It was rich farmland, thickly settled, for the most part by freemen of French-African descent. Many of the inhabitants were mulatto planters and plantation owners who owned slaves. The Northern troops were fascinated by these people, whose features were predominantly white rather than African. However, that did not prevent Smith's troops from destroying their homes and buildings.

Moving south, there was only one location where Banks's army could ford the Cane River—at Monett's Ferry on the southern tip of the island. Banks sensed that he was in trouble when he began encountering large trees felled across the road to obstruct his progress. Only then did it occur to him that rebels might be trying to trap his army on the island. His concern increased when he received a message from Smith that the Confederate cavalry had attacked his rear guard. Even as Smith struggled with Wharton's horsemen at the rear of the column, Banks was told that rebel troops were seen across the river, shifting forces toward Monett's Ferry.

There was even more bad news. Porter's fleet was stalled on the Red River with the damaged *Eastport* blocking the channel. Banks was on his own, confined by an army of unknown strength and without the support of his gunboats. The rebels might very well block his retreat and bottle up his entire army. Banks ordered his officers to quick-march their columns, hoping to beat the rebels to the ford at Monett's Ferry. What he did not realize was that he was racing against himself; the Confederates already occupied the high ground overlooking the crossing.

* * *

Meanwhile, Porter had his own problems. Some thirty miles below Grand Ecore, the *Eastport*, taking on water and listing badly, had ground to a stop against submerged snags in the river, once more blocking the channel. A frustrated Porter stubbornly ordered the pump boats *Champion 5* and *Champion 3* forward to attempt yet another rescue. Some of his captains urged him to remove the *Eastport* from the channel and abandon it, pointing out that they posed sitting ducks for rebel artillery. Porter responded that he would not be the one who abandoned the most powerful gunboat in the Mississippi River fleet. He insisted the *Eastport* be raised.

* * *

As dusk settled on Rigolet Du Bon Dieu, Banks continued to push his men toward Monett's Ferry crossing. They marched without a break, legs weary, faces caked with sweat and dust. Canteens were soon emptied. As night fell, the sky took on an eerie red glow from the fires left by A. J. Smith's troops. In some locales the flames had spread, setting fields and woods on fire. A Private Pellet with the New York 114th Regiment later wrote, "Destruction and desolation followed on the trail of the retreating column. At night the burning buildings mark our pathway . . . as far as the eye can see. The wanton and useless destruction has well earned [Smith's] command a lasting disgrace."

By midnight, men were dropping out of ranks, too exhausted to continue. Officers were nodding off to sleep in their saddles. Banks finally stopped the march at 2:30 in the morning, his advance elements still three miles from the crossing.

★ ★ ★

CLOUTIERVILLE, APRIL 23—Daylight revealed not only the charred devastation left by the Union Army but evidence of a brutal overnight march. As Wharton's horsemen trailed the Federals down the Cloutierville Road, they came upon troops sitting and lying beside the roadway—some of them asleep. The task of securing prisoners became such a problem that the rebels finally abandoned the practice and simply rode past the stragglers. A pall of smoke blocked the sun. Dead animals lay in pastures where they had been shot—cows, calves, hogs, horses, and mules. Every structure had been reduced to smoking ruin—barns, smokehouses, corn cribs, chicken houses, and cotton gins, as well as dwellings. Even fences had been torn down and thrown into the flames. Giant oak trees that once graced front yards stood singed and charred.

Catching up to Wharton, Taylor was appalled by what he saw. In his memoirs, he wrote:

> In pursuit we passed the smoking ruins of homesteads by which stood weeping women and children. Time for the removal of the most necessary articles of furniture had been refused. It was difficult to restrain one's inclination to punish the ruffians [Federal prisoners] engaged in this work; but they asserted, and doubtless with truth, that they were acting under orders.

Taylor had set the perfect trap for Banks at Monett's Ferry. Artillery on heavily wooded bluffs looked down on the bottleneck where Banks's troops would have to wade across the Cane River. Sixteen hundred dismounted cavalrymen under General Bee blocked the road at the crossing, and Polignac's infantry division stood by on his left flank, poised to attack any regiments that might survive the artillery barrage. With only forty-five hundred men at his disposal, Taylor had managed to trap twenty-seven thousand Federals in a narrow corridor between the Cane River on one side and marshes on the other. Short on supplies, Banks had no choice but to fight his way out.

General Emory, placed in charge of the advance forces by Banks, sent his cavalry ahead to attempt a crossing. The Union horsemen were met by a barrage of artillery fire and forced to retreat. Emory ordered a line of infantry skirmishers forward. The foot soldiers were likewise unable to reach the river. Banks sent word to A. J. Smith to send reinforcements to the front of the column. Smith sent the courier back with news that he was under threat of attack by Wharton's cavalry and might not be able to hold his own position, much less assist Emory.

At mid-morning the situation appeared bleak for Banks, but two unforeseen events conspired to save him. The first involved a local slave who happened to mention to Union soldiers that he knew a spot where they could cross the Cane River two miles above Monett's Ferry. As General Birge watched, the slave demonstrated by wading through waist-deep water to the other side of the river. Birge immediately began sending troops across the river—including a brigade under Colonel Fessenden and several regiments of the 13th Corps. As the troops came across the river, members of Colonel Baylor's Confederate cavalry spotted them.

Overwhelmed by superior numbers, Baylor retreated to a defensive position on a heavily wooded bluff. He was soon joined by several companies from Polignac's division. Slowed by rough terrain and a heavy fire from the rebels, Fessenden's brigade was pinned down, and the Union advance on the west bank of the Cane ground to a halt. At that point in the battle, General Bee made a decision that prematurely tripped the jaws of Taylor's trap.

Hearing heavy fighting on his left and seeing Union cavalry riding along the opposite bank of the river to his right, Bee became nervous and ordered a general withdrawal. Unknown to Bee, even as he withdrew, some of Banks's demoralized men, thinking they were surrounded by a large rebel army, were near mutiny and field officers were debating whether they should surrender. To the amazement of all, and especially Banks, the cork was suddenly, and mysteriously, removed from the Monett's Ferry bottleneck. Emory's troops poured across the river. Overwhelmed by numbers, Polignac was forced to withdraw, along with the artillery batteries overlooking the crossing. A disappointed Taylor continued to pursue the retreating Yankee columns with Wharton's cavalry and his artillery batteries until two o'clock the following afternoon before reluctantly breaking off the engagement.

Informed of Bee's action and considering his ill-timed attack at Pleasant Hill, Taylor censured him in his report and later removed him from command. He dispatched his cavalry to harass Banks's fleeing columns and sent Polignac's division to the Red River to attack Porter's stranded fleet. As the Union Army wearily marched toward Alexandria, Smith's troops continued to pillage and burn everything in their path. The first of Banks's troops staggered into Alexandria on April 25. A. J. Smith finally entered the city at the head of his army on the afternoon of the twenty-sixth. He was greeted by cheers from the 19th and 13th corps. Having saved the army at Pleasant Hill and held the rear guard on the long march from Grand Ecore, he was the hero of the hour. General Dwight waited for him with a lavish dinner arranged in Smith's honor. It included French champagne and the best cuisine from New Orleans. The hard-bitten Smith was duly impressed. Although he could hardly bear to sit at the same table with Nathaniel Banks, that did not prevent him from consuming more than his share of the general's champagne that night.

18

Blood on the Water

ON THE RED RIVER, APRIL 26—By the twenty-sixth it was obvious, even to Porter, that the *Eastport* could not be salvaged. Reluctantly, he ordered its destruction. Three thousand pounds of powder was placed throughout the vessel, and at 1:45 P.M. a huge explosion blew the *Eastport* apart.

Aboard the shallow-draft *Cricket*, Porter led his fleet down the river. He had gone less than fifteen miles when it seemed the gates of hell suddenly opened on him. From a wooded bluff at the mouth of the Cane River, no more than four miles from Monett's Ferry, a four-gun battery commanded by Captain Florian Cornay, supported by two hundred riflemen from the 28th Louisiana Regiment, sent a hurricane of metal into the *Cricket*. In seconds, its decks were covered with blood. Twenty-five men, half of the vessel's crew, lay dead or wounded. Within minutes, the *Cricket* was hit thirty-eight times by artillery shells. In his report to Gideon Welles, Porter provided a description of the action:

> [The shot] cleared all our decks in a moment. Finding the guns not firing rapidly, I stepped on the gun deck to see what was the matter. As I stepped down, the after gun was struck with a shell and disabled and every man at the gun killed and wounded. At the same moment the crew from the forward gun was swept away by a shell exploding and the men were wounded in the fire room, leaving only one man to fire up. I made up a gun's crew from the contrabands who fought the gun to the last moment. Finding that the engine did not move, I went into the engine room and found the chief engineer killed, whose place was soon supplied by an assistant. I then went to the pilot house and found that a shot had gone through it and wounded one of my pilots. I took charge of the vessel and as the battery was a heavy one, I determined to pass it, which was done under the heaviest fire I ever witnessed.

Although the *Cricket* managed at last to run past the ambush, some of the vessels that followed were not so lucky. *Champion 5* was riddled with shot and shell and slowly sank. Two transport steamers also went down, and three of Porter's tinclads were so badly damaged that they were rendered useless for duty.

Aboard the *Champion 3* a terrible tragedy took place. The boat was loaded with 175 slave-contrabands, picked up to perform menial labor for the boat crews. They were huddled below deck when a shell penetrated the boat's boiler, and the scalding steam killed all but three of the unfortunate passengers. The boat, with its grisly cargo, floated out of control, down the channel. Many of the bodies were dumped overboard so repair crews could reach the boiler.

Some of the gunboat captains waited until nightfall before attempting to run past the Confederate position, willing to take their chances with the channel rather than expose their vessels to daylight target practice. In the end it was a terrible day for the United States Navy. Porter had lost four vessels, including the *Eastport*. An estimated one hundred of his crewmen were killed or wounded and at least as many taken prisoner. The Confederates had only two casualties. One was Captain Cornay, the artillery commander who had orchestrated the havoc with just four field pieces and two hundred riflemen from the rag-tag 28th Regiment.

* * *

ALEXANDRIA, APRIL 27—With the coming of dawn on the twenty-seventh, David Porter was dealt another cruel dose of reality. During the eleven days he spent moving his fleet downstream from Grand Ecore, the river had fallen far more than he thought possible. Approaching Alexandria, he had anticipated difficulty getting his vessels across the lower falls. Now he found his progress impeded by not one, but two rapids.

The river's water level, having fallen some five feet, had created a shallow rapids at an outcrop of rocks above the first falls. There Porter could see bare rocks protruding from the river. A closer examination revealed a channel only twenty feet wide, with the water washing over the rocks less than four feet deep. Abandoning all rationale, Porter ordered the pilot of the *Cricket* to make a run at the falls. The pilot tried to discourage him, pointing out that, even if they were lucky enough to get over the first rapids, the channel at the lower falls was no more than three feet deep, and the bow could very easily plow into the rocks.

Porter would not be dissuaded. As the shallow-draft *Cricket* bumped and ground its way over the rocks on its way over the first rapids, Porter stood at the bow, chin thrust forward as if defying the fates. They made it safely past. Picking up speed, the bottom of the vessel scraped painfully, barely making it over the second falls. Although damaged, the *Cricket* had reached the safety of the deep water at the Alexandria docks.

The light-draft tinclads, stripped of their guns and all unnecessary weight, also made it over the falls. Cargoes were unloaded from the transport vessels and, one by one, they negotiated the rapids. But at day's end, ten gunboats remained trapped with no hope of crossing the falls without a considerable rise in the river. These were the pride of the inland fleet—the *Lexington, Fort Hindman, Osage, Neosho, Mound City, Louisville, Pittsburg, Chillicothe, Carondelet,* and *Ozark.* Boats from this fleet had fought at Memphis, Vicksburg, Port Hudson, and the Battle of New Orleans. They were the boats that ruled the Mississippi River and the bayous of Louisiana.

Most disturbing to Porter was the knowledge that, if he could not save his gunboats, he must destroy them. If such an armada fell into the hands of the rebels, the entire Gulf Department would be threatened.

Trapped with the gunboats at Alexandria was Banks's army, a captive of the general's pledge not to abandon the fleet. Banks deployed his troops protectively around the fleet and established a line of defense on the outskirts of the city. He had no choice but to wait for Taylor and hope for a rise in the river. To bolster his army, he sent a message to General J. J. Reynolds in New Orleans ordering more troops to Alexandria.

* * *

ALEXANDRIA, APRIL 29—The slightly built young man with the heavy beard sitting across from General Banks hardly looked like the savior of the Mississippi River fleet. He was Lieutenant Joseph Bailey, an engineer in the 19th Army Corps. General Franklin had arranged Bailey's introduction to Banks with the notation that he had a plan to get the gunboats over the rapids.

When they were at Grand Ecore, the lieutenant had approached Franklin with a plan to float the beleaguered *Eastport* over the falls at Alexandria. Having worked in the timber industry in Wisconsin before the war, Bailey had supervised the construction of wing dams to raise the water in streams high enough to float giant logs over shallows. Although he had never undertaken a project approaching the magnitude of the one at Alexandria, the principle was the same, and he was convinced it would work with a gunboat as well as logs. One only had to build larger wing dams.

Bailey's confidence impressed Franklin, and upon their arrival in Alexandria he arranged a meeting with Porter. The admiral promptly dismissed Bailey and his plan. "If a dam would get those boats over the falls, they would not be sitting there now," Porter said. Porter's rejection of the plan did not dissuade Franklin. He had been granted a leave of absence because of the wound he sustained at Pleasant Hill, but delayed his departure for New Orleans until he could arrange a meeting between Banks and Bailey.

Banks was skeptical the plan would work, but he was desperate enough to try anything. He issued orders for Bailey to proceed with the project.

* * *

JENKINS FERRY, ARKANSAS, APRIL 29—Like a bully pursuing a hapless victim, General E. Kirby Smith finally caught up with General Steele's fleeing army at the Saline River, some fifty miles south of Little Rock. Two days earlier Smith had written a letter to his wife stating his intention to "bag the entire army." By all appearances, Steele's army was ready to be bagged. Earlier he had lost most of his supply wagons to Confederate cavalry. Now he was bogged down in mud after two days of hard rains, and his troops were exhausted, short on rations, and low on ammunition. The mules and horses were so feeble from lack of forage they had difficulty moving his wagons and artillery caissons through the mud.

Although Smith had thirteen thousand troops at his disposal to deal with an army less than half that size, he had allowed his units to become scattered. In fact, he sent one cavalry division back to Oklahoma, thinking he would not need it to defeat Steele. Instead of bringing his army together for a coordinated attack, Smith directed a premature series of piecemeal assaults that proved disastrous. Backed against the Saline River, the intended victim turned on the bully with a vengeance. Every attack by Kirby Smith's forces was repulsed. Of the 6,000 Confederates engaged there, more than 1,000 were killed or wounded, while Union losses stood at 594 killed and wounded, 106 missing. It was a horrific defeat for Kirby Smith, as Steele resumed his retreat to Little Rock unmolested.

While Kirby Smith's dream of recapturing Little Rock and St. Louis ended on the muddy banks of the Saline River, his ambition and jealousy deprived Taylor of an opportunity to cut off and destroy Banks's army at Grand Ecore. Smith's incompetence as a field commander also contributed to the ranks of Walker's Texas Division being so badly cut up at Jenkins Ferry that the veteran unit saw little action following the battle.

However, in his report, Smith informed Seddon that he had won a great victory at Jenkins's Ferry.

★ ★ ★

ALEXANDRIA, MAY 5—Upon Banks's return to Alexandria, fearful that Taylor might attack him in force at any time, he issued orders to improve the city's fortifications. By May 5, two lines of breastworks complete with redoubts and artillery emplacements protected the north and west sides of town. Several regiments were also dug in at Pineville on the other side of the river. Still convinced that Taylor had a large army at his disposal, Banks strengthened his ranks with reinforcements from South Louisiana. By the first week in May, he had increased his troop strength to thirty-one thousand with more men on the way.

Indeed, Taylor did have a larger army than when he began his pursuit of Banks. Volunteers, inspired by his successes, had filled the gaps left by casualties and swelled his ranks to almost six thousand men. However, after dispatching troops to South Louisiana and the lower Red River, he still retained only about four thousand around Alexandria.

Not even Dick Taylor was so bold to attack an entrenched army of thirty-one thousand with four thousand men. Instead, he made Banks think he was surrounded. His cavalry rode up and down the Union lines, striking and retreating with enough frequency to convince the Federals they were under siege. In one of his reports, Taylor wrote, "I am compelled to 'eke out the lion's skin with the fox's hide.' On several occasions we have forced the enemy from strong positions by sending drummers to beat calls, lighting campfires, blowing bugles, and rolling empty wagons over fence rails."

Confident that Banks's troops had no intention of leaving their fortifications at Alexandria, Taylor began taking back lost territory. Vincent's cavalry went south to once more sweep the Bayou Teche and Lafourche regions clear of Yankee detachments. Northern overseers occupying confiscated plantations again fled to the safety of New Orleans. Confederate troops occupied Marksville, Fort DeRussy, and Simmesport. Within a week, all of Louisiana west of the Mississippi River was back in Confederate hands, with the exception of Alexandria, New Orleans, and the town of Plaquemines, just north of New Orleans. At Plaquemines, much like Alexandria, Federal troops were driven behind fortifications, where they remained, convinced they were under siege by a large army.

While Banks was fortifying and damming, Taylor sent General James Major with a small cavalry division to occupy David's Ferry on the Red River, thirty miles below Alexandria. He was accompanied by Colonel J. A. A. West with a four-gun battery consisting of two ten-pound field pieces and two howitzers. Their orders were to attack anything that moved on the river.

On May 1, as the Union transport *Emma* made its way down the river on route to New Orleans, a storm of shot, shell, and rifle balls rained down on it, disabling the vessel. Those crewmen who survived the attack fled to the opposite bank. The rebels promptly stripped the steamer of anything useful and burned it. Two days later, the troop transport *City Belle* churned up the river with seven hundred men of the 120th Ohio Infantry Regiment on board. The rebel gunners opened up, riddling the boat, killing or wounding more than one hundred soldiers, taking three hundred prisoners, and capturing the *Belle*. Some three hundred troops fled into the swamps.

On May 5, the transport *John Warner*, loaded with troops from the 56th Ohio on their way home, was being escorted downstream by the gunboats *Covington* and *Signal* when ambushed by the rebels. The *John Warner* became a slaughter pen. In a matter of minutes, 150 soldiers lay dead or wounded on its blood-soaked decks and the captain raised a white flag to stop the human destruction. The *Signal* was disabled and drifted helplessly as the captain of the *Covington* tried to tow it to safety. A shell damaged the rudder of the *Covington*, causing it to drift against the opposite shore. As West's howitzers literally tore the *Covington* apart and the crew scrambled to safety, Lieutenant George Lord bravely spiked the guns and set the vessel on fire. With the full force of the Confederate firepower then turned on the *Signal*, the captain quickly ran up a white flag.

In five days, Taylor's little force at David's Ferry had captured or destroyed three transports and two gunboats. More than one thousand Union soldiers and Navy crewmen had been killed, wounded, or captured. In the weeks that followed, scores of additional prisoners were taken as they tried to make their way across the country to Natchez and Vicksburg. In his report on the action, David Porter wrote to Welles that six thousand rebels and several batteries of artillery were involved in the attacks. The force actually consisted of less than one thousand Texas cavalrymen and four field pieces. The Confederates sustained not a single casualty in the five-day action.

As of May 5, when the carnage ended, Dick Taylor owned the Red River. Nathaniel Banks's army was cut off from all supplies and reinforcements.

* * *

ALEXANDRIA, MAY 8—When Banks entered Alexandria, provisions did not concern him. His staff assured him he had a three-week supply on hand for his troops. Thinking he would be able to resupply his army from New Orleans, he generously shared those stores with the hundreds of contrabands who had abandoned their destroyed plantations and trailed his army into the city. But by May 8, with the rebels in control of his supply corridor and Porter's gunboats still sitting above the rapids, panic set in.

Banks sent troops outside the city to forage for food, only to discover that the rural population had fled and Taylor had picked the country clean. Rebel cavalry ambushed his foraging parties, driving them back behind the Alexandria fortifications. During those encounters, Taylor noticed that some of the horses captured from the Yankee cavalry were little more than skeletons. Banks was out of forage for his animals and they were starving to death.

Without horse and mule power to pull his artillery caissons and supply wagons, Banks soon would be incapable of mounting anything resembling a large-scale offensive. Taylor also surmised that Banks's food supplies for his troops were running low. From that point, his strategy changed: "We played the game the Russians played in the [French] retreat from Moscow," he wrote. If he could not conquer Banks's army with bullets, he would starve it to submission.

As work progressed on the dams, the men were appalled when the bloated bodies of horses, mules, and humans came floating down the river. Many of the animals were from the transport *Alice Vivian*, carrying four hundred horses and mules when it went down at Blair's Landing. In addition to dead soldiers and Navy crewmen, a large number of bodies of contrabands from the ill-fated *Champion 3* floated down the channel. The smell of death on the river compelled the men to work even harder to complete the dams.

Banks and Porter argued frequently during this period. Nine of Porter's gunboats sat idle below the rapids at Alexandria, and Banks insisted that he send them downstream to clear the river of Confederate forces. Having already lost three gunboats, Porter suggested that, if Banks wanted the river cleared of rebels, he send his infantry. Neither was inclined to act on the suggestion of the other.

With the passage of each day, Banks seemed to lose more control of events. A. J. Smith did as he pleased, paying no attention to Banks at all and Porter and his staff had nothing but contempt for the general. And yet another chorus of concerned voices joined the growing panic. Banks came under siege by the cotton brokers, trapped with the army at Alexandria. They howled when he confiscated thousands of bales of cotton to use in the construction of Bailey's wing dams. Among those howling the loudest was Lincoln's old friend, Samuel Casey. When his cotton was seized, he protested to Banks. "I wish you would use somebody else's cotton," he told the general. "That's mighty fine cotton."

By May 8, the upper dam had backed up enough water to allow four of Porter's gunboats to run over the rapids. Before the others could follow, two sunken barges filled with rocks, a part of the dam, broke loose, and caused the water level to fall rapidly. Six gunboats remained stranded. Time and supplies were running out for Banks.

* * *

IN CAMP AT BAYOU RAPIDES, MAY 13—Time also was running out for Dick Taylor. Now that Kirby Smith's Arkansas adventure had played itself out, Taylor requested that Walker's and Churchill's divisions be returned to him. Smith's subordinates at department headquarters in Shreveport assured Taylor that reinforcements would be forthcoming from Arkansas.

However, in Smith's continuing effort to control the department, he had narrowed Taylor's command responsibility to the territory west of the Red River. On the east side of the river, the rebel force consisted of only about five hundred cavalrymen under John R. Liddell who, technically, was not under Taylor's command. In the early stages of the siege, Liddell could do little but harass the Federals on that side of the river because he had no heavy guns. Kirby Smith had borrowed his artillery for the ill-fated venture into Arkansas.

Day after day Taylor received reports of progress on the dam's construction without being able to do anything about it. "Like Sister Ann from her watch tower . . . we strained our eyes to see the dust of our approaching comrades arise from the north," he wrote.

The comrades from the north never came.

★ ★ ★

ALEXANDRIA, MAY 12—On May 9, Bailey began rebuilding the damaged wing dam at the head of the falls to save the final six gunboats. While Porter patiently waited for Bailey to complete the task, Banks watched his food supplies dwindle. He considered the consequence of putting his troops on short rations a time when they faced a forced march and the possibility of fighting a major battle.

Since troop transports could not be used, his army would have to march and fight its way some sixty miles overland to Simmesport. He told Porter on the ninth that he must get his stranded vessels over the rapids at the earliest opportunity. "With the march that is before us it will be perilous to remain more than another day," he said. Porter's rather blasé reaction did little to calm his anxiety. "I really see nothing to make us despond," he told the general. "You have a fine army and I still have a strong fleet of gunboats to drive away an inferior force in our front."

On the tenth Banks was upset to learn that the gunboats above the rapids were still loaded with cotton confiscated by the navy. He demanded that Porter dump the cotton and strip the boats of all unnecessary weight, including heavy guns and metal plating. Porter reluctantly complied. Grim-faced brokers solemnly lined the levee as if attending a funeral while cotton bales tumbled into the river. Dumped overboard with the cotton were eleven thirty-two-pound guns. Useful government equipment and the lighter guns were hauled on wagons to Alexandria and loaded on transports. Armor was removed from the ironclads and dumped in the river, exposing the wooden sides of the gunboats. Porter instructed his crews to coat the hulls and housings with tar so they would not become nighttime targets for Confederate sharpshooters.

The following day, the river rose slightly, and the men began laboriously winching and towing the stripped-down boats over the falls. Working day and night, it took two days to get all of the boats past the lower shallows. Meanwhile, General McMillan received permission from Banks to confiscate all private boats at Alexandria to haul military and government equipment. Most of those vessels were loaded with cotton and sugar purchased or stolen by speculators, and in some cases the boats themselves were stolen. McMillan, who had developed a genuine loathing for the cotton brokers, delighted in his task. "Fling overboard every damn pound of cotton," he instructed his men. "And if the proprietors protest, fling them with it!"

★ ★ ★

ALEXANDRIA, MAY 13—The citizens of Alexandria were awakened at dawn to the sound of Banks's legions marching out of town. It was a moment of relief mixed with apprehension. Most were glad to see the Yankees leaving, but there were rumors that General A. J. Smith intended to burn the city upon his departure. Concerned city leaders went to Banks, seeking assurance that he would not allow Smith to burn the town. Banks promised them that he would not permit such a thing to happen.

As the Union Army left town that morning, Dr. G. W. Southwick learned that some of Smith's troops had buckets of turpentine and camphene and were boasting that they were going to "turn Alexandria into hell." Southwick tried to find Banks but was unable see him. Instead, he received the following note from Banks's adjutant, General George B. Drake: "Sir: The General wishes me to inform you that Col. Gooding will, with 500 men, guard the town, and his force will be strengthened, if possible, in order to provide against the emergency you fear." There was only one thing wrong with Drake's assurance. Banks never issued an order for Colonel Gooding to guard anything.

About eight o'clock, Smith's troops began smearing turpentine and camphene on buildings with mops. Asked what they were doing, they replied: "We are preparing the place for hell!" Near nine o'clock, fires broke out in the business buildings along Front Street. In a subsequent investigation by Governor Allen, a citizen named Thomas Manning gave the following testimony: "The first building fired was a store on Front Street in the block next below the hotel. . . . I was standing on the levee in front of the store when it was fired by the soldiers, who first plundered it, and then, ascending to the second story, applied the torch."

The gothic old courthouse facing the river was the next to go up in flames, along with almost a century of public records and documents. The Episcopal and Methodist churches also were set on fire. As soldiers approached the Catholic church, Father J. G. Bellier, who had been a cavalryman in the French army prior to his calling, stood in the doorway and fearlessly berated them. The soldiers retreated rather than tangle with the enraged priest. His own church having escaped the holocaust, Father Bellier ran through flames to the Episcopal church to save the vessels used for sacrament.

As flames swept from building to building, A. J. Smith rode his horse through the streets shouting: "Hurrah, boys! This looks like war to me!"

One of the most graphic descriptions of the conflagration was provided in the writings of a Massachusetts soldier named L. Van Alstyne:

> Cries of fire and alarm bells were heard on every side. I think a hundred fires must have started at one time. We grabbed the few things we had to carry and marched out of the fire territory where we left them under guard and went back do what we

could to help the people. There was no such thing as saving the buildings. All we could do was help the people get over the levee, the only place where the heat did not reach and where there was nothing to burn. Only the things most needed, such as beds and eatables were saved. One lady begged so for her piano that it was got out on the porch and there left to burn.

Cows ran bellowing through the streets. Chickens flew out from yards and fell in the streets with their feathers scorching. A dog with his bushy tail on fire ran howling through, turning to snap at the fire as he ran. There is no use trying to tell about the sights I saw and the sounds of distress I heard. It cannot be told and could hardly be believed if it were told.

Crowds of people, men, women, children and soldiers, were running with all they could carry, when the heat would become unbearable, and dropping all, they would flee for their lives, leaving everything but their bodies to burn. Over the levee the sights and sounds were harrowing. Thousands of people, mostly women, children and old men, were wringing their hands as they stood by the little piles of what was left of their worldly possessions. Thieves were everywhere and some of them were soldiers. The provost guards were everywhere and, I am told, shot down everyone caught spreading fire or stealing. Nearly all buildings were of wood. Great patches of burning roof would sail away to drop and start a new fire. By noon the thickly settled portion of Alexandria was a smoking ruin.

As flames swept across the city, generals Emory and Grover were horrified. While Emory sent men to fight the flames, Grover dispatched his provost guard with instructions to shoot anyone stealing or setting fires. This resulted in exchanges of gunfire between Grover's troops and those of Smith. Emory tried to stop the flames and save part of the city by setting off a string of explosive charges, but the attempt failed.

Recruits from Alexandria who had signed loyalty oaths and joined the Union Army were well out of town when word spread that Alexandria was burning. Officers threatened to shoot anyone who broke ranks, forcing the men to continue marching even as they looked over their shoulders at the massive clouds of smoke, not knowing if their wives and children were alive or dead or if their homes still stood.

A Northern newsman reported that these wives of local men in the Union Army pleaded with officers to be taken on board the transport boats so they could follow their husbands to New Orleans: "[When] they were refused they became frantic with excitement and rage . . . With tears streaming down their cheeks, women and children begged and implored the boats to take them on board."

Also pleading for passage out of town were several prominent citizens who had openly embraced the Federal occupation. They also were left behind to face the wrath of their neighbors. Contrabands who had trailed the Union Army to Alexandria from the region's burned-out plantations stood solemnly on the banks and watched the steamers disappear down the river. Porter recalled the scene in his memoirs: "Out of the hundreds of negroes who had been promised transportation for themselves, their families and their effects, few got away. The last that was seen of these poor wretches, they sat down in despair upon the river bank where they had conveyed their all to escape the conflagration."

When the flames began to die down, there were moans and cries of anguish as mothers, children, and old men, black and white, ventured across the levee and searched through the smoldering rubble that had been their homes.

In less than three hours Alexandria, the third largest city in Louisiana, had ceased to exist. Twenty-two blocks were reduced to blackened ruins. All that remained of the once vibrant city was the Catholic church and a few houses on the windward side of town, mercifully spared by nature, not man.

* * *

YELLOW BAYOU, MAY 19—Leaving the ruins of Alexandria in its wake, the army marched down the river road toward Simmesport with the cavalry screening its long lines of infantry, wagon trains, and artillery caissons. Fighting a continuous rear-guard action against Southern cavalry, A. J. Smith's Midwesterners still managed to burn farms and plantations along the way. Progress was slow for the Union Army as advance units had to remove trees that Taylor's men had felled across the road. They did so under the fire of rebel snipers.

Although outnumbered more than six to one, Taylor stubbornly refused to let Banks go. At Mansura he spread thirty-two field pieces across the road and laid down an artillery barrage that halted the Federal column for most of one day. A surprise cavalry attack caused the advance units of Banks's column to fall back before reinforcements were brought forward to drive back the rebels. By now, reason and reality had abandoned Dick Taylor. Like a man possessed by forces beyond his control, he was trying to cut off an army of thirty thousand with one of forty-five hundred.

Having reached the burned out town of Simmesport on May 18, Banks's army still had to cross the Atchafalaya River to reach troop ships anchored on the Mississippi. He could ferry the men across, but faced the prospect of having to leave his artillery and wagons behind. The ever resourceful Joseph Bailey, having saved the fleet at Alexandria, rescued Banks once more. He built a bridge across the river by anchoring transport ships side by side and laying a bridge across them. When troops and artillery caissons began crossing, they came under fire from a small band of Confederates.

A. J. Smith sent General Mower with three brigades totaling some five thousand men to clear the area of rebels. Mower chased the snipers for two miles when he came upon a Confederate force of forty-five hundred waiting in a battle line at Yellow Bayou. The fight, though brief, was as vicious as any of the war. Fought in dense woods, Camille Polignac twice sent his small infantry division forward to engage in bitter hand-to-hand combat against a superior Yankee force. Placed on the extreme left of the Confederate line, the 28th Louisiana led both charges and suffered heavy casualties. The second charge drove the Yankees back and almost broke the Northern, line but Mower rallied his men and they held. Artillery rounds set the woods on fire and Taylor, realizing that he simply did not have enough infantry to defeat the Federals, ordered a withdrawal. Both lines ended up where they started. In the last major battle fought on Louisiana soil, the Confederates lost an estimated 600 men—the Yankees, 350. Mower withdrew and hustled his troops across Joseph Bailey's bridge to safety. Dick Taylor could only stand on the banks of the Atchafalaya and watch them go.

Thus came to an end the ill-fated Red River Campaign, one of the most ignoble defeats in the history of the United States military, and the last great victory of the Confederate States of America.

The official record lists 5,412 Union casualties in the campaign. However, these numbers are suspect, considering the large number of troops captured by the rebels. Dick Taylor estimated Union casualties at 10,000. The true number probably lies somewhere between. Confederate losses were estimated at 4,100.

During the campaign, Banks lost 29 field pieces, more than 400 wagons and 3,000 horses and mules. Porter lost 3 gunboats, 7 transports, and 28 heavy guns—and came close to losing his fleet.

When Banks reached the Mississippi River, General Edward Canby was waiting there to relieve him of command. Canby would have relieved him sooner but could not get up the river past Confederate guns. Banks's army was broken up and its troops sent to other theaters. A. J. Smith's troops rejoined Sherman and ravaged the Georgia countryside during their commander's infamous March to the Sea.

For practical purposes, the war in Louisiana ended at Yellow Bayou. In the wake of the failed Red River Campaign the state remained divided—almost as if by gentlemen's agreement. Until the end of the Civil War, the Federals contented themselves with controlling the region around New Orleans, the lower Teche, and banks of the Mississippi River, where troops protected Northern agents and "oath of allegiance" planters who supervised the production of cotton and sugar for Eastern markets. They did so under a system that blatantly exploited the labor of the very people they were supposed to free, a system established by Ben Butler and refined by Banks.

The war in Louisiana in general and the Red River Campaign in particular stood as such an inexplicable and ignoble Union defeat that some Northern historians, in their haste to glorify the events of that great conflict after 1865, were inclined to ignore it. The Battle of Mansfield and its aftermath proved an odd piece that did not fit into the overall puzzle of Civil War, and thus they discarded it, unintentionally enshrining the Trans Mississippi conflict as our forgotten war.

In another time and place, Dick Taylor's brilliant victory at Mansfield might have elevated him to legendary heights. In another war, the remarkable charge of Gray's brigade at Mansfield might have covered its ranks in eternal glory. In that charge, the brigade suffered heavier casualties than did the British in the famous Light Brigade in its charge at Balaklava in 1854. Regretfully, Alfred Lord Tennyson never took up the pen to record the uncommon courage of the poor dirt farmers, hill country herders, and lowland trappers whose blood stained Mansfield's dark and bloody ground.

****

19

****

Great and Noble Deeds

ALEXANDRIA, LOUISIANA, MAY 23—Having driven Banks back to New Orleans, Dick Taylor was bound to resign. He wrote a letter to the War Department, venting his rage at Edmund Kirby Smith. He then penned a general order intended as a farewell to his men. In the days that followed, officers throughout Louisiana assembled troops in the field and read the words:

HEADQUARTERS DISTRICT WESTERN LOUISIANA
IN THE FIELD

Soldiers of the Army of Western Louisiana!

On March 12 the enemy, with an army of 30,000 men, accompanied by a fleet of ironclads, mounting 150 guns, moved forward for the conquest of Texas and Louisiana. After seventy days continued fighting, you stand a band of conquering heroes, on the banks of the Mississippi. Fifty pieces of cannon, 7,000 stands of arms, three gunboats and eight transports captured or destroyed, sixty stands of colors, over 10,000 of the enemy killed, wounded or captured—these are the trophies which adorn your victorious banners. Along 300 miles of river you have fought his fleet, and over 200 miles of road you have driven his army. You have matched your bare breasts against his ironclads and proved victorious in the contest. You have driven his routed columns beyond the Mississippi, although fed by reinforcements of fresh troops, while many of your gallant comrades were withdrawn to other fields. The boasted fleet which lately sailed triumphant over our waters, has fled in dismay, after destroying guns and stripping off armor in its eagerness to escape you. Like recreant knights the ironclads have fled the field, leaving shield and sword behind.

The devotion and constancy you have displayed in this pursuit have never been surpassed in the annals of war, and you have removed from the Confederate soldier the reproach that he could win battles but not improve victories.

Along 100 miles of his path, the flying foe, with more than savage barbarity, burned every house and village within his reach. You have extinguished the burning ruins in his base blood, and were nerved afresh to vengeance by the cries of women and children, left without shelter or food.

Long will the accursed race remember the great river of Texas and Louisiana. The characteristic hue of his turbid waters has a darker tinge from the liberal mixture of Yankee blood. The cruel alligator and ravenous garfish wax fat on rich food, and our native vultures hold high revelry over many a festering corpse.

If the stern valor of our well-trained infantry was illustrated on the bloody fields of Mansfield and Pleasant Hill, this long pursuit has covered the cavalry of the army with undying renown. Like generous hounds with the game in full view, you have known neither hunger nor fatigue, and the hoarse cannon and the ringing rifle have replaced in this stern chase the sonorous horn of joyous halloo. Whether charging on foot, shoulder to shoulder with our noble infantry, or hurtling your squadrons on the masses of the foe, or hanging on his flying columns with more than the tenacity of the Cossack, you have been admirable in all. Conquer your own vices and you can conquer the world.

Our artillery has been the admiration of the army. Boldly advancing without cover against the heavy metal of the hostile fleet, unlimbering often without support, within range of musketry, or remaining last on the field to pour grape and canister into the advancing columns, our batteries have been distinguished in exact proportion as opportunity was afforded.

Soldiers! These are great and noble deeds, and they will live in chronicle and in song as long as the Southern race exists to honor the earth.

Informed that their commander had resigned, it is said that many a hardened soldier wept.

Epilogue

It is truly distressing to see the vast havoc war has
made on this country, which once abounded in
wealth and prosperity, but it is all gone now.

CAPTAIN ELIJAH PETTY
WALKER'S TEXAS DIVISION

THE AFTERMATH

In the final year of the war, Kirby Smith was content to remain in Shreveport, speculating in cotton, while rural Louisiana lapsed into a state of near anarchy. As troops on both sides were withdrawn and sent to other venues, opposing gangs of partisan rangers and jayhawkers roamed the countryside, fighting pitched battles over the meager spoils that remained. Outlaw gangs, some of them made up of ex-Confederates, and some from as far away as Missouri, terrorized the citizenry. The population's only protection came from poorly organized home guards and a few scattered units of Confederate and Union cavalry. In the waning days of the war there were even occasions when Union and rebel cavalry cooperated with each other in their mutual war against the roving outlaw gangs.

The Trans Mississippi was the only Confederate military district that was not conquered by force of arms. At the end of the war the Confederacy still controlled 90 percent of Louisiana, all of Texas except for Brownsville, and most of Arkansas. The rebel flag was not lowered at Shreveport until May 20, 1865, when the Trans Mississippi became the last Confederate military district to surrender.

Some 56,000 Louisianans served in the Confederate Army. More than 15,000 died in battle or of disease. Official records list 566 battles, engagements, or skirmishes in the state. Many of those who returned home found their lands confiscated and their futures determined by a new form of slavery that would keep Louisiana farmers, black and white, in bondage for another one hundred years. It was called share-cropping.

If economic and financial destruction is added to the physical devastation, no state except for Virginia suffered more than Louisiana. New Orleans was under Union occupation longer than any other major city. Federal troops arrived in Louisiana in the spring of 1862 and did not depart until the summer of 1877. At the beginning of the Civil War, Louisiana was the second wealthiest state in the Union in per capita assets. At the end, its economy was in shambles, and as predicted by James Taliaferro, "a withering blight" settled upon the state. Louisiana has not recovered, even until today.

★ ★ ★

RICHARD TAYLOR—Instead of accepting Taylor's resignation, Jefferson Davis promoted him to lieutenant general and placed him in command of a department that included Mississippi, Alabama, and a portion of Tennessee. With the move, one of the South's most brilliant military tacticians finished out the war as an administrator. With the army depleted, the people weary of war, and the country barren of resources, Taylor had no more rabbits to pull from his magic hat. What he did was unleash General Nathan Bedford Forrest, giving him free rein to wreak havoc on Union outposts, supply lines, and shipping points, prolonging the war in the Lower South for another year. On May 4, 1865, just twenty-one days after Appomattox, Taylor surrendered his department to General Edward Canby at Mobile.

Taylor arrived back in New Orleans without a coin in his pockets. He sold the warhorse that had carried him through all of his battles for enough money to buy passage to see his family at Natchitoches. He stopped at Fashion Plantation. Although the fields were in cultivation under the auspices of a Union overseer, the house was a shell, stripped of everything, its walls defaced and marked with soot from a fire that troops had started before their officers put it out. In his pocket he carried a single letter from his father that had been retrieved from a prisoner at Brashear City. It was the only document saved from his father's papers. Looking around the grounds, he entered one of the barns. There, stretched and nailed to a wall were several dry leather hides. One was white with brown spots. Another was reddish brown. They were all that remained of the children's ponies.

The Taylors moved in with Mimi's family. When he heard about the terrible conditions under which Jefferson Davis was being held in prison, Taylor went to Washington to work for his release. "If he remains in jail we all deserve to be there," he told a reporter. In New York he met Samuel Latham Barlow, a political kingpin, lawyer, and financier. Barlow helped Taylor convince President Andrew Johnson to free Davis. Impressed by Taylor's diplomatic skills, Barlow frequently called on him to handle business matters, affording him a much-needed income.

Taylor returned to New Orleans, and with financial help from his brother-in-law, Martin Gordon, became part owner of a canal company that eventually went broke. He managed the Metairie Racetrack for a while, dabbled in Democratic politics, helped reestablish the Boston Club, and became its president. In 1873 Barlow sent him to London on a business matter that extended into a stay of almost a year. As the son of a president, the Royal Family treated him virtually as one of their own. The Prince of Wales, soon to be King Edward VII, took a liking to him. He invited Taylor to live with his family, awarded him membership in the British Turf Club, and elected him an honorary member of the Marlborough Club, which was reserved for reigning princesses and their sons.

Upon Taylor's return to the United States, Barlow urged him to write his memoirs and even found a publisher for him. Unable to sit still for extended periods, Taylor developed a unique writing style. He would pace about the room, reciting the desired passage to himself, then go to his desk and put it on paper.

On March 3, 1879, while in Washington, D.C., lobbying for one of Barlow's railroad projects, he suffered a severe attack of rheumatoid arthritis. His conditioned gradually worsened, and his sister, Betty Dandridge, came from Winchester to nurse him. He died of cardiac arrest on April 12, at age fifty-three. Dignitaries from both North and South attended the funeral, including some who had opposed him on the battlefield.

"The extinction of slavery was expected by all and regretted by none," he wrote in his memoirs. He owned slaves, but Taylor never felt comfortable with that institution, and he insisted that he had fought for self-determination, not for the preservation of slavery. He blamed equally the fire-eaters of the South and the radicals of the North for the conflict that drenched the nation in blood.

Although historical speculation is a risky business, two *ifs* are worthy of exploration. Taylor went to his grave believing that if Walker's division had been released to him in 1863, he would have taken New Orleans and relieved the sieges at Vicksburg and Port Hudson. He was also convinced that if Kirby Smith had not taken away Walker's and Churchill's infantry divisions, he would have destroyed Banks's army and captured part of Porter's fleet. Had Porter's gunboats come into his possession, there is no doubt that Taylor would have wreaked havoc on Union forces controlling the Mississippi River. The replacement of George W. Randolph as secretary of war presents another *if* worthy of consideration. Once deprived of Randolph's support, Taylor not only had to fight Banks at his front, but Shreveport and Richmond at his back.

Taylor's book, titled *Destruction and Reconstruction,* had been released to critical acclaim a few days before his death. "I shared the fortunes of the Confederacy," he wrote, "and can say as Grattan did of Irish freedom, that I 'sat at its cradle and followed its hearse.'"

MIMI (BRINGIER) TAYLOR—Mimi never fully overcame the depression brought on by the deaths of her sons, and her health suffered as a result. In August 1874 when her husband returned from London, they met at Niagara Falls for a second honeymoon that extended for several weeks. They returned to New Orleans, and for a time Mimi seemed to recapture some of the youthful spirit that once marked her character. However, that January she became ill with a fever and died March 16, 1875. She had just turned forty-one.

EDMUND KIRBY SMITH—Having failed in his attempt to have Taylor court-martialed, Smith turned his attention to politics and cotton trading. He did not wait around to surrender his department at Shreveport in the spring of 1865. He fled to Houston, intending to rally enough troops to continue resistance in New Mexico or Arizona. On arriving there, he found that the Texas units already had disbanded.

General Canby, suspicious that Smith might be trying to rally troops in Texas, demanded that he sign the official surrender documents. He sent Confederate General Simon Buckner, Smith's second in command at Shreveport, to Houston with the papers. Smith signed them and immediately fled to Mexico. There, he and Governor Henry Allen established a colony for ex-Confederate politicians and generals—apparently financed by proceeds from General Smith's entrepreneurial endeavors in Shreveport.

Among those who fled to Mexico with them were Governor Reynolds of Missouri and generals Magruder, Bee, Price, and Buckner.

NATHANIEL P. BANKS—"General Banks looks dejected and worn and is hooted at by his men," one of his soldiers wrote during the army's flight from Alexandria. Relieved of command, at Simmesport, Banks never again was allowed to command troops. Reduced to little more than head clerk in Canby's army, he was assigned to handle political matters in New Orleans, a job perhaps more suited to his abilities.

In the spring of 1865, he was called to Washington to face an inquiry on the failed campaign. The harshest testimony against him came from David Porter. Although severely criticized by the Committee on the Conduct of the War, no action was taken and Lincoln sent him back to New Orleans to continue his efforts to establish a workable Union government in Louisiana. Andrew Johnson, upon taking office after Lincoln's assassination, fired Banks, allowing him to return to Massachusetts and resume a political career that fell far short of his ambitions. He died in 1894.

BENJAMIN BUTLER—Following his departure from New Orleans, Butler took command of the Army of the James in Virginia and came into conflict with General Grant. After the war he changed his political affiliation from Democrat to Republican and was elected to the U.S. House of Representatives. He served five terms, changing his political affiliation three times. Unable to get along with Republicans or Democrats, he helped form the Greenback Party. In 1882, he rejoined the Democratic Party and was elected governor of Massachusetts. In 1884 he ran unsuccessfully for president as the nominee of the Anti-Monopoly Party. He died in 1893 at age seventy-five.

HENRY GRAY—The little colonel who molded the "Rag Tag" 28th into the regiment that broke the line at Mansfield was elected to the Confederate Congress in the fall of 1864 in spite of the fact that he did not seek or want the office. Without his knowledge, supporters put him on the ballot against Kirby Smith's handpicked candidate.

Returning home after the war, he discovered that he was financially ruined and had lost most of his holdings. He was elected to the State Senate but resigned in 1866 when Eleanora died. When in his late sixties, Gray went to live with his daughter, also named Eleanora, at Corsicana, Texas. Upon her death, he moved in with his daughter Elvie (Gray) Stohard at Coushatta, Louisiana. He died there December 11, 1892, at age seventy-seven.

CAMILLE ARMAND JULES MARIE, PRINCE DE POLIGNAC—In June 1864, when Polignac's old brigade was detached from his command, the Texans who once called him "Gen'ral Polecat" held a farewell ceremony. They presented the little Frenchman a horse, "As a slight testimonial of our confidence in you as an officer and our esteem for you as a gentleman."

After the war Polignac returned home and served as a general in the French Army during the Franco-Prussian War, earning a knighthood in the French Legion of Honor. In 1899, when he was sixty-six years old, he became the father of a son. He named him

Victor Mansfield Alfred de Polignac. Camille Polignac died in 1913 at age eighty-one, having fought in three great wars. On April 8, 1925, his son visited the Mansfield battlefield for ceremonies dedicating a monument in honor of his father.

BRAXTON BRAGG—In spite of Bragg's irrational behavior and terrible performance on the battlefield, his friend Jefferson Davis stuck with him until the bitter end. In battle, Bragg had but one military strategy: Find the strongest point in the enemy line and attack it. The tactic worked well for General Grant, but he was fighting a war of attrition. For Bragg, it only hastened the destruction of two great armies—the Army of the Mississippi and the Army of Tennessee.

The worst of Bragg's many mistakes took place at Chickamauga, where he had a chance to destroy Rosecrans's fleeing army and alter the course of the war in the west, but failed to act. Following a defeat at Missionary Ridge that truly revealed Bragg's incompetence, instead of firing him, Davis removed him from command and brought him to Richmond as a military advisor.

Following the war, Bragg was financially ruined. He went to work as an engineer for the State of Alabama for a while and eventually moved to Texas. In September 1876, he was crossing a street in Galveston when he collapsed and died, the apparent victim of a heart attack.

JEFFERSON DAVIS—Pale, gaunt, and suffering from a severe case of influenza, Jefferson Davis fled Richmond just before Federal troops entered the city on April 3, 1865. Just eleven days later, Lincoln was assassinated and Andrew Johnson, who hated Davis for insulting him on the floor of the Senate, ascended to the presidency. He immediately accused Davis of ordering Lincoln's assassination and placed a one-hundred-thousand-dollar reward on his head, setting off a massive manhunt.

Traveling by ambulance, Davis and a small contingent of family, friends, and staff were camped in North Georgia when a Union cavalry patrol happened upon them. Northern newspapers portrayed Davis as a coward, fleeing in women's clothing when he was captured. In reality, he was wearing his wife's coat because it was warmer than his own and, instead of fleeing, he was trying to get to a pistol in his saddlebags when subdued.

Taken to Fortress Monroe, Virginia, he was placed in a dungeon cell. He was passive until guards tried to chain him, at which time he resisted and was severely beaten. It was the first of several beatings he would endure at the hands of his guards. Learning of the miserable conditions of his imprisonment, Taylor visited Davis and vowed to get him released.

Taylor enlisted the support of leading Democrats in the North, but Johnson stubbornly refused to free Davis for two years. In May 1867, a bond hearing finally was held in the same building where Davis once served as president of the Confederacy. He was released under a one-hundred-thousand-dollar bond, pending trial. Horace Greeley, the newspaper baron and an ardent abolitionist, was among those who posted his bond. No trial was ever held. Returning to the South, Davis engaged in several failed business enterprises and was living in Biloxi, Mississippi, when he died in 1889.

TOM STROTHER—Taylor's boyhood playmate and devoted servant, who stayed with him throughout the war, often at peril to his life, returned with the general to New Orleans after the war. Taylor helped Tom search for his family. His wife and children were found living in New Orleans. The only mention in Taylor's memoirs about Tom's postwar life noted that he became "quite prosperous."

WILLIAM SEYMOUR—The newspaper editor who wanted to be a soldier got his wish. Paroled from prison at Fort Jackson, he fled to Virginia and became a volunteer aide on the staff of General Harry T. Hays in the Army of Northern Virginia. He was in the battles of Fredericksburg, Chancellorsville, Gettysburg, and those of the Wilderness Campaign. After the war he returned to New Orleans and resumed his newspaper career.

Before leaving for Virginia, Isaac Seymour had told his son that, if he was killed, he wanted to be buried beside his wife at Rosewood Cemetery in Macon, Georgia. In 1868, William fulfilled his father's wish. He went to Virginia, exhumed Isaac's body and took it to Macon for interment. William Seymour was writing his memoirs when he died in 1886 at age fifty-four. Although incomplete, the memoirs provide one of the most vivid descriptions of the tumult and tragedy of America's bloodiest hour.

KATE BEARD—As the Battle of Mansfield raged, Kate Beard stood on her porch, just twelve miles away, and listened to the rumble of what sounded like distant thunder. As darkness fell, she anxiously waited for any news from Mansfield. Late that night neighbors informed her that the Yankees were beaten, but there was no word from James. Near daylight she heard a wagon coming up the road and went out to the yard. There she saw Ned and Alonzo waiting beside the team. In the back of the wagon, covered by a blanket, was the body of her husband. The pocket of his jacket held a packet containing a baby shoe, and he had among his belongings a lock of hair and a watermelon seed. He was buried at two o'clock that afternoon at Evergreen Church Cemetery, just down the road from Auburnia. Within a period of eleven days, Kate Beard had lost her husband and her infant son.

Widowed at age twenty-eight, Kate never remarried. After the war she devoted her energies to raising Corrine and being an active member of the Daughters of the Confederacy. She died at her home on November 15, 1917, at age eighty-two. Her obituary described Auburnia as "a refuge for the heart-weary and always a happy meeting place for members of her family and friends." The Kate Beard Chapter of the Daughters of the Confederacy is still active in Mansfield today.

THE NATIVE GUARDS—There were three regiments in the original Native Guards. When first organized, all line officers were African-Americans—most of them professionals and businessmen from the New Orleans area. Upon Nathaniel Banks's arrival at New Orleans, he received complaints that lower-ranking officers and men in the ranks refused to salute Negro officers or to take orders from them, creating discipline problems. Also, white surgeons refused to serve in black regiments.

Banks set up a bogus commission to "evaluate" the performance of black officers, its real purpose being to purge them from the service. Of the more than seventy African-American line officers in the Native Guards regiments, fourteen were evaluated and all "disqualified." Thirty-nine others refused to appear before the commission and resigned "for reasons of prejudice," including all sixteen line officers in the 3rd Regiment who resigned in mass. Of the remaining officers, three were killed in battle, two were dismissed directly by General Banks, one was kicked out for leaving his post, and one was removed for "cowardice." Ten received medical discharges, most of them wounded in battle. Only six remained in the service. Among them were Charles Sauvenet, who rose in rank to assistant quartermaster and who later became civil sheriff of Orleans Parish, and Captain P. Pinchback, who briefly became governor of Louisiana during Reconstruction.

Almost twenty thousand African-Americans in Louisiana served in the Union Army. Most of them never wore a uniform or touched a rifle. In fact, most were assigned to work on the same sugar and cotton plantations where they were slaves. Others constructed forts, repaired railroads, rebuilt burned-out bridges, and worked as teamsters or in the engine rooms of the navy's gunboats and transports. Native Guards regiments accompanying Banks during the Red River Campaign were assigned to guard General Franklin's supply wagons at the rear of the column. Those who were tested in action at places like Milliken's Bend, Donaldsonville, Port Hudson, Mansura, and Jackson acquitted themselves admirably in every case.

WILLIAM WALKER—The final resting place of William Walker was unknown until the spring of 1999, when members of the William Walker Chapter of the Sons of the Confederacy at Winnfield located the gravesite of the man for whom their organization was named. It was found in a small cemetery on the outskirts of Jonesboro, Louisiana, some thirty miles from Winnfield. On March 6, a memorial ceremony was held and a proper monument placed on the gravesite. The name of William Walker lives on each time members of the Winnfield Sons of the Confederacy meet or participate in a reenactment.

ST. VINCENT'S CONVENT—The convent building where Sister Mary and the orphans huddled in the hallway while shells fell on Donaldsonville, still stands today. Inside is a statue of the Blessed Virgin, minus the fingers that were severed by a shell fragment. Crowning the building is the cupola that was never used as an observation tower by Yankee or Confederate—none of whom were willing to tangle with Sister Clara.

THE WEST-KIMBRELL GANG—In the lawless last days of the Civil War in Louisiana, the West-Kimbrell outlaw gang began a bloody rampage that lasted for three years before its members were hunted down and shot or hanged. The leaders of the gang were John (Red) West and Laws Kimbrell, the son of Dan Kimbrell. West and Kimbrell served in the rebel army and were Federal prisoners at Vicksburg. Upon being paroled they returned to North Louisiana and turned to outlawry. The gang operated along the Harrisonburg road, killing, robbing, and dumping their victims in abandoned wells. Governor Henry Clay Warmouth became so alarmed he sent an agent named James Mabin to Winn Parish with instructions to form a vigilante posse and bring the gang to justice. Mabin carried fifteen pardons signed by the governor for those who would participate. In 1868 Mabin and local vigilantes shot and killed West and Kimbrell, and rounded up other members of the gang. Following a quick trial, they were executed.

As for "Dog" Smith, who terrorized the community following the departure of Sheriff Walker, he disappeared overnight and was never heard from again. There is speculation that he might have met the same fate as Rock and Ruler, at the hands of Winn Parish vigilantes.

MARTIN GORDON—Dick Taylor's brother-in-law and factor remained in New Orleans through the war, making deals with the best of the Eastern speculators. Although he could not save the Bringier fortune, he helped the family financially after the war. He also helped the Taylors. Although Dick Taylor never revealed his intelligence sources in New Orleans during the war, it is believed one of those sources was Martin Gordon.

LIEUTENANT CHARLES KENNEDY—The Union soldier who hated rats returned to Staten Island to the arms of his beloved Katie and their three children. He became a successful businessman and civic leader. He was instrumental in establishing a county-wide system of public education that became a model for other districts. He died in 1916 at the age of eighty-three.

FREDERICK LAW OLMSTED—The *New York Times* writer who praised Taylor in his writings gave up journalism in 1857 to become America's foremost landscape architect. He designed New York's Central Park, parks in Chicago, and the grounds of the nation's capital in Washington, D.C., and he became the first commissioner of Yosemite National Park in California. He died in 1903 at age eighty-one.

THE LOUISIANA TIGERS—In the Seven Days' Battles outside Richmond, the Louisiana Tigers Battalion suffered heavy casualties, the most notable being the death of its commander. Its ranks depleted and deprived of the guiding hands of Dick Taylor and Roberdeau Wheat, the unit became uncontrollable and was disbanded. The mysterious Captain Alex White, who originally formed the Tiger Rifles, survived the war and disappeared from history. Today, the Louisiana Tigers remain one of the most legendary outfits of the Civil War.

THE 28TH LOUISIANA REGIMENT—After the Red River Campaign, Gray's old regiment was sent to Arkansas for several months before returning to winter camp near Minden, Louisiana. On the morning of May 20, 1865, the last two Louisiana regiments—the 28th and 26th—held a ceremony at the flagpole in front of the Trans Mississippi headquarters in Shreveport. As a band played a solemn dirge, the Confederate flag was lowered. It was cut into small pieces that were distributed to the soldiers as keepsakes. The war over, the ceremony complete, the regiments marched out of town, one south, the other east. As each company came to the road that led home, it turned off until, finally, there were no companies left at all.

Bibliography

BOOKS

Anders, Kurt. *Disaster in Damp Sand: The Red River Expedition.* Indianapolis: Guild Press, 1997.

Arceneaux, William. *Acadian General: Alfred Mouton and the Civil War.* Lafayette: University of Southwestern Louisiana, 1981.

Ayres, Travis L. *Shiloh to Stone's River: The Story of Private John H. Sullivan of the 16th Louisiana Regiment.* Middletown, CT: Dixie Tales, 1996.

Bergeron, Arthur W. Jr. *Guide to Louisiana Confederate Military Units.* Baton Rouge: Louisiana State University Press, 1989.

————. *The Confederate General (Henry Gray).* Harrisburg: William C. Davis, 1991.

Biographical and Historical Memories of Louisiana, Vol. 1–3. Chicago: Goodspeed, 1892.

Briley, Richard. *Night Riders: The Inside Story of the West and Kimbrel Clan.* Montgomery: Mid South, 1963.

Civil War Series, Vol. 1–28. New York: Time-Life, 1983.

Cunningham, Edward. *The Port Hudson Campaign.* Baton Rouge: Louisiana State University Press, 1963.

Davis, Kenneth C. *Don't Know Much About the Civil War.* New York: William Morrow, 1996.

Dufour, Charles L. *Gentle Tiger: The Gallant Life of Roberdeau Wheat.* Baton Rouge: Louisiana State University Press, 1957.

Edmonds, David C. *Yankee Autumn in Acadiana.* Lafayette: Acadiana Press, 1979.

Garraty, John A. *The American Nation: A History of the United States.* New York: Harper and Row, 1979.

Gray, Lewis C. *History of the Agriculture in the Southern United States.* Washington, D.C.: Carnegie Institute, 1933.

Henderson, G. F. R. *Stonewall Jackson and the American Civil War.* New York: Konecky and Konecky, 1962.

Hicks, John D. *The Federal Union: A History of the United States to 1865.* Boston: Houghton Mifflin, 1937.

Hollandsworth, James G. Jr. *The Louisiana Native Guards: The Black Military Experience During the Civil War.* Baton Rouge: Louisiana State University Press, 1997.

Johnson, Ludwell H. *Red River Campaign: Politics and Cotton in the Civil War.* Kent, OH: Kent State University Press, 1993.

Jones, Terry L. *Lee's Tigers: The Louisiana Infantry in the Army of Northern Virginia.* Baton Rouge: Louisiana State University Press, 1987.

Kennedy, James R., and Walter D. Kennedy. *The South Was Right.* Gretna, LA: Pelican, 1994.

Linton, Calvin D. *The Bicentennial Almanac: 200 Years of America.* New York: Thomas Nelson, 1975.

Long, E. B. *The Civil War Day by Day: An Almanac, 1861–1865.* New York: Doubleday, 1971.

Love, Dahle, and Eugene Love. *History of Winn Parish, Vol. 1: The Lighthouses.* Winnfield, LA: E. F. Love, 1986.

McMaster, John B. *A History of the United States During Lincoln's Administration.* New York: D. Appleton, 1927.

Mobley, Frank. *El Camino Real: The King's Royal Highway through Winn Parish.* Dallas: F. Mobley, 1995.

Mosocco, Ronald A. *Chronological Tracking of the American Civil War Per the Official Records of the War of the Rebellion.* Williamsburg, VA: James River Publications, 1994.

Parks, Howard J. *General Edmund Kirby Smith, CSA.* Baton Rouge: Louisiana State University Press, 1954.

Parrish, T. Michael. *Richard Taylor: Soldier Prince of Dixie.* Chapel Hill: University of North Carolina Press, 1992.

Raphael, Morris. *A Gunboat Named Diana.* Detroit: Harlo, 1993.

———. *The Battle in the Bayou Country.* Detroit: Harlo, 1975.

Readings in Louisiana History. New Orleans: Louisiana Historical Association, 1978.

Spedale, William A. *Fort Butler 1863.* Baton Rouge: Land and Land Pub. Division, 1997.

Taylor, Richard. *Destruction and Reconstruction.* New York: D. Appleton, 1879.

Ward, Geoffrey, with Ric Burns and Ken Burns. *The Civil War: An Illustrated History.* New York: Alfred A. Knopf, 1994.

Weigley, Russell F. *A Great Civil War: A Military and Political History, 1861–1865.* Bloomington: Indiana University Press, 2000.

Winn Parish History. Winnfield, LA: Winn Parish Historical Society, 1985.

Winters, John D. *The Civil War in Louisiana.* Baton Rouge: Louisiana State University Press, 1993.

JOURNALS AND MAGAZINES

Casey, Powell A. "Confederate Units from North Louisiana." *North Louisiana Association Journal,* Vol. 6, No. 3, 1975.

Dabney, Thomas E. "The Butler Regime in Louisiana." *Louisiana Historical Quarterly,* XXVII, April 1944, New Orleans.

Jones, Terry L. "The 28th Louisiana Volunteers in the Civil War." *North Louisiana Historical Association Quarterly,* Vol. ix, no. 2, 1978.

Savas, Theodore P. "Colonel James Hamilton Beard and the Consolidated Crescent Regiment, A Death at Mansfield, Civil War Regiments." *A Journal of the Civil War,* Vol. 4, No. 2, 1994.

Taylor, Ethel. "Discontent in Confederate Louisiana." *Louisiana History Series,* Vol. II, New Orleans, 1961.

Taylor, Joe G. "Slavery in Louisiana During the Civil War." *Louisiana History Series,* Vol. VIII, New Orleans, 1961.

Vetter, Charles E. "William T. Sherman, the Louisiana Experience." *Journal of the Louisiana Historical Association,* Vol. XXXVI, No. 2, University of Southwestern Louisiana, Lafayette.

OFFICIAL RECORDS

Civil War Naval Chronology, 1861–1865. Naval History Division, Navy Department, Washington, D.C.

The Conduct of Federal Troops in Louisiana During the Invasion of 1863–64, Official Report Compiled from Sworn Testimony Under Direction of Governor Henry W. Allen.

Official Report Relative to the Conduct of Federal Troops in Western Louisiana During the Invasions of 1863–1864. Shreveport, 1865.

The War of Rebellion: The Official Records of the Union and Confederate Armies. Washington, D.C.

MEMOIRS AND DIARIES

"Arthur W. Hyatt Diary." Hyatt Papers, Louisiana State University, Baton Rouge.

Bearss, Edwin C., ed. *A Louisiana Confederate: Diary of Felix Pierre Poche.* Natchitoches, LA: 1972.

Bergeron, Arthur W. Jr., ed. *The Civil War Reminiscences of Major Silas T. Grisamore, CSA.* Baton Rouge: Louisiana State University Press, 1993.

"Diary of Captain W. E. Moore, Last Captain of the Shreveport Greys." *Shreveport Journal,* 1930.

Jones, Terry L., ed. *The Civil War Memoirs of Captain William J. Seymour: Reminiscences of a Louisiana Tiger.* Baton Rouge: Louisiana State University Press, 1991.

DISSERTATIONS

Everett, Donald. *Free Persons of Color in New Orleans, 1803–1865.* Tulane University Library, New Orleans.

NEWSPAPERS

Alexandria Daily Town Talk
Alexandria Democrat
Baton Rouge Daily Advocate
Lafayette Daily Advertiser
Natchitoches Union
New Orleans Commercial Bulletin
New Orleans Times-Picayune
Opelousas Courier
Shreveport Daily News
Shreveport Journal
Shreveport Times